25-16
uc

Bad Students
NOT
Bad Schools

Bad Students NOT Bad Schools

Robert Weissberg

Transaction Publishers
New Brunswick (U.S.A.) and London (U.K.)

Library of Congress Catalog Number: 2010002948
ISBN: 978-1-4128-1345-7
Printed in the United States of America

Library of Congress Cataloging-in-Publication Data

Weissberg, Robert.
    Bad students, not bad schools / Robert Weissberg.
        p. cm.
    Includes bibliographical references and index.
    ISBN 978-1-4128-1345-7 (alk. paper)
    1. Problem children--Behavior modification--United States. 2. School discipline--United States. 3. Classroom management--United States. I. Title.

LB3013.W4615 2010
371.93--dc22

                                                                2010002948

Contents

Preface

Bad Students, Not Bad Schools might be called an Emperor's New Clothes book—it says what everybody (or nearly everybody) knows to be true but is fearful of expressing in public—America's educational woes just reflect our current demographic mix of students. Today's schools are filled with millions of youngsters, many of whom are Hispanic immigrants struggling with English plus millions of others of mediocre intellectual ability disdaining academic achievement. Their lackluster performances are impervious to the current reform prescriptions regardless of the nostrum's ideological pedigree. In the past they would have just been pushed harder, and if that failed, they would be shown the door. Today, by contrast, schools have become the refashioned Great Society putting bread on millions of tables so slackers must be retained regardless of educational value. Worse, retention is embraced even if this impedes learning among their classmates. To be grossly politically incorrect, most of America's educational woes would vanish if these indifferent, troublesome students left when they had absorbed as much as they were going to learn and were replaced by learning-hungry students from Korea, Japan, Vietnam, India, Russia, Africa, and the Caribbean. In an instant, all the clamor for vouchers, smaller classes, additional social services, teaching the test, innovative pedagogy, recruiting better teachers, accountability, junking Progressive education, and all the rest would seem antiquated, perhaps akin to the once popular lament over America's youngsters being undernourished.

Putative experts refuse to confront this obvious truth, at least publically, so we lurch from one guaranteed failed reform to the next, squandering hundreds of billions while progress is, we are assured by opportunistic politicians, just over the horizon. Perhaps this neglect is explainable since our diagnosis raises the awkward issues of unchecked immigration plus the possibility of group-related differences in intellectual talent. Further facilitating this silence is that down deep Americans disdain educational excellence. Just ask any parent who has pleaded that funds for football should instead be reallocated to more AP math courses. Better yet, compare how we tolerate rampant grade inflation to obscure unexceptional academic accomplishment versus popular outrage over inflated sports performance. The latter has instigated fervent calls for federal probes into performance-enhancing drugs; the former goes totally unchallenged. Athletics is more important.

The good news is that America is exceedingly lucky, at least for the moment. Though horrific schools are everywhere, sufficient numbers of first-rate institutions exist, and their smart, motivated graduates get the job done. When highly intelligent, technically adroit foreigners are included in our domestic talent pool, America can certainly flourish though millions of students, including high-school graduates, can barely read or do simple arithmetic.

Indifference to academics was not always true. Compare the present situation to what occurred in 1957 when the "backward" Soviet Union launched Sputnik I and we realized that the Evil Empire possessed nuclear tipped missiles capable of annihilating the U.S. Only then did we get serious about world-class math and science but that commitment only lasted until the early sixties when urban violence made the Soviet threat less pressing. Uplifting the bottom, not rewarding the smartest of the smart, became the new official policy. Truth be told, mediocre education thrives because that's what we want and are unwilling to pay for the genuine article.

Writing a book is always an adventure, but *Bad Students, Not Bad Schools* has been a transforming experience. In the beginning, as they say, I was moderately optimistic about the future of reform, especially choice solutions, and I still support choice though I'm not convinced that it will improve performance. My categorization of the problem has evolved from the conventional "it's the bad system so let's tinker with it" to a far more provocative "it's the slothful sometimes disruptive students." This is a harsh, heretical indictment and one less amenable to government policy though it can be reversed if the political costs can be borne. Our characterization totally rejects both liberal and conservative panaceas since each side of the ideological divide ignores students.

My dreary assessment partially reflects first-hand experience. Though a native New Yorker I had not permanently lived in the city until 2004. My return reawakened memories of my own school experience from a half century back. Perhaps four decades doing social science had blinded me. Recall Groucho Marx's quip: who are you going to believe, me or your eyes? I had, obviously, ignored my eyes. I had almost forgotten about once academically stellar schools deteriorating almost overnight as students' populations shifted despite the same buildings, the same teachers, and the same central administration. In 1953 I briefly attended 7th grade at Booker T. Washington JHS on 101st Street on Columbus Avenue in Manhattan, a virtually brand new school already in serious disrepair, police stationed on every floor, a violent schoolyard, classroom with totally out-of-control students while the handful serious students were neglected so harried teachers could vainly try to control miscreants. This was a decade before the city's schools slipped into near disaster but it was clear to me that many of my fellow students, not buildings or textbooks (all of which had been stolen), were the culprits. After my mother daily heard my stories of mayhem bereft of any learning (other than skillfully avoiding schoolyard confrontations), her predictable response was *"genug est genug"* (enough is enough in Yiddish) and we moved to a nondescript, lower-middle class New Jersey town (East Paterson, now Elmwood Park) where I uncomfortably discovered that I was at least a year behind academically.

Some forty years later back in the city, I found that matters had hardly improved. In fact, when I described my experiences at Booker T. Washington JHS to a recent president of that school's parent-teacher association, she explained that matters had, unbelievably, sunk even further! I met NYC teachers who viewed their job as slow torture save those few students, usually immigrant children, who justified showing up for work. These teachers were good, intelligent people, no doubt capable of imparting knowledge to those who craved it, but their students were killing the spirit. They were marking time, trying to navigate sorrowful situations while cynically watching the "Education Mayor" and his hard-charging school chancellor build reputations by claiming to transform unruly dolts into dutiful scholars by just threatening teachers and "closing" so-called "bad schools."

These teacher tales were confirmed by casual strolls near several of Manhattan's schools. I observed swarming special school police and knots of rambunctious students milling about shouting an indecipherable version of English save a steady stream of the "F" word. (When I first encountered the police presence I had assumed a crime had been committed or a bomb threat; later I realized that this flooding was routine when school let out.) The disorderly behavior, plus what I could observe elsewhere in subways and fast food restaurants made the city's school tribulations crystal clear: it's the students, stupid, not the facilities or curriculum. By chance I also regularly observed several top-notch city schools like Stuyvesant High School only blocks from these calamities, and the contrast was inescapable—well-behaved, studious types speaking clear English without a police officer in sight. Same system, but totally different outcomes.

What finally instigated rethinking the problem was actually meeting many of America's notable educators: high-ranking public officials, top educational administrators, famous writers, Education School professors, and others trying to improve education. I had only read about them before, and now I could see them "in action," ask a question or two and watch reactions. I also spoke with other thoughtful people, including a few who privately finance educational experiments, and here too, the disappointments mounted. Most were smart, a few brilliant at making money, all serious and yet their "positions" on education were little more than heartfelt clichés, e.g., get rid of unions and learning will explode, pay teachers according to results and learning will explode, give parent more choice and learning will explode, tweak the curriculum and learning will explode, change the culture and learning will explode, and on and on. One academic expert earnestly informed me that the single most necessary improvement on today's agenda was to redefine "education." He wasn't sure about the end product, but he was convinced that redefinition was vital to progress. Perhaps he's correct.

All of the speechmaking was well-intentioned, nothing was absolutely wrongheaded but many of these self-appointed amateur experts, sad to say, had little curiosity about rival explanations let alone having pet nostrums challenged. Convictions resembled religious slogans to be endlessly repeated to fellow believers. Not a single pontificator put any blame on students themselves. Rousseau's worldview had completely triumphed—"good" students had been corrupted by "the system." The unpleasant possibility that students themselves hated school and their aversion was beyond remediation was, apparently, unthinkable, and voicing it breached decorum.

These experiences were eye-openers, and extremely disconcerting. Down deep, it seemed, few took education seriously even if they earned their livelihoods at it. Irresponsibility often reflected the personal irrelevance of these horrific outcomes for affluent New Yorkers who easily escaped the mess; other "experts" happily subordinated clear thinking to ideology. It is here where the mendacity theme coloring this book took shape: hearing distinguished speakers expertly twisting the truth, dodging awkward but vital topics and embracing much of what I call "Marxism-lite" that corrupts today's reform agenda. Actually, much of the speech-making resembled politics in the old Soviet Union ("full-bodied

Marxism," so to speak) where ambitious *apparatchiki* assembled in Grand Halls of the People to trade blatant lies about fulfilling quotas.

I became even more deeply convinced that old-fashioned stupidity and laziness, some of it benign, some more malicious, explained our national tribulations. I will never forget how one distinguished ex-governor was fêted and given a prize for suggesting that academic excellence required making sure that every person had a college degree. Perhaps he should have first asked college professors in his home state about how many of their current students, let alone those rejected from college for academic insufficiency, could actually do college work despite wide-spread grade inflation. I also listened to a Secretary of Education explain that high drop out rates among African Americans could be reversed by adding more Advanced Placement courses in schools where most students struggled with the basics. That these troubling encounters occurred often among "conservative" elite university graduates, deepened my pessimism. I already knew about how foolish radical egalitarians toiled to destroy America's education with their obsession with diversity, multicultural-ism, and aversion to standards, but to witness equally destructive (though different) nonsense from those ostensibly pragmatically committed to righting a sinking ship, was truly eye-opening. With friends like this, as the old saying goes, who needs enemies?

I was soon connecting dots that had heretofore remained unconnected. A Eureka moment. I have spent decades in the academy and I had seen, though did not fully appreciate, a similar pattern. There top administra-tors often distort a plain-to-see reality to score politically correct points and advance a career; appalling students expensively imported to an elite university and continuing their indifferent ways despite being showered with resources and pep talks; a willingness among "educators" to twist research so as not to offend disruptive, thin-skinned groups, among other malignancies. I also observed how "problem students" became standing justifications to hire more counselors and assistants, create futile program after program, and other schemes to bloat payrolls, all the while these recruits came and went academically scarcely touched. To be blunt, the university had, at least partially, evolved into a grandiose politically correct "make work" project that simultaneously helped advance radical political agendas. Whatever it was, it was not education.

I soon acquired a new-found appreciation for America's teachers, the "grunts" to invoke military terminology. Those I encountered might have been skeptical about imparting knowledge to their apathetic stu-dents, but I did not meet any who rejected that noble aim. They were not the zombies or callous pay-check collectors who mesmerized so many erstwhile reformers. They really did care (or once cared) and they were doing their best, often under horrific circumstances. But, all too often, they were cannon fodder, standing bogus excuses for ambitious higher-ups trying to make a career by blaming everyone save the real culprits, the students themselves. I began to fantasize that one day New York City's School Chancellor Joel Klein (and dozens like him) would spend a year trying to teach unruly, intellectually uninspired students who absolutely hated being in the classroom. And then have his before/after test scores put on the front page of the *New York Times*. This would be a return to the days when generals personally led their armies into combat versus issuing commands while safely in the rear.

This is a pessimistic book, some might say even excessively so. I, obviously, disagree. I prefer the "brutally honest" label. I would have said "inconvenient truth" but that catch-phrase is, I believe, already spoken for. Altering immigration and student retention policy would perform wonders but nobody seems willing to express these views, at least publicly. Nor are educators willing to take the heat when cracking the whip over self-esteem addicted students more accustomed to being told that their dreadful effort is first-rate. American education can be improved and dramatically but it is a question of wanting it badly enough. Like a lazy but rich dieter, we spend fortunes on gimmicks.

Over and above an irrepressible desire to tell the truth, what allows me to paint this dreary picture is that it was assembled under the auspices of nobody. I call them as I see them, as one baseball umpire once said. Indifference to political fashion and pressure, a let-the-chips-fall-where-they-may attitude is a great advantage in a field where nearly all research must placate various gods or at least not offend reigning check-issuing deities, liberal or conservative. This independence undoubtedly makes me "dangerous" but, as the mice agreed in the Aesop fable that begins Chapter 10, somebody has to bell the cat, and I figure it might as well be me.

K-12 education is a new field for me, and writing this book would have been impossible without the help of others who read my early drafts and kept me posted on education-related materials. Heartfelt thanks go to Mike Berman, Steve Goldberg, Rita Kramer, Elizabeth and Nino Languilli, Victor Porlier, and Irvin Schonfeld. And, as usual, the most heartfelt thanks are reserved for Erika Gilbert who carefully read and reread every word, making the most useful suggestions, and kept the entire project on track. Without her encouragement, including prodding me to take some long therapeutic walks, this book could not have been written.

1

Introduction
A Nation at Risk or a Nation in Denial?

Politics is the art of looking for trouble, finding it everywhere,
diagnosing it incorrectly and applying the wrong remedies.
—Groucho Marx

To see what is front of one's nose needs a constant struggle.
—George Orwell

Americans are increasingly alarmed over our nation's educational deficiencies, and though bewailing schooling, especially public ones, is unending, these tribulations are real. Expenditures have exploded, far exceeding inflation or even rising health care costs, but academic achievement remains flat. Many students cannot even obtain a dumbed-down high school degree and if they do make it into college, they are forced to take remedial courses and often flunk these. Why the widespread disappointments despite fiscal extravagance, let alone hundreds of "guaranteed" reforms? The answer we submit is simple and can be summarized under four awkward truths.

First, though there are ample exceptions, millions of American students from kindergarten to college are intellectually mediocre, lack ambition, and anti-intellectualism is rampant. In most communities sports far outshine academics and this passion is true even at many elite universities. Conceivably, moreover, America's intellectual capital is declining as schools increasingly attempt to teach recently-arrived immigrants, many of whom struggle with English, from nations lacking strong educational traditions.

Second, educational failure is generally more profitable, financially and otherwise, than success though every well-paid school administrator, foundation executive, and vote-hungry politicians will deny this damnation. Falling test scores only beget more money, more jobs, and more lucrative foolishness to keep the failed educational industrial complex afloat. "Helping the children" is today's Great Society welfare colossus.

Third, the true cost of academic excellence—hard work, diligence, repeated failure—is too burdensome, so despite our collective wailing, our fear of overseas competition, we relish academic mediocrity because it is easier. Gift grades and gratuitous praise often painlessly help keep the peace. Given a choice between unearned self-esteem and earning it the hard way, the former is irresistible.

Finally, we are a nation in denial about why America's schools perform poorly. With relatively few exceptions, Americans refuse to look in the mirror and confess personal responsibility. Students and parents readily accept high grades for mediocre work. We live in a world where schools (buildings, desks, books) but not the students in them "fail." If junior can't read, somebody else is to blame, the government should fix the problem and don't tell me otherwise! Who wants to admit that one's offspring is not too bright, poorly motivated, and that lavish spending for continued failure only serves to put bread on millions of tables?

The apt parallel is how Americans wrestle with obesity. Both schooling and dieting reflect a common mind-set: spend generously to minimize painful exertion so fortunes await pundits promising easy alternatives to a strenuous regimen. In the case of weight loss, the basic, serviceable formula of eating less, exercising more is too arduous for millions unable to control appetites; substituted instead are cosmetic plastic surgery, stomach staples, diet pills, hypnosis, and gimmick meal plans by the dozens promising instant, effortless slimness. Trying to lose weight often becomes shifting from one promised elixir to the next, just as in "reforming education." Older readers may recall the "smart pill" that instantly brought erudition with zero effort or, lacking this pill, just place books under the pillow so as to wake up smarter. Today the "smart pill" has been replaced by vouchers, abolishing teacher tenure, multiculturalism, small theme-based schools, boosting self-esteem, paying students to learn, laptop computers for everyone, national standards, business-like accountability and dozens—if not hundreds—of similar painless but guaranteed-to-fail quick fixes.

The Academic Accomplishment Formula

Progress requires a broad understanding of what education entails, and while hardly simple, key ingredients and their relationships can be summarized by the following formula:

$$\text{Achievement=intelligence x motivation x resources x pedagogy x instruction}$$

This shorthand formula for academic achievement integrates the major elements in today's education debates. It hopefully overcomes the blindfolded men all trying to describe the elephant problem—those focusing on one item typically neglect others. In words, students achieve academically if: (1) they are sufficiently smart; (2) are motivated and possess decent work habits; (3) have books or whatever else required for mastering the subjects; (4) the instructional format makes the material accessible given their ability; and, (5) teachers properly explicate lessons. Failure occurs when dull, lackadaisical students daydream in chaotic classrooms lacking resources presided over by an incompetent teacher. The recipe has been recognized for centuries and perhaps its plain-Jane nature makes it easy to ignore.

The formula has powerful implications for educational progress. Elements are *multiplied* so *if any term is "0," the final result is "0."* It is *not* an additive formula; one cannot compensate for a "0" (or close to "0") anywhere by upping values elsewhere. If the billions wasted on educational tinkering tell us anything, it is that students who hate school will not suddenly shine if bused to palatial schools or will the innumerate relish math if handed free programmable calculators. Conversely, smart motivated students excel in decrepit buildings with out-of-date textbooks. With these five components in place, the next step is to assign weights regarding the contribution of each to achievement. This must be a bit speculative but the following weighting seems plausible:

$$\text{Achievement = 8 Intelligence x 4 Motivation x Resources x Pedagogy x Instruction}$$

This "human capital" model says that student intellectual ability has a huge impact (a value of 8) on academic accomplishment, followed by motivation (a value of 4) while resources, pedagogy and instruction (1 each) have far less force though are scarcely trivial.

Intelligence means the mental capacity to reason, plan, solve problems, think abstractly, comprehend complex ideas, learn quickly, and profit from experience. IQ scores roughly, but not entirely, summarize cognitive capacities. The scientific evidence on the relevance of cognitive ability for academic performance is overwhelming. Writing in the late 1990s Arthur Jensen notes that *Psychological Abstracts* lists some

11,000 studies linking IQ and educational attainment, and the connection is indisputable (Jensen 1998, 277-82). The average correlation is 0.5, a figure quite high by social science research standards though, as one might expect, variations exist across studies. This relationship is *not* simply a function of socio-economic status—brains strongly affects school performance even within families where siblings all share the same economic advantage, and while having rich parents helps, the correlation between family income and education is much lower. An overview of almost 200 studies of this connection conducted in 1982 found that the correlation between parental economic status and their children's educational success averaged about 0.22 (White, 1982).

Heavily weighting motivation, a summary term for discipline, tenacity, organization, fortitude, and work ethic among other "Calvinist" traits derives less from scientific studies than history and commonplace observation. An old Indian expressed it perfectly: when the student is ready to learn, the teacher arrives. The world abounds with examples of high achievers with no more than above average intellect who triumphed thanks to drive and formidable work habits. A recent analysis of six successful schools largely teaching Native Americans, Hispanics, and inner-city blacks found that a strong emphasis on discipline, diligence, delayed gratification, politeness, and other middle class "character" factors could produce stellar academic outcomes (Whitman 2008). Teachers observe this daily and upping commitment is one of the profession's main tasks. Obviously, sheer tenacity cannot overcome low intelligence otherwise dullards could be doctors. Still, mediocre intellects can succeed in countless fields by just paying careful attention, putting in long hours, endlessly practicing, and otherwise being "a grind."

This unequal weighting, including the low values assigned to resources, pedagogy, and teaching and the absolute importance of the student characteristics is easily observed though its implications for educational progress are seldom openly acknowledged. New York City during the 1930s, 40s, and 50s was renowned for its superb public schools, and Ivy League colleges imposed strict quotas (usually 5 percent) to stem the flow of bright, ambitious (and mainly Jewish) New Yorkers. Then in the early 60s the city's once admired system "collapsed" as blacks, most freshly arrived from segregated, under-funded Southern schools, increasingly enrolled though the pedagogy, resources and teachers scarcely changed.

More recent has been the arrival of at least 15,000 students to New York City's schools from rural Dominican Republic, Tibet, Central America, and elsewhere who barely had any prior schooling, are illiterate, speak halting English and are extremely poor (Medina, January 25, 2009). Many lack the most rudimentary school-related skills, e.g., knowing how to ask a question. To insist that the usual "educational reforms" (e.g., school choice, better teacher pay, administrative accountability, modern technology, etc., etc.) will succeed when even those in the early grades are years behind is fantasy. It is estimated that 5.1 *million* students in the US (a 60 percent jump between 1995 and 2005) currently struggle with English (and 77 percent of these are Spanish-speaking). According to experts, it will require five to seven years before their English will permit them to read a novel or understand a scientific process at a level comparable to their English-speaking classmates (Thompson, 2009). It is no wonder that many flee school as early as possible—their lessons may be indecipherable. Yet one more time, *students,* not the schools, are the crux of the problem.

The next step is to assign values to each learning-producing factor, e.g., the motivation level at a given moment. To simplify, assume that each factor has a range of 1 to 10 with "5" being average and 10 the highest possible score. Thus, a typical class would have "5s" across the board—nondescript students with ordinary motivation, commonplace resources, nondescript pedagogy, and middling teachers. Given the unequal weights of these five factors, a modest increase in intellectual talent and motivation would substantially alter overall outcomes; by contrast, importing a gifted teacher or drastically reducing class size would barely help. To boost test scores, the best practical solution would be to replace most below average students with ambitious budding geniuses.

Misallocating Resources

This human capital model and possible values understood, the next question is how best to invest scarce resources to maximize educational attainment. It is here that America's tribulations become apparent. Paradoxically, it is the equation's right side—the *least* important contributors to achievement—that mesmerizes today's reformers. Huge sums are invested in building over-the-top schools, developing cutting-edge pedagogy, and trying to improve instruction while, as subsequent chapters will demonstrate, the formula's first two elements—brains and motivation—are largely neglected. Yet it is obvious that millions spent on cutting-edge textbooks are pointless if students refuse to read them or are befuddled by the book's ideas. In business terms, contemporary educational tinkerers misallocate investments. *Cognitive talent and mo-*

tivation are the places to invest. In sports this would be as if a basketball franchise with inept, lackadaisical players tried to reverse its fortunes by constructing a spectacular new arena, adding high-tech training facilities, inventing clever new plays, and hiring a Hall of Fame coach. This patently foolish strategy would immediately enrage fans paying to watch ineptitude and lack of hustle. But this is *exactly* what occurs in American education.

Emphasizing the last three relatively less critical elements reflects political expediency, not sound educational policy-making. This is the path of least resistance in today's world of dysfunctional "reform." Nobody is angered when educators keep silent about slackers more inclined to socialize than study. Add the promise of immense tax-payer generosity—billions for new facilities, millions for technological gimmicks and teacher bonuses, and all the rest that "helping the children" entails. Conservatives with their pet nostrums—charter schools, vouchers, accountability—are equally guilty of misdiagnosing the problem and avoiding giving offense. Do these "experts" really believe that if lazy students can go school shopping they will be miraculously transformed into accomplished, motivated learners? Focusing on the last three elements also offer excellent rhetorical opportunities for ambitious office-seekers—one can quickly become "an education mayor" by promising new school construction with state-of-the-art Internet facilities stocked with hundreds of newly-hired counselors, administrators, role models, daycare workers, and learning coaches. A campaign built on "its time to kick some butt in our schools" will attract far fewer voters.

Dwelling on the last three elements demonstrates a remarkable inattention to return on investment. Educators and a gullible public seem ever willing to spend lavishly though progress fails to arrive. The upshot of reaching a plateau is not, however, rethinking future allocations. Instead, as traditional, sensible remedies fail, and the latest expensive gimmicky panaceas likewise come up short, "experts" increasingly gravitate toward more bizarre, more desperate solutions, e.g., free cell-phone minutes for doing homework. This is particularly visible in the fads afflicting pedagogy: American schools have gone from teachers sternly imparting knowledge and punishing slackers (hardly fun but effective) to teachers helping students "discover" what they "already knew" to classrooms where ignorance is flattered to strengthen self-esteems or racial pride which, we are assured, will somehow inspire a thirst for knowledge. If students refuse to read books, add spiffy pictures; if that fails, add color; if that, too, falls short, pay them to read or replace textbooks with video games; and if that, too, is unsuccessful, denounce book learning as only one path to knowledge and hardly suitable for all children.

Upping Human Capital and Boosting Motivation

National cognitive talent levels may initially appear permanent or at least beyond manipulation. In reality, however, school smarts are *readily manageable if public officials and those who vote for them are willing to pay the price.* Unfortunately for champions of academic excellence, the *political* cost is far too burdensome. Given a choice between "controversial" policies that offend versus academic mediocrity, the latter is *always* preferred. What makes this choice tolerable is America's ability to import brains as we now import oil—why crack the whip on lazy Americans when smart, disciplined foreigners arrive daily? And, unlike foreign oil, the overseas pool of talent seems limitless, cheap (at least for the present) and buying it off the shelf from India or China is less painful than pressuring Junior to master calculus.

Charles Murray speaks this awkward truth when he notes that America can readily solve its educational woes by once again limiting educational access (Murray, 2008). It is the "democratization" of schooling—a diploma for nearly everyone—that brings those into the classroom who can barely master the material and, critically, to insist that these youngsters can be proficient is romantic foolishness. Critics gleefully recalling an earlier era of 8th graders doing today's college-level work conveniently forget that those students intellectually far out-shined today's 8th graders. If one single genuine "magic bullet" cure for American's education decline exists, it would be to eliminate the bottom quarter of those past 8th grade. Unfortunately, the "democratization" of education seems to be irresistible as educational reformers increasingly call for enrolling semiliterates in college as if a degree itself certifies proficiency. New York City tried this in the late 1960s with "open admission" to the city's elite universities and it was disastrous, a cure worse than the disease. Perhaps the financial gain from this foolishness explains it all.

Revising America's immigration standards could dramatically improve our school populations. Canada, Australia, and Singapore, among others, explicitly tilt their immigration policy towards the academically adept and the U.S. could certainly follow suit though the political heat would be intense. To be sure, accusations of "racism" would be immediate but, as we note below, some of America's top college students are black though they (or their parents) were born overseas. Foreign engineers can be enticed with citizenship, not H1-B temporary visas. Even more controversial, though certainly feasible, would be deporting the families of students here illegally, many of whom are academically troublesome, and this might even include offspring born in the United States.

Even without touching the hot-button immigration issue, America's schools could be intellectually upgraded by encouraging academically overwhelmed students to depart voluntarily after 8th grade or pursue more economically-useful vocational training in proprietary schools (with government paying tuition). Additional resources might also be poured into schools catering to the very bright, a tactic that is widely ignored despite its obvious potential. All of this might economically benefit everyone, from the newly technically-skilled workers to consumers who complain about long waits to have their cars repaired.

Student academic indifference is likewise pushed off the public agenda though schools are hardly defenseless against lethargy *if they so choose.* For decades American schools successfully prodded students but in ways largely verboten today—namely, the threat of corporal punishment, ridicule, shame (the Dunce cap and public tongue lashings), calling in parents to terrify slothful offspring, and countless other proven though politically-incorrect remedies. The bad news is that in their place are iffy "kinder" gimmicks concocted by Education School professors that more resemble entertainment than imparting discipline. This is a world where helping students means shielding them from purely psychological discomfort, let alone harsh criticism. Even forcing youngsters to sit still and silently concentrate as a precondition for learning, a practice central to Japanese schools, is "unacceptable" in today's climate more attuned to "exciting" students' "natural" curiosity.

A 175-year-old Catholic grade school, the Transfiguration School, in New York City's Chinatown exemplifies how stellar achievement is possible on near starvation budgets when smart students are driven to excel. Outward material conditions would predict problems: class size far exceeds the City's average, it lacks a library, a nurse's office, and art and music rooms (the cafeteria doubles up), and the gym is outdoors, a small local crowded park. Teachers are not some elite corps drawing exceptional salaries. Finances depend on tuition and gifts, most students are eligible for free or reduced price lunches, a third receives scholarships while the City chips in a grand total of $57 annually per student for textbooks (a bit more for those with limited English). The cost—$4,800 per year—is less than half the public school figure. Though Catholic, and one class per day is devoted to Catholicism, only 20 percent of the students are Catholic, so "foreign" values are being imposed. The school is also run by those of Italian extraction who instruct largely Chinese students, many of whom travel long distances to attend, and at parental expense.

Measured in terms of student performance, and fierce competition for admission, the school is a resounding success. Many students "apply" at birth and the wait lists are long. There is zero school violence and classrooms are quiet with children in uniforms paying rapt attention to their teachers. Test scores are extraordinary and many graduates enter New York City's elite high schools where only test scores count (Shapiro, 2008). This all occurs in a city where school budgets have soared while test scores have gone nowhere.

Sadly, cheaply-produced academic excellence where smart students diligently labor rarely attracts public notice. The Transfiguration School story appeared in the *Downtown Express,* a small community newspaper for lower Manhattan. The lessons here—disciplined students anxious to learn, carefully listening to their teachers and absorbing strong moral messages about love and compassion, even regularly praying according to a religion most do not accept—are probably anathema to Education School "experts" seeking miracles. Perhaps these experts know that cloning this school is impossible given its smart, motivated students. "Good news" for contemporary educational tinkerers is when a "sexy" extravagant program targeting horrific under-achievers offers a glimmer of hope. No office-seeker would hold a press conference at the Transformation School and offer it as a guide for those more tempted by sports or socializing.

The Liberal Alternative

To appreciate this "conservative" Human Capital perspective, consider a weighing more in tune with today's prevailing liberal educational orthodoxy. It's the same set of factors differently weighted as follows:

$$\text{Achievement} = \text{intelligence} \times \text{motivation} \times (5) \text{ resources} \times (4) \text{ pedagogy} \times (4) \text{ instruction}$$

The exact numbers are, again, speculative but these they generally reflect prevailing liberal thinking. This is not a straw man to be easily demolished; it only *appears* to be one when made explicit, and rest assured, this is what the education reform literature insists upon. Foolishness only appears when this vision is made plain. In words, student cognitive ability and motivation are relevant but subordinate to resources, pedagogy, and teaching skill. Or as Bill Gates put it when announcing his

$3 billion Education 2.0 plan to an audience of top educators and CEOs, "We need to give all teachers the benefit of clear standards, sound curriculum, good training, and top instructional tools" (Wallis, 2008). Of the utmost importance, students, especially with regard to racial and ethnic backgrounds are essentially interchangeable so replacing academically-driven students of Chinese ancestry with recent academically-indifferent Mexican immigrants makes scant difference though accommodations may be required for language skill and other factors irrelevant to ability and motivation.

Thus, to boost performance for an average class the allegedly most efficient investment is adding resources followed by improved pedagogy and upping teaching skill. Moreover, and this is absolutely critical, the values for the last three elements are currently not only low (say 3 on a 10 point scale) but substantial benefits flow from this intervention. Put differently, America is under-investing in resources while applying poor pedagogy and instruction techniques. That is, if $9,000 per pupil is augmented to $15,000, or star teachers replace today's average ones, performances would increase notably, far more than upping intellectual ability or cracking the whip over the indolent. Variations across socioeconomic or racial/ethnic groups are largely explainable by unequal values for the last three elements so, for example, rich kids do better because the values for resources and teachers are higher

Given the depressing results generated by this formulation over several decades, this resource-heavy vision doubtlessly misreads reality. The low value given to cognitive talent is clearly preposterous. No college admission officer, let alone a teacher, believes it. Past experience is most damning, however. Today's educational landscape overflows with expensive failures targeting this end of the equation, everything from ineffective palatial high schools to major pedagogical disappointments like President Bush's once heralded, multi-billion dollar Reading First Program. At best, these innovations show small initial benefits, but harbingers never produce the promised major upswing. In fact, tiny progress often declines with time, suggesting a Hawthorne affect (intervention itself instigates improvement regardless of what is done) or, in some instances, data fudging. Right side interventions also seem to help only those at the very bottom, and it is unclear whether they persist. It is not that the last three elements are trifling; rather, they are less valuable than intellectual ability and motivation and possible benefits have long been maximized. To exaggerate only slightly, if a $500 laptop does little good, updating it with a $1,000 model is pointless. Similarly, if drastically cutting average class size, as has occurred in recent decades, shows no appreciable academic gains, it is wasteful to reduce the number of students yet further.

No Pain, All Gain

America has become remarkably adroit at hiding hypocritical appetites for painless educational gimmicks and this destroys clear thinking. Surveys endlessly show that parents think education is "important" and even parents whose offspring lag well behind fervently hope their children will graduate college. In one especially revealing set of surveys, mothers of American first-graders were far, far more likely to be "very satisfied" (40 percent) with their children's education than mothers in China or Japan. The same huge difference also existed in fifth grade. American mothers even believed that their children outperformed their Chinese and Japanese counterparts when reality was exactly the opposite. Remarkably, according to one compilation, education reports issued in all fifty states described local students as "above average" (Stevenson and Stigler, 1992, Chapter 6).

Though "improving education" is always near the top of problems facing America and politicians happily exploit this anxiety, enthusiasm wanes when the bill is to be paid. "Doing something to improve schooling" often means holding a boisterous public rally to demand politicians and educators "do something" about education. If that fails, just vote for the candidate promising to spend the most for the "schools we deserve." In Washington, DC a frequent tactic to protest dismal student performances is to keep Junior at home, a ploy perhaps secretly welcomed by teachers. This naturally rewards lazy teachers—the worse the outcomes, the more students kept home, the less there is to do, and so on. This is win-win sloth.

A passion for good outcomes acknowledged, how many "concerned" parents would endorse the Japanese school year of 240 days (versus 180 in the US), with a five and a half day school week, in which no vacation lasts longer than three weeks, with assignments given over the holidays (Peak, 1993, 43)? Or spend each morning checking that backpacks are well-organized and contain the required supplies and assignments? Japanese parents even patrol shopping malls on weekends to insure students are home working. American teachers rightfully complain that few parents are involved in their children's education and grumble if assignments interfere with family vacations. The same parents probably "demand" schools to perform wonders.

Professional educators often encourage the all-gain-no-pain hypocrisy. According to one account, at least some teachers of English even reject learning proper English (Allen, 2007). Instead of forcing students to master conventional rules on punctuation, grammar, and even how to write legibly, the virtues of independence, self-expression, and creativity are promoted. A few professors *encourage* writing errors as a sanctioned rebellion against the "tyranny" of Standard English. One in particular—Sandra Wilde of Portland State University—has even proclaimed a "Speller's Bill of Rights" asserting that one's worth as a human being exists regardless of spelling ability (cited in Allen, 2007, 30). In 1993 the National Council of Teachers of English pushed this odd notion of personal autonomy to its logical end by endorsing the right of students to their "own language" whether it was hip-hop, Spanglish (an ad hoc mixture of Spanish and English), Valley Girl-talk or that of any other community or personal identity. Bible readers recall that God punished Babylonians constructing a tower that dared reach the heavens by making people speak multiple languages so as to frustrate communication. Perhaps some pedagogues for this reason envision themselves as doing the Lord's Work.

Meanwhile professional pedagogues typically loathe daily drill and memorization, though history demonstrates the value of this hard-nosed approach. "Experts" instead insist that the repetitive exercises incapacitate learning by deadening the brain (derisively labeled "drill and kill"). In their place, are "fun" activities that not only are virtually content free but fail to develop tenacity, and without resolve, future failures are inevitable. That these "fun" pet nostrums fail is irrelevant; they are supposed to produce, and promise is more important than results. Further add a long-standing ideologically-motivated aversion to "elitist" testing where some students outshine doltish classmates (derided as "teaching the test"). One renowned education professor even called matching letters with sounds "the flat earth view of the world" (cited in Allen, 2007, 29).

Underlying Pathologies

The foolishness afflicting America's education system, nearly all of it self-imposed and in principle reversible, is immense. Subsequent chapters offer an autopsy-like analysis but certain themes are ubiquitous, and it might be useful to highlight a few in advance. These might, perhaps whimsically, be called the "Four Debilitating Mental Habits of Highly Incompetent Educators" currently guiding public (though not necessarily private) educational discussions.

Invisible Marxist-Lite

It is often said that a fish has no concept of water. The same holds for nearly all contemporary policy-makers inventing nostrums for our educational ills—remedies inevitably reflect countless clichés, bogus scientific assumptions, even stipulated "facts" and empirical connections "so obvious" that they are judged axiomatic. That understood, much of what permeates today's educational thinking oddly resembles Marxist beliefs regarding the "right" environment's power to transform human nature. Just provide resource-rich settings and inspired teachers (or least teachers terrified of being fired) and learning will flourish regardless of natural ability or motivation. This is the equivalent of Marxists insisting that after a few years of collective farming peasants would lose cravings for private property and greed. Educators reject the pessimistic view that schooling is not a natural inclination and thus must be imposed, and this can be unpleasant.

If a single phrase encapsulates Marxist-lite thinking, it is "children cannot learn in a 'bad school'" and "conservatives" hardly object. Make schools "good" and like wilting plants watered, youngsters will blossom. This is counterproductive anthropomorphic thinking, as if tables and chairs, not students, flunk tests. From this dominating perspective, students themselves, regardless of ability or background, are totally blameless since they are not born disruptive, lazy or immoral, let alone hating schoolwork. Rather, these unproductive traits are socially acquired, imposed by a "bad society," and thus, in principle, reversible by tinkering with environments. Improving education thus becomes reengineering surroundings to unlock blocked natural virtues. It is no accident, then, that early intervention, e.g., Head Start, school lunches, early counseling, are favored by today's Rousseau-influenced educators. The 1960ish slogan "It's society's fault" may have departed our vocabulary, but the underlying worldview still flourishes.

As with Marxism itself, educational efforts should be egalitarian and uplift the least competent regardless of repeated setbacks. This leveling is ideologically-inspired and totally dominates the entire ideological spectrum right to left. Even conservatives now call for enticing the best teachers to the worst schools or creating an educational Marshall Plan to help the least proficient, as if pushing up the bottom would magically uplift American education more generally. And, at least for some, leveling can be legitimately accomplished by hampering the top by, for example, insisting that AP courses admit those who can barely do the work or dumbing down tests to ensure that everybody receives an "A." Education becomes an upside-down world and shifting money into schools for the gifted while reducing help for illiterate chronic troublemakers now appears morally abhorrent, if not "cruel."

The indolent thus must be rescued, not condemned and this may even require some violence. A recent proclamation from sixty leading academics, school administrators and civil rights activists called on Washington "to squeeze" teachers to boost academic accomplishment among blacks and Hispanics (Dillon, June 12, 2008). For the uninitiated, "to squeeze" is criminal argot to denote physical intimidation. Perhaps these reformers will next "put out a contract" on inept teachers or make them offers they cannot refuse. When reading scores remained low despite President Bush's once-heralded billion-dollar "Reading First" program, the president was *personally* blamed as if he were a negligent parent. Critics accused the president of everything from advocating terrible pedagogy to cronyism in awarding contracts. Newspaper accounts of his alleged failure *never* mentioned the possibility that the students themselves were at fault.

The Race Taboo

The fear of offending is vital to social life so countless words and ideas are totally impermissible, save among the most trusted friends in whispered conversations. In education the great taboos are racial differences in cognitive ability. Though the topic draws careful scientific attention, these statistically-dense conclusions are rarely broached in *public* education-related discussions. The essence of the race taboo is that Asians are generally slightly smarter than whites, and these two groups are, on average, smarter than blacks. Acknowledging this taboo regarding differences says nothing about the mix between nature and nurture in causing differences. Its mere existence is what matters and, furthermore, *all* attempts to level them have failed. It is not a function of test biases since even IQ tests that do not rely on vocabulary or culture uncover the overall racial pattern.

And, as our "human capital" formulation made explicit, cognitive ability is only one factor in academic accomplishment and those of middling intelligence, regardless of race, can shine academically thanks to diligence, superb teachers, and excellent curricula. If smoking gun proof of this is needed, just witness the extraordinary academic accomplishments of black students born abroad or those who have immigrant Caribbean or African parents. Like past ambitious newcomers, many of whom skimp and save for quality schooling, they rush to take advantage of educational opportunities. While these "immigrant blacks" comprise only 13 percent of all blacks in the U.S., they comprise 27 percent of those African-Americans at top-notch colleges (Jaschik, 2009). Indeed, these immigrant blacks are proportionally more numerous than whites at selective colleges and a few native-born blacks worry about being pushed aside by these ambitious youngsters. Think Colin Powell, Barak Obama, and countless other children of immigrants.

Moreover, averages can easily obscure storehouses of cognitive talent since every demographic group contains outliers, regardless of averages. According to the U.S. Census Bureau there will be about 3 million African-Americans of grade school age in 2010. Given normal IQ distributions, this translates into about 69,000 youngsters with IQs of 115 or higher (two standard deviations above the mean), a figure that could fill dozens upon dozens of high-achieving all-black grade schools. Scattered about, these students would dominate honor rolls at hundreds, perhaps thousands, of schools. If we take the entire African-American school aged population (5 to 19) eligible for school in 2010, and look at the extreme right side of the intelligence distribution (IQs of 130 or higher), there are over 12,000 of these super-bright youngsters. Given that super-smart kids of any background are exceedingly atypical, it is bizarre to suggest that achieving academic excellence among African-Americans requires ignoring IQ data.

A 1994 *Wall Street Journal* article (Gottfredson, 1994) following in the wake of *The Bell Curve,* signed by fifty-two leading researchers in this field, affirmed that group-related variations in intelligence are real, are at least partially genetic, are accurately measured by IQ tests across all subgroups, and have real world consequences. Again, they do not reflect unequal resources; even American blacks from wealthy families generally have lower IQs than whites from poorer families. These experts also add that the race gap is not closing, we do not know how to narrow IQ differences, and this pessimism about narrowing gaps is confirmed by the failure of ambitious billion-dollar efforts like Head Start (Spitz, 1986 catalogues these attempts).

Let us be clear: all these findings, in various degrees, rest upon empirical research but are by no means certified, indisputable Scientific Law. Nor are these findings ammunition to deprive anybody, rich or poor, black, white or Hispanic, male or female, from the best possible education. Recall that there are lots of young African-Americans whose IQ would fast track them to Ivy League educations. Still, an honest effort to improve schools would be well-advised to consider these facts along with countless other hypotheses about unequal cognitive ability. To dismiss them as "unthinkable" or "racist" regardless of the evidence can only impede possible solutions. Japanese schools permit youngsters to run wild for ten minutes between classes to relieve the pressures, and this might help America's young hyper-active black males blow off steam and concentrate, which in turn, would alleviate a huge waste of talent (in fact, a recent study of 11,000 third-graders found that black youngsters were more likely than whites to be cooped up but those who had a fifteen-minute recess had fewer classroom behavior problems). Alas, adding a racial element to this disruptive behavior problem hints at some biological element in black behavior, so it is more polite to suggest instead that schools hire more counselors, even prescribe Ritalin.

These findings hardly doom blacks to educational insufficiency and this sanguine conclusion does not require disputing IQ test validity or even claiming that race lacks any scientific meaning. Differences across racial groups are ubiquitous, and inequality of talents across demographic groups is just a fact of life. Whites are not outraged that Asians outscore them on SATs or are disproportionately admitted to elite universities. The historical record clearly shows that millions of blacks have benefited immensely from superb schooling so today's dismal record is hardly inevitable. Progress requires *honest* inquiry and looking at what is learned given abilities, not making envious comparisons. Thomas Sowell's review of pre-civil rights movement of black education uncovers places like Washington DC's Dunbar High School that instructed its students in Latin while sending countless graduates to elite schools where they performed as well as their white classmates. Today, Dunbar is a classic inner-city educational disaster. Elsewhere "no-nonsense" black majority schools, many of them Catholic, produce well-educated students who excel in demanding universities (Sowell, 1993, especially 10, 96, 282).

If native-born blacks, unlike many of their immigrant compatriots, initially lack Calvinist virtues, schools can certainly help inculcate them. This is superbly illustrated in schools like KIPP (Know is Power Program), Cristo Rey Jesuit High School in Chicago, Amistad Academy in New Haven, Connecticut among a handful of others where students, many of whom are just middling in intellectual ability, achieve impressive academic results thanks to teachers imparting a strong work ethic, strict discipline, and unyielding high standards (Whitman, 2008). What these findings on group differences counsel is that education should be directed at achieving the best possible results for each individual, not trying to level group differences.

The damage that can occur by refusing to confront awkward racial differences is sadly illustrated in battles over Massachusetts's mandatory teacher certification exam. Blacks fail at a rate twice that of whites, especially the writing test that focuses on grammar, punctuation, an ability to write an essay, and reading comprehension. The test can be taken repeatedly, and a single pass secures certification. Predictably, the test has been attacked as biased and a state task force has been appointed to study ways to overcome these unequal failure rates. And, of course, a lawsuit is pending (Jan, 2007). Nobody will publicly admit that these unequal pass rates might just reflect unequal ability or that flunking the test should encourage teachers to study harder so as to substitute diligence for less cognitive talent. At least for many educators and activists, equal proficiency is just assumed and it is "better" to waste millions in legal fees and test revision than confront the unwelcome news. More important, totally off the agenda is that students will be harmed by hiring semi-literate teachers regardless of their race. Politeness trumps student learning, so an illiterate black teacher is better than a literate white one insofar as "helping" blacks.

Sloppy Science

The physical sciences required centuries to achieve today's technological marvels, and this was not easy. Unfortunately, it is difficult to imagine worlds as far apart as "education research" and what transpires in today's physical sciences. It is an open secret in today's research-oriented universities that their Schools of Education attract the least talented faculty, the least proficient students and what passes for research there would rarely pass muster elsewhere in the university. Among educators shoddy science is not only tolerated, it is often venerated. Not all educational research is scientifically inadequate, some of it actually does satisfy rigorous standards, but the bulk of it, to be frank, is terrible.

Unlike medicine where mistakes bring death and thereby inspire public demands for tougher standards, absolutely *nothing* can impede the deplorable proliferation of education nonsense. Educational quackery is also First Amendment Protected. Add to the confusing mayhem economic self-interest. In physics careers may flourish if one hypothesis triumphs over another, but money is never paramount. Education differs profoundly—competing solutions typically have major economic consequences, and this predictably fosters bending even seemingly-scientific truth, and slanting occurs across the ideological spectrum. The National Education Association, the largest union of K-12 educators, is hardly a disinterested party when dissecting the impact of union rules on test scores. Taxpayer organizations are, naturally, skeptical of studies calling for higher teacher pay. Hundreds of interests have financial stakes in educational policy, and many hire well-paid professional advocates to conduct self-serving research. Government choices may thus reflect a group's political savvy and electoral weight.

The almost pathetic quality of "educational research" was laid bare in the battle over President Bush's multi-billion dollar No Child Left Behind (NCLB) (Viadero, March 5, 2008). In more than 100 instances the legislation itself calls for educational improvements to be based on "scientific research." The entreatments are deceptively telling—imagine space exploration, energy, and medical legislation "insisting" upon scientific methodology. Paradoxically, NCLB is filled with nostrums that either reject science or are shaky. And, pushing for science-based research occurred a *year or two* before Bush assumed the presidency and was institutionalized by the Education Science Reform Act of 2002 (ESRA). In other words, it is only after decades of relentless failure and hundreds of billions, that Congress acknowledged the need for more scientific rigor.

But, the promised land of scientific precision may not have yet arrived. ESRA's re-authorization has generated disputes over what, exactly, is the "scientific method" and some members of Congress actually reject the tough methods used in fields like pharmacology. In particular, the gold standard random experiment has been challenged as the best approach and in 2008 Congress explicitly rejected a $5 million random assignment-based study approach to assess the Upward Bound Program designed to help disadvantaged students enter college (legislation also forbid *future* use of this venerable scientific technique). To be sure, not all is lost and in 2008 Congress did authorize twenty-three large scale evaluation projects, of which eighteen included randomized assessments. There are also efforts to fund research-training for education specialists.

Nonetheless, even this weak embrace of science was too much for today's educators. As the Obama administration took shape the anti-science clamor soon returned. Calls reappeared for applying lessons from successful, innovative projects without all the tedious, time-consuming investigations into why it works with that particular student population (Viadero, 2009). For these advocates, including a close Obama education advisor, the pathway to academic achievement lay in innovation and experimentation, not complicated investigations into the "why?" question. So, if video games boosted reading in one school, just use them elsewhere. To be blunt, this approach is closer to folk remedies than scientific medicine—a hit or miss strategy disdaining any understanding of why, exactly, some potion cured the illness.

Informed outsiders might be flabbergasted when following today's debates in education. Consider the ongoing controversy over the "value-added research method" (Viadero, May 6, 2008). The gist of this quarrel is whether *individual* student performance data should gauge academic progress versus *aggregate* grade or class data. In other words, by the end of fifth grade is Johnny—and only Johnny—further along than when he exited fourth grade? Since aggregate indicators are fraught with imprecision, individual level data should be the gold standard. After all, most of a fifth-grade class might have fallen backwards compared to when they left the fourth grade, but if a few smart students were added (or dummies excluded), higher average fifth-grade scores misrepresent progress. Aggregate measures are clearly second best rough approximations.

Remarkably, though this focus on individual students is occasionally used, and easy to calculate, education experts still doubt its relevance. An entire 2008 conference sponsored by leading education-oriented foundations debated it, and resistance seems rooted in how such information might be used in, say, judging teachers. Other critics speak of it as being "untested" or over-sold. To a scientifically attuned interloper, this is appalling messenger shooting—collecting vital data is being subordinated to insulating teachers and administrators from potential bad news. Perhaps education "researchers" dislike the truth, desire rubber yardsticks, and shaky fuzzy measures suffice by making it almost impossible to certify what succeeds or fails.

One can also spend days reading this research literature without encountering any discussion of causality, the chicken and egg problem, an absolutely critical quandary when imposing reforms. So, if the wealthy have schools with better students it is just blithely assumed that wealth promotes academic excellence. That affluent parents demand superior schools and willingly finance them, and may even have smarter children than the poor, is unspeakable. Similarly, that motivated students inspire teachers, not the opposite, never seems to occur to those demanding better teachers to light fires. Recall the days when a hearty appetite was a sign of health so the sick would gorge themselves to get better.

Ignoring science can be remarkably cost-free in education. Unlike commerce or medicine, no penalties exist for promoting what is purposely misleading—terrible research is not yet a crime akin to faking drug test data. Schools of Education hardly need legal departments to clear faculty publications to avoid costly class action litigation. An education professor whose ill-conceived strategy to improve literacy failed will *never* be punished for malpractice nor will angry parents sue for damages. No greedy attorneys advertise on New York subways, "Has your child been mis-educated as result of faulty pedagogy? If you believe so, call our toll-free hotline. Last year we won $5 million for a similar suit." To be blunt, education may be *par excellence* a field of professional irresponsibility. This cacophony, most of it totally unscientific, means that it is impossible to learn from mistakes, so the same doomed-to-fail proposals reappear endlessly. The blind lead the blind and prosper doing it.

Dishonesty

Though we may expect educators to speak truthfully, misrepresentation, even outright lying, has become endemic. Much of this begins with deceptive euphemisms to soften an unwelcome reality and these white lies can debilitate clear thinking. Tough exams to identify accomplished students are called "barriers" to those who fail as if the under-performers were being artificially hampered in acquiring knowledge or a diploma. Students struggling for years to learn English are inoffensively called "English Language Learners" (ELL) though a more accurate label might be "English Language Non-Learners." Those in over their head academically are "challenged" as if they could do the work if only they tried harder while today's strugglers who can avail themselves of multiple social service programs and counselors are labeled "disadvantaged." Disruptive students heading towards a life of crime become "at risk," not troublemakers or, as was popular in the 1950s, juvenile delinquents. Students in one Seattle school with abysmal test scores were called "scholars" as if this flattering label could change an unpleasant reality (Johnson, 2009). Common in all these euphemisms is the effort to help the miscreant avoid personal responsibility—barriers must be removed, more help provided to those skipping English lessons, ever more resources committed to the "disadvantaged" and risks reduced for the "threatened." This is feel-good denial of an uncomfortable reality.

Daniel Koretz has studied the falsification of education test data for decades and strongly suggests that deception, much of it verging on outright fraud, has almost become a way of life (2008, Chapter 10). He calls the misrepresentation the dirty secret of high stakes testing and sadly notes that there are firms who prosper selling juice-the-numbers materials to hard-pressed school districts. So common is this fabrication, that it has its own name—Campbell's Law—which says that the higher the stakes for public policy, the greater the cheating. In some instances this may entail outright dishonesty, e.g., teachers changing wrong answers into correct ones, but cheating is often less visible and more borderline. Separating legitimate help during a test from actually giving away the correct answer may be an impossibly murky distinction. Practice sessions can use items from the test itself. It is easy to test only on what is taught or just teach the test, a strategy encouraged by the public's willingness to accept tests developed by those whose careers are affected by the outcomes. Another favorite ploy is to manage the test-taking population to exclude those known to be low scorers.

Pressures for falsifications abound and there is little to stop it. Parents upset over shoddy education cannot sue to stop number cooking—they move, home-school, seek out extra help for junior or otherwise escape the deceit and thereby leave it in place. As animals lacking predators may overrun a territory, reality-twisting demagogues quickly dominate debate—who wants bad news about tiny progress? In today's odd incentive structure openly lying to co-believers can demonstrate political trustworthiness since the blatant falsehood assures supporters that the speaker will do *anything* to advance the cherished cause. Who can predict what an honest office seeker might say, and so why risk uncertainty? That the public desperately craves easy miracles entices yet more deception. Recall the parallel with bogus diet programs—people crave illusions.

What Is to Be Done?

Reformers anticipating an easy magic bullet cure for America's educational woes will be disappointed by what follows. Our analyses demonstrate the emptiness of today's education reform menu, and this is equally true for liberal and conservative panaceas. If there is a sure-fire solution, it is the very difficult one of enrolling smarter, better-motivated students while letting those uninterested in academics depart. This prescription is, we admit, hardly exciting and certainly will upset those seeing education as a cornucopia of jobs and contracts. It will also disappoint those students and parents who believe that attending school should boost their self-esteem regardless of academic accomplishment. We speak painful, unwelcomed messages, but these are the unvarnished truths.

2

Bad Students, Not Bad Schools

There is an old joke about a newly opened luxurious restaurant tottering on bankruptcy. A meeting was called of all involved and each offered their cure. The lawyers suggested revising articles of incorporation to achieve tax breaks. Bankers preferred financial re-restructuring and new loans. The advertising agency wanted an expanded media campaign. A real estate expert suggested moving to a new location. Decorators advised fresh color schemes and trendier furniture. Then, way in the back, a voice rang out from an unnoticed nobody, "What about the food?"

Analyses of our educational woes abound with stupidities, but if one had to choose the most damaging, it would be that America is plagued by "bad schools." So, if semi-literate students make zero progress, just move them to a "good school" and, *voilá*, test scores will soar.

This diagnosis and proposed solution are flat out wrong, and offers a politically-convenient definition of our trouble that soothes delicate sensibilities. It is the equivalent of claiming that America's expanding waistlines are caused by "bad restaurants" so close McDonald's, Burger Kings and the rest, and Americans would be fit and trim. This popular betterment route only makes matters worse: bad *students,* not dreadful schools more than any other single factor are the culprits.

And by "bad students" we mean all predilections inimical to learning, everything from passive sloth to violent criminality.

What Begets What?

In the language of social science, a troubling causality quandary exists —the chicken and egg problem—when linking atrocious schools to shoddy academics. Do awful students produce dreadful schools *or* are these students created by bad schools? Current mainstream "expert" thinking *always* asserts schools are the evil-doer—naturally hungry-to-learn students are corrupted by their awful environment. The opposite is far more plausible, however, and if bad students cause bad schools, our entire effort to boost educational performance by changing school environments is pointless. Rehabilitating dilapidated buildings is one thing; transforming an inherently anti-intellectual youngster is quite another.

Deplorable conditions inimical to learning are not present at creation. Buildings are not constructed with broken windows, graffiti covered walls and violence-inducing corridors. Police are not assigned randomly regardless of circumstances nor do schools needlessly invest in metal detectors and surveillance cameras. Inoperable equipment, tattered or missing textbooks, overflowing toilets, and the like conditions do not mysteriously appear. *In each case students are largely responsible.* Supposedly dedicated students are not "victimized" by lifeless objects to the point of distraction. Administrators rationally react when students, not things, are the miscreants. Why buy the latest textbooks if they are quickly stolen? Talented teachers rationally flee perilous settings, and to insist that schools under-perform since they have "bad teachers" is but a duplicitous way of admitting that rambunctious students can drive out frustrated skilled teachers enjoying flight options. Even capable instructors who persevere can be indistinguishable from zombie colleagues. Such potential high-performers may go through the motions and thus appear "bad" but, if transferred to classes filled with quick learners, may be reborn. Return them to previous schools, and they will again go "bad."

By refusing to confer personal responsibility for failure we anthropomorphize tangible things, as if desks and chairs—not their occupants—flunk spelling tests. This is yet another triumph of that pernicious 1960s's "don't blame the victim" mentality and, for good measure, it incorporates into national policy the corrosive mentality debilitating the impoverished (i.e., it is "society's fault"). According to this alluring official cosmology, a once "good school" can "go bad" as if an impersonal toxic plague-like force—not new students—struck it.

Protests against "bad schools" can have a 1950s civil rights flavor when African-Americans were forced to accept second-rate back-of-the-bus facilities while whites received first class treatment. Back then blacks demanded access via sit-ins and marches and ultimately succeeded—they could now sit at the front of the bus. This mentality apparently lingers on though wholly inappropriate. In anticipation of the 2008 school year a Chicago civil rights leader, James Meeks, sought to resurrect this give-us-first-class-facilities strategy for education, as if education could be acquired like a consumer good (Tarm, 2008). Under Meek's tutelage thousands of inner-city black students traveled to Winnetka, IL and tried to enroll in New Trier High School, one of the state's premier academic (and largely-white) institutions. (A September 5, 2008 *Washington Post* follow-up story told of these inner-city students unable to take their science books home since the school lacked sufficient numbers. Zero was said about explaining this shortage, e.g., books were stolen, destroyed, or misplaced by inept teachers.) That most of these unprepared students would suddenly be overwhelmed by the work, and lacked any legal right to enroll, made no difference. It was *déjà vu* all over again—the whites had the good stuff like snazzy books and computers and blacks just wanted to get their share of this "good education."

Haplessness in the face of "bad schools" misconstrues the problem. If refurbishing run-down, crime-ridden facilities with stellar facilities with police officers every ten feet would cure "bad schools," they would have vanished decades ago. Grumbling aside, dreadful physical conditions—including criminality—are often tolerated. Walter Williams, a sociology professor, depicts one such museum-quality bad school, Frederick Douglas High School in Baltimore, MD. At one time the school turned out a parade of distinguished graduates including Thurgood Marshall, judges, and members of Congress. Today, most of the students are far, far below grade level in reading and math, about a quarter of the students fail to show up on a given day and many of those who do, don't attend class—they just wander the halls. Those in class often just laugh, joke, and tussle with one another. Others have heads on desks, apparently sleeping. The educational establishment "solution" to this disaster, a rightly skeptical Williams notes, is more money, smaller classes, and newer buildings (Williams, 2008).

Perhaps on slow news days the city editor tells an unoccupied reporter "visit some inner-city school and get a horror story, we haven't run one in six months." One such account concerned the overwhelmingly black and Hispanic I.S. Roland Hayes School in Brooklyn, NY (grade 6 to 8) where the reporter saw graffiti-covered mutilated books thrown into plastic crates, student lockers made unusable to prevent them from being used as weapons and some classes being held in hallways since students refused to calm down (some had never quieted down and thus never entered the actual classroom). There are no recesses since anxious teachers park their cars on the playground. Teachers are particularly worried about flirting between students and teachers and among students themselves, and this in a school of eleven to thirteen year olds (this tale comes from insideschools.com, April 2005). Academic results are, predictably, dreadful.

These tales *never* cause experts to think "well, maybe it's the students, not the schools." A 2008 *Newsweek* story tells of a reporter stopping in at Washington, DC's Cardozo Senior High School (Wingert, 2008). He found countless class-skipping students noisily lolling about the halls with scarcely any attempt to return them to classes, tales of brutal violence including a substitute teacher beaten by three freshmen girls for shushing them, and a totally trashed classroom abandoned by the intimidated teacher. As a security measure all bathroom save one were locked and the school's fire alarm was routinely set off. Other than patrolling the metal detector, the school's security force was invisible. But, how does the author account for this anti-learning mayhem? It's obvious: after talking to some of the students he concluded that their dreadful behavior is just a reaction to a dysfunctional educational system.

On a National Public Radio program dealing with inner-city schools Frank Burd, a Philadelphia math teacher, spoke of "opening yourself up," developing trust with these students, being sensitive to cultural nuances, and using gentle inoffensive language to solicit obedience (Grabar, 2008). Sadly, a few months before the interview, Burd suffered a broken neck, brain damage, and a shoulder injury when he "incorrectly" asked a student to turn off his noisy iPod. Burd's colleague, music teacher Ed Klein, similarly attempted to be sensitive to his students by replacing Eurocentric music with rap. But, when he called in a parent "one too many times" to deal with an unruly offspring, Klein suffered a broken jaw due to his efforts. In previous encounters with this "concerned" parent he was sprayed with a fire extinguisher and threatened with death. Ironically, Burt still calls his attacker a "beautiful-looking" kid with just a bad home environment. Klein, by contrast, is unable to say much since he cannot remember the incident having lost his short-term memory.

These schools are hardly inescapable Hurricane-like natural disasters. A neighborhood *truly* craving a first-rate institution can certainly assist the police by identifying drug peddlers, document gross incompetents, or file complaints about dangerous conditions or filth. If officials dawdle, parents can discipline unruly children, make sure junior arrives promptly, side with teachers, not their "innocent" off-spring in disputes, and supplement the school's meager resources either by raising money or volunteering. Recall the School of the Transfiguration mentioned in Chapter 1—superb results on a broken shoestring. Terrible schools do not push educationally-motivated parents into indifference; the opposite causal chain—chaos arising from indifferent parents is more plausible.

What are "Bad Schools"?

Complaining about "bad schools" probably began with formal education. Socrates ran a "bad school" by corrupting Athenian youth, and authorities, like modern bureaucrats, gave him the death penalty though in this instance it was literal. Make no mistake, "bad schools" are real, not another fanciful idea cooked up by radical education professors. Millions of parents annually endure financial sacrifices or relocate to send their children to "good schools" while "bad schools" undermine property values. But, while this terminology suffices in ordinary conversation, matters grow murky when this concept comes under the scientific microscope.

Almost *anything* about schooling has been, and quite properly, attributed to this killer of learning. Especially popular are physical deficiencies, insufficient supplies, overcrowding, distracting noise, hungry students unable to concentrate, large factory-like facilities, among myriad visible impediments thwarting learning. More modern educators seem especially partial to instructional materials as the culprit: antiquated boring "irrelevant" textbooks, non-inclusive "too white" curriculums and lousy pedagogy such as (for conservatives) whole-word reading instruction, (for progressives) teaching mathematics by rote learning, or (for everybody) one-size-fits-all lessons. Other inventory updates focus on personnel, notably unqualified teachers, certified instructors lacking "cultural competence" (i.e., sensitivity to black or Hispanic culture), teachers holding pupils to soft standards, "hidden" staff racial prejudice, administratively-weak principals, unmotivated tenured teachers hiding behind union protection, the lack of merit-based pay, tenure, and too few social service professionals vital for today's diverse, often psychologically-troubled student body.

Lastly, and most central for our purposes, though bringing up the rear in the public eye when today's educational evils are put on parade, are "bad students" making "bad schools." Most prominent are traits that subvert education for everyone, even classmates keen to learn—bullying, sassing teachers, and otherwise impeding learning. More extreme are gang warfare, drug peddling, inflammatory vulgar language, thievery and shakedowns, even rape and assault. But, far more commonplace though never officially recognized statistically is just garden variety contempt for academic achievement—mocking "A" students, emphasizing sports or flirting over studying, a penchant for cheating or just sleep-walking through classes.

The Wages of Anthropomorphizing "Bad Schools"

Current "bad schools" discussions invisibly slide back and forth between collectives and individuals. This is a familiar social science quandary—the level of analysis problem—where collective and individual traits may be dissimilar despite a common label. For example, Japanese people are remarkably peaceful but Japan was for half a century highly aggressive as *a nation*. Mexico is the opposite—an international pacifist with a sky-high domestic murder rate. Garbling this distinction is allowable in everyday conversation but it can be disastrous when forming public policy, and unfortunately, this is *exactly* what occurs among today's reformers.

Certification of school—not student—success or failure often merely reflects clever negotiations, a knack securing administrative waivers or adroit managing of school population, among other factors, none of which have *anything* to do with imparting *individual-level* knowledge. Words like "failure" thus become meaningless and putative fixes are lost in fogs of confusion. For example, several Michigan high schools with otherwise excellent academic records "failed" the federal standard when a handful of special education students flunked their tests. If these institutions had fewer than thirty special-ed pupils, the special-ed students would not have been singled out, and the school would have passed with flying colors. Other schools elsewhere failed since the proportion of students taking the test fell slightly below the 95 percent requirement, regardless of how, say 94 percent performed. A California study similarly found that schools with four or more legally-defined student categories were five times more likely to be classified as "failures" than those with more homogeneous student populations, even if these "failing schools" had strong average test scores. The phenomenon has even acquired a name—"the diversity penalty" (Schouten, 2003). Elsewhere schools survive by showing "progress" toward meeting standards (Adequate Yearly Progress or AYP in gov-eduspeak), so a savvy administrator will be wary of large but unsustainable performance jumps (MacDonald, 2004).

A similar perplexing outcome occurred at Hinsdale South High School, an outstanding academic institution located in an affluent Illinois suburb where parents obsess over gaining admission to prestigious colleges. It "failed" when a few disabled enrollees came up short. As required by law, the school notified parents advising them that, because of this blemish, school officials would help them transfer their children to "better" schools though, as every parent knew, Hinsdale was top-notch. Some parents worried that the "failure" stigma would hinder entrance to first tier colleges and undermine property values.

Well-intentioned administrators navigating this Alice-in-Wonderland world confront several catch-22s. If principals boost standards or impose tough discipline, some students will gain academically but others will be truant or drop out. Alas, this exodus risks "failure," regardless of absolute progress elsewhere since compelling thugs to show up versus rightfully expelling them can bring a collapse into anarchy when miscreants realize that for the school to "pass" they must be prevented from dropping out. A clever gang leader might say, "If I stay home or drop out Mr. Principal, you're toast!" Or, if white academically-proficient suburban schools voluntarily recruit inner-city blacks (as now occurs in some Virginia schools outside Washington, DC), they risk being shuttered due to unacceptable race-related achievement gaps, no matter how admirable the motives or black progress. The latter possibility suggests a rational aversion to racial integration regardless of non-academic benefits. Why risk unemployment by importing struggling students?

Adept cynics could effortlessly "solve" the "bad school" quandary by manipulating bureaucratic rules, specifically transferring every underperforming student, including the disabled, to a single district or state mega institution. If such under-performers resist relocating, entice them with free meals, clothing allowances, and other enticements, all of which are cheaper than upgrading academics (note: NCLB prohibits transfers from good schools to bad ones, but our new entity—Bart Simpson High—is not yet bad since schools are given time to reform). In an instant, institutions shedding these troublesome folk become "good." Wait three years until this newly-created disaster receives the death penalty, move the entire population across the street, rename the school Beavis and Butt-head Tech, and *voilá*, an educational miracle, and savvy politicians will immediately brag of their magisterial power. Three years later, order an exodus back to the old building, and keep it up *ad infinitum*. Construct a national campus—Hieronymus Bosch Academy of Earthly Delights—where armies of low-performers toil and America is totally cured.

The opposite scenario is also possible—closing bad schools (the "death penalty") destroys, not improves, decent education everywhere. Washington DC's schools illustrate the perversity of this "enlightened" policy but the process can occur anywhere. Here's how the dynamic works. First, as parents sensibly flee the crime-ridden District's schools, declining enrollment means fewer schools. Now, the current Chancellor (Michele Rhee) who clearly accepts this "bad school" theory of educational calamity shutters the worst performing facilities. But, since students are legally entitled to schooling, they are shipped elsewhere. Unfortunately, many of these "bad schools" refugees are gang members and so now confront rival gangs, and the turf wars begin (Ali, 2008). Violence explodes, more students flee, more schools receive the death penalty, the buses roll with refugees, turf wars intensify, and like an atomic chain reaction, enrollments sink. Eventually the Washington, DC school system may consist of only a few prison-like facilities where nobody learns anything since every school is a "bad school."

Ostensibly benign racial segregation is particularly appealing as a means to jimmy the numbers. Several cities are toying with black male only schools, a move that would perform statistical wonders for city-wide test score gaps at the school (but not individual) level. One Westchester County New York school district (Ossining) now runs a voluntary K-12 black male only program that entices enrollees with varied perks including free trips to Knicks and Mets games to practice counting skills. There is even a black male only college preparatory program for high schoolers (Hu, 2007). Keep in mind that these "solutions" lack any demonstrable *individual* academic gain. But, and this is critical, removing struggling blacks from the district's regular schools makes the entire district "much better" according to the good school/bad school cosmology.

Not all "Bad Schools" Are Bad, at Least for Their Customers

When government seeks to upgrade educational standards by shutting awful schools, two particular problems arise. The most evident, though less pressing for our purposes (though not for parents), is the mismatch between today's singular, government-supplied test score definition and a range of individual conceptions. Parents, students, teachers, administrators, tax-payers all likely possess quite distinct if not contradictory visions—obsessing over admission to prestigious colleges or perfect SAT scores is not universal. Few may publicly confess to favoring football over AP calculus, but observation of what transpires across thousands of schools confirms this variability.

Zero guarantees exist that government-certified deplorable schools are atrocious for all students or parents. It just depends on what is *personally* desired and a "good education" does not mean that traditional academic learning—even literacy—is a priority. Godwin and Kemerer (2002, 37-40) offer some intriguing interview data across several settings about

African American parents who initially attended good "choice schools" and then voluntarily returned to their original "bad schools." These were substantial (often 50 percent or higher) and reflected a variety of perfectly understandable motives. In some instances their children just felt socially uncomfortable in these new schools with their "white culture," others objected to newly imposed discipline, receiving poor grades, and failed to make new friends. The cost of transportation and travel time were also common explanations. A national survey taken in 2004 found that 85 percent of parents favored keeping their children in neighborhood schools, even if these schools were deficient—only 14 percent wanted the transfer option (data cited in Whitman, 2008, 25-6).

More important, the costs of accomplishment, no matter how prized, are not always worth paying and may be decidedly negative. In the interview data reported by Godwin and Kemerer (2002, 39-40) some of the parents of students returning to the old school told of the extra academic demands made on their offspring and teachers recommending that junior might be academically happier elsewhere. In other words, it was just easier to go back than up the effort. A parent whose doltish child somehow sneaked into the hyper-pressurized New York City's Bronx High School of Science might reasonably conclude the Bronx Science was a catastrophe and his son would be happier in one of the City's "worst" crime-ridden schools where he would quickly master the class material and rise to class valedictorian. Academics can have a downside if mediocre students in high pressured settings drop out or seek comfort in alcohol, drugs, or the rebellious youth counterculture.

The escape from grueling academics is not necessarily limited to African Americans avoiding "white" schools. A *Wall Street Journal* story told of middle-class white parents fleeing the two public high schools in Cupertino, CA (Hwang, 2005). Cupertino has recently attracted many education-obsessed Asians and even a "B" average in these pressure cooker settings means being in the bottom third of the class. As these Asian youngsters dominate advanced courses in math and science, white students fall behind and anxious parents sent them off to less demanding, often private schools (this makes perfect sense since colleges look at class rank and grades). One of these schools—Monta Vista High School—is among California's top academic high schools, yet it is a "bad school" for many whites. Whites abandoning a school (i.e., "white flight") rather than face cutthroat competition have also occurred in Rockville, MD and other communities seeing influxes of Asians.

This is a consumer sovereignty "defense" of awful schools, and we admit that these anti-academic inclinations may be injurious. Still, as the history of reform demonstrates, top-down imposed academically-centered remediations concocted by experts are easily resisted if unwelcome. Not everybody heeds officialdom's advice regarding eating vegetables, exercising more, or not smoking. Again, desiring the supposed benefits of a "good school"—high income, prestigious jobs and all else on the enticement list—is seldom sufficient to reverse unwise inclinations. Shuttering a low-performing school, *without altering the underlying preferences driving this insufficiency* almost guarantees that the same woeful outcomes will be repeated elsewhere. Beneficiaries of such largesse may actually want to return to the "misery" of indolence.

Making "Bad Schools" Better Academically

Analytically linking "bad schools" with dismal academic achievement is critical if "good schools" are to solve America's educational troubles. The NCLB and comparable other government initiatives make this link central yet the *precise* connective tissue is hardly self-evident. The parallel is medical diagnosis—a sick person may display multiple signs of illness, but what are causes versus mere symptoms? Precisely linking symptoms to illness can be extraordinarily difficult. After all, we saw that "bad school" can entail multiple unsavory traits, but what, in particular, makes the evil-doer so destructive? Sloganeering and lurid journalism aside, disentangling this quandary is a research nightmare all too easily avoided as the next election looms. Further add the problem of ideologically-driven research, for example, the NEA, America's largest teachers' union, is always happy to report research showing that bad schools are over-crowded so more teachers should be hired while conservatives hail a study depicting the miracles of merit pay. Sadly, today's pontificators favoring magic bullet quick fixes of "bad schools" ignore these complexities.

To link bad schools to bad performances first requires translating possible culprits—surely in the hundreds—into precise statistical indicators and this opens the door to ideologically-slanted findings, findings whose particular tilt will be privy only to those intimately-acquainted with the study's actual construction. That unsophisticated policy-makers (and media reporters) inclined to executive summaries seldom venture beyond highlights only exacerbates the possibilities for mischief. This partiality need not be conscious or reflect financial sponsorship. Pushing outcomes in certain directions more likely reflects a deep-seated *Zeit-*

geist rendering favored results "plausible" while other possibilities are judged "unthinkable." An AIDS researcher who explained this disease as "god's punishment" would be mocked; when it comes to explaining "bad schools," however, standards are more lax, and the upshot is maddening confusion and ill-devised reforms.

Kinder, Gentler "Bad Schools"

To illustrate how "bad schools" can be "safely" (i.e., inoffensively) scientifically linked to academic achievement to minimize awkward press coverage, consider one notable investigation of this complicated subject—Chubb and Moe's *Politics, Markets and America's Schools* (1990). The authors are distinguished academics not ideologues, the respected mainstream Brookings Institution published it, and it is a model of exacting social science. It is also a remarkably transparent, expensive, laborious project entailing two large-scale surveys.

In brief, an enormous amount of data about students, teachers, parents, and the schools themselves were collected (for example some 60,000 sophomores and seniors in 1,015 high schools were interviewed). Data from all types of schools were collected and were even asked if there were more than 50 books and pocket calculators at home. Additional probes concerned discipline, questions about cutting classes, punishment for school rule infractions, fighting on school grounds, disrespecting teachers, and the like. Data on school violence were also obtained—robberies, alcohol and drug use, possible rapes, and weapons on school grounds. Teachers were interviewed on wide-ranging factors obviously related to "bad schools," for example, how many students completed homework, whether students "fooled around" during instruction and several queries pertaining to how administrators facilitated learning. Questions covered teacher control over students and curriculum and if teachers felt that their efforts made it worthwhile. Whether schools had exit tests and implementing a racial desegregation plan was included. These data were complemented by multiple economic resource indicators (e.g., spending per pupil) plus racial/ethnic composition data. The key measure of the academic outcome certifying a bad versus good school were gains in student achievement across select academic subjects.

This is attention-getting research. The authors' prestige, the publisher, and imposing data analysis seemingly renders it definitive. But, this conclusiveness is not as rock-solid as it might appear. Despite all the factors hypothesized, this menu is hardly complete, and it is unclear just why these particular explanatory factors were selected for in-depth treatment versus drawing from an entirely different menu. Of critical importance, the statistical terminology and various manipulations are mind-numbing, and only the most technically-sophisticated readers will grasp the complicated pathway necessary to these conclusions, let alone recognize how slightly different procedures could alter results (particularly given the finding's often small magnitude). And while these data are publicly available, it is doubtful that amateurs are up to challenging the authors' conclusions.

What do Chubb and Moe uncover? Actually, their book abounds with varied conclusions, some straightforward others exceedingly complicated if not confusing, and those looking for quick magic bullet answers will leave frustrated. Relatively early on (99) the authors announce: "High performance schools differ in goals, leadership, personnel and educational practices from low performance schools. Their goals are clearer and more academically ambitious, their principals are stronger educational leaders, their teachers are more professional and harmonious, their course work is more academically rigorous, and their classrooms are more orderly and less bureaucratic." Later on (187) they reaffirm the importance of assorted organizational features as the pathway to academic success: staff autonomy, strong educational programs, clear and ambitious academic goals, workforce harmony and coordination, teacher professionalism, and similar bureaucratic reforms that will unleash pent-up academic productivity. As for immediate concrete policy changes, the authors recommend enhanced administrative freedom via more school choice as the pathway to ridding America of terrible schools.

Remarkably, factors typically arising in plain-folk talk regarding "bad schools" evade elaborate statistical analysis. A visiting Martian encountering this study would surmise that American students crave first-rate schooling, possess the requisite talents but, alas, organizational insufficiencies having zero to do with students themselves block attainment. The preverbal educational nightmare—the inner-city graffiti-covered jungle of gang violence where students are just lucky to survive *never* appears in this magisterial tome. As one reads *Politics, Markets and America's Schools* one is reminded of the "it's the food" tale at the chapter's beginning. Everything is put into the police lineup except the students themselves, an approach that would surely baffle most parents shopping for a "good school." The book's bottom line recommendation is that "change the rules and the children will learn." Only if educational reform were so simple.

The hot-button race issue is carefully skirted. Chubb and Moe conclude (126-7) that school racial composition is unrelated to academic gains among students, and no doubt, the data, as crunched here, confirm this contention so, at least here a school's shifting racial composition makes no difference. This race-is-irrelevant argument is ludicrous. Massive "white flight" over the last half century where white parents flee schools upping lower-class black enrollment is exceptionally well-documented. Are millions of whites deluded in their lemming-like migrations? To speak plainly, the largely lower-class black school often epitomizes the "bad school" and many middle class blacks likewise flee the arrival of lower class black students. That numerous urban school districts now have miniscule white enrollments and efforts to entice whites to "black schools" usually fail despite excellent facilities, clearly contradicts this "race doesn't matter" conclusion. Nevertheless, in a world where social scientist experts can manufacture reality via including and excluding variables and choosing what to correlate with what, this counterintuitive conclusion becomes statistically-certified wisdom. To put this conclusion into crime language, "the fix is in."

Bad Students

Given today's ideologically-suffocating "don't blame the victim" mentality, assembling the evidence to convict this alleged culprit—students—is arduous, not unlike convicting the hit-man in a professional Mafia execution—no witness recalls anything, at least publicly. There is also official collusion in covering up loathsome student behavior (versus "the school's" guilt). In the weird logic of NCLB, administrators are *personally* punished for having unruly schools so self-interest encourages lying. Consider the violence plaguing countless schools. For the school year 2003-04 only *26* of the nation's 91,000 public schools were officially labeled "dangerous" according to NCLB figures, but this compilation excluded one Los Angles High School that had 17 robberies, 25 batteries, 11 assaults with a deadly weapon, and three sex offenses. Washington, DC did not have a *single* unsafe school in that period though the DC Office of the Inspector General admitted that there were some 1,700 "serious security incidents" in the District's schools (cited in Snell, 2005). No doubt, these police-based figures grossly underestimate the mayhem bedeviling myriad schools and no records are kept of other, milder, student behaviors inimical to learning, e.g., dozing during class, petty vandalism, harassing decent students, and all the rest frustrating learning.

Other types of evidence are also limited in securing a conviction though they help build a case. Dismal National Assessment of Educational Progress (NAEP) test scores together with the occasional lurid exposés of widespread student ignorance strongly corroborate student insufficiency but only indirectly. In particular, to certify indolence from test results requires first establishing baselines of possible attainment given individual intellectual talent. Conceivably, the slothful beleaguered by Algebra I may be functioning at the top of their academic game given innate cognitive abilities, and outward signs of anti-intellectualism are merely predictable though unwise psychological reactions to awaiting failure. Thus, in one sense "bad students" are guilty as charged for disdaining learning but, in another sense, innocent since they cannot perform better and reasonably blame their noxious behavior on overly ambitious task-masters. In legal terms they are "not guilty" by reasons of innate incompetence.

Better evidence would come from the frank testimony of exasperated teachers regularly trying to motivate apathetic students. According to one 2007 *New York Times* story, some 41,291 teachers have fled the New York City school system since 1999 (Gootman, 2007) and while it may be impossible to say that troubling students fully explains this exodus, daily confronting dozens of difficult-to-teach students undoubtedly hasten flight. One particularly insightful investigation of this possibility covers all Texas public elementary schools from 1993-96 (Hanushek, Kain, and Rivkin, 2004). The study conducted by three economists included teacher salary data, student test scores, school characteristics, and school racial/ethnic composition data and carefully tracks teacher employment patterns, among multiple other factors that might explain the choice to leave a school or shift careers. To condense a long story, student attributes are often decisive in teacher's decision to quit or transfer, and this factor far outshines monetary incentives, especially for female teachers and holds across all years of experience.

Specifically, as the proportion of black and Hispanic or low-income students rises within a school, white teachers jump ship (by contrast, black teachers gravitate to "black schools" as these factors shift). White teachers who continue teaching are, critically, drawn to high-achieving schools, and transfers typically occur within the same urban school district, a relocation unrelated to teaching smaller classes and pay incentives since pay schedules tend to be uniform within districts. According to the authors, moreover, upping salaries (so-called "combat pay"), at least within feasible ranges, cannot entice teachers to engage low-achieving minority students, let alone attract fresh recruits from elsewhere. At best, male teachers in a certain age range might, however, be slightly more tempted, a pattern perhaps explained by the lure of greater retirement pay.

What drives white teachers to flee low-performing, black and Hispanic schools in favor of white, better achieving schools? Student quality is a highly plausible explanation—it's discouraging trying to impress laggards and, after years of futility, it is tempting to leave. If student characteristics were irrelevant we'd expect transfers and exits to be fairly uniform across schools, and they are clearly not. Note well, in principle this motivating factor would apply regardless of race or ethnicity, but in the Texas context, this means blacks and Hispanics (see the Vietnamese boat people account below). It is no secret that these minority/low income schools overflow with unruly, occasionally violent, unmotivated students regularly making life miserable for anyone, of any race or ethnicity. Recall Baltimore's Frederick Douglas High School and this school is hardly unique. Even a committed teacher would surrender after years of talking to the walls and reading atrocious essays, let alone tackling daily disciplinary eruptions. For women the risks are more serious, and the data reflect these. Rival explanatory factors—insufficient instructional supplies, indifferent principals, broken audio-visual equipment, and similar resource-related deficiencies—undoubtedly pale in comparison to being irrelevant in dangerous, even life-threatening, circumstances.

Another clue to our school versus students question is survey-based. Here the most comprehensive analysis is Laurence Steinberg's *Beyond the Classroom* (1996). Steinberg is an expert on adolescent development and he and his university-based associates surveyed more than 20,000 teenagers in 9 quite different ethnically diverse high schools in Wisconsin and California between the late 1980s and early 1990s plus hundreds of parents and dozens of teachers. Focus groups were also used and students were re-interviewed over time. The research probed less formal elements of schooling, especially what occurs beyond the school's walls, not directly captured by test scores and other objective indicators, but these dispositions absolutely underlie academic accomplishment.

What does Steinberg uncover? Are intellectually ambitious students frustrated by inadequate schools? Students are clearly the problem. Steinberg finds that commitment to schools is at an all time low, and this indifference is not just centered in the notoriously under-performing inner-city schools. An extremely high proportion of students fail to take school seriously—they spend countless hours "goofing off" with friends, often cheat on tests or rely on the homework of others. For many attending classes is just a nuisance—between a third and 40 percent admit they are not paying attention or not trying hard. Teachers routinely report having classes where half the students seem "checked out." Furthermore, little non-classroom time is devoted to academically-related activities. Homework, even when minimal, is clearly secondary to athletics, socializing, or employment. Academic achievement is not highly valued, and is often demeaned. Less than 20 percent believe that good grades bestow social prestige (accomplishment is often a liability, and this is not just rampant among blacks) and a reputation as "a brain" appealed to only one in ten. Significantly, parents similarly despair academic accomplishment though, naturally, insist that a "good education" was desirable. Students frequently said that low grades failed to bring parental rebuke and one third indicated that parents had scant idea of their school progress.

Student indifference and outside distractions creates a downward spiral of low achievement. Faced with bored students, many tired from work, teachers stop making the extra effort to inspire, even just to impart the basics, and this, in turn, confirms to students that schooling is just a waste of time. Meanwhile, professional pedagogues who sense the disengagement attempt to make learning "exciting" with bedazzling textbooks and ancillaries, films and other attention-grabber "fun" stunts to jump-start enthusiasm. Though students might welcome the vacation from "dry" academics, these novelties totally fail to address deeper defects, notably a lack of discipline or an ability to concentrate. And without these essential "grind" qualities, subjects like math and science are "too hard" and academic motivation further wilts. In a sense, by competing with tricks to spike academic curiosity, schools abandon their traditional and inescapably tedious educational role though administrators can readily defend themselves as "trying to be relevant in today's attention-deficit disorder culture." If juicing things up fail, just keep reducing the assigned readings and homework to make schooling more palatable, just as a TV producer might dumb-down a TV sitcom and add a few sex jokes to sustain a dwindling audience.

Steinberg's analysis is a devastating critique of American education but it should not obscure numerous outposts that do embody the highest standards. Though relatively few in number, they annually graduate thousands and are spread across the nation, including many smaller towns hardly enjoying reputations for academic excellence. They range from world famous large urban schools such as New York City Bronx High School for Science and Boston Latin in Boston, MA to the Oxford Academy in Cyprus, CA. One in particular, the Preuss School in La Jolla,

CA enjoys an outstanding academic reputation though its student body is largely black and Hispanic, two populations often associated with academic failure. If one adds in the innumerable academically top-notch private schools, the supply of intellectual accomplishment in America's school is enormous.

Natural Experiments

Fortunately, the "bad students versus bad schools" hypothesis can be examined in the realm of academic achievement though, we admit, only by approximation. This is the "natural experiment" approach whereby the school (and this includes everything from teachers and facilities to the curriculum) is "held constant" while the student body changes. That is, if new students arrive at a "bad school" and excel it is implausible to insist that the school itself inherently destroys learning. A second natural experiment entails permitting students from a "bad school" to relocate to a "good school." In practice, the latter experiment is what most racial integration is about—inner city black students will, supposedly, flourish once they have good teachers, top-flight equipment, and all the rest possessed by "good schools." Chapter 4 examines desegregation's impact on academic achievement but suffice it to say, racial integration rarely rescues struggling new arrivals from insufficiency. For the present we concentrate on the first natural experiment—what happens when smart, motivated students arrive at a "bad school."

Immigrants and Bad Schools

The United States has recently experienced massive immigration and newcomers have generally settled in impoverished localities dominated by troubled schools. Add unfamiliarity with English, few economic resources to compensate for public school shortcomings, and all the other problems bedeviling newcomers and one would reasonably expect immigrant children to be prime victims of those terrible places that have historically under-served millions of impoverished African-Americans. But, matters are complex: student performances in these oft-dreary, run-down sometimes violence-plagued settings varies widely, and these dissimilarities are often so spectacular, that the "bad school did it" crime theory utterly collapses.

On one side of the performance divide are Hispanics, particularly those recently arriving from Mexico plus Puerto Ricans who have for decades resided on the mainland. Their academic attainment is, on average, dismal, and thus seemingly offers perfect smoking gun proof of the bad school-begets-bad-students hypothesis. On the other side of the accomplishment ledger are the "boat people" refugees fleeing to the United States beginning in 1978. Most were ethnic Vietnamese with a fair number of Chinese and Laotian ancestries. They had suffered horrendous conditions in Thai and Cambodian refugee camps, often arrived sick and malnourished. They had fled Vietnam by sea on tiny boats or by long on-foot treks through jungles and with barely any material possessions. Few spoke English though a handful began English lessons in the refugee camps. Prior imprisonment by the Communist regime was common, families were broken up, and half or more initially escaping by sea died en route while countless survivors of this journey were raped and robbed by marauding pirates, frequently after first-hand seeing family members killed. Unlike the first wave of Vietnam better-educated more urban refugees fleeing Saigon in 1975, most in this second wave lived at the bottom of the socioeconomic hierarchy and lacked modern skills or adequate education. Upon landing, significantly at a time of a nation-wide economic downturn, they received only modest public and private welfare assistance supplemented by help from friends and family who briefly preceded them. Volunteer religious and charity groups often sponsored them since private sponsorship was government required. As is true for countless past impoverished newcomers, refugees gravitated toward rundown neighborhoods where their children typically attended dismal public schools (our analysis is drawn from Caplan, Whitmore, and Choy, 1992).

The boat people numbered about half a million and generally settled in California (especially Orange County near Los Angeles) plus a scattering of other cities, notably Chicago, Houston, Washington, DC, and Boston. Significantly, despite years of trauma and separation, family structures remained reasonably intact with few single, unrelated adults comprising a household. Eventually unattached adults often joined larger families and contributed economically. Large families were the norm. After a brief adjustment period, labor force participation soared though typically in low-paying jobs. Welfare dependency dropped sharply though modest government financial assistance frequently remained. Still, the overall escape from poverty was relatively fast. Sufficient family income was generated by having multiple household members work, commonly for long hours, all the while caring for children.

How did the refugee offspring perform academically? Keep in mind that English was not their native language, and most lived with families where nobody spoke English fluently, if at all; all had missed a year or more of school, and faced staggering problems of cultural adjustment. By all standards, the children of the boat people did *exceptionally* well, typically outperforming native-born Americans (and students from other immigrant groups) who at least superficially enjoyed superior resources. In California their overall high school grade point average was about a "B" but in math nearly half (46.7 percent) were "A" students (only 6.3% averaged "D" or less). They excelled in science and spelling, though less so for fields requiring English proficiency.

The absence of local competition cannot explain accomplishment since comparable results occurred on California's state-wide academic achievement test (the CAT)—a bit above average overall with striking results in mathematics, science, and spelling. Even those who had lost years of school in transit performed admirably and these students were the same ages as their American classmates. Of the utmost importance for our purposes, these performances show no significant variation across different school systems, *including schools normally associated with low achievement and student disruptions* (81-82). In the words of Caplan *et. al.* when discussing the implication of their findings, "The schools across the country, even in low resource urban areas such as those attended by the refugee children, respond remarkably well to *children who come prepared and willing to learn*" (162, italics added).

Teacher reports help explain this remarkable accomplishment. From kindergarten onward teachers witnessed an enthusiasm for learning and pleasure in mastering lessons. School administrator interviews and actual transcripts reveal almost zero disciplinary problems, virtually no suspensions, or drug use. In one Orange County, California area popular with refugees they comprised some 20 percent of the school enrollment but were twelve of the fourteen high school valedictorians. And, contrary to what might be expected, children with three or more siblings out-performed those from single-child families. English proficiency had no impact on academic accomplishment in fields beyond English itself, something to ponder in the bilingual education debate.

What explains these amazing performances? Today's "experts" fixating on dreadful academic achievement with the school itself as the primary culprit would be bewildered. The boat people children certainly did *not* benefit from the usual remediations prescribed for laggards. No Marshall Plan bestowed ethnically-sensitive curriculums, role models and mentors, diversity specialists, high-tech gadgetry, culturally-competent teachers speaking Vietnamese dialects, edifying museum trips, intensive preschool intellectual enrichment, one-on-one coaching, or material incentives to entice slow learners. Boosting self-esteem as a precondition to learning was off the agenda while parents did not form advocacy groups to sue school officials to assure high test scores. There was no attack on "root causes" that might, supposedly, inhibit academic progress, i.e., eliminate immigrant poverty, cleanse society of xenophobia towards the Indo-chinese ("gooks"), or pry open the government-controlled flood gates of free health care, affordable housing, and affirmative action imposed middle-class career opportunities.

Disentangling all the success-inducing factors is complicated and can never be absolutely conclusive, yet one element is paramount: cultural values. In terms of our formula depicted in Chapter 1, this is motivation though we also suspect that cognitive talent was high. Caplan *et. al.* (especially Chapter 4) probe deeply into these forces, and the ubiquity of certain desires versus rivals is unmistakable. Foremost, the commitments to education and achievement, a cohesive family, and hard work were unanimous (42). Closely following were values associated with Confucian/Buddhist virtues: respect for family and elders, high standards of morality and ethics, fulfilling obligations, restraint and discipline, among others (43). These values were often drilled into children, and this included parents insisting that children help with household chores at the earliest age possible. Diligence training was nonnegotiable and work typically occurred without direct parental supervision. Parental involvement was intense almost everywhere so lackluster grades would disgrace a family, and where difficulties arose, family intervention was immediate.

These parents typically viewed well-educated children as old-age insurance, and that children clearly internalized this expectation provided formidable motivations. At the *bottom* of the boat peoples' value hierarchy were "fun and excitement" and "material processions." Interestingly, when respondents, many of whom resided in low-income neighborhoods, were asked to judge what motivated their non-refugee neighbors, the latter two values were said to be decisive! Though from a culture light years from current American standards, these refugees strongly embraced our "old-fashioned" anti-hedonism Protestant work ethic.

The boat peoples' academic achievement is remarkable but historically hardly unique. Celebrating our immigrant past is an oft-told saga but it is seldom recounted in its fullness. *Some* impoverished immigrant groups have achieved amazing successes while *others,* often exact contemporaries facing comparable obstacles, fall behind. "Bad schools" cannot possibly explain both outcomes since the schools scarcely differed. To repeat, people and their values, not the school's physical attributes or teacher traits are decisive. For example, in the early twentieth century, non-English speaking immigrants from Eastern and Southern Europe arrived in New York City, attended schools run by the same central administration with identical books, and yet variations in performance were enormous. Jews typically thrived academically while their Italian and Slavic compatriots fell behind (and the Irish who had arrived decades earlier likewise never excelled academically). So great and extensive was this academic accomplishment that Ivy League schools imposed religious quotas lest they be "overrun" with underprivileged, loud, boisterous slum-dwelling Eastern European Jews (no anti-Jewish quotas previously barred highly assimilated more sedate German Jews with similar passions for education).

The variability across immigrant ethnic groups remains as observable as before. Consider what now occurs in California where Asians, especially the Chinese, have flocked to elite schools while African-Americans and Hispanics lag behind despite Herculean efforts on their behalf including lowered admission standards. For example, in the Fall of 2006 students of Chinese ancestry outnumbered their black classmates by a ratio of five to one at Berkeley. There were even more first year students of Korean and Pakistani/East Indian backgrounds than blacks (University of California, Office of the President, 2007). And these numbers minimize academic discrepancies given graduation rates, classroom performances, and major fields of study (Asian immigrants gravitate to more demanding majors like molecular and cell biology versus sociology or ethnic studies). Their flagship Berkeley campus is hardly exceptional. According to a newspaper account published in 2006 the University of California at Irvine (UCI) was about 40 percent Asian, leading it to be nicked-named "The University of Chinese Immigrants" (Kelly, 2006).

Explanations for success are readily apparent. Despite radical rhetoric, those gaining entry into elite schools are not "privileged." Asians clearly outperform whites in their academic preparation, and enrollment would include even more Asians if merit were strictly followed. Nor are these Asians benefiting from wealthy "establishment" parents. Data from Berkeley in 1999 show that these immigrants are more likely to have parents with incomes below $40,000 and half (versus 22 percent on non-immigrants) had mothers who never went beyond high school. Immigrant students were also less likely to have fathers with four-year college degrees (Office of Student Research, 1999). Keep in mind that the major wave of immigration occurred after 1965, so these students typically grew up in homes facing the tribulations of economic and cultural adjustment where English fluency was rare.

Tracing university-level success stories back uncovers a familiar pattern—relentless parental pressure toward academic accomplishment. A visit to Orange County outside Los Angeles with its dense concentration of varied Asian groups reveals a by now recognizable story. Asian parents are proud of the academic competition faced by their children, even noting that non-Asians avoid "Asian schools" due to intense rivalry. Obsessing over schooling even begins before kindergarten as parents maneuver to enroll offspring at outstanding competitive nursery schools. At one local high school that is 41 percent Asian (mostly Chinese) the academic scores put it in the top 2 percent of all California's schools. Interviews with parents reveal a near obsession with educational advancement as opposed to extra-curricular activities, save cultural heritage, after-school Chinese lessons, tutoring, and SAT preparation. Many parents display a keen interest in their children's school progress anticipating future admission to Stanford, Harvard, or Yale (Kelly, 2006).

Three thousand miles east from Orange County are the Russian immigrants who beginning in the late-70s arrived in the U.S. only to confront the customary problems of learning a strange difficult language (with a confusing alphabet, to boot) and reestablishing themselves economically. Again, the enthusiasm for education translated into newsworthy success stories almost overnight. An almost cliché quality surrounds the tales, for example, how thousands of émigrés moved to Milburn, New Jersey, an affluent community with expensive housing but one offering first-rate public education. Residency entailed major sacrifices, e.g., renting small apartments and commuting considerable distances to jobs, and when their offspring graduated, many relocated to more affordable housing (James, 2002).

Across the Hudson River are Russian immigrants who have remade once decrepit Brooklyn's Brighton Beach into a vibrant neighborhood with public schools graduating star students. These immigrants and their children have revitalized the city's university system, a return to decades past when Jewish immigrants excelled at this "poor man's Harvard," as it was nicknamed. City University of New York (CUNY) has now again joined the ranks of elite universities producing Rhodes Scholars, two in 2004 and both of whom emigrated from the former Soviet Union. One, Lev A. Sviridov, lived near Chernobyl during the time of the nuclear meltdown and began his early years in New York homeless with an unemployed mother and helped support himself by scavenging for cans and bottles in trash cans.

First-generation immigrants are generally overrepresented among Rhodes winners—students named Andrew Kim, Yong Hwa Lee, Swati Mylavarapu, Anastasia Piliavasky, and Kazi Sabeel Rahman (Arenson, 2004). Figures from comparable academic competitions tell the same story. Of the 2004 Intel Science Talent Search, seven of the top ten receiving awards were foreign born or children of foreign born. In the previous year three of the top four were immigrants or children of immigrants. Students from these backgrounds are also disproportionately found on the US Math Olympiad and US Physics Team (Jacobs, 2004).

These *selective* success tales cut across the racial divide. Many blacks who have recently arrived from Africa and the Caribbean typically settle in dreary urban areas and begin with lowly jobs, but, of the utmost importance, demonstrate the same zeal for education as do the boat people, the Chinese and Russians. A recent *New York Times* account reported that children from this group were twice as likely as native-born blacks to be at the top twenty-eight universities. Within the Ivy League, African and Caribbean blacks made up 41 percent of all black freshmen (Anna, 2007). In 2000 some 43 percent of African immigrants had a college degree, far higher than the proportion of even whites or Asians (cited in Page, 2007). Given that these newcomers previously lived mainly in societies with a slavery tradition and racial discrimination, it is hard to argue that educational attainment results from artificial "privilege." More plausible, like so many—but not all— émigrés, they prize hard work, personal responsibility, and schooling over undisciplined consumption.

What is especially noteworthy about selective immigrant success in "bad schools" is how contemporary education "experts" ignore these extraordinary accomplishments. Though often celebrated in our national folklore, one could read countless professional "sure-fire cure for educational woes" and never encounter these upbeat lessons of poor kids from "bad schools" rising to the top. With scant exception, expert-supplied remedies are either just empty assurances or have proven useless, e.g., bilingual education, culturally inclusive curriculum, lavish funding for smaller classes, high-tech innovations *ad infinitum*. Bad schools are to be cured by more resources, more resources, and yet more resources. Carefully examining what produces learning, independent of physical setting, and then applying it more generally never occurs to these authorities. One can only imagine if modern medicine embraced this muddle-headed thinking—the sick would receive magic potions and die, but, rest assured, the great miracle elixir, genetically engineered super-Eye of Newt, is just around the corner.

When the Best Schools Are Not Good Enough

A second "bad school" hypothesis test derives from when African-Americans enjoy every advantage imaginable in a "good school" including learning side-by-side with smart white students. Does this really change matter? Such circumstances are rare but do occur, and the results confirm a familiar message: school facilities exert minor, if any, independent impact. Consider Shaker Heights, Ohio schools, a poster child for wealth and deep educational commitment. A sizable African-American population resides there, many of whom have middle class or above incomes. Educational spending here far exceeds the national average, and the school system justifiably boasts of its acclaimed excellence. Boundaries are even drawn to insure racial integration. This is as close to educational paradise as can be imagined: modern libraries and state-of-the-art computer facilities, plus a commitment to special programs across multiple fields, from Kindergarten to 12th grade for students of every interest and background. Advanced placement courses are the norm, and students usually pass them with flying colors for college credit. Teachers, most of who have Masters Degrees, are the best of the best and together with various other professionals offer specialized, one-on-one help for almost any problem imaginable, academic or otherwise. National academic awards are common and over 90 percent of its graduates go on to college (www.Shaker.org/about/).

How do African-American students, many from well-off families, perform in this stellar setting? The answer is: not well. A 1998 *Washington Post* article (Fletcher) paints a disappointing picture. Black students comprise about half of the school population but account for 82 percent of those at the school failing Ohio's ninth-grade proficiency test, and 84 percent of those receiving a "D" or "F" in at least one major subject post fifth grade. Despite administrative encouragement for blacks to take AP courses, most prefer less-demanding subjects. In the four previous high school graduating classes, blacks were greatly underrepresented at the top and overrepresented at the bottom. Average race-related differences in SAT scores are actually *larger* than holds nationally. In 1999-2000 a mere 4 percent of Shaker Heights blacks passed Ohio's state proficiency test with honors, a figure comparable to blacks statewide, the vast majority of whom lacked these prodigious resources (cited in Thernstrom and Thernstrom, 2003, 122). Dismal outcomes have persisted for years and, more remarkably, equally apply to children from the most prosperous neighborhoods.

Significantly, the usual explanations for these dreary outcomes fall short. Careful on-site investigations find that among blacks no stigma exists for "acting white," and, in fact, black students with good grades were admired by other blacks and lackluster performers were teased. Black parents also had high aspirations for their offspring and no relationship existed between what teachers expected and race, parental income, or parental education. One black researcher extensively observed actual classroom behavior, and did not witness a single instance of a black being held back by "European culture" or "European pedagogy" (Ogbu, 2003; Ferguson, 2001). Black students just performed poorly.

Shaker Heights educators deplored these gaps and have made an extra effort to narrow them over and above in-place stellar programs. To head off future failure tutors work with small groups of lagging kindergarteners to build language skills; special art classes exist to boost self-esteem; low-achieving but high potential students are singled out for extra attention; and those about to take state proficiency tests receive further tutoring. A student race relations group promotes racial harmony. Since these Shaker Heights educators cannot possibly blame "bad schools" for disappointing outcomes, they instead offer up a medley of (unverified) explanations stressing culture, especially black peer group pressure to "act white," which translates into doing poorly in school. Though these alleged culprits have been found innocent, they still are repeated; perhaps facing reality is too difficult.

Shaker Heights is perhaps the most noticed of these unanticipated outcomes, but it is hardly unique. The pattern reoccurs in other towns and cities, many with prestigious universities whose presence creates a strong pro-education, pro-integration atmosphere in which residents lavishly fund education. The outcome in Princeton, NJ closely mirrors what occurs in Shaker Heights: huge commitments to academic excellence (twenty-nine AP courses), virtually everybody going on to higher education and an affluent, well-educated community committed to civil rights. There has also been political pressure from local blacks to have more black teachers and school board representation. Still, the racial gaps are sufficiently large to run afoul of NCLB though Princeton can hardly be accused of short-changing its black students (Freedman, 2005).

So counterintuitive are these dreary outcomes that several such localities in 1997, under the auspices of the College Board, created the National Task Force on Minority High Achievement to scrutinize the problem and develop solutions. By 2005 some twenty-five communities were involved. Members are generally middle-class communities with ample educational spending, and include Berkeley, CA, Chapel Hill, NC, Evanston, IL and Amherst, MA (Belluck, 1999). This anomaly has also resulted in black parents creating websites so as to find ways to take advantage of these opportunities, for example, holding study sessions prior to a big test or organizing field trips (deVise 2007).

Unintended Consequences of Closing Bad Schools

What might happen if, as reformers hope, every "bad school" is shut? Would test scores soar? As we noted, if a beauty contest were held for the "most facile educational quick fix" this reshuffling miscreants to better schools solution would win, hands down. The Century Foundation, for example, recently issued a report entitled "Helping Children Move from Bad Schools to Good Ones" that suggested that this route would insure NCLB's success and thereby solve the "most serious" challenge facing America. This nostrum's favored catchphrase is "socio-economic integration" and the Foundation's account highlighted several school districts already moving in this direction (Ascribe Newswire, 2006). One bill recently introduced in the Texas legislature would grant vouchers to students at risk from dropping out, enrolled in special education, or with limited English proficiency from districts with at least 90 percent economically-disadvantaged students to be used only at private schools (Sadowski, 2007). In other words, first solve the legal and logistical problems of shipping every pupil every which way, and children will learn. A musical chairs pathway to learning.

More probable would be no overall change; matters might even deteriorate. At a minimum, given that what is a "bad school" for some is "good" for another and vice versa, resistance to these well-intentioned marching orders, including from many now mired in alleged rotten places, may instigate a counterrevolution. American education's localism virtually insures this rebellion. Remember the Boston mess after 1974 when Judge W. Arthur Garrity, Jr. ordered massive busing to integrate Boston's segregated ethnic neighborhood schools? During the Judge's supervision total enrollment dropped from 93,000 to 57,000 and the proportion of whites shrank from 50 percent in 1965 to 9 percent in 1998 (Richer, 1998). Visualize the outrage of parents who suddenly find their slothful offspring relocated to an academically "good school" who, for the sake of boosting test scores, suffers algebra rather than basketball or cheerleading. What about the reaction of homeowners residing near decent schools with well-behaved students suddenly encountering kids from horrific schools loitering nearby? Defending local autonomy would be a no-brainer for ambitious politicians, whether campaigning in the white suburbs or an inner-city African-American community. What comes into being via politics disappears via politics.

School administrators contemplating a reshuffling of accomplished and underperforming students face a seldom-appreciated painful choice since this tactic can sharply reduce overall enrollment and thus reduce state funding. A recent San Francisco skirmish perfectly illustrates this dilemma. First, as a result of escalating housing costs many African-Americans are leaving to the suburbs and schools in their neighborhood are being closed as enrollments fall. Remaining black parents are understandably upset. Meanwhile, on the other side of town "high-performing schools" with white and Asian students are overcrowded. Black parents have suggested that some of these students be transferred to the underutilized facilities in their neighborhood. For Myong Leigh, the district's chief of policy and planning, the matter is more complicated. He delicately explains that parents cannot be forced to send their children to black neighborhood schools and if this were attempted, many of these parents would desert public education altogether, further reducing state aid, aid critical to schools with heavy black enrollment since they consume extra resources (Knight, 2006).

To be blunt, shifting troublesome students to "good schools" will almost certainly subvert performance at recipient schools while scarcely uplifting those, allegedly, victimized by rotten instruction. The outcome could be nightmarish. One San Diego area school district has seven elementary schools, five of which are failing. Since students from the five can now legally transfer to the remaining two, the influx of refugees has outraged parents who paid a housing premium to enroll their offspring in the nearby superior school. Not only do these local residents face overcrowding, but their high-quality school is suddenly plagued by a physical violence and "purple language" thanks to these new arrivals ("Seeking Excellence/ Bad Schools vs. Good Schools Not a Solution," 2007). Can one honestly insist that bullies and petty thieves will mend their ways if only sent to crime-free schools? A more likely scenario is that they will be energized by easy pickings. This is, sad to say, the equivalent of transferring the sick to a healthy setting and expecting the ill to catch "health."

Let us consider a more fruitful but ideologically-awkward remediation. Prior to students from a "failing school" being shipped off to Top

Notch High they are assembled and told of their academic inadequacy. Applicants must therefore first complete an academic "boot camp" to acquire discipline, regular study habits, self-control, a knack for dealing with authority politely and all else needed to thrive in awaiting surroundings. Failures will be left behind. Needless to say, this almost never occurs; not a single move-the-student plan even contemplates this vital corrective. It is blithely assumed that essential traits will just magically appear when move-in day arrives. The opposite pathway is doubtless more realistic—if osmosis exists among today's youngsters, the direction typically flows from bad to good. Skeptics need only examine the growing popularity of profanity laden Hip-Hop music and sloppy attire captivating rural adolescents miles from urban ghettoes.

To appreciate the foolishness of this upgrade-via-osmosis mentality, consider what happened when the 1975 Individuals With Disabilities Education Act required (where feasible) inserting disabled children into regular classrooms. The law's aim was to help the disabled acquire "normal" behaviors from their new peers, and this policy has been followed so that by 2005 some 54 percent of the disabled spent most of the school day in normal settings. Leaving aside the benefits to these students, this idealistic plan has proven troublesome more generally, often resulting in high teacher turnover, classroom disruption, school violence, and disciplinary problems. In Massachusetts, for example, Special Ed students are 17 percent of enrollment but are more than half of all those responsible for weapons assault or physical violence. According to 2001 statistics compiled by Washington's General Accounting Office, those in Special Ed were more than three and a half times more likely than normal classmates to be violent, including bringing weapons to school. Even program defenders acknowledge these problems but insist that more funding for extra help could solve them (Tomsho and Golden, 2007).

An even worse historical parallel to this uplifting by osmosis is the scattered site housing nostrum a quarter century back. According to that era's experts, the urban underclass owed its pathologies to overcrowded "bad housing," i.e., bleak Soviet-style urban apartment buildings warehousing the impoverished. The "obvious" solution was to tear down these monstrosities, and relocate occupants to "good neighborhoods" to "naturally" absorb a passion for cleanliness, law-abidingness, attentive parenting, avoiding narcotics and alcohol, and all the other socially-valued middle-class instincts.

This policy proved disastrous and perhaps nothing better illustrates this flawed thinking than the highly publicized destruction in 1972 of

St. Louis' colossal Pruitt-Igoe public housing complex, the public policy equivalent of sacrificing 10,000 goats to please the gods. In 1994 the US Department of Housing and Urban Development (HUD) undertook a massive, five-year-long experimental project involving low-income families with children in five cities (results are reported in Sanbonmatsu, Kling, Duncan, and Brooks-Gunn, 2007). Thanks to a complicated system of housing vouchers, more than 5,000 randomly-selected children now had the opportunity to live in "good neighborhoods" that, naturally, had "good schools." The outcomes were carefully examined, including detailed interviews with parents and children, plus data on the schools themselves, to assess progress in reading and math. To condense a long story, and though there are tiny exceptions here and there, no academic progress occurred, and this included scores for younger children who had spent relatively few years in the high poverty neighborhood. Tellingly, few of the voucher-winning black and Hispanic parents relocated to largely white neighborhoods though this move was legally possible. One suspects that other values besides education, for example, preferring to be among people like themselves, trumped cravings for first-rate schools.

Conclusions

If this were a trial to convict schools themselves for shoddy education, it should be clear that "bad schools" are blameless. To insist that "bad schools" wreak their havoc *selectively*, only on certain demographic groups, principally blacks and Hispanics, grossly overreaches. There are just too many exceptions of economically-deprived students, many still mastering English having experienced severe hardships, flourishing in these allegedly horrible places, and placing laggards with high performers amidst stellar physical facilities failing to produce miracles. Trial over, jury dismissed. Alas, as schools accused of "bad behavior" do not harass accusers, school buildings found innocent do not have boisterous celebrations to be reported by the press.

Relentlessly censuring inanimate objects—"bad schools"—while absolving human beings from insufficiency may be outlandish, but it makes perfect sense in today's politically-"sensitive" climate. This cosmology almost seems inevitable, an enduring testament to the massive cultural infiltration emanating from the 1960s. Abandoning personal responsibility for "it's society's fault" is so complete, so ingrained in our national DNA that to broach earlier explanations of educational inadequacy is taboo. This "something else is the problem" is the official orthodoxy and even opinion polls on curing our educational woes avoid the "students themselves" on the what-is-the-problem menu. No doubt, clever lazy youngsters will tell their parents, "How can I pass geometry when my school suffers an administratively-weak principal." Woe to the office-seeker whose "education plan" entails tough discipline for disruptive students and hiring no-nonsense teachers. He or she would be booed off the stage as cruel, mean-spirited, and judgmental.

This private silence, this abandonment of the public square will no doubt increase as parents secure more free market or even Internet options. An odd paradox will soon emerge: parents (and students) increasingly find "good schools" (however defined, including rotten academic ones) but the call for tackling "bad schools" will swell as dreadful test score outcomes resist every imaginable cure. Anthropomorphically-inclined reformers will be exasperated. Nothing seems to help though Talmudic data readings always unearth glimmers of hope. After all, we now spent far more than ever before on education, showering schools with the latest technological gadgets and obtaining endless court orders to pursue social engineering, so the only "solution" is more and more, tripling the wrong medication to cure a misdiagnosed disease. To be blunt, it's the stupid, stupid or, as we initially said at the top of this essay, it's the food.

3

Motivating Students
or
You Can Take a Horse to Water *and* Make a Dehydrated Equine Feel Better about Herself

A traveler once spied a man and his mule stopped in the middle of a stream. The man was futilely pushing the stubborn animal. The traveler dismounted, walked down and offered to help. "You try," said the mule's owner. "You have to reason with the mule," the traveler opined at which point he picked up a 2 x 4 and smashed it across the mule's head. "But," said the mule owner, "I thought you were going to reason with him." "I am," said the traveler, "but first I need to get the mule's attention."

I doubt whether classical education ever has been or can be successfully carried out without corporal punishment.
—George Orwell

Recall that the academic achievement formula requires a high positive value for "student inclination." Nothing, whether glittering technology or racially-balanced schools, can surmount penchants to cut class, sleep, or otherwise disregard lessons. Instilling thirsts for learning is perhaps the most formidable obstacles facing today's educators. Here we examine what leading pedagogues counsel to reverse widespread academic indifference. The question is not what in fact occurs in classrooms (modest attainment judged by depressing outcomes) but how appetites can be improved by instructors seeking authoritative counsel.

Unfortunately, the pedagogical "How to" literature generally shows guidance to be vacuous, unscientific, and probably more vocationally-beneficial to the advice-giver than exasperated teachers. Efforts to arouse students are hardly doomed; thousands of teachers regularly intellectu-ally awaken the academically lethargic. But, feats acknowledged, a huge gulf separates what is feasible *independently* in thousands of disparate settings where clever teachers utilize personal bags of tricks versus formulating *general public policies* to remediate a national tribulation. It is applying general expert-formulated prescriptions that concern us. What do specialists recommend to extol thousands of Johnnies and Janes to study though many would rather play video games? This can be truly maddening and repeated failures may explain why this topic draws scant public discussion.

Formidable Obstacles

Enlisting public schools to light intellectual fires is an uphill battle, and impediments deserve recognition. The place to begin is to acknowledge that a "one size fits all" nostrum is probably doomed. Successful strategies undoubtedly must be fine-tuned according to age, culture, subject matter, teacher and school characteristics, family life, and just about every other factor instigating achievement. What suffices with, say, students from backgrounds drilled to obey authority would probably fail with unruly confrontational youngsters. Not all cultures equally prize future economic success, so holding out the allure of lucrative careers may be talking to the walls.

Elsewhere potentially successful tactics may be legally or morally impermissible so today's motivator struggles with a severely limited repertory. If past achievements are any guide (and they are), the ever-present threat of punishment or shame may be the superior motivator for many children. Regrettably for those attuned to the whip, not only is corporal punishment (even if mild) generally legally impermissible, but perfectly legal though vigorous rebukes for indolence, e.g., biting sarcasm, may bring unwelcome accusations of abusiveness or insensitivity that contravene today's prized educational "caring" ethos.

The aversion to corporal punishment was illustrated in a 2008 study conducted by the American Civil Liberties Union and Human Rights Watch. The study found that corporal punishment was widespread in southern states and African-American and Native American students were more than twice as likely as whites to be paddled. It also raised issues about males spanking females and condemned the humiliation and shame it brought. Left unsaid in this all-too-familiar charge of racial discrimination was (1) whether the recipients deserved harsh punishment and (2) whether it helped either the miscreant or fellow students by facilitating learning. Indeed, paddles were described in tedious detail (including how acquired) but nothing was said about educational outcomes. Physical punishment was bad and no need to explain why. As the Human Rights Watch glibly put it, "Likewise, parents and even children want orderly, safe school environments in which students can learn. But corporal punishment is not the answer. The practice hurts students, it damages the cohesive school culture that they need in order to learn, it is discriminatory, and it teaches violence as an appropriate response to problems" (*http://www.hrw.org/reports/2008/us0808/1. htm#_Toc206220327*). Clearly for the ACLU and Human Rights Watch, the possibility of racial discrimination outweighs learning. (The Report also said that poverty was at the root of this "violence" and that curing poverty and more resources would make paddling unnecessary.)

To appreciate just how far American schools have drifted away from brutal punishment, consider one rural 1820s New York teacher "motivating" an older student abusing younger classmates. Walking to school one morning he cut several birch whips, five foot in length, and as large as his thumb at their base. Called outside, the miscreant was then whipped ten times with as much strength as the teacher could muster, and when the student showed signs of resisting, the blows were vigorously applied to the head and face. Despite the student's new-found submission, the beating continued. He was ordered to remove his coat, and fifteen more lashes were applied, and when the evil-doer tried to escape, the teacher gave hot pursuit, caught him, and administered a severe tongue-lashing. End of problem. Though this demonstration occurred only once it sufficed, and the rest of the school year was marked by kindness towards the ever-attentive students (recounted in Finkelstein, 1989, 155-57).

Nor is it permissible to energize the slothful by terrifying them. Save for children at strict traditional religious schools, contemporary youngsters are impervious to sermons about slackers rotting in Hell. This is a far cry from the early days of American education when schools forcefully taught self-control and morality to suppress the passions detrimental to reason. Students in that era then memorized hymns and studied the Bible while those challenging authority paid a high price (Finkelstein, 1989, 11-12). Today, by contrast, imparting guilt for sloppy work habits—you should be ashamed of yourself—might be deemed too psychologically damaging for young children. The once reliable, "I'm going to speak to your father about your cursing" may be meaningless to pupils from fatherless homes or where parents habitually defend Junior. The days of community stigma are long gone, especially where criminality is omnipresent. Once feared after-school detention (and missing the school bus) has now been transformed into resource-rich programs designed to *help* at-risk students or at least shield them from the mean streets. Laggards quickly realize that in today's kinder, gentler educational atmosphere, threats of unpleasant retribution are empty gestures.

The obstacles to stigmatizing bad behavior were sadly illustrated in a Texas School, Gonzales High School, when the school decided to ban certain types of clothing. If in-school suspension failed to impress students, the deputy superintendent threatened that the miscreants would have to wear prison-style blue jump suits. Unfortunately, students hearing of this punishment have threatened to glorify these jumpsuits as a sign of their rebellion, even purchasing their own overalls to be "in fashion" (Kriz, 2008). This is no different than the "prison look" so popular in many big cities, baggy pants, undone shoelaces, that occurs when prison officials confiscate belts and shoelaces.

Lurking behind the motivation quandary are unruly classrooms. Just keeping a lid on things, not promoting academic excellence, is sufficiently praiseworthy in many troubled schools. Violence is a serious threat—in 2007 New York City employed some 5,000 "school safety agents," 200 of whom were armed (Zimmer, 2007). Establishing the orderliness necessary to learning can become a bureaucratic burden. New York City's September 2007 disciplinary guidelines run for 37 pages, much of it lawyer-like prose, and a quick trigger for issuing suspensions may prematurely end a career. Persistent punishment for humdrum sloth, no matter how noble the ultimate educational aim, today can invite scrutiny from local activists endlessly seeking victimhood or government inquiries regarding civil rights violation ("singling out only minorities"). Critically, educators, not students, are often reprimanded for crimes as part of school accountability and students certainly grasp this upside-down incentive structure. Overly-protective parents may threaten litigation if Junior-the-wise-guy is inconveniently sent home for a week. Why risk annoying gossiping students? Calming troubled classrooms to inspire academic excellence thus becomes an unaffordable luxury.

Further add today's culture of heightening self-esteem coupled with relishing personal autonomy in which criticism, let alone painful punishment, is judged debilitating. Students don't doodle during math; they explore artistic creativity. Teachers quickly discover that inflated grades and undeserved praise painlessly keep the peace. The adage "no pain, no gain," is transformed into "no pleasure, no gain." If students eventually flunk government-mandated tests, expert-certified convenient excuses are always handy: outside assessments are unfair or culturally biased, instructional resources were inadequate, expectations are unreasonable, students are handicapped, and so on. By the time a coddled student arrives at high school and is unlucky enough to be rebuked for indolence—no matter how justified and gentle—this experience may be traumatic and justify his or her failing to learn!

Further add today's rampant cultural anti-intellectualism. Though, fortunately, many exceptions exist, ours is a society of low-brow TV, grammatically-incorrect music, dumbed-down books and magazines (and even then too boring to read), and a culture far more infatuated with hedonistic painless consumption than difficult-to-achieve erudition. "I consume, therefore I am" is often the motto among youngsters. By contrast, Japanese schools forbid students from frequenting distracting places like malls or pin-ball parlors, and many parents cooperate with school officials to enforce these "no go" zones. Most Japanese schools also ban students from owning cars or riding motor bikes to reduce teen socializing while powerful norms discourage holding outside jobs. High-school dating is rare and these dates are brief (cited in Peak, 1993).

In the U.S., by contrast, controlling after-school activities has been an uphill battle. In 1984 Texas barred students with less than a "C" average from playing football ("no pass, no play") plus other extracurricular activities and this enraged parents. Other states have joined the no-pass, no-play bandwagon, even tying drivers' licenses and family welfare benefits to academic performance, but rules often contain convenient loopholes and are circumvented by sports-minded parents and school officials. Critically, evidence suggests that threats were ignored—not even surrendering a drivers' license can push many students to "Cs" let alone to become bookworms (Webb *et. al.*, 1993).

In sum, the awaiting obstacles to upping motivation are severe. Students must be cajoled, enticed, and rewarded for progress no matter how slight. Picture the unpleasant fate awaiting a hard-nosed "tough love" teacher who flunked his or her bungling students, loudly scolded them for stupidity, assigned hard-to-read books, and kept them after school until each had written a cogent 500-word paper free of spelling or grammatical errors? And then refused to grade above "B" while posting egregious student papers for public ridicule? And this terrifying ritual would be repeated daily for a month. Students would undoubtedly improve and cherish the teacher long after graduation, but this triumph would surely be overshadowed by the teacher's new-found "Nazi" reputation. Many students would flee. Parents might complain that their child was "distraught," even cried and was being deprived of Little League. Alarmed school administrators would quickly stop this "torture" since aggravated students might drop out and thus cost everyone their jobs under NCLB guidelines penalizing schools with high drop-out rates. Better to praise the "original voice" of this incoherent jumbled scribbling and give everyone a gold star.

Assessing Motivation Boosting Nostrums

Those who advise "follow this motivational recipe and students will thrive" must be held accountable both for what they advise and the ultimate outcomes. Ideally theories would be tested experimentally and those receiving the intervention (the E group) should outperform the control (or C) group. Second, successes must persist. This is the bane of countless educational interventions, particularly with young children. It is relatively easy to achieve short-term performance jumps, and this can bring enthusiastic program expansion followed by future disappointment (e.g., Head Start). Programs begun in grade school where habits are more malleable might thus require monitoring until high school, with the same students, where more serious learning occurs. This may require a decade or more, and educators seldom have this luxury.

Calibrating success further requires a baseline of what is achievable for each student, in each subject, at that particular age. Without a multi-dimensional yardstick, judging success or failure is unattainable. Youngsters are not infinitely malleable clay—as the old adage goes, you can't get blood from a turnip. Consider teaching math to two apathetic students whose abilities markedly differ. Dick, who has a modest knack for math, responds well to entreatments and moves from "C" to "B" work, his ability limit. Jane, on the other hand, is far brighter but remains largely unmoved though likewise progresses from "C" to "B." The identical upward movement, then, reflects widely unequal impacts, and the motivational intervention might even be judged a failure for Jane given her superior potential.

Most troubling for calibrating success concerns the end product of heightened enthusiasm—retained content. Upping motivation is not an end in and of itself though it often becomes that; it is only *a prerequisite necessary to master difficult, challenging subjects that will not be conquered without this thirsting.* Motivated students ingest hated bitter medicine. The gauge of a successful intervention is *not* that once listless students now rush to and fro talking of Michelangelo. It is what undertakings are about not gushing passion per se. Motivating students to excel at cheerleading is not comparable to getting them master calculus. The world's most determined students may strike classroom visitors as dour, humorless, and absolutely listless, i.e., "unmotivated." But, closer inspection may reveal that these gloomy fifth-graders, despite fearsome obstacles, were diligently conquering non-Euclidian geometry and loving every minute of it. Or will love it years hence.

Falsely conflating bubbling enthusiasm with a genuine passion for *hard* learning effortlessly seduces reformers desperate to invigorate academic strugglers. Upbeat media tales abound of delighted visitors witnessing once disdainful third-graders now gleefully reciting Shakespeare. Alas, animation only suggests, but does not certify, newly-acquired appetites for learning. Everything absorbed may be superficial and ephemeral. Youngsters can readily appear "motivated" if everything is playful fun where nobody is criticized, everybody excels, and rewards are every-where. Teachers facing a class of totally bored math students could undoubtedly send pseudo-motivation skyrocketing by setting up a gambling casino where students calculate odds and those in green eyeshades count wads of cash.

Professional educators may find these criteria exasperating. We obviously disagree. The modern medicine parallel *is* appropriate though, admittedly, nobody dies from pointlessly haranguing the listless. It is just a question of whether education is really desirable—if "being educated" is on the same plane as dressing fashionably, then our criteria are surely excessive. We also will accept as valid their likely excuse, "What you ask is just too difficult." But, just because today's educators cannot satisfy these requirements or overcome fearsome obstacles, does not render our benchmarks irrelevant. In any case, we now turn to what today's motivational experts counsel.

Expert Scientific Counsel

What expert advice might a teacher receive by scrutinizing ostensibly scientific, empirically-based research? Two broad approaches inform this enterprise: "external" versus "internal" strategies. External motivation is applied by an outsider, usually the teacher. It may be positive or negative. Positive incentives include good grades, material incentives, and prizes while on the negative side are bad grades, scorn, humiliation, corporal punishment, and other punitive mechanisms to *force* learning. Proponents assume that youngsters are naturally *dis*inclined to master tough subjects, are quickly distracted and teachers—not students themselves—best dictate knowledge objectives. It is an authoritarian orientation, long on drill and enforced discipline, in which progress is defined by conquering specific objectives, and mastering substance outweighs all other educational aims, including student happiness. The venerable adage, "Spare the rod, spoil the child" reflects the spirit. Compulsory learning, it is argued, will, hopefully, eventually provide the building blocks for future original accomplishment—those dutifully (and often unhappily) mastering logarithms will be tomorrow's can't-wait-to-get-to-work rocket scientists.

Internal motivation, by contrast, stresses creating the fire within. Now, students will learn because they *want* to learn not because they must learn or else. Rejected is that students must be initially forced to learn before the fires can start burning; one starts and ends with igniting the inner passions.

Historically, the external approach had dominated and still remains popular in many traditional schools and in education-obsessed nations like Japan and Korea. Its justification is largely that it has worked for generations and still performs. Surprisingly given this admirable record, today's scholarly motivation literature widely *condemns* this "external" approach as part of the problem, not part of the solution (see Powell in Fuhrman and Day, 1996, 35 for an assessment overview). Balance is not the issue—the judicious mix of carrots and sticks versus lighting inner fires. According to this new expert-certified orthodoxy, sticks no matter what thickness or how frequently administered are unambiguously bad though it is conceded that some sticks, notably grades, are legally inescapable. Ryan, Connell, and Deci (1985) assemble a litany of negative outcomes of external-based motivation, all—supposedly—resting on empirical research. Damaging consequences include a diminished inner appetite for learning, increased aversion to school work, a lower sense of competence and self-worth, heightened anxiety, and greater attribution of success or failure to authority figures (projecting blame), and unproductive coping with failure. The *coup de grâce*, according this overview, is that the externally-goaded are underachievers as measured by standardized tests and teacher assessments.

Writing some seventeen years later when educational attainment had gone nowhere and the "do something" clamor grew louder, Deci and Ryan (2002) reiterate this mantra even more forcefully in their aptly titled, "The Paradox of Achievement: The Harder You Push, the Worse It Gets." They agree that proficiency is deteriorating and must be reversed but holding students accountable via standardized tests—hardly the *über* draconian punitive measure—"…essentially deform school climates with their narrow focus and pressuring methods, resulting in less than excellent experiences…." (62). Relying on more recent research (though reiterating past research-based rebukes), the authors add fresh condemnations of exterior-based motivation: it stifles creativity, hinders problem-solving, and undermines navigating more complicated tasks. Even "punitive" expressions like "You should..." undercut learning.

Deci and Ryan conclude that external pressure actually *reduce* motivation, especially for grade-schoolers though less so for college students—"spare the rod, spur the child" is the new, expert-certified adage. In their words, "It is possible to motivate people with rewards, that is, to motivate them externally, but this is not self-motivation, and thus is not the type of motivation thoughtful educators hope to engender in their students" (67). That this exterior motivation in these confirming studies was exceedingly mild, namely just simple performance tests (in artificial circumstances) and deadline pressures, one can only imagine the truly horrific impacts if malingerers received tongue lashings or spankings.

That the real world rests on plain-to-see external motivation never enters the discussion. A Martian encountering this scholarship might surmise that millions of people hold jobs, mow lawns, and otherwise perform drudgery because they love doing it rather than needing to earn a livelihood, risk embarrassment, or just want to get into Yale. This is a truly bizarre view of reality for it is one thing to suggest that internal pressure may outweigh exterior rewards and threats but quite another, as is the case here, to insist that external stimuli are irrelevant or counter-productive.

So overpowering is dedication to internal motivation as the singular legitimate force in academic accomplishment, that even the most self-evident, powerful stick must be purified into students autonomously wanting to learn. The authors discuss the well-known case of pre-med students mastering organic chemistry, a grueling essential step toward an MD (71). They concede that students frequently possess little natural appetite here but still labor for future pay-offs. Nevertheless, in the authors' complicated analytical framework, all is not lost since at least some pre-meds will eventually acquire a taste for carbon-based molecules and thus, happily, again demonstrate intrinsic motivation's superior power. Whether this "learn to like broccoli" versus "eat it or stay at the table" strategy is the ticket to medical school and, eventually, better medical skill is, of course, another matter. To continue this diet parallel, it is as if the stomach could distinguish broccoli on the basis of reasons for eating it.

How can dozens of researchers, all with reputable institutional affiliations, arrive at conclusions that seemingly contradict obvious reality? Is

Japan slouching toward the Stone Age despite currently graduating eighth graders doing U.S. college level math? Establishing this odd, lopsided perspective is no small accomplishment. The starting point is redefining the school's mission, and this means rejecting traditional learning as the central undertaking. Deci and Ryan (2002) typify this reformulation effort and commence by proclaiming that "truly excellent education" for most parents and teachers involves more than what today's standardized tests require in reading and math (no data support this point, however). Students, they continue, must "…achieve their full potential, learning material that is deep, meaningful, and of lasting value and developing a greater capacity to think critically and creatively about problems" (62). Students are, moreover, assumed to be curious, and committed to learning, not just grade grubbers, and will surely acquire a sense of self-confidence and competence while they absorb their lessons. Youngsters must also learn to be respectful, and be respected, and be contributing, well-rounded members of the community. Let there be no misunderstanding of this mission: "Having students attain high achievement test scores is but one criterion for excellent education and, despite pervasive rhetoric, *it may not even be the most important*" (62, italics added).

This twisting of academic accomplishment into something else can be surrealistic. The *Handbook of Research on Improving Student Achievement* (Cawelti 2004, 3) is a serious, research-based compilation of "best practices" and carefully considers strategies across multiple subjects with a major emphasis on underachievers (especially African-American students). How might black underperformers excel in science? The *Handbook* concedes that scientific knowledge is a worthy aim but it is also imperative that these often underperforming students learn to like science and take more courses in science. Furthermore, exposure to science also enables these struggling students to value human diversity while increasing minority student access to social networks that facilitate entry to higher education. In other words, science education is less about mastering the mechanics of photosynthesis than, say, acquiring some vague social panache necessary for college admission.

This expansive "learning" conceptualization opens the door to manipulating "motivation." Traditional education stipulated clear, often just-beyond-reach aims, and the teacher's job was to press students toward quantifiable objectives, and success was demonstrated by performance *on tough subjects* and too many giggles might reflect insufficient whip. Reading at grade level meant reading at grade level as measured by well-worn objective standards—those struggling with *Friends and Neighbors* when they should be breezing through *More Friends and Neighbors* clearly required reprimands. But, if reading proficiency serves as only one of multiple valid goals, teachers might congratulate themselves for boosting this laggard's self-esteem and respectful community commitment. This is target shooting when bulls eyes are drawn afterwards. Now, a fifth-grade teacher can *honestly* brag that thanks to his or her encouragement, little Johnny is inspired to detect "deeper" mysterious meanings in *Dick and Jane* or, in the case of black students barely completing Science I, "success" is just being able to name-drop Isaac Newton.

"Science" to the Rescue

Can science justify these iffy conclusions? The answer is "yes" but only according to what passes for "research" among today's education experts. One common tactic is an experiment with a well-defined short-term task and varied instructions or options. A typical example (cited in Ryan *et. al.* 1985, 21) demonstrated that students excel when given choices of tasks. Specifically, two groups received puzzles to solve in thirty minutes, only one group, however, could select which particular puzzles to solve, and the researchers happily report that those enjoying choices continued on even after the experiment officially ended. This convenient puzzle/multiple instructions format has grown quite popular with investigators, and has even been extended to cross-national and nursery school settings.

In some instances the empirically-based justifications for relying on internally-driven motivation to jump-start learning are, to be frank, impenetrable and useless despite contrary assurances. Corno and Rohrkemper (1985) summarize multiple studies that seemingly validate what they call "self-regulated learning" (SRL). SRL entails a series of steps, from tracking information to linking new to old information, to "applying motivation control strategies" (61). One successful illustration of this method showed that SRL students behaved more comprehensively and systematically during a computer game. Elsewhere fifth graders taught mathematics in a large group were asked to recall their thinking during the lesson. Happily, those who claimed to "try to understand the teacher and the problem" did well. Other recounted studies further confirm the utility of SRL. How this common sense advice that is just jargon for learning itself (e.g., "discriminate among stimuli") builds appetites for knowledge remains totally unclear, though this is what investigators assert.

What about studies scrutinizing actual classroom practices? The gold standard "inspire from within" exemplar is deCharms and associates'

1960s study conducted in one large inner-city, largely-black school district involving eleven schools, thirty-two classrooms and 1,200 children (deCharms *et. al.*, 1976). This well-funded, expertly-advised project trained sixteen randomly-selected teachers, received ample administrative cooperation, and followed students from the end of fifth grade until they left eighth grade. The experimental/control group design was carefully followed. Ironically, training teachers to adopt this "made-in-the-academy" intervention occasionally met resistance, and researchers had to push their method on teachers, a tactic hardly consistent with the project's philosophy stressing the superiority of self-originated inspiration. Frequent adjustments also resulted from teacher turnover and student attrition plus practical problems common to all schools, notably insufficient time. Students could receive varying levels of the "E" condition, as well. Perhaps for these reasons, aims were regularly scaled back. Measurement of success was further complicated by the sudden arrival of a federally-sponsored anti-drop out program. Still, as research into self-generated motivation, it doesn't get better than this.

Varied exercises were supplied to help students recognize their own motives, set goals, strengthen their self-concepts, develop an appreciation for accomplishment, and observe teachers exhibiting these traits. Teachers were told to nurture academic appetites, not command them into existence by, among other tactics, encouraging children to see achievement as central to personal identity. In sixth grade, for example, each student made a creative picture poster of his or her name, cut the poster into ten jigsaw-puzzle pieces, and then added one piece per week to the classroom's bulletin board so as to build a "total picture" at the end of ten weeks (67). Students detailed their achievements in stories and were told to visualize accomplishments beforehand. In spelling exercises children identified their own goals to reduce frustration. Each child also had an exercise-filled "Origins" manual marked "confidential" listing daily goals. This busywork predictably soaked up considerable time and teacher attention, time perhaps better spent on learning substance.

Did this labor-intensive, costly enterprise actually boost motivation to learn what otherwise would not be learned? In ways that foretell future studies, the authors stretch the success yardstick to assess "motivation thinking" and goal setting plus secondary benefits such as attendance. Even then, however, the evidence that appetites (apart from tangible accomplishment) can be enhanced via expert intervention is weak (104). As for hard-edged academic benefits, the authors begin by noting the obstacles to sorting everything out, including acknowledging the possible Hawthorne effect (142). Nevertheless, using the Iowa Test of Basic Skills that measures several academic proficiencies, answers are offered. The overall news is upbeat but as a solution to what ails many inner-city schools, it falls well short.

What about *academic* progress? In a nutshell, these students, who began well behind national averages continue to fall behind as they mature, but the good news is that those receiving the experimental training now fall behind at a slower rate. Celebration may, however, be premature. Positive outcomes were erratic, for example, greater progress followed the sixth grade and this tapered off by the seventh grade, and increased learning varied by subject areas. The intervention also performed better for boys than girls. Reading progress—the key to future learning—was, sadly, impervious to intercession. All and all, this highly-sophisticated study suggests that academic indifference is remediable, but only selectively, very modestly, and with extensive effort, and whether the benefits persist into adulthood is totally unknown. Nor is it clear what national averages on the Iowa test substantively signified. More telling, this huge project has seemingly been forgotten. A statistician might argue, however, that these results are generally consistent with random fluctuation, not the program itself.

The deCharms *et. al.* study is, at least by comparison, exceptionally well-done social science, a model for future work. Unfortunately, subsequent explorations have failed to build on this template. Consider one study (summarized in Ryan *et. al.*, 1985) that seemingly goes to the core of the motivational strategy debate, that is, do external pressures (e.g., prizes) outperform nurturing internalized desires to excel? The data consisted of both teacher and student interviews in thirty-five classrooms in fourth through sixth grade. Teachers were classified according to their control versus autonomy inclination while children were asked about motivation and perceived competence. Not surprisingly, children's dispositions reflected teacher views, so students in classrooms taught by teachers inclined toward autonomy exhibited higher feelings of self-worth, heightened perceptions of cognitive competence and claimed greater motivation. A similar study reports that over an eight-week period students in classes with "controlling" teachers showed a decline in these feelings. Comparable classroom-based studies with varied formats all confirm this insight: where teachers shun outside pressure in favor of autonomous motivation, children internalize these "good" values.

But, do these self-perceptions of self-confidence, etc., translate into better academic performance? Their review of several experimental studies Ryan *et. al.* (1985) argues that internally- versus externally-driven students did better on standardized tests, classroom tests in the case of college students, and learning unfamiliar material on neurophysiology. This news is less conclusive than it appears though perhaps persuasive to those unfamiliar to exacting scientific procedures. Whether "internals" are matched to "externals" in academic ability and gains survive are, unfortunately, unnoted in upbeat summaries (matching requires detailed ability assessment, even IQ data). Nor is it possible to discern if gains constituted genuine erudition as opposed to, say, going from "C" to "C+" on an easy-to-pass test. Let us not confuse "making progress" to absolute proficiency.

Assessing the Science

The academic research literature on motivating students is immense, and we admit that our brief tour is incomplete and, conceivably, biased though our exploration fails to uncover worthy gems. Still, have these experts helped those desperate to ignite intellectual passion? Recall that a key criterion was successfully pushing indolent students to show progress on *tough* material, not just be energetically engaged or perceive themselves as craving knowledge. Content is critical—progress on easy subjects is meaningless. What is remarkable—at least to an outsider—in literature is the pervasive disconnect between the researcher-supplied task and the school's core, often legally-mandated mission. Students are "motivated" to perform tasks whose value is unclear while yardsticks often lack any clear calibration. This may just reflect the nature of laboratory experiments but a "content-free" approach is hardly inevitable. In one such experiment (cited in Ryan *et. al.* 1985, 25) college students read "a passage" while another praised study just concerned accomplishing something that "required intelligence" (Ryan *et. al.* 1985, 26).

Admittedly, a few classroom undertakings resemble puzzles, e.g., geometric proofs, but most properly taught lessons entail arduous work over the long haul. To repeat, motivation means getting students to absorb bitter medicine and do so over years. In designing a study it is thus essential that materials to be learned are curriculum-based, require exertion (not just fun), and progress occurs in the context of what each student can reasonably accomplish given aptitude and circumstances, i.e., the motivated student should now function near the top of their unique abilities, and this inescapably differs from student to student and subject to subject. Somebody who cannot be inspired to crave puzzle-solving may thrive when prodded to read poetry. A complicated, multi-faceted measurement format is, apparently, nowhere to be found in this literature and it is therefore impossible to know what is *usefully* accomplished by these interventions.

Assume that the experts here have at least uncovered a grain of truth—some inner directed learners, in some subjects occasionally outperforming schoolmates inspired by the whip. It does *not* therefore follow that the motivator's tasks should be about converting those profiting by external pressure into students cherishing learning for its own value. A more plausible scenario is that some learn best by external pressure, others learn better via intrinsic motivation, and effect can vary by subject, and the overall average outcome easily obscures these personal net effects. Perhaps the massive study undertaken by deCharms *et. al.* should also have included a second experimental group—students prodded by strict discipline to assess the net comparative value of their "push from within" strategy.

More generally, the focus on external versus internal substitutes the pathways to learning for measurable learning itself, and this quest, unfortunately, seems more to reflect a grander philosophical agenda regarding human nature. Children attend school for arduous academic substance, and this is the bottom line, so, of the hundreds of tactics to boost intellectual appetites, the real question is which *specific* ones work, for what children under what circumstances, for downing the bitter medicine. Sweeping generalities about the evils of prizes or rebukes gets us nowhere other than to score irrelevant philosophical points. The causal pathway may also be iterative, not one or the other as these pedagogues aver. A student who masters reading thanks to repeated humiliation might eventually gain proficiency and *then* become a voracious, self-directed reader. Or, just as likely, internal passions grow cold and periodically require a kick in the butt. Complicated empirical questions abound and, unfortunately, they are neglected in these inquiries.

Matters become especially tricky when dealing with those least inclined to learn prescribed lessons, a topic that grows ever more central as educators attempt to inspire the least competent. Limiting tactics to inspire an inner passion for knowledge among disadvantaged students may be futile and, more important, ultimately harmful. At best, this "inner" strategy may be appropriate *after* rudimentary knowledge and good habits have been forcefully instilled. Cultivating inner passions may require years of nurturing and, to be frank, this may be impractical especially as youngsters fall behind. Better to inflict pain early and impart basics rather than wait for innate curiosity to awaken. Strict multiplication table drill in second grade may appear "subversive" to experts, but it is foolish to expect early ignorance can be autonomously overcome years later when the former daydreamer encounters algebra. He or she is more likely to regret earlier inattention—I should have been *forced harder* to learn it!

Assuming that research does demonstrate some boosting of motivation, what evidence exists that it begins the long pathway to educational attainment? As one robin does not make for spring, fiddling with a puzzle after the experiment ends does not certify a decade-long commitment to serious learning. The most authoritative answer remains the deCharms *et al,* fifth- to eight-grade study but even here the evidence is murky and certainly cannot be extrapolated into early adulthood. Elsewhere answers are even less satisfactory. There is no follow-through to see if lessons survived for, at best, more than a few months. These experts perhaps believe that whetting an appetite for learning is akin to starting a forest fire with a single match—once underway, it can be all-consuming.

What about targeting motivational strategies to target specific populations that, *a priori,* might seem to warrant unlike treatment? Oddly, especially in light of modern educator's infatuation with treating all students as unique individuals, potentially-vital personal differences are neglected. That schools themselves collect much of theses data, and family background and personal experience data are readily gathered, makes omission inexcusable. One five-year empirically-based study begins by asserting that "(L)earners are distinct and unique" (xiii) and subsequently lists multiple factors distinguishing students (e.g., demographic traits, ability, economic class) that teachers must recognize, but these potentially relevant factors are *never* connected to motivational strategies (McCombs and Whisler, 1997, 81-2, 112-14). At most, references are periodically made to commonplace demographic categories but even then, usage is frustratingly casual, imprecise, and incomplete. It seems inconceivable to these experts that race/ethnic characteristics may be subordinate to factors such as home life or cognitive ability. Or that these labels may disguise distinct social groups, for example, native-born blacks versus Caribbean-born immigrants. More relevant for uncovering a cure, this stereotypical lumping together can obscure significant variation—the high-achieving African-American student from deplorable conditions—whose experience might provide valuable insights into what pushes students to strive.

What is remarkable about this "one size fits all" penchant is that any experienced teacher knows this crude counsel to be mistaken. Teachers recognize that even siblings react differently depending on native ability, maturity, personalities, and countless other traits. Professional helpfulness would seem to be about providing a full repertory of motivational ploys, customized to targets, versus glibly announcing, for example, that group praise outshines individual gold stars. This is exactly what doctors do—prescribe treatments based on the patient's age, family history, allergies, vital signs, and dozens of other highly-specific traits. Even over-the counter medicines target specific ills, not just "sickness."

Practical Advice

What about "hands on" guides to boost motivation? One prominent example is *Overcoming Student Failure: Changing Motives and Incentives for Learning* (Covington and Teel, 1996) published under the distinguished American Psychological Association's (APA) imprimatur. Everything about this handbook, its reliance on up-to-date research (copiously cited), a small army of assisting experts, preparation time (six years), and utilizing actual classroom experience suggests authoritative wisdom. The clear, step-by-step style and format, including Q and A exercises, checklists, suggested activities, and straightforward style clearly reveal its target audience to be teachers wanting to galvanize the lethargic.

The guide begins by honoring contemporary pedagogical orthodoxy: past practices offer an *ir*relevant guide to future success, modern education theorizing holds the key, progress requires a rethinking of what motivation is all about and, predictably, while some external pressure (e.g., grades) may occasionally be justified (though rarely), the proper pathway is to light fires from within. Students themselves must crave knowledge and, significantly, all students can benefit equally from this draw-from-within strategy (called "motivation equity"). The authors offer three seemingly common sense-based myths *impeding* progress: (1) students who do not try are unmotivated; (2) competition enhances achievement; and (3) the greater the reward, the greater the effort. Centuries of ostensible educational wisdom must therefore be junked and, the authors admit this will be arduous, but America's educational decline requires stern measures.

How is this to be done, and without all the traditional punitive tactics that have proven so effective in the bad old days? The path begins by castigating grades, perhaps among the more gentle corrective measures available to teachers, as subverting the impetus to accomplishment, creativity, and intellectual risk-taking. While adults, including college admission officers, may treat them seriously, for students they are "exaggerated," "threatening," and a false indicator of self-worth (10). At best, grades should be a feedback mechanism, not a bribe. Grades create an atmosphere of surveillance and unequal power; they are also physically dangerous since child abuse is more common when report cards are sent home. If that were insufficient condemnation, grades may encourage cheating, poison trust between teachers and students, and are often subjective and unfair while "artificially" classifying students into ability groups (14). Admittedly, grades (and other tangible rewards) cannot be eliminated, but their role can be sharply reduced.

With grades brushed aside, the book castigates "the ability game"—the commonplace practice of students competing via ("narrow") academic accomplishment. This is an essentially false activity, the authors insist, since real learning need not reflect official inducements. The ability game, with its stress on avoiding mistakes, even hurtful sanctions, is subversive because it "stratifies" classrooms while promoting a zero-sum learning atmosphere (25). In fact, assigning students to hierarchical ability groups (falsely) encourages students to believe that poor performance reflects differences in ability while, for those at the bottom, engendering hostile attitudes towards school and lowered personal aspiration (26). Citing Howard Gardner's well-known multiple intelligences theory, this manual advises teachers to recognize distinct forms of communication—music, drama, dancing, and other non-verbal, non-written methods. By expanding possible avenues to displaying learning, more students can succeed, and so teachers achieve success where there may have only been failure (25). From Covington and Teel's perspective even the distinction between academic and non-academic activities is harmful, and thus to be rejected. The conventional classroom's "ability game" also drives students to avoid failure via disengagement, faking involvement, procrastinating, setting unrealistic goals, and bogus excuses.

Still, how are low-achieving disinterested students prone to skip assignments, be chronically late or garble instructions to be turned around? Positive advice begins with recognizing that these low performers *are* really motivated *but* are expending great energy to protect self-worth rather than pursuing valuable accomplishment (29). In other words, the "traditional" classroom, not laggards, is the problem. The solution grows clearer: redirect unproductive self-defense energy towards mastery, including, but not exclusively, academic accomplishment. The impetus for learning must be altered—out with the pressure, in with the passion from within. It is axiomatic that students possess deep, expandable reservoirs of ability and these talents must always be in the forefront—the sky's the limit, but only if students are properly nurtured (37).

And this brings us to the "equity game" guaranteed to transform laggards into achievers. Specifics include eliminating competition among classmates so pupils are measured only against what teachers want; instilling pride as result of one's own accomplishments regardless of how others perform, honoring as many diverse abilities as possible (including "non-academic" skills); permitting alternative incentives though, of course, these will decline as motivation becomes internalized; and make assignments engaging with novelty and surprise (46-8). The familiar spelling bee—the epitome of head-to-head classroom "survivor" competition--provides a horrific illustration of what is wrong with traditional approaches. In the New Classroom Order each student selects words from a menu of varied difficulty—easy, moderately tricky, and hard items—and levels reflect each student's past performance or words not yet taught (64-5). The choice, it is claimed, forces students to evaluate their own proficiency, and mistakes mean failing the test. With no two students having the same words in the same categories, nobody competes against anybody else and, it is assumed, the possibility of boredom will push students to internalize desires for spelling proficiency. Self-diagnosis of academic strengths and weaknesses is also encouraged to build accurate goal setting on the way to greater motivation (67). There is also a suggested "work contract" between teacher and student so as to enhance a sense of personal motivation apart from what classmates seek. Student are even encouraged to make a checklist of their "multiple abilities" so they can improve their acting and dancing along with reading and writing (83).

Perhaps bowing to reality, the authors acknowledge the tangible incentive may still be vital (and grades are legally mandated) in today's classroom. But, if used, they must be applied according to certain rules to build "authentic" motivation. Among other factors, the rewards should reflect student preferences (extra computer time vs. candy) and the conditions for earning rewards. Incentives are also to be bestowed infrequently, should reflect unique situations, and never in a class competition since losers will feel socially inferior, and may involve (unspecified) non-school benefits (84-90). Naturally, as Marxists predicted the withering away of the state, these experts predict a withering away of cookies and cupcakes as indifferent students transform themselves into well-behaved self-starters.

Overcoming Student Failure does address particularly troublesome, seemingly-incorrigible students, often from slum conditions, who might seem impervious to this approach. What can be done here? The authors confess that a little extra pressure might be justifiable, but only of the gentlest sort. High standards are appropriate but these can elicit failure so pupils ought to feel safe when trying to advance. Students must therefore exercise some control over their learning agenda, goals should not be too intimidating and incentives should be personalized. What about the bottom of the bottom, those who are disorganized and totally clueless about performing well? Motivating them, the authors confess, will be trying. Nonetheless, teachers will require patience to help students learn basic skills and, for the long run, encouraging the "…underlying skills of originality, independence of thought, and autonomy that sustain an equity focus" (106). The book substantively ends with one final, large type caution: "Competition destroys the will to learn" (108).

The APA guidebook's recommendations are hardly unique in today's catalogue of professional advice, and to illustrate the mentality a bit more, consider Merrill Marmin's *Inspiring Active Learning: A Handbook for Teachers* (1994). This is likewise an authoritative treatise, published under the auspices of the Association for Supervision and Curriculum Development (ASCD) that overflows with scholarly citations plus nine single-spaced pages of bibliography and recommended readings. The Ph.D. Professor of Education acknowledges the help of some 164 teachers and academic experts in distilling wisdom. The book claims to supply proven best practices to motivate youngsters, while helpful tips drawn from real life classrooms are everywhere.

The handbook's goals are certainly alluring. After duly acknowledging America's troubled schools, it asserts that academic accomplishment should not detract from creating classrooms with a new spirit where students value themselves, respect each other, and act reasonably (ix). The book's aim is to *inspire* (italics in original) students and drawing on superior business practices, stresses cooperation (not bossiness) and commitment. Nor is failure to be feared. Just follow the recipe and, month by month, students will become mature, responsible members of a pleasant, thriving learning community (1). Now, all students will complete assignments promptly, at-risk students will acquire self-management skills, misbehavior in and out of the classroom will be reduced, classrooms will run smoothly, and motivation will shift from extrinsic to intrinsic, among other benefits. In a catchphrase, the goal is "an inspirational classroom."

And how will students daily behave if all goes as planned? In "an inspirational classroom" students begin with a thirst for learning, are proud of their abilities, possess an inner strength, are full of energy waiting to be applied, are self-motivated, and thus do not require detailed orders. Nor are they self-centered and resentful. If this were insufficient, they are comfortable in dealing with authority, are alert, creative, diligent, and able to concentrate (3-4). A detailed target checklist is then provided to assess progress to this blissful condition. Notably absent in the educational virtues catalogue is *any* academic yardstick. To rebut charges that this lofty agenda is unreachable for low-performing youngsters mired in inner-city chaos, the authors approvingly cite Marva Collins—also explicitly mentioned in the Acknowledgements—for her magnificent, against-all-odds accomplishment with troubled students. Unfortunately, some twelve years *prior* to the guidebook's publication, Marva Collins' astonishing claims were exposed as fraudulent along with her bogus credentials (Spitz, 1985, 82).

The pathway into motivation Shangri-La has innumerable steps together with countless exercises and extended realistic illustration, so we can only provide a sampling. Lessons are to move quickly to prevent boredom, even if students fall behind; lectures include varied material (but not too diverse to heighten anxiety) so there will always be some attention-getting material; shift topics when sensing growing boredom; do not wait until students are attentive to begin talking since they will catch up; and avoid repetition so as not to turn off students (but return to the subject later if necessary). Equally important is to engage all students, and several tactics are suggested. For example, call on students to speak to an issue sure to generate interest; have students write one-sentence summaries of what they have just heard; teach material to only half the class and have these students instruct the unexposed; rather than prod slow pokes, give more enticing examples to stimulate curiosity; kindle engagement by frequent votes on what some student said about the material; encourage students to seek help from friends to build a cooperative spirit; elicit group responses ("a choral approach") to help students memorize facts; provide ample visual presentations, role play, and use demonstration to pique interest; insert "provocative" topics when discussions drag; talk aloud when solving a problem to provide insight into problem solving; and move from easy to difficult problems to instill excellence.

This motivational approach strives to build self-confidence, and teachers receive a cornucopia of tips to help strugglers feel better about their abilities. Suggestions include posting positive signs on classroom walls, "Everyone needs time to think and learn" or "Everyone makes mistakes" versus discouraging ones like "Raise you hand before speaking;" and rely on a "cushioning" strategy to reduce unhealthy anxiety, comments like "its okay to make mistakes" or "hunting for right answers is more important than right answers."

Compare these messages to what occurs in Japan where classroom posters announce "Become a child who can persevere" or "Hang in there" (cited in Peak, 1993). To return to Marmin's advice given to U.S. teachers, praise and rewards can motivate, but only if properly utilized. Approval must be honest (not manipulative) and bestowed widely, preferably to the group as a whole. Where students err, a brief acknowledgement without the "distracting emotion" of the misstep suffices. Calling on a second student to supply the correct answer is unwise since that makes the first student feel inferior (and ignoring mistakes is often advised). This flight from exposing student errors is radically different from what happens in Japan and China were student mistakes are openly noted so other can learn from errors (Stevenson and Stigler, 1992, 193).

So that students do not become "addicted" (unhealthy "bribery") to approval, comments should be akin to "thank you for showing me your work." A suggested alternative to praise is "honest delight" and, judged by the examples, these avoid cognitive accomplishment, e.g., "What bright eyes you have today, Zack" (72). Similarly, inspirational admonitions (75-6) are more about life in general than what ought to infuse a school classroom—upbeat compliments about energetic speaking, sticking to something, listening to others, being alert, asking for help, or displaying confidence.

What about achieving *academic* excellence? Teachers should begin by giving students challenges, but these should not be chores or boring; rather, they must be "...exciting, adventurous, stretching opportunity, a chance to be undaunted by obstacles, to reach and conquer" (78). (And it goes without saying that everyone in the class somehow gains rewards for conquering.) Teachers can help by playing cheerleaders and holding high expectations, and this includes accepting non-performance since there must be a valid reason for it and, anyhow, it will be done next time around. Another helpful tactic is to sprinkle lessons with undemanding but stimulating challenges, for example, tell students to pace themselves, eat well, and walk briskly (84).

Much of *Inspiring Active Learning* concerns humdrum classroom mechanics, details like how to begin and end a lesson, distributing assignments, arranging chairs, managing classroom time, creating groups, dealing with homework, and all else that goes into teaching generally.

What about the demonstrable academic payoffs from this strategy? A chapter on testing and grading (Ch. 11) offers some insight here. The goal, it is announced is to de-emphasize grades to: (1) put more emphasis on "learning and developing life-long learning habits;" (2) reduce the discouragement coming from receiving low marks; and (3) allow for alternative ways to assess student achievement (142).

The disjunction between grades and learning is central and infuses the entire chapter. Useful practices to build excellence include having students assemble work portfolios to develop self-management skills; assess performance with an eye to its possible impact on the student's future life; invite parents to classrooms to demonstrate that students are working hard and using a "reverse report card" to entice parents to monitor student progress. In Chapter 13 we are told how to "stimulate thinking" and methods include sorting things into categories, finding similarities between similar appearing items, making predictions, solving a problem, and brainstorming alternatives. The book concludes with how to teach beyond the facts, and here we receive familiar advice: collect facts into generalizations, use values to link subjects, and post on classroom walls important concepts, things like courage, friendship, whole self, and candor (181).

Assessing Practical Advice

Our tour has been quite brief, but rest assured, these two exemplars are hardly unusual. Skeptics might want to peruse *150 Ways to Intrinsic Motivation in the Classroom* (Raffini, 1996); *The Will to Learn: A Guide* (Covington, 1998); *How to Reach and Teach in the Inclusive Classroom* (Rief and Heimburge, 1996); *Motivation for Achievement: Possibilities for Teaching and Learning* (Alderman, 2004, 2nd ed.); *The Learner Centered Classroom and School* (McCombs and Whisler, 1997); *The Passionate Learner: How Teachers and Parents Can help Children Reclaim the Joy of Discovery* (Fried, 2001) among countless other "how-to" manuals embracing this "sticks are bad" since they hurt learning, "self-esteem good" vision. What can we say about these recommendations to a teacher daily confronting students unwilling to learn? Most evidently, other then unverified self-congratulation and citations galore, they offer *zero* scientific evidence that recommendations perform as claimed, and we can be absolutely certain that if confirming data existed, they would be heralded. They are not cures for our national tribulations, and if they were diet books, threatened litigation might compel the publishers to withdraw them or post disclaimers on the cover.

Worse, minimal documentation is a nonissue, an omission that speaks loudly about professional irresponsibility. A *profound* anti-intellectual, anti-merit mentality infuses these remedies. One essay in a well-pedigreed anthology (Darling-Hammond in Fuhrman and Day, 1996, 149) seemingly rejected the idea of real Platonically-objective achievement, placing quotation marks around—"high performance"—to depict certain schools as if the label just reflected something unreal. A certain postmodern vocabulary twisting mentality also appears so cognitive ability is often repackaged as beliefs about cognitive ability, not actual accomplishment. Meanwhile, demonstrated achievement becomes a desire to excel independent of what was done. Though each guidebook begins by recognizing today's educational insufficiencies, this boilerplate is absolutely disingenuous, a throw-away line to (hopefully) placate critics. Prescribed "cures" are guaranteed to exacerbate our woes by subordinating arduous learning to psychological uplift. Attending school is to be made fun, an adventure, a cost-free opportunity to explore one's own opinions ("learner centered" in this jargon), and thus, by implication, if it is too hard, it's not learning.

Rejected is the time-honored principle that some materials, no matter how hard or boring, are vital to education and thus must be imposed regardless of bitter taste. It is dogmatically claimed that student, not teachers, should guide learning and this surely will boost appetites. Raffini (1996, 17) is typical and argues that instilling intrinsic motivation first entails a sense of autonomy, and this, in turn, requires that students be able to choose learning activities (and goals), as if all options lead down the same path. Even classroom procedures are occasionally open to individual choice. Given that youngsters can scarcely judge how best to learn anything, this is the equivalent of letting small children choose their meals since all food, in some sense, contain nutrients. Why memorize vocabulary when singing might suffice? Another guidebook (Fried, 2001) blithely proclaims, a la Rousseau, that children are born passionate learners but are corrupted by today's schools.

Schools here resemble group therapy, not the historic understanding of how knowledge is conveyed. This aversion to arduous, traditional learning at the expense of self-esteem and all the "touchy-feely" is hardly surprising given what America's schools of education now preach. Two university experts, after a five-year empirical study concluded that traditional modes of schooling are obsolete, and students are frustrated by a lack of caring, especially for black students who find race and culture a source of alienation. A more accommodating, race-sensitive approach is counseled (McCombs and Whisler, 1997, 61). Rita Kramer has carefully documented this aversion to substance from top education schools like Columbia's University Teachers College to obscure institutions at the bottom, and nothing indicate a flight from muddle-headed "theorizing" and a social working mentality (Kramer, 1991). These authorities would undoubtedly be horrified at what transpires overseas or in local religious academies where fearful students master complicated subjects by paying rapt attention to revered teachers.

To appreciate the toughness of what occurs elsewhere, consider the following episode that occurred in a Japanese elementary school where children were learning to draw three-dimensional cubes (Stevenson and Stigler, 1992, 16). One boy having trouble with the task was asked to go to the blackboard to draw the cube. After five or ten minutes he asked the teacher if he had it right and the teacher asked the class's opinion. The classmates shook their heads—no. He continued to struggle but showed no signs of emotional distress. Happily, by the end of the period he got it right and the entire class applauded. No doubt, many Americans would see this episode as hurtful public humiliation, not a lesson to instill the virtue of persistence. (Also add that grades are public in Japan and China, another "attack" on the fragile self-esteem of underachievers).

Make no mistake—these made-in-America motivation nostrums constitute energetic, gushing *anti*-intellectualism to pursue an egalitarian ideological agenda. If the recommendations are heeded, truly stellar students will be ignored, if not condemned as curve busters, since rewarding high achievement will, say these authorities, make others feel less worthy, less capable, and thus drive unhappy souls yet further into failure. Hailing bright students as heroes, it is alleged, also creates the "false" impression that some forms of achievement outrank others. Predictably, tracking by cognitive capability is harshly denounced. According to one expert (Alderman, 2004, 8) ability grouping denies some students exposure to college- or job-related rigorous material while also depriving them of high-achievement peer pressure. The intellectual cost to bright students by diluting advanced classes or abolishing them altogether is, naturally, a non-issue.

Those outside today's peculiar pedagogical world will quickly discern a futile attempt to alter human nature. For these professors, Darwin never wrote a word. It is "Marxism-lite" at its grandest and reflects the egalitarian dumb-down ideology infusing today's academy. Do academic experts honestly believe that teachers can extinguish the competitive spirit, keep order among youngsters only by jazzing things up, and achieve universal academic excellence by proclaiming that every child craves arduous assignments and appetites that will surely arrive *mañana*? Education School lifers might buy this fantasy but, paradoxically, students themselves will see through it. First-graders obviously sense that some classmates outshine others and that honoring everybody for even the most academically-irrelevant talent, e.g., bright eyes, is feel-good trickery. Insisting that teachers refashion human nature invites disrespect for the profession—how can anybody be so stupid as to proclaim that competition destroys learning?

Imagine a talented university mathematician spending a year teaching fifth graders was told to master these "how-to" treatises so as to inspire students? Just scanning the oft-contradictory, cliché-filled, hopelessly vague material might cool enthusiasm for this career shift. Nor is there any cumulative benchmark wisdom so everything is an endless smorgasbord of tips, none better than any other. Further envision if his or her "motivating" lectures were periodically checked by the *au courant* Head of Instruction to insure that everything conformed to the jumbled orthodoxy. The former college instructor would be responsible for insuring that no child felt inadequate while he or she made the Pythagorean Theorem personally relevant and entertaining. And watching out that his or her praise was dispensed in just the right amounts and only in "healthy" ways. Even a novice in probability theory could predict that this idealistic adventure would quickly end, and next year's math teacher would be more attuned to students' needs for respect and community involvement, even if shouted-out answers were incorrect. It is no wonder that bright, talented college students avoid K-12 teaching.

As far as can be determined, today's motivation experts just supply "how to entertain" advice, not guidance on making the lethargic daydreamer master difficult material. Sesame Street appears to be the model: keep it short and constantly shift topics, jazz it up, emphasize novelty, have lots of animation and, most of all, link learning to fun. Classrooms are thus filled with youngsters pontificating on current events, collecting material from varied sources, brainstorming, setting unique learning objectives, even confessing feelings (see Raffini, 1996, 58-60) and, naturally, playing with the latest computer and audio-visual technology. Juicing up once-dull subjects with music has become a thriving industry. One Michigan-based website includes songs from some 200 artists to help teach core subjects, foreign languages, even special education (*http://SongsforTeaching.com*). Other music sites specialize in science and math while the national Science Song Writers' Association produces albums for future Einsteins. Now teachers play the guitar rather than write on blackboards and one Virginia teacher has composed a rap song "Document Dudes" about the Founding Fathers (Chandler, 2007).

A former Department of Education researcher (Tomlinson, 1993) characterized this arrangement as a tacit "bargain" in which teachers ease up in exchange for better classroom deportment. A recent *Washington Post* exposé told of a Washington, DC school where math students clipped pictures of motorcycles from magazines. One interviewed graduate (who did enter college but soon flunked out) said she did not complain since she received an "A." The school was in the middle of the pack academically among DC schools, even offering ten AP courses (Haynes and Jain, 2007). Hopefully, experts assume that the classroom will now outshine the TV or mall as superior entertainment, and as preteen mall rats move from Claire's (cheap flashy jewelry for teenagers) to sophisticated adults buying *haute couture* at Neiman-Marcus, easily distracted third-graders will mature into joyous Talmudic scholars. Even if this strategy fails, why oppose fun?

Japanese Schools

Compare the "make learning fun" mentality with what transpires in Japanese grade schools. Here parents of incoming first graders are informed that children must develop perseverance to perform unpleasant tasks. Teachers thus stress building good habits (e.g., fixed homework periods), and parents must reinforce the practice, practice, practice mentality. Physical education classes require long hikes and other challenging activities, and students keep personal logs to measure progress. Every step, including organizing one's desk and checking backpacks the night before, is achieved by relentless, precise drill. Winter classrooms are minimally heated and parents are urged to dress children in shorts to build resolve. All Japanese schools have statues of Ninomiya Kinjiro and all school children are familiar with how he was always with his school books, used every possible moment to study all the while gathering wood and helping his mother around the house. In China the comparable celebrated figure is Lei Fend, Mao's "good soldier" known for his stalwart dedication (Stevenson and Sigler, 1992, 86-7).

With ample teacher engagement, the value of discipline is eventually internalized and relentlessly reinforced (glossy Japanese fluff teen magazines admonish readers to get up early and be prompt). To improve concentration, students practice sitting still quietly, staring at a circle on the blackboard, and records are kept for the exercise. With diligence, first graders can join schoolmates in assemblies where everyone engages in staring for as long as ten minutes. Youngsters learn meticulous note-taking and by fifth grade have mastered it (Peak, 1993). One can only imagine the howls of outrage if American schools attempted these "unhealthy" "mean-spirited" practices. Cold classrooms with students in shorts would be scandalous, and responsible parties might be forced to commit professional *hara-kiri.*

Conclusions

Though our tour of "expert" counsel shows it to be of little theoretical or practical value, readers should not despair. Thousands of teachers surely stimulate students using strategies unlikely to enter the academic literature and, to be fair, made-in-the-academy nostrums may indeed perform as advertised though unlikely and certainly not across the board. There are also hundreds of public and private schools where accomplishment-driven American students could certainly compete effectively with their overseas peers. More important, schools are only one setting where students can gain an appreciation for learning, and are perhaps the least important. Family life, as stereotypically exemplified by hard-nosed, education-obsessed Jewish and Asian parents, undoubtedly far outranks schools, and not even teachers belittling knowledge can subvert this home-based pressure. Those parents unable to pressure Junior also have options such as private tutoring or enrolling him or her in private schools known for intensive motivation. A parent prizing academic doggedness is not hapless when little Tim reports, "Ms. Smith says that it is more important to feel good about me than learning how to read." Let us not confuse awful professional advice on upping motivation with what actually transpires in thousands of schools and millions of homes.

Further keep in mind that comparisons between today's indifferent student and yesterday's strivers can easily be exaggerated. Beware of apples to oranges comparison. Robert Hampel's careful historical overview shows that past motivation insufficiency was routinely "solved" by mass exoduses not some now-forgotten pedagogical tricks (1993). Nineteenth-century schools were under no pressure to retain malingerers, and the vocational standards and economic conditions of the day encouraged flight rather than staying on to diagram sentences. A return to this "if you don't like it, there's the door" would undoubtedly transform many classrooms into thriving learning enterprises, but a modern-day exodus would also bring unacceptable levels of professional unemployment.

Shoddy advice about imparting a passion for academics is hardly harmless however; it may occasionally be catastrophic. Damage assessment begins by acknowledging that numerous traditional, *proven* motivation tactics are available to teachers. Perhaps early educators were on to something when insisting that progress first required controlling passions versus today's belief that innate desires can by themselves instigate learning. Admittedly, nothing in the storehouse is the perfect cure-all, and all require effort, and some may require legislative tinkering, but reading educational history will surely uncover useful remedies that can at least be successfully applied to some students, some of the time, and can be conveyed to thousands of teachers frustrated by rampant intellectual laziness.

Contemporary motivation handbook advice is a totally unnecessary take-no-prisoners "war" on the punishment repertory as if a few unrealistic experiments, informed by a mish-mash incoherent egalitarian ideology, could contravene thousands of years of proven pedagogy. Students are all too easily absolved from responsibility. One expert, Blankstein (2007), even condemned schools—not students—for "creating a truancy problem" by locking school doors at 7:35 a.m. As an alternative he describes a school providing a first-period experimental class for late-comers awarding physical education credit. The students loved it, he notes, but nothing is said about students learning the value of promptness. "Loving it" trumps everything, apparently.

The real losers of this ill-advised fashionable pedagogy are students, disproportionately African-Americans arriving from environments disparaging academics who face daunting odds in acquiring decent educations. To insist, as per orthodoxy, that these youngsters possess an innate intellectual curiosity, can't wait to do fractions, or otherwise hanker after difficult, often boring tasks is a destructive fantasy. Make no mistake: this self-motivating passion can be instilled, at least for some, but a vast gap separates "instilled" from "drawn out" and this cannot be done immediately. Better to take no chances and start tough instruction early.

The relentless attack on competition and individual achievement while celebrating "feel-good" cooperation may be inimical to what boys, particular black boys, gravitate towards. To be blunt, today's practical recommendations reflect the feminization of motivational psychology, the aversion towards aggression and competition, the emphasis on sharing, and all else striking young boys as "girlie." This feminization may well explain why the academic performance of young black males continues to deteriorate. The title of a recent book—*The War Against Boys: How*

Misguided Feminism is Harming Our Young Men (Sommers, 2000)—tersely sums it up. These expert-supplied "culturally-sensitive" strategies clearly clash with what can be daily witnessed in the schoolyards where aggression and competition among boys are normal.

Today's schools abound with irony, and none is greater than the contrast between classroom tactics to master demanding tasks versus athletics. That high school sports, especially football and basketball, unlike academics, are *serious* enterprises with unambiguous, highly-valued outcomes. A high school football coach who inspired his players by relying on innate curiosity to learn positions, refused to let them sprint 100 yards in full gear without resting because many would feel winded, and insisted that even the proverbial 90-pound weakling could excel at defensive end due to his unique non-football verbal talents would be a joke. If he justified defeat after defeat with, "the score is only one measure of accomplishment and perhaps the least important," a trip to the school psychologist for therapy would be in order.

The contrast between football and the classroom is huge, and that the same students are involved only enhances the paradox. Football coaches (at least successful ones) typically yell and scream at bumblers, force weaklings to toughen up by inflicting pain, humiliate daydreamers in front of teammates ("you dummies play like *# !!@#** sissies"), kick players off the team for petty infractions, and otherwise behave in ways guaranteeing instant dismissal if such outbursts occurred in classrooms. Coaches with reputations for abrasiveness who relentlessly push middling players to excel are admired while warm and caring types, those happy to achieve "moral victories" are viewed contemptuously.

Many players fondly recall this abusiveness, though only after graduating—Coach Attila gave me discipline, taught me to strive and provided the self-confidence that comes from mastering thirty-five basic plays, using eight formations with each one having at least three options. I truly thank that wonderful no-good SOB who turned my life around. Perhaps this calls to mind an early 1950s tale regarding the incoming president of the University of Maryland, a school then more famous for championship football teams than academic excellence. His goal, he said, was to build an academic program that the football team could be proud of. He succeeded.

4

Closing the Racial Gap in Academic Achievement

A society that puts equality—in the sense of equality of outcomes—
ahead of freedom will end up with neither equality nor freedom.
—Milton Friedman, *Free to Choose*

During times of universal deceit, telling the truth becomes a revolutionary act.
—George Orwell

That African-Americans on average lag behind whites in academic proficiency is exceedingly well-documented. Divergences begin before kindergarten, persist, and are ubiquitous across all academic subjects and resist all remediation efforts. By age seventeen this amounts to two to three years of schooling. Nor has the expansion of the black middle class ended this awkward fact—even poor whites outperform black children from affluent families. For the last half century the quest to eliminate gaps has been a national priority; some might say an obsession, across nearly the entire ideological agenda and money is, apparently, no object. Liberals are deeply concerned about the economic inequality that gaps bring while acknowledged conservatives like Abigail and Stephen Thernstrom in their heralded *No Excuses: Closing the Racial Gap in Learning* label disparate attainment *the* civil rights issue of our day (2003, 1, 274). E.D. Hirsch calls this gap the "new civil rights frontier" (Hirsch, 1996, 43). President Bush's No Child Left Behind (NCLB) legislation made elimination of racial disparities absolutely central.

Today's "official" public consensus is that victory is possible if we re-energize commitment, spend yet more, and seek innovative cures. President Obama even made closing racial disparities in education a priority in his February 2009 nationally-televised speech before Congress. In April of 2009 a highly publicized report from McKinsey & Company calling for major efforts to close this race-related gap and estimated that its closure would save America between $310 and $525 billion a year (McKinsey & Company, 2009). Conveniently omitted from these calls was the awkward fact that such billion-dollar efforts have existed since the 1960s, and progress has been zero. In fact, less than a week after the *New York Times* uncritically reported on the McKinsey & Company call for closing the gap (Hernandez, April 23, 2009), another *New York Times* story headlined "'No Child' Law Is Not Closing Racial Gap" (Dillon, April 29, 2009).

Eliminating inequality in outcomes would be wondrous, but, to be politically incorrect, this doomed-to-fail enterprise imposes liabilities far exceeding spending untold billions more. The aim should be the best possible education for every student regardless of personal trait, not leveling attainment across every imaginable demographic category. This quixotic quest subverts *all* education and *if educational progress is the aim, we should end the bridging-the-gap enterprise.* Achieving racial equality in outcomes and simultaneously boosting academic proficiency more generally are, as a practical matter, *inherently contradictory* and, for good measure, the quest also harms struggling African-American students. To repeat: you cannot both close gaps and promote academic excellence, at least with current public policies. Pessimism holds even if we set aside race-related IQ differences though this plausible assertion—if true—inescapably thwarts equal outcomes regardless of government pressure or resources. This futile, self-destructive pursuit puts a politically-driven moral high above genuine educational attainment.

History of Failures

Educational outsiders are generally unaware of America's long-standing commitments to narrowing racial differences, and it might be helpful—if a tad repetitious—to highlight this enterprise. In 1966, James S. Coleman and associates, in a model of careful social science methodology, using extensive national data (some half a million students, 4,000 schools, and 60,000 teachers), found that pouring ever more tangible resources into schools scarcely improved student performance. Obviously, money is vital, but beyond adequacy, yields were marginal. Somewhat surprisingly, material differences between predominantly black and predominantly white schools were relatively small so equalizing expenditures was not the solution. Nor did racial balancing much improve matters. Good teachers could help black students learn, but overall Coleman and his associates found that parental background, by contrast, was decisive.

Coleman's 1981 follow-up investigation was more optimistic about schooling, but this largely reflected the benefits of private schools, Catholic and non-Catholic. That these were generally safer, stressed discipline, required regular attendance and homework while often having smaller classes made the difference (Ravitch, 1985, Ch. 7). Private schools were also more demanding and pushed students harder. Nevertheless, whether these learning-boosting practices can be successfully exported to public schools remains uncertain (especially since private schools can more easily expel extreme trouble-makers). Questions also exist regarding the similarity of students in private versus public schools. All and all, however, these lessons from the 1981 report have proven of little value as subsequent billions in failed compensatory education have come to naught.

In 1965 Congress passed the Elementary and Secondary Education whose Title I authorized ample federal support to help low-income students achieve academic parity with children from wealthier families. After forty years and $200 billion showered on countless communities (50,000 schools and 12.5 million students currently receive Title I funds) and innovations galore, studies consistently show gaps remaining virtually unchanged though narrowing temporarily occurred during the 1970s and 80s. Actually, the news may be worse than officially reported. One major 1988 study found that academic standards in schools with impoverished students were substantially lower than in high achieving localities, so a grade of "B" in a largely black school might only be a "C" in a majority white school (Kosters and Mast 2003).

Also from the upbeat 1960s was the then famous (but now almost forgotten) "Milwaukee Project" run by Professor Rick Huber and other University of Wisconsin-Madison associates. In terms of targeted effort—$14 million on relatively few participants over fifteen years, with one-on-one mental stimulation to very young children at risk from mental retardation—this is the Mother of All magic Bullet-like interventions (Page, 1986). It began with children from impoverished homes shortly after birth and continued until school age. IQs of the targeted twenty children were raised thirty points, an incredible jump! This miracle predictably bestowed notoriety and political access on Huber and his colleagues, and quickly entered college textbooks unchallenged. The popular media, including *Time* hailed the project as demonstrating the power of a decent environment to work miracles.

Unfortunately, celebration was premature. For one, the study's countless serious technical problems cast serious doubt on the findings. It was often impossible to know what had transpired and measurement standards periodically shifted. Evidence strongly suggests teaching the tests and investigators often ignored required scientific guidelines. Second, the authors shielded the buoyant news from closer scientific scrutiny, publishing vague, non-technical reports, all the while refusing to answer critics. The investigation's messiness ultimately resulted into criminal charges against Huber and his colleagues for embezzlement and tax evasion. Huber was sentenced to five years for fraud and stripped of his University of Wisconsin responsibilities. Interestingly, though the successes received far-reaching publicity, the promised miracle's subsequent collapse totally escaped mass media attention. No wonder beliefs about easy-to-manipulate environmental factors linger in the public's consciousness.

The hugely-expensive Kansas City, Missouri experiment during the late 1980s and early 1990s repeated this we can't-miss-if-we-only-spend-the-money saga (see Thernstrom and Thernstrom, 1997, 345-6). If there was ever an example of throwing limitless money at a problem, Kansas City is perfect. The school district (KSMSD) was two thirds black with about 5 percent Hispanic enrollment and achievements were dismal. Though the school was well-funded by Missouri standards, this was deemed insufficient to a local judge who, citing years of fiscal neglect vis-à-vis wealthier suburban schools, told school officials to "dream" as if money were no object, even if judge-imposed tax increases might be constitutionally questionable. Local school official claims that massive spending could not alleviate underlying problems hindering achievement, e.g., single parent homes, were tersely dismissed. Also rejected were claims that shabby facilities could be readily repaired at a reasonable cost. The judge said, "Dream" and dream they did.

And on the Second Day the Judge said "and let physical facilities be palatial." And this came to pass. Myriad upgrades included air-conditioned classrooms, planetariums, animal rooms, a twenty-five-acre farm and a twenty-acre wildlife area, a model UN assembly equipped with simultaneous language translations, radio and TV studios, movie editing equipment (with screening rooms), a temperature-controlled art gallery, a $5 million indoor Olympic-sized swimming pool, fencing taught by the former head coach of the Soviet Olympic fencing team, and a plethora of high-tech gadgetry. Field trips were made to Mexico and Senegal, the director took a "good will" trip to Moscow, and the student-teacher ratios dropped to 13 to 1, the lowest in the nation (Ciotti, 1998). Nor were academics slighted: schools offered concentrations on international affairs, multiple foreign languages, even instruction in ancient Greek. Eight schools in the system now specialized in mathematics and science. This did not come cheap, and by 1993 this extravagance had added an additional $1.3 billion to an already large annual budget, $36,111 per pupil *extra*. In 1995 the U.S. Supreme Court ended this failed social engineering.

Despite $2 billion in over-the-top facilities, the expected uplift failed to arrive. Drop-out rates moved upward while scores on standardized tests measuring reading and math dropped. Administrators stole while construction costs far exceeded all reasonable standards. Critically, the racial gap remained unchanged. These lures, all the NFL-class weight rooms, extra teachers, and specialized learning opportunities, even sending taxis to get white students not on bus routes (cost: $50,000 per month)—failed to bribe white suburbanites to stay for more than an interlude, and so KSMSD was just one more disappointment at ameliorating racial gaps, albeit on a grandiose scale.

The popular Head Start program was initiated in 1965 as a sure-to-succeed panacea to insure that poorer children (especially African-Americans) received all the benefits, from cognitive stimulation to medical attention that would permit them to catch up with middle class cohorts. The estimated cost has been $100 billion since inception, and annually serves some 900,000 deserving children and while its popularity suggests accomplishment, it has failed in its primary mission of boosting academic achievement though it has provided other worthwhile benefits like better health care.

This sorry conclusion has—as is legally required—been repeatedly documented. A 1985 U.S. Department of Health and Human Service analysis found that the program's claim of long- term benefits were exaggerated, and this included increases in cognitive test scores and academic benefits plus such non-academic benefits as reducing crime, teen pregnancy, and unemployment (Hood, 1992). A more recent overview summarized a detailed study from 383 sites of 4,600 children that found "No gains were detected in such important measures as early math learning, oral comprehension, motivation to learn social competencies" (cited in Husock, 2007). If Head Start did perform in some mysterious fashion beyond the ken of crude social science methodology, ranges in achievement should have steadily narrowed over the last forty years, and this is certainly not true.

Some black leaders insisted that academic progress would arrive when blacks themselves assumed political control of educating their children, and the government often agreed. In 1967, for example, a federal judged abolished Washington, DC's white-dominated, federally-appointed school board and blacks assumed control. The results over four plus decades have been an unqualified disaster and even many blacks agree. Appointed administrators (almost all black) have brief tenures, physical conditions were terrible, sometimes violating the fire code, record-keeping was often chaotic or non-existent, corruption rampant and, more critically, DC's children still lagged behind. Litigation over running the district has consumed millions of dollars but to no avail. Nearly every reform gimmick has been tried by DC's administrators and met with failure. Parents who can flee DC's schools, including many middle-class African-Americans often do, and schools are just as racially segregated as before court-ordered integration (Witt, 2007). Similar disappointments have occurred in other largely black cities, e.g., Newark, NJ, East St. Louis, IL, Gary, IN, where African-Americans dominate—gaining control of schools brings zero educational gain.

These failures have only driven blacks to more desperate and questionable "solutions." After years of disappointing outcomes, African-American educators and community activists in Pittsburgh, PA have embraced a more racially-sensitive approach to boost performances (*Teacher Magazine*, Dec. 8, 2008). Measures include adding more African material to history lessons, even using African art to teach social studies and math, a greater stress on black cultural identity, sensitivity training for white teachers, and racial quotas for calling on students in class and meting out discipline for infractions. Tellingly, reforms reflect a settlement with local activists, not proven scientific research.

The election of Barack Obama in 2008 seemed to re-energize this close-the-gap impulse and newly-supplied solutions again flowed (and recall that this quest was made explicit in his February 2009 speech before Congress). A *USA Today* forum of expert teachers and heads of advocacy groups offered an impressive medley of solutions. These included more federal funding to bring high-quality teachers to inner-city classrooms, enhanced presidential leadership, teachers who demand the very best from students, a greater understanding of the crisis, eliminating socioeconomic inequality, and financial incentives for good suburban schools to take in low-achievers. One expert, Jeanne Allen, the president of the Center for Educational Reform even said that a solution could be implemented in months, not decades (Toppo, 2009). Meanwhile at a symposium in New York City the city's school chancellor said the gap could be closed by empowering families, increasing expectations, fairer allocation of financial resources, a longer school day and school year, and more school choice (*NYC Public School Parent*, January 8, 2009). What is revealing about these "expert" suggestions is that they are *ad hoc,* exhibit almost no overlap, are bereft of details, and reflect zero scientific evidence. This is after forty years of wrestling with the problem and hundreds of billions invested. It is inconceivable that this lackadaisical non-scientific mentality would prevail if the gap were an alarming national medical condition.

All these intervention failures are absolutely typical. Ronald E. Ferguson, in a careful overview of the most methodological rigorous studies, offers scant hope for magic bullet solutions. Admittedly, occasional successes do occur but "obvious" solutions such as early intervention, eliminating tracking, using more black teachers, intensive remediation all disappoint (Ferguson, 1998). Abigail and Stephen Thernstrom in their *No Excuses* (2003, especially Chapter 4) catalogue similar disappointment for once "guaranteed" solutions. Jay P. Green and associates likewise show that unremitting fiscal bountifulness generally comes to naught save in a tiny number of cases, and even here the results are small (2005, Chapter 1).

Conservatives have also joined this quest with such "cures" as school uniforms, banning gang symbols, prohibiting baggy pants, creating same-sex schools, drug-free zones surrounding schools, zero tolerance for disciplinary infractions, spending a day inside businesses to whet appetites for future achievement, even scary visits to jails to see the wages of dissipation. Several troubled schools have adopted the "SchoolStat" system modeled after the New York City Police Department's anti-crime "Compstat" program that minutely tracks problems so school administrators can react immediately (Hu, 2007). A few conservatives advocate somehow altering the black lower class anti-intellectual mind-set, though it is unclear just how this is to be accomplished.

A *New York Times* story illustrated just how far those trying to help black students might go—all the way to Antarctica, it turns out (Rimer, 2008). Stephen F. Pekar, a Queens College geology professor (who is white) believes that too many African-American students disdain science and math, and to boost curiosity he has convinced Shakira Brown, a black middle-school teacher to join his scientific expedition to Antarctica. This adventure, Pekar claims, will provide a role model for black students though twenty-below-zero temperatures, horrendous blizzards, and primitive living conditions are hardly fun. The National Science Foundation is sponsoring the trip with additional help from Harlem's Children Zone, Urban Science Corps, and the American Museum of Natural History. Ms. Brown's students are fascinated, though whether her excursion will help them master difficult college-level courses required for a scientific career remains iffy.

The Magic of Racial Integration

If there is one single, supposedly-guaranteed historic cure for narrowing the academic divide between blacks and whites, it has been racial integration. Though pushed pursued with a vengeance it has failed to perform. The "logic" seems mesmerizing: transfer those allegedly injured by shoddy instruction (i.e., blacks) to superior, learning-positive facilities occupied by whites. Now, it is argued, exposure to high-quality teachers in resource-abundant settings plus interacting with more motivated classmates, newcomers will thrive as might a starved person be rejuvenated at an all-you-can-eat buffet. In practice this means mixing African-Americans, many of whom test noticeably below whites (though exceptions do exist), with better-scoring whites. The blending, critically, assumes that low black performance principally results from inadequate schools though the legal impetus for integration usually has little to do with physical facilities, teacher qualifications, money spent, or other tangible qualities—segregation itself qualifies a school as "bad." This segregation is-the-culprit thesis historically dominates close-the-gap remedies, and compared to alternatives seems almost cost-free, save overcoming huge political resistance from white parents hostile to racial mixing plus many black parents wanting neighborhood schools.

David Armor (1995) has thoroughly probed this subject, reviewing hundreds of separate studies relying on multiple analytical techniques, and judicially concludes that if this remedy does perform as claimed, the empirical evidence does *not* confirm it though, to be sure, sifting mountains of research reveals a glimmer or two of hope (76). It is certainly undeniable that massive racial integration of public schools beginning in the early 1970s has failed to eradicate racial gaps in academic achievement. Furthermore, its coercive nature often reinstitutes segregation as whites flee rather than see their children attend racially-mixed schools.

Consider some typical examples of this alleged solution. In Pasadena, California the white school board under pressure from residents steadfastly resisted racial integration but litigation followed litigation, political turmoil heated up, and then finally in 1970s, black students entered formally all-white schools. The initial test score gaps were substantial—whites scored on average at the 59th percentile, blacks at the 27th percentile. Researchers monitored the same students over four years, from first to fourth grade, and while black scores jumped a bit in second grade, they soon reverted to previous low levels, and remained there until the fourth grade, at which point the investigation ended. As was common elsewhere, whites quickly fled the school system and the Pasadena system soon became overwhelmingly black.

Outcomes were no better in Norfolk, VA where, too, political turmoil and litigation surrounded school integration. Again a substantial achievement gap initially separated blacks and whites, and scores for both *declined* immediately after forced busing and efforts to juggle neighborhood school composition to avoid resegregation. This downturn was substantial—nearly 20 percentile points for whites and a parallel decline for blacks so the latter now scored at the 12th percentile measured against the national average. Faced with truly dismal and unexpected outcomes, administrators instituted an intensive basic skills program and, happily, scores for both races rose and soon returned to pre-integration levels. Though sizable race-related gaps persisted, black scores did show a small increase over their pre-segregation days.

Armor's exemplars are typical, and extensive other overviews of the alleged benefits of racial mixing show comparable outcomes though, again, glimmers of hope occasionally appear. In 1984, for example, the National Institute of Education assembled experts to assess what they considered the very best studies of the benefits of racial integration. Nineteen studies were selected as satisfying the highest scientific standard. Overall, the outcomes were decidedly mixed—several positive, several negative but certainly no magic elixirs emerged. Some African-Americans attending integrated schools demonstrated small gains in reading and mathematics; others showed *declines* in both subjects as a result of racial integration vis-à-vis those in segregated facilities. Translating the improvement into time, gains, and losses were typically about a month out of an entire school year though in a few instances the gain exceeded half a school year. Attempts to separate situations yielding gains versus losses, for example, whether integration was coerced or voluntary, proved largely unsuccessful. Huge quantities of political capital were thus expended for a few tiny academic gains (and a few setbacks, too).

The intellectual industriousness expended by experts to "demonstrate" the merit of this racial-mixing-begs-black achievement is prodigious, an almost religious-like commitment in the face of uncooperative evidence.

Between 1971 and 1990 the racial gap in reading and math scores on the National Assessment of Educational Progress (NAEP) has declined somewhat though is still substantial. Given a general parallel movement toward racially-integrated schools, desegregation champions hail these upbeat results as confirming the benefits of integrating schools. Yet, as Armor points out (94-6), if these data are subdivided according to school racial composition, versus just assuming universal integration, the results are less sanguine. Blacks did move upward in reading during this period, but gaps between integrated vs. segregated schools were nearly nonexistent. Ironically, black math scores showed greater upward movement in largely minority settings. As for the overall achievement gains of African-Americans, Armor (96-8) plausibly argues that economic progress, not mingling with whites, boosted black test scores. That is, black parents now enjoyed access to greater resources, and this translated into superior academic outcomes for their children, regardless of school racial composition.

Today's Educators and Politicians Can't Learn, Either

Past unproductive outlays do not, alas, suggest a learning curve regarding financial extravagance or other government-supplied remedies to close race-related disparity. A cynic might reasonably argue that financially rewarding failure naturally teaches people how to manufacture disappointment. Between 2003 and 2005, for example, federal spending for the disadvantaged increased from $11.25 billion to $14.64 billion (*US Statistical Abstract 2007*, Table 207). President Bush's No Child Left Behind (NCLB) has generated widespread controversy but absent from these debates is whether its central aim—transforming the bottom via pressuring and bribing school officials—is even achievable. It is inconceivable that congressional Democrats (and a few Republicans) so skeptical of Bush's Iraqi strategy would have imposed similar provision to this quest—demanding a fixed timetable for Department of Education bureaucrats to withdraw from local classrooms or face defunding.

The soldiering on in the face of endless setbacks can drive public officials to almost desperate claims. A handsomely-produced brochure from New York City's Department of Education called "Fair Student Funding" once claimed that dreary schools (read high concentrations of black and Hispanic students) could be fixed via "fair and transparent" funding. Current New York City spending decisions, it was alleged, reflect ages-old "subjective" criteria and, shame of shame, some schools in the system receive as much as $735 *per child* (italics in original) more than others, a tiny fraction of overall spending per child (New York Department of Education, 2007). Implied is that inequality of outcome woes would vanish if each student in every school received identical allocations. Even on technical grounds, let alone mountains of contrary empirical evidence, the proposal is pure demagoguery. Not only is this cost per student figure an accounting nightmare given apportioning sunk capital costs and central administrative overhead, but re-assigning senior teachers to equalize payrolls violates union contracts and might well bring a massive exodus from high performance schools if teachers were forced to relocate to dangerous inner-city locales.

Meanwhile, multiple movements are afoot drawing heartfelt support from sundry do-gooders, teachers unions, and others feeding off education budgets to guarantee equal educational outcomes as a matter of (state) constitutional right (provisions guaranteeing some type of "adequate schooling"). Owing to sympathetic judges, multi-billion-dollar judgments to bring everyone up to speed grow commonplace. In December of 2006 a New York State judge, thanks to a lawsuit by the Campaign for Fiscal Equity, ordered the state legislature to up its educational spending by $2 billion, considerably less than the $6 billion the suit demanded. Thus far the state is dragging its feet (Warner, 2007) and the economic crisis of 2008/9 has virtually abolished this court-ordered windfall. A Connecticut group calling itself The Connecticut Coalition for Achievement Now wants to shift $1.3 billion in state funds from "reactionary" spending to "preventive" spending to boost minority accomplishment. It proposes a grab bag of solutions—greater accountability, more charter schools, recruiting teachers to urban areas, more frequent monitoring of student performances, and various budgetary reclassifications, among others—to accomplish this mission though it remains unclear how this concoction of therapies can be successfully implemented (Crompton, 2007). All and all, as of early 2007, there were some 125 court cases pending aimed at squeezing legislatures for additional educational funding (Warner, 2007).

The sophistry to concoct spend-your-way-to-closing-the-gap arguments is embarrassingly transparent, especially since success only requires convincing a few judges—not accountable legislators—who may not grasp the horrendously complicated policy issues. In some instances judges are told of extreme atypical circumstances, for example, Alabama students still using outhouses or New York students required to pass courses with non-existent laboratories to graduate (Levin and Herszenhorn, 2007). Fresh government largesse also always attracts political constituencies such as teachers' unions and firms supplying new buildings or expensive electronic gimmicks. Further add the remuneration received by advocates, much of it state paid. In particular, two professors (Lawrence Picus and Allan Odden) run a consulting firm (Picus and Associates) and have successfully billed several states hundreds of thousands (in some instances over a million) dollars in fees to advance judge-coerced generosity (Hanushek, 2007).

This is truly awful social science though politically persuasive (see Hanushek, 2007 for details). The recipe is simple. First, single out few upbeat studies as "relevant" though their applicability is grossly exaggerated (and conveniently ignore contrary results or the study's own qualifications). Second, assert a causal relationship, not mere correlation so, for instance, demonstrating that better paid teachers and superior results are related is construed as "paying teachers more makes kids smarter." The same logic is then applied to summer programs, full-day kindergarten, smaller classes, one-on-one tutoring, and professional development (among other interventions). Now, since each of these programs "causes" academic success, and if each is applied over a student's entire school career, the promised benefits will, it is alleged, be spectacular though extraordinarily expensive. But, who can resist helping the needy? Totally ignored is that the interventions often fail or are cost ineffective given likely meager benefits. Nor do advocates recognize the ceiling effects of these cure-alls. That nations spending far less than the U.S. outperform American schools is irrelevant. Advocates similarly ignore evidence from religious schools thriving on starvation budgets. The solution, "obviously," is more manic spending until the equality plateau is finally reached—Sisyphus on court-ordered steroids.

American universities that have failed for decades to boost black academic performance, using every possible remedy (even those of dubious legality) likewise keep trying. Harvard University in 2005 organized the interdisciplinary Achievement Gap Initiative (AGI) to be run by Harvard professors and immediately sponsored a forum to highlight research useful for narrowing racial differences (Bautz, 2005). In late 2007 eighteen state college and university system leaders unveiled an eight-year plan, financed by two private foundations—Access to Success—that would, once more, try to help black students catch up. The Chancellor of the University of Maryland, William E. Kirwan, said that if higher education cannot close the racial achievement gap, "…our nation is going to suffer tremendously." Suggested tactics included redesigned remedial courses, synchronizing high school and college curriculums, greater financial aid, and sharing of information and "best practices." Goals can be very ambitious, for example, New York's SUNY system hopes to boost minority enrollment by 50 percent in eight years, an aim that guarantees admitting barely competent students.

Bogus Solutions Make Matters Worse

The consequences of these failures can far exceed fiscal profligacy. Shielding under-performing African-Americans and Hispanics from the bad news has deeply corrupted American education. Close-the-gap laws like NCLB and the threat of litigation are guns to the heads of educators, and with no legitimate solutions in sight, the incentives for dishonesty are often compelling. And for good measure, add black and Hispanic violence-prone agitators clamoring that government could close these gulfs "if it really wanted to." It may get worse—a lawsuit in Tampa Bay, FL, threatens to make racial gaps illegal, and if civil rights activists win school officials might face the option of cheating, dumbing down tests or face fines or jail time (Tobin, 2007). This is a perfect storm whereby those skilled at manipulating statistics or flattering those desperate to hear good news, survival-of-the-fittest style, rise to the top. Hard-nosed realists, by contrast, will be shunned or forced into silence. Eventually, like some super-predator, charlatans will proliferate and America will painlessly slouch towards stupidity.

A straight-talking public conversation about education when it wanders into the racial/ethnic minefield is nearly impossible. Lying is endemic; explanations of why African-Americans do poorly can be near mystical. Seattle, WA, has for years unsuccessfully spent millions to make blacks academically proficient, and the district's official explanation for failure is institutional racism, officially defined as "an indirect and largely invisible process that operates automatically and results in less access to services and opportunities of a society based on race" (quoted in Fryer, 2007). Now, just try banishing what is undetectable.

The most inane nonsense goes unchallenged lest it offend ideological sensibilities. In 2007 four thousand people attended a California conference offering 125 panels, all on closing the black-white academic achievement gap. It was a feeding fest of nonsense, but the grand prize must go to Jack O'Connell, California's chief of public schools. He announced the gap's true cause—black youngsters attend churches encouraging parishioners to clap, speak loudly, and be a bit raucous, behavior deemed inappropriate in schools. So, according to O'Connell, if teachers take more sensitivity training to "appreciate" this style, test performances among African-Americans will rise. Not one iota of scientific evidence was offered, including how many young blacks actually attended loud churches. That many whites attend rock-em-and-sock-em Pentecostal churches also went unnoticed. Other conference experts explained the gap with post-traumatic stress disorder (PTSD) due to school violence, fewer AP courses, Eurocentric tests, teacher inexperience and cultural ignorance, over-crowding, and lack of access to preschool programs (Asimov, 2007). To exaggerate only slightly, this close race-related gaps passion encourages people to embrace stupid fantasies, a huge self-imposed millstone in educational progress. One might draw a parallel with cynical Marxist functionaries who survived the Evil Empire's final years thanks to skilled fabrications and public lying but at least they knew what they were doing.

The pressure to show that "gaps can be closed" is so great that even truly wondrous outcomes can be subordinated to this ideologically-driven passion. A particularly egregious example is David Whitman's *Sweating the Small Stuff: Inner-City Schools and the New Paternalism* (2008). This study shows how several inner-city schools catering to blacks and Hispanics had achieved breathtaking outcomes thanks to imparting a no-nonsense Calvinist work ethic that entails a longer school day, three weeks of summer school, dedicated teachers (who work longer hours than peers elsewhere and can be more easily fired), far fewer classmates, a dress code, a more demanding curriculum, a forceful principal, strictly-enforced discipline, and no social promotion among multiple other benefits. Unfortunately, upping academic achievement among blacks and Hispanics is not good enough in today's egalitarian times. Otherwise impressive news is distorted into even better news so as to honor the egalitarian gods. Results from the Calvinist treatment are not compared to white schools receiving the same treatment but to black and Hispanic students in nearby schools who lacked exposure to this Calvinist work ethic. The correct conclusion is that this treatment helps blacks and Hispanics vis-à-vis other blacks and Hispanics. It is thus technically impossible to aver that racial gaps can be closed with these measures. Conceivably, the same help given to white students may exacerbate the achievement gaps.

Lowering Standards to Hide Unwelcome News

Twisting unwanted reality into something more flattering is a long-standing American tradition, and the impetus for ersatz accomplishment is hardly surprising when assigned tasks are likely unreachable. To appreciate ease of accomplishment, one must realize that no Bureau of Standard-like measures exist for educational proficiency. Experts have ample leeway in, say, selecting test items, scoring answers, deciding cut-off points, and what abilities to measure. That unchallenging tests exhibit little dispersion while tough ones produce a much wider range can greatly facilitate this deception. A high school spelling exam using "dog" or "cat" will inevitably demonstrate across-the-board spelling excellence. But, substitute items like "pneumatic" and "antediluvian" and the range of scores widens. Now for the political bottom line: *given racial differences in academic accomplishment (for whatever reason), the tougher the test the wider the race-related gaps.* Tough tests bring unwelcome news to racial egalitarians, *always*.

Thus, if narrowing racial gaps is paramount, and nothing seems to work, just include only easy-to-pass items (e.g., spell "cat") and nobody cries foul. In 2007 the New York state Regents exam, which certifies high school graduates as earning the highest academic degree, carried this principle to absurd lengths. The exam was once a highly-regarded gauge of New York State's outstanding educational system but unacceptable race-related disparate outcomes have gutted it. Significantly, much of the test involves pictures and cartoons, and correct answers are so obvious flunking it requires willful stupidity. The 2007 version, for example, contained several historical pictures of women marching and picketing for the vote. The exam question asked students for *one* method by which women sought the vote. Other questions inquired why women wanted the vote, and these reasons were plain to see in the posters carried by suffragettes (Epstein, 2007). The 2008 exam continued this dumbed-down approach. One picture showed students outside of Little Rock's Central High in 1957 with troops guarding the door. The caption tells of a white student being admitted while a black student (Elizabeth Eckford) was turned away. A second picture shows this black student surrounded by a mob. The exam question is: What happened to Elisabeth Eckford when she tried to attend Central High School? A different photograph from this event is captioned "On September 25, 1957, federal troops escort the Little Rock Nine to Central High School." The question is: "Based on this photograph, what was the job of the United States Army troop in Little Rock, Arkansas?" (Epstein, 2008).

Absent access to the actual items, skullduggery is almost fool-proof if not undetectable. The above stories were written by a New York City school teacher who has been grading Regents exams for thirteen years. He further explains that the scoring system is so Byzantine that making the politically-correct numbers is a snap. The economic parallel is inflating the currency so everyone is a "millionaire," a preposterous solution to poverty but, alas, one that seems tolerable in education as pressures mount for proficiency on the cheap. Why should those with the "prestigious" Regents degree complain?

The repertory of handy educator tricks is immense. Administrators terrified of exposing race-related differences can replace tough fact-based tests with mushy personal portfolios, reject standards of conventional English when grading essays, cover failure with euphemisms (report cards with "ready to learn" versus an "F") and use infamous social promotions. Portland, OR, like other cities with minority students challenged by high school exit exams now permits would-be graduates an options of three exit exams—a national one, the state version, or a local one that might include just a portfolio (several other states are, too, toying with this option). In Newark and Camden, New Jersey, both of which have high concentrations of academically-troubled African-American students, administrators have *de facto* surrendered to reality and now award "alternative diplomas" for those failing the regular tests (Silverman, 2008). Exams can be endlessly taken and retaken with only the highest scores counting (and this may include tests for the high school diploma); curves shifted and minimum passing scores lowered; and if that comes up short, award "extra credit" for trying hard. Thus, with scarcely any effort, all students, from the dull to the exceptional, can be lumped into meaningless mile wide "proficient" categories.

An employer demanding a high school diploma is probably oblivious to this academic counterfeiting and new tricks are being devised. One third of all states now employ "credit recovery" where students unable to graduate can "make up the work" via brief, supposedly intensive sessions (Gootman and Coutts, 2008). Its popularity in New York City may reflect that these extra sessions are loosely supervised and with a student "graduating," the school, including the overseeing principal, may receive a cash bonus. That "credit recovery" is increasingly being applied with computerized online testing obviously invites wholesale fraud. Several New York teachers requesting anonymity called this practice a dirty little secret, a joke, that hardly substituted for classroom work but it happily shows that many struggling blacks and Hispanics do "graduate."

Recent efforts to make Advanced Placement (AP) courses more racially inclusive further illustrate racially-motivated pernicious dilution. Now administrative tinkering can easily certify a marginal student "advanced" and few will complain. In Loundon County, Virginia, for example, the threat of NAACP litigation has motivated a doubling of black students in AP courses in just four years, a truly remarkable increase in cognitive ability (Chandler, 2007). Note well: this is just sitting in the AP class apart from assessing actual learning and it is the college, not the high school, that decides the pass standard, so inflating the numbers is cost-free for under-the-gun high school administrators. That this inflation might hurt legitimate AP students while bewildering struggling African-Americans is undoubtedly secondary to avoiding an expensive lawsuit. Bubbling below the surface is an expert-led movement to make African-American history an official Advanced Placement course, a policy that would cause "blacks enrolled in AP" numbers to skyrocket while avoiding awkward absences in physics and calculus (Jaschik, 2007).

Bogus baselines can be a godsend to those worried about dreary test performance, especially if African-Americans perform poorly. How is a parent to discern that their offspring is a functional illiterate if classified as "average" given classmates equally unable to read or write? In Georgia, for example, a student need only pass 17 of 40 questions to advance to fourth grade, and 16 of these items are classified as "easy" by the state's department of Education. In Texas the state's accountability exam can be passed by correctly answering 29 of 60 questions. When Michigan found that it had 1,500 "failing schools," officials promptly adjusted the pass standard from 75 percent to 42 percent correct, and the number of failing schools dropped to 216 (Ladner, 2004). Firms supplying and scoring tests also have scant incentives to sustain a high fixed standard; better to keep clients happy with "good news." Years back the Educational Testing Service (ETS) became alarmed as some colleges dropped their SAT requirements since scores exposed large racial disparities that complicated diverse admissions. To "solve" this deficiency, and keep the testing fees coming, the ETS systematically eliminated individual items with sharp racial disparities. Though SAT results continue to be unequal, differences are now undoubtedly smaller.

The twisting of "proficiency" is readily apparent as lawmakers interfere in testing in response to racial activists happy to bury yet more bad news. Further add the need to append built-in statutory loopholes and escape provisions as the price to be paid for legislative enactment. Educators are a huge voting bloc and hardly welcome career disrupting legislation, so just kill the bad news messenger. Statutory language may tacitly encourage deception—the NCLB required tests to be "challenging" yet this is never concretely defined and surely invites political meddling. Unusual variations in state "pass rates" are often the tip off. For instance, for the 8th grade English assessment test, 30 percent of South Carolina students were rated "proficient" while just across the border in North Carolina the figure was 88 percent (cited in *http://tc.edu/new/ articlehtm?id=5955&tid=119*). Another study found dramatic variability in "pass standards," for example, students in Colorado could pass a reading test with scores between the 9th and 18th percentile nationally; in South Carolina and Wyoming "pass" was in the 70th percentile nationally (Fessenden, 2003). Statistical manipulation, often justified with technical jargon such as "confidence interval" is commonplace so as to transform magically-failing schools into Great Leaps Forward. Indiana, for instance, once interpreted a figure of 40.0 percent as "really" a passing grade of 58.8 percent when the "margin of error" was incorporated into the analysis (Redelman, 2003).

A little thought will show that the most efficient, surefire, so simple that even a caveman can do it way to equalize test scores across all groups is *to educate everyone into stupidity*. If learning equality across all demographic groups is the single paramount goal, the *only* guaranteed, honest, non-manipulative solution is to return to prehistoric conditions where *nobody* could read or write, let alone solve quadratic equations. If this sounds too extreme, and a tad too embarrassing, just force everyone to enroll in remedial classes, a situation that often *de facto* occurs when teachers endlessly repeat unchallenging lessons so the least adept can stay abreast. A cynic might even demand that these classes be labeled "advanced" just as the smallest toothpaste tube is "large." These dumbed-down measures would truly exorcize racial inequalities.

Old-Fashioned Data Cooking

If the lowest of the low cannot be deemed "proficient" by the above handy tactics, just cheat. NCLB rested on political accommodations and the resulting "flexibility" virtually guaranteed dishonesty. For one, schools typically administer tests themselves with minimal outside oversight. Strict financial controls are ubiquitous when spending public money but have no equivalent in testing. In a pinch, teachers can just tell students answers or exclude laggards from the test-taking population by classifying them as "learning disabled" (Snell, 2005 catalogues these ruses). Add the handsome personal financial rewards accruing to "miracle workers" plus near nonexistent punishment if caught, and it is a wonder that anybody is honest. In fact, with rampant dishonesty, it is rational for an honest educator to cheat since without an artificial boost, they may lose their jobs due to "poor performance" if they are unlucky enough to compete against cheaters. The contrast with business legal regulations, and sports for that matter, sadly confirm America's indifference to educational excellence. Imagine fan outrage if an NFL football team exaggerated a running back's total yardage? Not so for reading and math scores—lies in education are rarely challenged.

Given that inflating test scores is not a criminal offense, that far too many schools exist to permit thorough investigations, and many administrators profit from fraud and are thus motivated to keep silent, precise statistics are lacking. Actually, like drinking during Prohibition, relevant data are probably uncollectable given public indifference. Moreover, much of this is accusations, not a result of courtroom trials, and often reflects a teacher ratting on colleagues, but that being said, the evidence, though largely anecdotal, suggests that American education is slipping into a culture of mendacity. This is less flat-out lying than shading and shaping the data—spinning, so to speak. A Google search "NCLB cheating" uncovers a treasure trove of incidents across the entire nation. The subject has surfaced in congressional debates surrounding re-authorizing NCLB though legislators are unsure of solutions. A private firm (Caveon) exists to probe accusations and their website, caveon.com, offers copious examples of educational fraud.

Smoking gun proof is often of the "too good to be true" variety. For example, Camden, NJ is an historic educational calamity, the worst of the worst, but a *Philadelphia Inquirer* story revealed how its test scores suddenly shot up to be among the highest in NJ, and this decidedly-implausible outcome triggered a state investigation (one can only wonder why the state did not initiate the inquiry). Suspecting out-of-control test fraudulence in its schools, the Chicago schools hired two professors of economics to investigate, and they found evidence of cheating in 70 classrooms. In 2004 Texas suspected cheating in 400 schools and the state plus a private firm dug further (Kummer, 2006). Doris Alvarez was a former national Principal of the Year (among other honors) at San Diego Preuss School where low-income and minority students had achieved spectacular academic results. *Newsweek* rated it 10th of the nation's top 1,200 high schools. Alas, a review of the school's transcripts found that three quarters had at least one grade altered. Teachers also complained of pressure to push unqualified students into AP courses (Toppo, 2007). Similar tales of data cooking have appeared in Boston, MA, Columbus, OH, plus various school districts in Indiana. One might suppose, however, that this particular cheating was found out since it violated cheating's cardinal rule—don't over-do it or you will be discovered. A series of small "adjustments" would probably have passed unnoticed.

A recent New York State spectacular great leap forward has likewise raised "too good to be true" suspicions. Here scores in both reading and math jumped virtually overnight even in cities with chronic academic insufficiencies. New York's educational officials predictably hailed these outcomes as proof of their wise policies (Medina, June 24, 2008). Celebration may be premature, however. These upswings were not mirrored in national tests administered to New York students. Several academics with no stake in these outcomes also expressed reservations about the data, even suggesting that scores just reflected inflation. Note well, these outcomes were not state audited so everything was on the honor system (Green, June 23, 2008). One upshot of this putative uptick was greater attention of a particular noted miracle worker, John Hughes, who had built a reputation for quickly turning around underperforming schools. According to teachers at his schools, however, they were routinely asked to "help" struggling students by telling them that their answers were incorrect. Elsewhere teachers have observed that students arriving with excellent test scores are academically unprepared (Green, June 30, 2008).

Make no mistake: this fraud is typically rooted in trying to disguise racial differences in academic achievement. If critics complain of dreadful graduation rates of blacks vis-à-vis whites, a few obscure administrative changes can result in printing up diplomas for hundreds of semi-literate graduates. If too few blacks are admitted to college, just loosen local community college entrance requirements to enhance "opportunities" albeit for many students unable to master high school work. After all, "students going on to college" says zero about them learning anything or even getting a degree though it sounds wonderful. Meanwhile, states worried over racial imbalance at elite state colleges increasingly make high school graduation rank, regardless of other indicators such as test scores predicting failure, as *prima facie* evidence of admission worthiness.

Trying Harder Only Makes It Worse

The last several decades have seen a paradox in American education: we invest billions, develop endless promising pedagogical innovations and yet we seem to be going nowhere, even backwards. This paradox is predictable since we glibly confuse what is supposed to work with what actually does work. Some of this is intentional since failure is nothing more than humdrum wasteful pork-barrel politics. Still, incredibly sloppy thinking is also a culprit and here we'll highlight some gap-closing "solutions" akin to earlier medicine when cures were far deadlier than diseases.

Misallocating Resources

A favorite nostrum for the gap obsessed entails shifting resources away from well-performing students to those "who need it the most." It is tacitly assumed that the academic adroit will continue to flourish on diminished diets while, to continue the food parallel, the educational starving will now prosper from redirected "calories." The most forceful version of this mentality, often labeled "fairness," is that equal outcomes require unequal resources given unlike starting points so underachievers will now receive better-qualified teachers, smaller classes, state-of-the-art technology and all else to lift those lagging behind. Beliefs about the power of material resources, versus human capital (i.e., the students themselves), are central, and comparable to insisting that inept basketball teams could become champions if only given better practice facilities or nicer uniforms.

At least two major miscalculations infuse this thinking. First, it falsely assumes a universality of resource impact across varied settings: what performs in school A performs equally well in schools B through Z. Most notably, a stellar teacher in one setting will have similar uplifting impacts elsewhere, no different from, say, Boyle's Law working everywhere. Unfortunately, as every experienced teacher learns, what succeeds with one class may fall flat next period with roughly comparable youngsters. Make students and environments more dissimilar and unequal outcomes, regardless of identical books, lesson plans, and all else, are inevitable. A dynamic teacher who inspires gruff working-class white kids may terrify introverted Asian children from recently-arrived immigrant families. Admittedly, some truly gifted instructors, like high-paid basketball coaches, may transform losers into winners anywhere and under any circumstances, but it is unrealistic to expect widespread transferability of talent.

If this interchangeability of resources were, indeed, correct, the massive court-ordered racial integration schemes of the last forty years should have long narrowed educational gaps, and clearly, as we saw, they have failed. Each student takes something different away from the same teacher, the same books, and the identical lectures. This equal-resources-brings-equal-outcomes delusion is particularly visible at prestigious universities overflowing with stellar learning opportunities where less talented students largely survive by gravitating toward easier majors, taking remedial classes and finding sympathetic instructors. Keep in mind that almost every major university has at one time implemented race-related outreach programs keyed to the low achievers only to abandon or severely modify them.

A second, and ultimately more important, flaw in this shifting argument concerns net *overall* educational gains, not just helping the bottom. As pressure mounts to uplift those lagging behind, it is tempting to fixate on progress at the bottom and, in fact, NCLB made this fixing imperative lest federal funding be withdrawn. But, this bottom fixation need not bring *overall* educational progress. The same resources allocated to the top may be far more productive than identical resources provided to strugglers. Moreover, targeting the weakest students can easily mask setbacks elsewhere, i.e., underperforming good students who slip to just average thanks to their competent teachers assigned to ghetto schools. Similar invisible costs can occur if basic computers are given to gifted students so as to guarantee computers for those barely able to use them. If maximizing educational attainment were the aim, a far superior solution would be giving the smartest students the best machines and tell the less able that their machines will come when they reach proficiency.

The Adding Resources Paradox

Race gap closers inevitably demand additional funding. The logic superficially seems solid: those lagging behind must catch up with more affluent, better-performing classmates, so extra money to reward excellent teachers or buy cutting edge technology, etc., etc., eventually levels the playing field, and with everybody now equal, gaps will vanish. This vision has become an unchallenged cliché among radical educators: familiar tales of dilapidated urban schools while wealthy whites enjoy suburban opulence. That the link between school expenditures and performance is virtually nonexistent scarcely matters to these advocates since, as we saw, they willingly invest huge sums to secure tiny benefits. But, the disappointing news awaiting gap closers is even more depressing: across-the-board fiscal generosity, even extra money to the disadvantaged, virtually guarantees *widening* gaps.

To condense a complicated story, given unavoidable inequalities in cognitive talent (regardless of sources—nature or nurture), the greater the resources supplied, *the greater the gap in accomplishments*. Since people differ in talents and abilities, equal resources *ensures* unequal outcome—children are not identical seeds that flourish equally if watered and fertilized equally (see Sarish and Miel, 2004, 258-62 and Hirsch, 1996, 44-6 on this paradox). It would be as if two people of unequal natural athletic ability relentlessly practiced golf, in a year's time the more naturally talented would be even further ahead. Give professional equipment, more practice time and equal expert instruction to both, and the performance gap would widen even further. For egalitarians, the grim message is that equality of resources brings inequality of outcomes.

These counterintuitive outcomes have been carefully catalogued across myriad areas involving multiple government-funded early intervention programs (Ceci and Papierno, 2005 summarize these). The pattern has even acquired a name—the Matthew Effect, after the Biblical preacher who spoke (Matthew 13:12) of faith growing stronger among true believers while declining among the less faithful. The phrase "the rich get richer" is the economic version. One cited study described how good readers become even better readers than those initially only a step behind. That is, the initially superior reader reads more, builds a larger vocabulary, prefers reading as a leisure activity, associates with fellow book worms and requests books as gifts. The less adept reader, by contrast, avoids books and so by adolescence once small gaps have become cumulative.

Studies of young children find that this "Matthew Effect" applies to using cognitive strategies, comprehension, memory tasks, academic performances, and vocabulary acquisition among other skills. Ironically, summer enrichment programs, often heralded as a way to help the disadvantaged catch up disproportionately benefit middle class attendees. The multiplication effect increases with age, so that as children progress through school, the smarter become more knowledgeable than less able classmates. Thus, if all students spent only three months in a dilapidated single-room schoolhouse with only McGuffy's reader with a semi-illiterate teacher, and outside study was impractical, end-of-year test scores would show slight (but still some) dispersion. Now add better textbooks, computers, a library, capable teachers, a nine-month school year, science labs, and all the rest. The outcome would *necessarily* be wider gaps, as brighter, more motivated students better utilized newly-available resources.

The implications for today's gap equalizing nostrums are dreadful. If by some miracle schools hire only inspirational, smart teachers this will aggravate differences even further. By contrast, staffing schools with incompetents will disproportionately hurt brighter students (given their higher potential) and thus flatten inequalities (though extraordinary students may eventually still flourish independently). A smart, inspiring teacher will, however, have a much larger impact on intelligent students since they can absorb far more. So much for the "quality teacher" magic bullet to smooth outcomes though, in a sense, egalitarians are correct about the relationship between teacher quality and achievement gaps—if ineffectual teachers instructed brainy pupils, achievement would fall and thus level outcomes courtesy of incapacitating the smartest.

Ceci and Papierno argue that the Matthew Effect can only be prevented by stopping the already advantaged from participating in uplift-the-bottom interventions. Income barriers to access (e.g., Head Start) or explicitly targeting the "at risk" (who are usually poor) are two common exclusionary strategies. Unfortunately for egalitarians, these prohibitions are constrained since the political price for enacting generous legislation often requires extending eligibility to middle-class children. Other enrichment programs are applied without regard to cognitive ability though helping the bottom is often the program's impetus. The perfect example is Sesame Street, which was originally designed to narrow group-related cognitive differences but has actually *widened* disparities.

That middle-class parents are typically more proficient at utilizing these "help-the-disadvantaged" programs only compounds the egalitarian's woes. Studies of college scholarship programs designed to help "the needy" such as the GI Bill and Hope Scholarships in fact were disproportionately utilized by the more affluent. Funds targeted for the disadvantaged may also be allocated on a district-wide basis (e.g., magnet schools, community resource centers) and, again, smarter students, thanks to keen-eyed ambitious parents, may better utilize these opportunities. Ironically, initiatives to entice smart people into teaching to revitalize dreadful inner-city schools may backfire for egalitarians if these talented individuals eventually relocate to academically-oriented schools. A truly dedicated egalitarian would be wise to pay bonuses for bonehead teachers to teach the smartest students.

More telling, however, is that government's assisting the disadvantaged, even explicitly baring the advantaged, cannot deter ambitious parents from privately countering government intervention. Such is the nature of educational capitalism and not even the Soviet Union could thwart bourgeoisie parents from overcoming biases favoring young proletarians. No laws prevent middle-class white or Asian parents pursuing comparable, if not superior enrichments, and a cognitive "arms race" may ensure. Faced with ghetto schools supplying free SAT help, striving parents might hire Stanley Kaplan tutors, add home computerized instruction or elect private schools to maintain their lead as those below try catching up. A *New York Sun* story told of how affluent New Yorkers by the scores willing to pay up to $400 for an hour and a half of SAT tutoring, even thousands for tips on college application essays (Weiss, October 22, 2008). Keep in mind that success relative to government-assisted upstarts only requires comparable resource commitments, not superior efforts, given already initial advantages in ability and motivation.

Going one step further, even if such gross resource misallocation were tried, government must stop brighter students from acquiring knowledge on the sly. The totalitarian road is inevitable. Smart students attending resource-starved schools must now be legally *forbidden* to read too many books, enroll in cram academies, or surf the Net to overcome artificial shackling. Perhaps egalitarian champions would develop a special paint ("fairness yellow"?) that instantly peeled from the ceilings to impede ambitious nerds. A secretive black market in after-school activities might emerge, a network of educational speakeasies. Though a casual connection is uncertain, it is indisputable that as New York City school officials toil to help lagging black and Hispanic students, the demand for elite private school places with skyrocketing tuition has soared.

This analysis poses an awkward dilemma: pouring money into education *will* often (though not always) assist the disadvantaged but, if there are gains to be made, they will be made *disproportionately* by those already several steps ahead. And these multiply the greater the educational investment. One cannot have it both ways: progress for the bottom will be "paid for" by even wider gaps. This paradox need not be immoral and it is certainly not inimical to America's national interests. This is comparable to explosive prosperity producing huge wealth gaps while the poor enjoy what were once luxuries. To insist that burgeoning race-related gaps are morally reprehensible is, to invoke the old adage, cutting off one's nose to spite one's face. Unfortunately, the dilemma's true nature and its hidden benefits are typically ignored, and the upshot is confusion as to why we spend ever more and fail to narrow racial differences.

The Morality of Coerced Academic Achievement

Proponents of closing race-related achievement gaps assume that (1) academic excellence is universally desired; (2) it is intrinsically worthy, personally or for America as a nation so, therefore (3) imploring everyone to excel in school is a moral imperative. That is, blacks *should* try to achieve at white and Asian levels, and to reject this quest is a personal failing and, going one step further, a national calamity. These well-meaning if not commendable assumptions are only superficially applicable and, more importantly, bring undesirable outcomes.

Surely everyone wants a first-rate education but, that acknowledged, it does not follow that this is a person's highest priority, especially when requiring prodigious effort. Recall the parallel with being fit and trim on the cheap. If erudition came out of a bottle, everyone would buy it. Academics *über alles* probably applies to only a small sliver of the population (certainly less than 20 percent). By this logic it is equally legitimate to insist that everybody should be passionate about physical fitness or dressing stylishly. America rests on multiple cultural inclinations, but a passion for learning is *not* ubiquitous. In a nutshell, the black culture so often castigated by paternalistic whites for its indifference to academic attainment deserves a modicum of respect provided, as with all subcultures, it remains within the law. Cultural sanctity is a general principle, and violating it requires serious justification. Nor are African-Americans unique compared to other Americans in this disdain for grueling academics. New York City teachers decades back acknowledged that Irish and Italian children lacked the academic drive of their Jewish counterparts, and even among today's whites, anti-intellectualism is rampant.

When academically-unresponsive blacks are reprimanded for believing that academic accomplishment is "white," critics miss the point though, we admit, such crack-the-books, do your homework advice is sensible for those prizing future economic gain. Far more is being requested than meets the eye and exceeds exerting a few extra hours per week. Good grades and test scores are necessarily interwoven with multiple deeply-rooted Calvinistic inclinations—eschewing momentary pleasures, patience for drudgery, a knack for forced concentration, a tolerance for repeated failure, among others—and, let's be frank—these *are* "white" cultural attributes though non-whites, especially Asians, Indians ,and many blacks often master them (and millions of whites are clueless). Might the identical logic dictate that academically-indifferent black students tell white classmates that they should act more "black"?

New York City's effort to close Canarsie High School, a "failing" school largely catering to blacks perfectly illustrates this dilemma (Medina, Dec. 24, 2007). By all objective measures Canarsie is a troubled school—low graduation rates, low daily attendance, poor test scores and all the rest. Still, both parents and students have fought to save the school. Parents spent two and half hours hectoring representatives of the city's Education Department, accusing them of a double standard for white and black schools. Alumni have also mobilized to keep the school open, and many recall fond memories of their Canarsie experiences. Students have picketed with signs reading, "Let us keep our school" and "Leave the doors open bring in the freshmans [*sic*]." To be sure, closing will probably have no academic impact on student lives, but the outpouring of attachment is undeniable.

More generally, that many blacks demand that schools build self-esteem poses a formidable obstacle to academic attainment. Note well, there is absolutely nothing improper about demanding schools heighten feelings of self-worth but this inflated sense of competency hurts, not benefits, learning. Specifically, those who overestimate their ability in a task typically fail to monitor their performance correctly, acknowledge errors or assess correctly the means necessary to accomplish the task (see Kruger and Dunning, 1999 regarding the pernicious impact of overestimating competence). Equally important as our chapter on motivation argued, teachers shielding delicate egos also shield students from acquiring the tenacity necessary for future success. No psychological harm means no gain. Reducing mathematics to simple addition may do wonders for sense of worth but this "help" guarantees innumeracy.

In any case, we can argue forever regarding what culture is "best" individually or collectively, and the horrors of cultural relativism, but conclusions aside, judgments do not justify *imposing* a culture, especially a highly encompassing one, against the recipient's will. This is, to exaggerate only slightly, tantamount to a forced religious conversion. American education, after all, ultimately rests on parental consent and has always recognized the need for varied educational institutions. In the final analysis, a white student who refuses to dress in the Hip Hop style despite peer pressure is morally no different than a black student who refuses to devote untold painful hours to mastering algebra. We can plead with the latter, offer enticements, marshal supporting scientific evidence, and threaten punishment if sloth violates state statutes, but the coercive menu is constrained. To deny this argument opens the door to cultural imperialism of *every* variety, and who can predict which version will ultimately triumph? There is certainly no reason to expect that the bookish recipe that well-intentioned educators recommend will outshine rivals for each particular individual.

The tribulations of force-feeding an "academic culture" on those disdaining it was illustrated in a New York City charter school quarrel (Herszenhorn, 2007). The school, Beginning with Children, is partially though generously funded by Joseph and Carol Reich, and these patrons insist on traditional academic excellence as reflected by superior test scores. Since the numbers remained flat, the Reiches fired several school board members and demanded administrative changes. They further complained that terminated board members paid too much attention to the local constituency, not lagging test scores. As expected, several parents and teachers are outraged over these imposed hard-nosed standards, protesting that they are being excluded in hiring decisions and choice of reading program, plus being used by the Reiches to burnish their philanthropic image. No doubt, as wealthy whites increasingly fund charter schools as the route to educational proficiency these conflicts over core values will escalate.

Conclusions

To recap: (1) race-related gaps in educational attainment are substantial, ubiquitous, and enduring; (2) they have resisted countless expensive remediation efforts; (3) pushing harder to close them can dumb down learning and corrupt efforts to find genuine solutions; (4) shifting resources from decent students to troubled ones only undermines educational progress generally; (5) pouring more money into schools likely exacerbates gaps; and (6) no moral imperative exists to eliminate racial discrepancies and may be unwelcome by intended beneficiaries. All and all, *trying to close race-related gaps and promoting academic excellence are administratively incompatible and this serves no useful purpose other than to placate a few egalitarian ideologues.*

Absolutely nothing about these conclusions implies that America should abandon struggling black (or any other) students or reduce expenditures; helpfulness and gap closing are theoretically independent though in current practice they are inversely connected. Academic proficiency for blacks and Hispanics is certainly within reach but the path to this goal does not entail gap closing. Still, given the immense popularity of close-the-racial-gap quests, and for good measure, the awkward issues raised by conceding defeat, our effort for a ceasefire may seem as futile as actually producing authentic equal outcomes. This is an admittedly uphill battle but abandonment costs *are* tolerable. Consider the potential anger among those currently advancing this Quixotic crusade. The prospect of disgruntled professional educators rioting is remote. Hardly any putative expert will hurt economically though mission statements may shift (and these experts are skilled at sniffing trends). Helping the less able is politically sacrosanct but the precise form of assistance is hardly chiseled in stone. One has only to observe how programs like Head Start flourish despite its failed original egalitarian intellectual mission. Skinflint Republicans behave generously when legislation targets struggling black students regardless of private doubts. Subsidizing iffy programs is a long, honored American tradition—bridges to educational nowhere, so to speak—and we can certainly afford it. Costs far above and beyond fiscal wastefulness are what concern us: the duplicity and the counter-productive misallocations that come with this doomed-to-fail crusade. This harmfulness far exceeds fiscal waste.

Ironically, egalitarians might welcome abandoning this enterprise since surrender means being relieved of the pressure to achieve near-impossible outcomes. Though the actual NCLB Sword of Damocles threat was in practice slight, future measures, including lawsuits, to penalized schools lagging behind may be more severe. But, a ceasefire will now relieve administrators from the need to falsify data to "show" progress on nar-rowing racial differences, and a modicum of honesty is always welcome. Moreover, one might guess that if teachers and principals surrounded by inept students could choose between (a) trying to raise test scores and then gain financially if successful but terminated for failure or (b) continued employment with a dismal status quo, "b" would win hands down.

Redirection also helps many marginal teachers (many of whom are black) to keep their jobs. Mounting pressures to level outcomes will likely (but not inescapably) bring heightened demands for superior teachers necessarily calibrated by standardized test score results while simultane-ously firing failed test-takers. Given past performances, legally-required upgrading will inevitably disproportionately hurt black and Hispanic educators. In fact, the more strenuous the professional certification, the more blacks and Hispanics culled. The Thernstroms (2003, 204-5) con-vincingly demonstrate this most unwelcome news. If "quality teachers" is the elected route to gap narrowing, a scorched earth campaign to uplift the bottom would virtually guarantee a lily white and Asian teaching pro-fession. In New York City the proportion of newly-hired black teachers in the school system dropped from 27 percent in 2001/2 to 13 percent in 2007/8, a decline attributed to a 2003 New York state law required all new recruits to pass a certification exam (Green, Sept 25, 2008).

What about calming easy-to-anger ideologues fixated on this aim, those who fume about academic gaps as a scandalous blight on democracy and a civil rights embarrassment? Heated rhetoric aside, the bark here is far worse than the bite. At least some passionate egalitarians already acknowledge the quest's futility and suggest shifting gears. The promi-nent radical educational theorist Richard Rothstein and his associates, working out of Columbia University's Teacher College's "Campaign for Educational Equity" in their analysis of NCLB (in a paper aptly titled "Proficiency for All—An Oxymoron"), confess, "There is *no date* by which all (or even nearly all) students in any subgroup, even middle class white students, can achieve proficiency" (italics in original). Rothstein *et al* agree that closing the gap is a worthy aim, but accomplishment both within groups and between groups is "extraordinary difficult" even "inconceivable" (Rothstein, Jacobson, and Wilder, 2006). There is absolutely nothing inevitable about this close-the-race-gap crusade and like so many failed schemes, it may pass into history as yet one more well-intentioned but flawed nostrum.

One final item. The current obsession with narrowing racial gaps assumes that somebody other than African-Americans will perform the heavy lifting. Personal responsibly is totally immaterial, if not condemned. So, for learning to occur courts might order integration; legislatures allocate heftier budgets; mayors hold principals accountable; philanthropists sponsor innovative schools; and so on and so on. Somebody, *somebody* will rescue those unwilling to pay attention. The chair of the University of Georgia's "African-American Male Initiative" to attract more black males to college explained their absence by their failure to be "mainstreamed," that is, these innocents were pushed off college-track programs, reprimanded, disciplined, and ultimately suspended for negative behavior, which, in turn brought unemployment, even prison (cited in Arenson, 2003). Left unsaid is the role of these students themselves, the lack of dedication and focus let alone bad behavior. This expert-certified flight from personal responsibility can only call to mind the old adage about the road to hell being paved with good intentions.

"A Plan for Success," (nd) a manifesto issued by Campaign for High School Equity, a group funded by Melisa and Bill Gates forcefully reaffirms this "somebody else do it" mentality. It recounts the familiar poor academic performances of "communities of color" and offers a catalogue of solutions, *all* which required committing more government resources plus countless schemes (e.g., role models, accountability, recruiting better, more sensitive teachers, diversity, and raising expectations, among several dozen suggestions) that have *all* previously failed. But, what is relevant is that *nothing, absolutely nothing* is said about students themselves who, by implication, are totally blameless. According to the Report, an unequal educational system (underfunded, segregated) denies a decent education to students of color. In other words, unequal proficiency is no different from feeding students meals that differ in nutrients, so progress depends on forcing the system to provide banquets to everyone. It is perhaps no wonder, then, than millions of troubled students passively await the educational Messiah, just as the Gates Foundation promises.

5

The "War" on Academic Excellence

A story is told about a promoter who approached the great violinist Isaac Stern for a concert. When asked his fee, Stern replied, $15,000. But, said the impresario, Jascha Heifetz, the acknowledged world greatest violinist only receives $10,000 per concert, why do you demand more. Well, said, Stern, Heifetz is much more talented than I am, and for him playing is easier, so I need more money.

Give me a smart idiot over a stupid genius any day.
—Samuel Goldwyn

If educational achievement were America's paramount aim, investing in the intellectually talented is the indisputable superior, economically-efficient strategy. Unfortunately, we neglect the smartest while lavishing billions to uplift the bottom, and the inevitable failure here only inspires greater effort. What saves America from calamity is we import brains to compensate for home-grown deficiencies. But what if China, Russia, and India decide to embargo intellectual talent? Or their expanding economies soon soak up once exported brains? Picture panicked Microsoft executives when this day finally arrives: "you mean we now have to hire inept Americans? Where are my Indian software engineers?" Bill Gates will rue the day he gave $120 million to barely literate Washington, DC students so they could attend college.

The "War" on Gifted Education

Today's educators wage a truly senseless contemporary "war" on intellectually-gifted students. Given the tiny numbers of intellectually-superior students, and how little is required to educate them well, more is involved than just saving money. Hostility overwhelmingly rests on demographic imbalance: students in traditional gifted programs are disproportionately white and Asian, while blacks and Hispanics are rare. This discrepancy is, in fact, so embarrassing in today's egalitarian world that even the pictures in the National Society for the Gifted and Talented's membership-seeking pamphlet exaggerates the number of blacks and (apparently) Hispanic enrollees. Meanwhile, Del Siegle, the president of the National Association for Gifted Children, at the group's national convention called for modifying No Child Left Behind (NCLB) so as to provide more help for minority gifted though, as we shall see, the federal government's "gifted" programs already target this group at the expense of non-minority gifted (Cho, 2008).

Add a healthy dose of anti-intellectualism among many of today's leading educators and the recipe for aversion, not celebration, is complete. If the U.S. were uniformly white and Asian, or if gifted classes mirrored the population or academic distinction could be accomplished effort-lessly by anybody, the "war" would never exist. Attacks are relentless, emotionally charged, and entail an ingenious Orwellian, "war-is-peace" ideologically-motivated twisting of the educational vocabulary.

Finessing Genetics and Group Differences in Intellectual Ability

The education establishment's overwhelming liberal if not radical character makes it nearly impossible to confront honestly this demo-graphic imbalance. Even vague allusions are rare, but when this topic does surface, the devious deceitful wordplay can be remarkable. Consider, for example, an essay in a scholarly anthology about the gifted. The author, James J. Gallagher, an eminent education professor at the prestigious University of North Carolina, Chapel Hill, summarizes varied debates surrounding this field (Gallagher, 1997). He offhandedly notes that Jews and Asians are over-represented in traditional gifted programs. That readily available IQ data shows that these two groups far outshine blacks seemingly explains this difference—Jews and Asians are on average just smarter. And since the pattern holds across millions of people, persists across generations, and in wide-ranging economic circumstances world-wide, this superiority is likely to be at least partially genetic.

These facts, however, even if hedged by qualifiers, are today unspeak-able. Instead, the professor glibly asserts that this gap just demonstrates that others must be brought up to speed so as to equal Jewish and Asian accomplishment (13). That is, if everybody, including blacks and Hispan-ics idolized learning, read books, everyone would be smarter, and gifted classes would mirror America.

What does Gallagher say about the possible genetic basis of IQ across varied racial/ethnic groups, a critical element for making gifted programs more racially inclusive? After all, a sizeable, scientifically-respectable literature shows that IQ is substantially inheritable, and varies by demographic group, so perhaps Jews and Asians received their smarts mostly from parents, not the family library. As is routine in this egalitarian literature, the alternative of biological factors shaping group differences is "settled" by a naked, totally-unsupported declaration. Gallagher observes that the claim that intelligence is totally determined by heredity has been discredited, an odd assertion since no researcher has *ever* offered this lopsided view. Even those favoring nature over nurture admit that environment plays a substantial role, so this "refutation" accomplishes nothing other than to display ignorance. Now, with this cartoonish heredity argument banished, he simply says that we should consider environmental factors i.e., the advantages and disadvantages people enjoy (13). That's that—it's the environment 100 percent since genes are not 100 percent.

Gallagher accomplishes more than just personally expressing an unsupported, scientifically-dubious opinion. The *Handbook of Gifted Education* (1997, second edition) by virtue of its distinguished contributors and scholarship sets the authoritative tone in this enterprise. Now, for those glibly wanting to reject any genetic explanations of group differences, no matter how modest, life is simple: just cite Gallagher. That he is at a prestigious school, and is endlessly honored, and this wisdom appears in an authoritative *Handbook*, renders this "truth by acclamation" almost indisputable. Why argue?

Tellingly, one *Handbook* contributor is a distinguished, well-published *bona fide* geneticist—Robert Plomin (1997). He offers a brief, well-versed tour of genetics but perhaps realizing what is politically permissible, he judiciously avoids offending egalitarian sensibilities. He repeatedly (and accurately) states that while genes are important, they are not totally determining, and they certainly cannot establish the "ought" in social policy. Genes, save in rare circumstances, are about probabilities, and today's knowledge remains incomplete, so let us not jump to any premature conclusions. But, like the proverbial non-barking dog, *zero* is said about racial/ethnic differences being biologically rooted, and this omission must be conscious since this possibility is clearly central to gifted education debates. Indeed, it is perhaps *the* topic undergirding discussions over inclusiveness. Explicating it could take only a paragraph or two and might help settle this contentious issue. Plomin does admit that biology shapes IQ, and IQs run in families, but this message barely hints at the next step, group differences. This snippet is also easily lost in a presentation of research findings permitting even a pure environmentalist to find confirming tidbits. In short, an ideologically-awkward subject remains taboo and so *Handbook* readers may never grasp that their quest for racial equity may be hopeless.

Egalitarian Champions of Gifted Education

The battle against gifted education is a multi-front war and one of the major lines of attack involves "elitism." That is, dividing youngsters by cognitive talent creates (not merely recognizes) an elite and this is somehow harmful and undemocratic. One Syracuse education professor (Mara Sapon-Shevin) is blunt: "Given the current crisis in education, I don't see creating more schools [for the gifted] that will be elitist, de facto segregated, and won't contribute to the overall improvement of the school system. I don't doubt that schools are not serving gifted kids. But they're not serving anyone else either" (quoted in Vanderkam, 2003). By this flawed logic, America's university system ranging from Harvard to Bronx Community College should be transformed so everybody attends the same classes, all with mediocre professors, and receives identical degrees, if not the same grades.

This aversion to educational "elitism" often entails converting the ordinary to "superior," the equivalent of Martha Stewart selling "exclusive luxury" in K-Mart. It is just a matter of wordplay to fool those craving elite status sans the hard work. In 1995 the Educational Testing Service re-centered its SAT tests to boost test scores without added difficulty so, for example, what was a 425 became a 500. More telling, one could now get a "perfect" 800 with what was previously a 730. When combined with high school grade inflation, it is no wonder that elite schools have problems sorting out applicants—unlike their parents, today's applicants appear almost uniformly-terrific academically. Likewise, conceivably to overcome the "stigma" of catering to exceptionally-bright students and simultaneously avoid political tribulations, the number of high school courses classified as "Advanced Placement" (AP) has soared 150 percent in the last decade though evidence strongly suggests that many are "advanced" in name only (DeVise, 2007).

Education outsiders can barely imagine the educational establishment's deep-seated aversion to bright students. Media accounts routinely quote some gifted program chief executive about "how America must up our brain power to be internationally competitive" but this rhetoric is deceptive. The reality—at least what is said in public—*is just the opposite.* Dumbing down is celebrated. The Director of the Jack Kent Cook Foundation, which promotes gifted education, was hardly ashamed of a metaphor suggesting dishonesty when certifying intellectual excellence. In his words, "If what we are trying to do is measure not accomplishment but giftedness and talent, then putting your thumb on the scale or adding point for kids from low-income backgrounds re-equalizes things. The question is how heavy should the thumb be?" (Quoted in Meyer, 2008). In this Newspeak, cheating becomes "equality" as if schooling was golf and players all had handicaps to ensure competitiveness.

Consider, for example, how the Teachers' College Record (TCR), the citation rich research-oriented website of Columbia Teacher's College, treats top performers. An outsider would conclude that they don't exist, at least according to these experts at America's premier education school. Searching thousands of articles uncovers just two on teaching gifted students. One is a 1941 descriptive account of programs while the contemporary essay challenges the very idea that gifted children can be easily identified. Not unexpectedly, these two items (one of which is hostile) exist in a sea of heartfelt pleas, many verging on crackpot, to remediate those suffering untold disadvantages. One TCR treatise entitled "Merit and Difference" boldly insisted that "...the concept [intellectual merit] has no meaning in itself" and just reflect the way institutions assign individuals to hierarchically-ordered social classes. The author further suggests that it may be counterproductive to think of individual merit, so "merit" should be examined by asking how institutions bestow it (Baez, 2006). The education establishment's antagonism is often so convoluted as to be embarrassing—schools for the smartest, it is alleged, will produce students unable to survive a diverse world or that teachers should be trained to challenge all students, not just the brightest.

The National Education Association (NEA), the nation's largest teachers' union, is often in the forefront of this anti-intellectual campaign. Immediately after Congress enacted George W. Bush's NCLB with its stress on reading and mathematical proficiency, the NEA attacked even the effort to promote core academic skills, the gateway to proficiency. The NEA instead prefers "multiple measures," all of them "soft," notably portfolio assessment (often amalgams of drawings, writing, and varied projects) bereft of right or wrong answers (Holland, 2007). The NEA president, Reg Weaver, condemned NCLB's tests as nothing more than measuring an ability to regurgitate facts, as if facts were unimportant. That states that tried this murky approach abandoned it as unwieldy and plagued by idiosyncrasies (and vulnerability to cheating) makes no difference—learning dates and places is just bad and, one might hypothesize, an unwelcome burden on unionized teachers.

The demagogic populist rhetoric further implies that bestowing the gifted label *per se* hurtfully stigmatizes those excluded, as if students themselves fail to recognize that some classmates are "brains" while others are dummies. In 2008 the Montgomery County (MD) school system dropped the term "gifted" from its vocabulary though its actual instruction and testing remained unchanged. This labeling, in their expert opinion, was arbitrary and unfair since it stigmatized those excluded (deVise, December 16, 2008). A little digging into this label avoidance predictably showed that "the problem" was demographic imbalance—just too few gifted blacks and Hispanics. According to this twisted feel-good logic, excluding certain groups only exacerbates academic problems by lowering self-esteem, so a vicious cycle is created: rejection from a prestigious program diminishes academic performance as the humiliation sinks in, and yet more rejection as academic performance drops yet further. Better to disguise the hurt with euphemisms.

Other critics of traditional gifted programs challenge the very idea of "intelligence" as if the sorting was accomplished via meaningless standards. This hostility is ideological, not science. While barely conceding that "something" called "intelligence" may exist, that it can be correctly established using standardized tests is rejected although, in fact, accurate measurement has successfully existed for decades. Donna Ford, a prominent, often cited academic expert on gifted black students, takes a particularly ingenious approach to discrediting the standard, IQ-based approach to assessing giftedness via cognitive testing (Ford 1996, Ch. 2). She reviews multiple definitions of "intelligence" and since no two are worded exactly alike, she concludes that its meaning is sufficiently fuzzy, if not vacuous, so that almost any attribute can be twisted to signify "intelligence."

Fuzziness established, Ford then asserts that black children can be gifted though not according to existing flawed definitions. Then for good measure, she throws in "potential giftedness" to suggest that even those not currently identified as "gifted" may, indeed, be undiscovered treasures. In other words, "intelligent" and "gifted" may not exist, but some students may have these traits without showing them. Her *coup de grâce* for traditional gifted programs is her claim that many blacks are disproportionately endowed with certain under-recognized, under-appreciated abilities qualifying them as intellectually superior. These include a knack for expressing emotions, a language rich in imagery, a skill at improvisation, a superior sense of rhythm, a flair for humor, expressive body language among other "gifted" talents. Other positive but overlooked intelligence attributes include a keen sense of justice (and sniffing out injustices), altruism, and a proclivity for novel analyses plus a preference for focusing on people, not things (Ford, 1996, 14-5). As for traits traditionally defining "gifted," i.e., aptly solving complex problems, these are all there, she blithely asserts, and at requisite if not superior levels, according to Ford but "…may be hidden due to sub-standard educational experiences" (15). These are not the musings of an outsider—Ford is a board member of the National Association for Gifted Children and has served on varied journal editorial boards of academic journals focusing on gifted children where, no doubt, she has helped legitimize this anti-intellectual perspective.

Definitional tinkering hardly ends the quest. Enrolling African American students in programs for academic stars further requires cleansing schools of deeply rooted "atmospheric" deficiencies invisibly debilitating smart blacks (Ford, 1996, 3-4). According to Ford, and without a scintilla of proof, black students learn to be underachievers by being sensitive to social injustices, astutely witnessing the contradictions between academic learning and life experiences or growing wary of schools that celebrate merit. This is further compounded by ubiquitous racism, negative stereotypes among teachers and school administrators, and if these were inadequate to thwart academic mastery, black students come to see the racial, class, and gender discrimination in both their schools and the larger society. All of these ideologically-flavored pathologies "demotivate" gifted black students. Thus, if black students are to progress, the schools, if not American society, require a radical transformation.

Writing a few years later Ford pushed a distinctive "black intelligence" even further. She and her colleagues (Ford et al, 2004) speak of black students possessing a unique learning style that must be recognized (and appreciated) by both teachers and researchers to ensure educational progress. She compiles multiple commendable "black cultural styles," notably spirituality, oral tradition, harmony, communalism, and expressive individuality. Paradoxically, this race-sensitive cosmology justifies the very segregation that most blacks revile. Racially-distinctive psychology would certainly justify excluding many blacks from traditional programs largely attracting whites and Asians. The most helpful solution, it would seem, is apartheid—paralleling traditional classes for whites would be black-only gifted classes where pupils can progress quickly thanks to culturally-sensitive accommodations.

Particularly pervasive in this anti-merit crusade is the notion that the IQ test and similar instruments are culturally biased to reflect the dominant white culture, or merely echo socioeconomic status. Blacks and Hispanic are "culturally deprived" (e.g., have fewer books at home, watch fluff TV programs) or are raised in environments disdaining intellectual accomplishment, so the upshot are lower IQs and eventual exclusion from gifted programs. Deborah Meier, an education professor, boldly stated this misleading if not factually incorrect view during one of the annual debates in New York City over the lack of minorities in the city's gifted program. For her, "IQ tests by themselves are very poor means for labeling children and separating them from other children...... They're enormously reflective of class and race" (Meenan, 2008). Similarly, the University of Virginia education professor, Carolyn Callahan, who heads up the National Research Center on the Gifted and Talented, endorsed this approach when she explained the absence of black and Hispanics from gifted programs by their supposedly lack of adequate preschooling and decent nutrition (Mehta, 2007). She also added that "societal messages" lower the self-esteem of minorities, and this, too, keeps them out of gifted programs. That Washington has poured hundreds of billions into early intervention, e.g., Head Start and subsidized meals for poor children, with scant success, went unnoticed by this professor (nor did she notice that self-esteem among many blacks is unrealistically sky-high). From this insufficient resource perspective, unequal access to gifted programs is to be solved by the usual medley of "root cause" anti-poverty and early enrichment programs.

That IQ scores are race and income related is indisputable. What is unclear is the causal nexus, and those loathing IQ tests axiomatically assume that poverty, etc., cause low IQs when it is just as plausible, if not more so, that low IQs cause poverty. Thanks to America's meritocracy, smart children from impoverished families move up economically while those with lower IQs and poor parents lag behind. In fact, the relationship between environment and IQ increases with age as smart people choose their environments, so a smart kid with parents on welfare can shape his or her resources by visiting libraries or watching educational TV, let alone absorb more from schools lessons. To insist that poverty inhibits intelligence and eliminating poverty can increase it, it simply false, except in extraordinary circumstances (e.g., severe malnutrition) and this is well-documented. If anti-poverty programs could boost IQ, low IQs would have vanished decades ago thanks to America's prodigious social welfare spending and early intervention programs.

Messenger shooting has now defied all reason; that some blacks and Hispanics might benefit from testing is irrelevant unless the news is 100 percent good. An almost Kafkaesque example comes from Tampa, FL, where a worried principal banned a high school newspaper essay depicting the school's racial gap in academic achievement (Stein, 2006). That these data are required under NCLB, and are readily available elsewhere, and are undoubtedly plain to see among students themselves, was irrelevant. According to the principal, "If it is something that has the potential to hurt students' self-esteem, then I have an obligation to not let it happen." The students were further told not to talk about the article. In this world a failed test makes students dumb, not dumb students fail tests.

Egalitarian Newspeak rhetoric aside, testing all students for inklings of giftedness *helps* those from impoverished backgrounds who otherwise might be overlooked. This was the SAT's original justification: locate bright students from third-rate high schools since the requisite brain power exists but outward signs may be absent. The advantage is particularly true for culture-free tests—a bright ghetto youngster may be unfamiliar with "regatta," but might quickly solve a complicated spatial relations puzzle. Alas, the idea of extensive, objective testing seems anathema to many professional educators who condemn it as "elitist." They know that the messenger will bring a low average score and this trumps good news for a few economically-disadvantaged students who perform well. When New York City sought to expand gifted programs into poorer neighborhoods by screening all kindergarteners, a step that would surely uncover some undetected smart but poor kids, the Dean of Stanford's School of Education denounced this effort with "Testing young children for gifted classes most likely will increase inequalities" (Gootman and Gebeloff, 2008). From this egalitarian perspective, either everyone moves up or nobody moves up.

The anti-testing argument not only ignores mountains of contradictory research regarding the absence of cultural bias (see Jensen, 1980) but the inconvenient fact that non-verbal, culture-free IQ tests display identical unwelcome patterns. A similarly-awkward fact is that even black and Hispanics children from affluent homes able to afford books, quality health care, and nutrition are underrepresented in IQ-based gifted programs. Nor are critics able to explain why "biased" tests accurately predicting academic success, similarly foretell future earnings, illegitimacy, criminality, accidents, and propensity to be on public welfare, among other non-academic outcomes. Rather than dispute standard IQ measures on scientific grounds, a technically-demanding task, equality across racial/ethnic groups is often just boldly asserted with religious-like conviction. IQ tests are sometimes depicted as "barriers" to giftedness as if they were stairs preventing a wheelchair-bound person from entering a hospital for vital medical care. One professor of educational psychology glibly reaffirmed the official orthodoxy regarding why few blacks are in gifted programs with, "There is no logical reason to expect that the number of minority students [assumedly black and Hispanic] would not be proportional to their representation in the general population" (Frasier, 1997, 498). One can only imagine what "logic" means here.

A less overarching challenge concedes that IQ tests do measure something real, but these data are only part of the story (often a tiny part) and should not be the exclusive admission criteria. The enemy here is often depicted as "the one size fits all" intelligence test. To affix a modicum of scientific gloss to this clamor, calls are made for "multimodal" screening procedures that are "multidimensional" (not "unidimensional") versus evil approaches that are "narrow" or "exclusionary." Meanwhile, substituting personal judgment for objective testing data is called "being more sensitive" to overlooked abilities since they rely on "nontraditional" or "sophisticated" techniques. A moral imperative is also frequently added with calls to desegregate gifted programs as if they are a lingering vestige of Jim Crow. Admittedly, this view is not without some merit given that IQ is not everything, i.e., creativity, diligence, among other traits, do shape achievement. Still, without a sufficiently-high IQ all the inventiveness and tenacity comes to naught, and substituting vague, impressionistic data, e.g., "lively," or "ambitious," opens the door to bias far exceeding the alleged flaws of IQ testing.

The hero in this "IQ is not everything" argument is Howard Gardner, a frequently-honored, endlessly-cited, Harvard education professor. His theories of intelligence are ubiquitous in the gifted literature and always celebrated as rock solid scientific truth though there is far more speculation here than hard evidence. Gardner posits eight "multiple intelligences"—linguistic, visuospatial, logical-mathematical, musical, interpersonal, intrapersonal, and bodily-kinesthetic (this list grows as Gardner discovers additional "intelligences"). The terms reflect his definition of intelligence, a "psychobiological" ability to solve problems or create products of value in a culture. In Gardner's cosmology "intelligence" reflects a *particular* culture, not universal adaptability, so among the Navajo, a talented basket weaver is considered "intelligent."

This formulation potentially certifies everybody as "gifted" and thus, in effect, destroys gifted education's historic meaning. These eight traits also may only be the first step, so the expansive possibilities are huge, particularly since everyone craves to be "gifted" one way or another. The slow-witted parent with an average child can now invoke an illustrious Harvard professor's prestige to get her middling offspring upgraded—Junior is off the charts when it comes to intrapersonal skills! The outcome is likely to be disastrous, however. A classroom of these freshly-reclassified grab-bag "gifted" children may now include those struggling to read but who display great talent for drums and tubas. Meanwhile, a shy young girl capable of college-level math will unlikely ever learn anything new as loud talkative boys obsessed with break dancing (bodily kinesthetic intelligence) dominate the class.

In principle, there is nothing inappropriate about accepting Gardner's alternative universe but these traits should not be called "intelligences" as in "gifted programs for highly intelligent students." Many lack any statistical relationship to cognitive ability and are hardly "a type" of mental facility. A more appropriate label would be "talent" and many large cities offer special high school programs for drama, music, and art. Schools routinely hold auditions for bands and plays, and nobody complains that these are elitist, undemocratic, or unfair. The school marching band is, in effect, a class for the musically talented. Perhaps the most ruthless talent screening occurs in sports, and to insist that "everybody should be on the football team since every one is equally talented, albeit with different skills and all proficiencies contribute" might be construed as a sign of a dangerous mental illness.

Where frontal assaults on the primacy of intellectual ability fails, destruction might be accomplished via administrative tinkering. One such destructive approach abandons IQ testing in favor of evaluations by parents, teachers, and students themselves as well as traits such as "emotional strength" and then "race norm" the outcomes. That is, classifying all students by race, sex, and parental income, and then choosing the top scorers within each of these wide-ranging categories to create a "representative" classroom (Richert, 2003). Needless to say, multiple, foggy admission criteria coupled with racial/ethnic quotas undercuts the very purpose of time-honored gifted programs. Nobody will be excluded, no matter how slow. Facing the prospect of multiple tests with ambiguous criteria, pressured school administrators will undoubtedly declare all students "gifted" so, thankfully, entire schools may escape the stigma of failure and bask in the gifted label though zero has changed from "pre-gifted" days. This is the equivalent of making everybody a millionaire by inflating the currency.

This "race norming" call recently surfaced in New York City when a uniform "test only" admission standard was first implemented for gifted programs (Gootman and Gebeloff, 2008). Though the cut-off point had been lowered from the top 5 percent to the top 10 percent to increase black and Hispanic enrollment, the newly imposed system-wide uniformity and objectivity brought an unwelcome outcome: the number of white children from affluent neighborhoods soared, from 25 percent to 39 percent of all those admitted, and these students comprised a mere 14 percent of the city's school population. Ironically, imposing city-wide standardization and objectivity was originally justified as a step toward helping blacks and Hispanics by removing alleged capriciousness.

Test performances in the city's poorest areas were so low that many local classroom seats set aside for the intellectually superior remained empty. Joseph S. Renzulli, head of the University of Connecticut's National Research Center on the Gifted and Talented who advises the city in this area, naturally faulted this racial/ethnic imbalance. He suggested instead that "gifted" be neighborhood defined, so smart kids from slums, regardless of test scores, would be admitted. In all fairness, this "neighborhood-centered" admission process closely resembles college admission practices in Texas and California where a fixed percentage of each high school graduating class (which is neighborhood-centered) is automatically admitted to certain colleges to guarantee diversity. Still, that this call for dumbing down comes from the head of a program for the gifted, located at a research-oriented university, should be noted.

The race norming, inclusionary mentality is hardly limited to educators. The private sector can fall prey to it though the costs of being "an intellectual elitist" or "anti-democratic" would appear minimal. Surely corporate CEOs do not have to face voters complaining about the "too white" classes for high achievers or worry about parents angry over Junior not making the cut. They can just award grants to gifted programs, no strings attached. Alas, the egalitarian pressure is almost irresistible. For example, the financial giant Goldman Sachs has endowed 403 scholarships for those from disadvantaged minority backgrounds to study at the Center of Talented Youth, an organization founded by Julian Stanley, a renowned no-nonsense advocate for exceptionally-bright children (Stanley died recently and one wonders if this would have occurred under his leadership).

As expected, to avoid outcomes attracting unwanted political scrutiny and protests, less fortunate children were excused from traditional testing *(http://cty.jhu.edu/about/history.html)* and instead were quizzed about their aspiration, whether they believed top grades were important, whether they enjoyed learning, beliefs about how they would perform academically, and similar "soft" measures. The rationale was that such measures were also used for those admitted by stellar test scores (*http: jhu.edu/research/wwkunder_rep.html*). No doubt, this well-intentioned inclusiveness held back the truly gifted whose classes had to be slowed to accommodate those whose intelligence may be illusionary. These putative beneficiaries are probably also academically overwhelmed, so everybody loses, smart and not so smart alike.

Imagine if Goldman Sachs invested exclusively according to such fuzzy criteria, for example, asking CEOs of potential investment targets if they wanted to be successful or whether profit was personally important? The deceitfulness here verges on the comical. An academic-style paper justifying Goldman's help for supposedly gifted minorities (called "scholars") stated, "In our fast-paced, technological-based society it is becoming increasingly necessary for all our students to excel. It is not enough to simply be an average kid; one must be well above average...." (Lohrfink, 2006). The analysis also insisted that some merely repeating lessons would increase scores on standardized tests, a blatantly false claim (if true, NCLB would have been a rousing success). Obviously, Goldman Sachs' legal department was excused from customary due diligence, suggesting that Goldman knew that this was charity, not investing in America's future.

That those admitted may lack required academic ambition seemed irrelevant. It was just happily assumed that upping intellectual rigor is thus akin to offering extra nutrients to the famished. In fact, "helping the gifted" has often become a new-found ruse to pour additional funds into chronically-struggling students. This sales pitch was undoubtedly the aim when Nashville, TN, a troubled system according to NCLB, appointed a new head of the metropolitan gifted program, an experienced local educator named Beth O'Shea (Mielczarek, 2008). When assuming her position she announced that what was good for gifted children is good for all children, so all children should have access to superior resources. And this will include advanced level courses such as pre-algebra and foreign languages. That many Nashville pupils, according to NCLB, cannot currently master the basics, one can only wonder how pre-algebra will boost math proficiency among those perplexed by arithmetic.

Champions of racial/ethnic inclusiveness also assume that once the doors are pushed open, and excellence is within reach, the once excluded will shine. But, as our tour of motivation demonstrated, you can take a horse to water.... Excelling may require brains but it *also* requires diligence, self-discipline and an appreciation of intellectual accomplishment. It may conveniently be assumed that children from economically-disadvantaged backgrounds are chomping at the bit to master trigonometry while classmates down the hall struggle with fractions, this thirsting may be absent, and a lack of appetite dooms efforts to remove barriers. The news here is not good. Almost everything we know about lower-class life, its emphasis on short-term consumption, prizing sociability over intellectual pursuits, suggests that lighting fires demands far more than exposure.

A Pittsburgh, PA-area newspaper account highlights this horse to water quandary. Project SEED is a four-year-old venture sponsored by the American Chemical Society and generously funded by corporate donations teaching advanced chemistry to high school students. It targets low-income families and even pays students $3,200 for attending the summer session (Puko, 2008). Unfortunately for SEED administrators, relatively few applications arrive for a program that by its very nature must be highly selective. The Center for Talented Youth at Johns Hopkins University has similar difficulties attracting kids from low-income families, an obstacle attributed to low social support for attending highly-charged academic settings. All and all, it is a long road between funding these expensive ventures (and corporations happily give) and transforming low-income students into future scientists.

Self-Esteem, Not Knowledge

Beneath this dilution of "gifted" is a craving for psychological gratification, image improvement, so to speak, without the commensurate intellectual attainment. Unfortunately, fans of self-esteem *über alles* fail to demonstrate how this refocus improves learning unless one redefines "learning" to include "believing that one is smart." Perhaps twisting language or redefining standards is easier than mastering difficult subjects. In a society where genuine academic skill really does count, this is pure delusion. The opportunity costs for this feel-good exercise are substantial, especially if students are enticed to escape hard work since they are already "highly talented."

A potential danger lurks here extending far beyond watering down gifted programs to achieve demographic proportionality. Manipulating standards can also irresponsibly transform troublesome, if not personally dangerous, traits into seemingly-positive ones. A near paranoia about imagined racially-tinged insults, hardly a workplace asset, can readily become the praised "sensitivity to racial justice." Perfecting one's bodily-kinesthetic gifts may the polite way for students to waste time at sports while they should be mastering algebra. Redefining and expanding "gifted" also subverts genuine learning by rationalizing anti-intellectualism, sloth, insubordination, and rejecting "Calvinist" traits vital to academic success. Especially for below average students, this invites disaster. It is all too easy to imagine Mr. Lazybones proclaiming, "The schools are racists, my teachers have too low expectations, we lack adequate funding, merit is culturally defined or Howard Gardner better recognizes my big mouth as 'highly developed verbal skill.'" All of this, obviously, just confirms the old adage that the road to hell may be paved with good intentions.

Guerilla Warfare against the Gifted

The ideological assault on gifted programs is hardly idle academic chatter. Academic pronouncements inevitably filter into countless communities without raising much alarm. Though the long-term impact of these battles may be huge, they hardly qualify as a "crisis" in today's educational environment. The Davidson Institute for Talent Development (*www.davidsoninstitute.org*) promotes gifted education and its Web site carries pertinent local newspaper stories, which have an almost generic quality. Typically parents of precocious children wanting extra effort from the local school are pitted against school administrators, varied egalitarians, other parents, civil rights activists, and academics who insist that targeting extra bright students undermines public education. The battle is seldom about educational excellence; it's about ideology.

The costs of protecting gifted programs can be deceptively burdensome. Schools can face costly litigation if classes lack the requisite number of blacks and Hispanics, and few schools can afford a protracted battle. That the ACLU has now enlisted in this anti-intellectual crusade adds to potential litigation, particularly since it has hundreds of chapters nationwide. For example, it recently threatened legal action against California's Tustin Unified School District since those enrolled in its gifted program failed to mirror the racial/ethnic/economic composition of the general student body (a typical California and national pattern). Defending IQ-based testing against an ACLU-led suit might entail paying experts to travel and testify, and even if the suit might be won, cost-conscious school administrators might prudently act to preempt suits by "diversifying" gifted programs which, in effect, will seriously undermine them.

The campaign's anti-intellectual spite has been especially visible in New York City school politics though the big Apple is hardly unique. Consider just one of several targets in the anti-merit crusade—the city's elite science/math-based high schools where admission is only by grueling objective test (only a little more than 10 percent of test-takers gain admission). Graduates of these schools have often had distinguished careers, including several Nobel Prizes and similar awards. Unsurprisingly, the enrollment is overwhelmingly white and those of Asian descent (many of whom are recent immigrants) with blacks and Hispanics far below their proportion of the city's overall school population. According to a chorus ranging from radical race-baiting rabble-rousers to top education officials, enrollees are little more than beneficiaries of unearned white privilege advancing up the economic ladder thanks to culturally-biased tests.

David Dinkins, before being elected New York's mayor, suggested that elitist education hindered those at the bottom, so if these talented selfish grinds eased up a bit, everyone would benefit (MacDonald, 1999). Such thinking, and Dinkins is hardly unique, almost conceives of academic excellence as a zero sum competition, so students at elite institutions mysteriously "steal" perfect SAT scores from blacks or Hispanics "confined" to dreadful, resource-starved schools. That some of these top schools flourished in dilapidated settings, often with run-of-the mill teachers goes unnoticed. Likewise, according to this perspective, a student "gets" a world-class education not by hard work and brains but just by attending a world-class school, just as one gets a gourmet meal by going to a three-star restaurant. Even to suggest that stellar mathematical accomplishment is earned might "offend" sixth graders struggling with decimals. Why should nerds hog all the best teachers, science labs, and computers to as to "get" smarts?

What protects NYC's Bronx Science, Stuyvesant, and Brooklyn Tech is a 1971 state law requiring objective tests to be the sole admission standard. Even so, the pressure to "diversify" (i.e., add more blacks and Hispanics) admission standards are intense, and legally barred from adding impressionistic criteria (e.g., "committed to helping the community"), educators have sought numerous remedial and coaching solutions. A Specialized High School Institute (SHS) exists for this purpose and offers prospective elite high school applicants test-taking skills and extra lessons. In 2006 SHS enrolled nearly 3,800 students in 17 locations, and supplied 16 months of admissions test preparation. Selected "underrepresented" students can begin in sixth grade trying to qualify for these demanding tests. Ironically, although SHS was intended to be "minority only," increasing numbers of ambitious whites and Asians have enrolled (strict race-based admission was declared illegal) while the proportion of blacks and Hispanics declined (Grootman, 2006). The city also offered several smaller specialized high schools targeting minorities that attempted to replicate outstanding school math and science outcomes while avoiding cut-throat academic standards (they failed). The elite schools themselves recognize this lopsided demographic issue, and administrators periodically voice the need for more racial/ethnic inclusion but are legally powerless to relax standards. Meanwhile, non-legally protected but academically-superior New York City high schools have also felt bureaucratic pressures to admit marginal students so as not to appear excessively elitist.

The fragility of intellectually-elite schools is made clear by the tribulations faced by similar schools lacking New York's legal protection. Boston's renowned Boston Latin School fell to the egalitarian crusade when a federal judge in 1975 imposed racial quotas on admission (Mac-Donald, 1999). Likewise, San Francisco's academically-excellent Lowell High School had "too many smart Asians" and similarly succumbed to court orders to add less able minorities, and this battle has lingered for decades. In this upside-down Newspeak world, a school graduating budding geniuses can invite trouble since its accomplishment may energize egalitarians to destroy it to achieve "fairness." "Success" in terms of garnering resources may now require enrolling the most troubled students, not future Nobel Prize winners. New York City has changed fundamentally from the 1940s when the *New York Times,* today's strident champion of race/ethnic educational equity, defended an academically-elite school threatened with closure for its "rigid entrance requirements," its "homogeneous body of able students" where the gifted were not held back by dullards (MacDonald, 1999).

Matters at the city's grade schools are hardly any better. One New York City school district superintendent even banned spelling bees, competitive science fairs, honors programs, and classroom ability groupings so as not to rattle anybody's self-esteem (and she moved up the administrative career ladder after promoting these policies). One suspects, naturally, that protecting self-esteem would be less pressing if blacks and Hispanic students carried off most academic trophies. The recently-retired Deputy Chancellor for Teaching and Learning reaffirmed the official anti-merit orthodoxy when she opined that all children are gifted in one way or another, and it is unfair to single out a particular group for special treatment. Under pressure from parents to have a least some measures of academic achievement, one Bronx educator re-instituted science fairs (after previously abolishing them) but banned prizes to protect participants' egos (Wolf, 2006).

Ridding gifted classes of smart kids who tend to be white and Asian can verge on deceit. In one instance an announcement for a Bronx gifted program openings appeared in newspapers catering to Latinos and blacks, but not those favored by middle-class whites. Still, white and Asian youngsters flocked to these classes but to promote "equity," class size was sharply expanded so as to include more blacks and Hispanics. To obscure the absence of specialized classes for the gifted, the phrase "whole school enrichment" was concocted to suggest that now everyone would receive this extra special academic attention (Wolf, November 16-18, 2007).

New York City's experiences are typical. In Lodi, California where, as usual, school administrators are trying to enroll more minority children in gifted classes that are too white and too male (Reid, 2006). The gifted program's director "solved" the problem by first expanding the admission criteria from the top 2 percent of the intellectually capable to something else but is silent on what, exactly, this "something else" is. The pool of "gifted" happily expanded to include more minorities and girls but since the spaces for these children remained constant, some of the more capable had to be denied places in the program. This, in turn, was "solved" by lottery so that "everyone has an equal chance" of being "gifted."

Portland, OR, which has long operated under a court order to diversify its program, has pursued a different strategy. Here the selection process at low-achieving, largely-minority schools is heavily weighted toward non-academic abilities like art, music, and even humor plus recommendations from parents and teachers (Parker, 2006). Compared to standard IQ testing, the selection process is labor intensive since the work of each individual student must be assessed for his or her special talent. Interestingly, the reliance on parental judgment is justified on the grounds that many poor parents have themselves attended enrichment programs and thus may be able to identify especially-talented children. This expensive outreach also sends teachers and administrators to conferences on how to identify gifted minority students.

Denver, CO is undergoing a comparable twisting of "gifted" so as to achieve cosmetic equality. The facts are predictable: about two thirds of the Denver school population is black and Hispanic and until recently they comprised only a quarter of the test-defined gifted program (Meyer, 2008). But, under a recently enacted change, the numbers of blacks and Hispanics are substantially on the upswing and the usual "adjustments" explain this expansion. Now poverty and lack of English skill are explicitly part of the evaluation progress along with teacher evaluations.

Art and writing will soon be added to the assessment process. In fact, under the new standard, a child who only makes it into the top quarter of cognitive test outcomes can be "gifted" versus the usual cut off point of the top 5 percent. One Denver school principal justified this expansion by claiming that underserved students are bright but were intellectually handicapped, for example, they did not know what "plaid" is or might never have ridden on an escalator. No corroborating evidence is presented and a skeptic might argue that nearly every American youngster, the poor included, has visited a mall displaying lots of plaid and seen escalators. These Denver educators also claim that broadening the "gifted" program will not exclude those who would have entered using more conventional criteria, a mathematical impossibility since the program's size has not kept pace.

Cutting Funds

The most effective tactic to destroy gifted programs is simply to defund them. Here, too, media accounts have a generic quality and in many respects resembles a silent epidemic, perhaps akin to Dutch Elm disease, slowly spreading from one town to the next with scarcely anybody noticing. Bit by bit, like dying elms, gifted programs wilt and then disappear altogether. To continue the epidemic parallel, the first signs of desolation were noticed around 2004 and it was not until a few years later that it drew some national attention.

A 2004 *New York Times* article might have been the first to call national attention to this "defoliation" (Schemo, 2004). It recounted tales of woe for gifted programs sweeping the nation. For example, in 2002 Michigan aid for the gifted fell from $4 million a year to $250,000. In Illinois funding collapsed from $19 million per year to zero while New York also dropped from $14 million to zero. Oregon's commitment likewise dropped to zero after years of funding. In Connecticut one in four school districts abandoned gifted programs altogether. In Missouri the state subsidy for gifted went from 75 percent to 58 percent of local outlays. Two years later the carnage continued to mount. An *Associated Press* account told how a total of eight states offered nothing (Palvesky, 2006). Another six states spend less than $500,000, not even a pittance in today's educational world. Clearly, something is happening over and above the usual educational establishment's aversion to intellectual precociousness.

In 2008 two studies released by the Thomas B. Fordham Institute pointed the finger more forcefully: President Bush's No Child Left Behind law. The gist of these findings is that NCLB's relentless pressure to uplift the bottom and close racial gaps in achievement has emaciated gifted programs. Chalk up another confirmation of the Law of Unintended Consequences—when NCLB was enacted, supporters hailed it as rescuing American education and while it *may* have helped push dismal students towards marginal mediocrity, much of this uncertain progress has been "paid" with neglecting future academic stars. Since this distressing pattern was easily predictable, one can only wonder what the Bush administration had in mind when it decided to target the bottom.

Still, in all fairness to NCLB, there is no smoking gun proof of this nefarious impact. Conceivably, nothing, including all the NCLB money, would have helped high IQ students do any better. Cautions acknowledged, consider the following data. Most plainly, while the math and reading scores of the bottom 10 percent have shown some modest (and uneven) improvement since NCLB, scores of the top 10 percent have remained virtually flat. All the extra billions, administrative edicts, volumes of paperwork, pressures for accountability, and countless other burdens have had zero impact on the brainiest students in exchange for small gains at the bottom. It also remains to be seen if these modest improvements survive amidst America's anti-intellectual culture or whether they improve workforce quality.

Meanwhile, surveys of teachers in grades 3 to 12 operating under NCLB report that teachers felt pressured to concentrate on the needs of the least able, in particular, about 60 percent said that low achievers are a "top priority" versus 23 percent giving comparable attention to high achievers. Some 40 percent of the teachers agreed that the honors and accelerated classes have been watered down or lacked rigor. Eighty-one percent admitted that struggling students are likely to receive one-on-one attention versus 5 percent of the academically talented (even average students were almost totally neglected so as to help those at the bottom). Perhaps the best news from this survey of teacher attitudes is that the vast majority *reject* the idea that improving the bottom should take precedence over helping all students. Obsessing over the very worst at the expense of all else has not yet become pervasive pedagogical dogma.

Will the Fordham report reverse this "defoliation"? Probably not. The education landscape is littered with dozens of similar the-sky-is-falling, we-must-improve, reports, all written by distinguished experts, all largely forgotten save for a cursory citation. Americans have probably become inured to this gloom and doom since, as Chapter 1 made clear, the public embraces an "all gain, no pain" mentality. The report will draw heartfelt political support from only a *tiny,* helter-skelter constituency, and this will be *crushed* by the millions feeding off helping the least able students. No matter how much money is squandered on the bottom, acknowledging this wastefulness and suggesting that smart kids deserve a few crumbs from the table is unthinkable in today's egalitarian political climate. That public school classes for the gifted are vanishing may hardly attract much media attention either, especially since parents of these children enjoy options: just quietly turn to home-schooling or just move to those few communities offering classes for the truly gifted.

Federal Government Help for the Gifted

The federal government (and many localities) seemingly spare no expense to uplift academic strugglers and even when the term "gifted" is applied, it is just another way of helping the less academically able. Deception was not always the case. Following America's humiliation in 1957 when the "backward" Soviets launched Sputnik, helping the smartest of the smart was genuine. Pushed by such military notables including Admiral Hyman Rickover and a worried Congress and with nuclear annihilation ever present, Washington quickly assembled world-renowned scientists to fix American education. Meanwhile, panicky newspapers and magazines condemned America's inability to match Russians brainpower (Clowes, 1981, Ch. 1). A Gallup Poll reported that 70 percent of Americans believed that their high school students must work harder. The contemporary news media also relentlessly condemned the equality fetish and making school fun while polls echoed the public's new-found infatuation with tough standards (Clowes, 1981, Ch. 9).

With the alarm sounded, the National Defense Education Act (NDEA) of 1958 allocated money to states for testing programs to identify the intellectually talented, and counseling to encourage these students to attend college, especially in the fields of science and mathematics. Given shortness of time and lingering reservations about a suddenly expanded federal role in education, the outcomes were impressive. Student loan programs were established in some 1,200 colleges; 1,000 fellowships were awarded at 23 universities and 12 foreign language institutes were created. Some $33 million was spent on new equipment. But, perhaps more than anything else, solid math and science education were suddenly appreciated as nationally vital, not a pastime for a few oddball geeks. Perchance, anxiety over low self-esteem of those excluded from gifted programs or race-related gaps was an unaffordable luxury when faced with a nuclear-armed enemy possessing operational intercontinental rockets.

These scientists (not education professors!) energetically sought to toughen up secondary education. Not every proposal succeeded, but the focus on the very best was indisputable. Nobody saw educational upgrading as a stepping stone to higher political office and one can only imagine campaigning on a platform of saving America from communism by pouring money into students who could barely read. A famous book deriving from this project—*The Process of Education*—repeatedly called for enlisting the "best minds," "eminent men" or "best people" so as to restore the glories of American science (Gallagher, 2000). Today, of course, this type of mobilization is unimaginable, almost politically embarrassing, and it would surely be resisted by putative experts as "too elite."

Once the post-Sputnik panic was replaced by the Great Society and burgeoning racial turmoil, Washington's compassion for academic stars wilted. The NEDA, the great federal instrument to protect America from Russian missiles soon expanded to cover business administration and nursing. Federal money poured into education, but the gifted barely received crumbs. In 1972 a report submitted by the federal Commissioner of Education, Sidney Marland, called for Congress to support programs for the intellectually talented but the report accomplished little (Wickstrom, 2004). (Interestingly, the Marland Report explicitly noted the hostility of teachers and educators to smart students.) Legislation enacted in 1974 did create the Office of Talented and Gifted with the US Office of Education, provided various resources to assist educators and authorized federal appropriations not to exceed $12.5 million (the original figure was $80 million, still a pittance compared with funds for disadvantaged students). This final figure amounted to $1 per eligible student per year. In 1978 the Gifted and Talented Children's Education Act became law and helped states fund gifted programs. Alas, in 1981 under President Reagan the initiative was effectively ended when these funds were combined into more general federal educational assistance.

The next "help" installment was the 1988 Jacob J. Javits Gifted and Talented Students Education program (named after the liberal Republican Senator from New York). While the Act seemingly incorporated the Marland Report's earlier recommendations, it greatly, and explicitly, extended "gifted" to target children who were economically disadvantaged (at least half the funds), had trouble with English, or had disabilities. Again, the sums were paltry (it began with $10 million, a rounding error for helping the barely literate) and, critically, did nothing to actually help establish programs for the gifted. Descriptions of the funded programs make it clear that this was indistinguishable from commonplace anti-poverty programs (see Ford, 1996, Ch. 10). Nonetheless, even a few micro crumbs were too much and President Bush's FY 2006 budget *cut* all grants from this program (*http://www.ed.gov/print/programs/javits//index/html*).

Nevertheless, in 2008, the Javits Program was back on track but, to be blunt, its mission has, again, very little to do with helping those with exceptional IQs. A better description might be that they were anti-poverty programs providing jobs for middle-class educators. The term "all students" (not the smartest students) was frequently invoked in sponsored programs, as are remediations typically associated with helping laggards—mentoring, off campus service learning, summer programs, and peer tutoring—versus, say, upgrading science equipment for those bored with antiquated technology. North Carolina's The Project Bright IDEA 2: Interest Development Early Abilities initiative is typically Orwellian. Like programs expressly targeting the bottom, it speaks of closing the achievement gap and directs research on gifted programs for "underrepresented populations." The demonstration project spoke of changing the "dispositions" and capacities of teachers now trying to push these "excluded" students into gifted programs (in Edu-speak "dispositions" means pursuing egalitarian social justice, above all eliminating racial/ethnic/socioeconomic disparities). Interestingly, the program's aim is to encourage "gifted behavior" among disadvantaged students, not necessarily browbeat them into learning, say, how to write.

An examination of grants awarded in 2006 demonstrates a wondrous Newspeak *patois*. Page, AZ, for instance, received $340,000 for "Buried Treasure," a project that, among other goals, sought to uncover gifted children equally across the school districts' demography, i.e., gifted quotas. Meanwhile, Denver, CO got $123,000 for "Take Five," which involves coordinating efforts among multiple government agencies and university faculty to increase the number of gifted children from low-income and/or high-minority groups. Iowa educators received $319,000 to help the "twice exceptional child," that is the youngster who is both intellectually talented but learning disabled. Similar grants to help disadvantaged gifted students have been awarded to schools in Maryland, Massachusetts, Minnesota, New York, Texas, and Wyoming.

A scan of these brief announcements suggests that America has exhausted extracting brain power from the genuinely smart and, like distilling gasoline from coal, must now spend fortunes on expensive, low-yield projects. Elsewhere an observer might suspect LSD in the water supply. So, for example, when Washington awarded $2 million to

Western Kentucky University (WKU) to find 120 low-income/minority children for a "gifted program" stressing math and science, WKU's president intoned, "This is the kind of thing government does to help ensure higher quality of life for its citizens" (Baker, 2008). In fact, it was hoped was that these students would eventually enter WKU's honor program. That this $2 million will probably accomplish nothing and could have been better spent on more pressing needs or tax reduction seems beyond the president's intellectual capacity. Two million is, after all, two million (WKU is, however, getting a new building out of the deal).

An equally-pointless pledge to help the gifted education is Math Now: Advancing Math Education in Elementary School. The program offers all the usual verbiage about increasing U.S. global competitiveness, math's key role in today's technological world and, naturally, how we as a nation lag behind our overseas rivals. In 2006 as part of this American Competitiveness Initiative President Bush proposed $260 million for various math programs targeting students in early grades and middle schools. Middle School students would have their math deficiencies analyzed and intensive instruction would help them move ahead to more advanced topics. A National Mathematics Panel would be created to evaluate "best practices" in teaching math so, finally, Americans can reach the heights now occupied by Chinese, Japanese, and Koreans.

A more recent incarnation of this "gifted" science/math effort is the Science, Technology, Engineering and Math (STEM) program, and as of 2007 some 57 federally-funded STEMs were in operation nationally. A similar program targeting youngsters is SMART—Science and Mathematics Access to Retain Talent. SMART's purpose is to encourage youngsters to take challenging math instruction early on so they can excel at demanding college-level classes in math, technology, engineering, and even foreign languages. By the lavish standards of NCLB and similar uplift-the-bottom ventures, these clever acronym-named programs are cheap but, given American students' woeful math and science performance, it might be argued that every little drop helps.

Unfortunately, and quite predictable in today egalitarian climate, the initiatives generally target struggling "disadvantaged" students. The "soft" remedial strategies so favored by today's progressive educators—cooperative learning, peer tutoring, parental outreach, the need for more women and minorities in science etc. etc.—infuse these projects. The importance of discipline, let alone using IQ tests to identify potential one-in-a-thousand academic stars, is nowhere to be found. Both in theory and practice these initiatives are absolutely indistinguishable from the scores of (failed) anti-poverty programs. New is the hijacking of the word "gifted" plus some banalities about Americans needing every ounce of intellectual talent to fend off our economic competitors.

Almost nothing, even horrific budget cutbacks for genuine gifted programs, let alone a record of 100 percent failure with these pseudo-gifted programs, can slow this colossal wastefulness. In October 2008 The University of Virginia Curry School of Education announced that two of its faculty had received a $2.2 million dollar US Department of Education grant to promote STEM education for youngsters (Curry School of Education, 2008). Were the researchers targeting smart students? Of course not! The project intended to uncover STEM talents in previously underrepresented groups and then devised "learning units" and instructional strategies to turn these heretofore lagging students into tomorrow's scientists and engineers. A local school superintendent participating in this $2.2 million program called this venture the cornerstone of twenty-first-century education. Naturally nobody asked if even a tiny handful of these students could master calculus and similar tough-nut prerequisites for scientific careers.

The almost invisible shift in thinking about "gifted" that occurred between Sputnik and today's egalitarianism is indisputable. Helping a few Whiz Kids master quantum mechanics so as to protect us from Soviet rockets became inch by inch moving the entire school population, but especially those at the very bottom, up a few notches. A 1993 Department of Education report deceptively entitled *National Excellence: A Case for Developing America's Talent* spoke of how we as a nation were squandering intellectual talent, and this wastefulness was especially severe among the economically disadvantaged and minority students. This is pure early Bolshevik speech-making about turning the children of proletarians into brilliant scientists. One might guess that stupidity is infectious, so experts endlessly fussing over dullards succumb to muddled thinking.

Ironically, federal funding for Javits, National SMART Grants, and the other bogus "gifted" programs may *destroy* the few existing programs for bright children. The "free" federal money lure may further dilute remaining traditional gifted programs and thus holds back the truly smart. Imagine young Newtons suffering while the exasperated teacher explains why geometry requires mastery to those disdaining math? Ambitious educators who once considered upgrading skills to teach trigonometry to brainy fifth graders may retool to instruct struggling "but gifted" sixth graders with pie charts using real pies to be more culturally appropriate. Meanwhile, thanks to the all-too-familiar Newspeak linguistic corruption—"gifted" may well become a euphemism for "slow learner" just as "exceptional" replaced "retarded," which in turn, supplanted "feeble-minded."

Importing Brains

America has a nearly schizophrenic view of gifted education—we disdain helping them in favor of the least able but relish their contributions. This was perfectly illustrated by pronouncements by Melinda Gates whose foundations (with husband Bill Gates) has poured hundreds of millions into assisting the least able. In an April 2007 National Public Radio discussion Melinda was asked about a Gates Foundation's website statement claiming that *all* U.S. youngsters would earn a high school diploma and *all* these graduates would possess college-relevant skills and *all* then would attend college (emphasis added). When asked if this were possible, she emphatically said "yes." To further emphasize the point, she told the interviewer of recently visiting a largely black and Hispanic Chicago school, and concluded that with the right teachers and expectations, 95 percent to 98 percent would be enrolling in college. This might take time, she admitted, but it was feasible and the Gates Foundation would do everything possible to achieve that goal. Left unsaid, of course, was that the federal government had invested hundreds of billions (far more than the Gates Foundation had) over nearly a half century to advance that goal but to no avail.

Less than a year later husband Bill testified before Congress. Here the message differed a bit though in principle was not contradictory. He pleaded for more government money for science and math education so the U.S. could sustain its competitive technological innovation (Hart, 2008). But, promoting more programs for the intellectually talented was not on his agenda. Instead, he told Congress that many of the most able graduates in math, science, and engineers are temporary residents and cannot get the visas necessary to take jobs with U.S. firms. He advised raising the number of H-1B visas that permitted companies (like Microsoft) to hire needed scientists and technicians. (Currently some 65,000 H-1B visas are awarded and by lottery another 20,000 for those with advanced degrees. Applications are usually double the number available.) He added that neglecting this awaiting overseas talent meant the U.S. was missing a great opportunity.

Gates' beseeching was hardly unique. A steady stream of high-tech executives annually visit Congress pleading for additional foreign brain power. It has not been especially successful (Pear, 2007). Not even personal one-on-one talks from CEOs of Microsoft, National Semiconductor, Intel, and Seagate among others have opened the gates to huge reservoirs of foreign intellectual talent. Nor has intensive, well-funded lobbying worked its magic and the same can be said for floods of letters, telephone calls, and e-mail. Resistance often comes from those preferring American workers, not Indians or Chinese, or fear that foreign techies will undercut American-born rivals. Others are anxious that temporary residents will return home with new-found skills and become overseas competitors.

In principle this dilemma is easily resolved: expand homegrown talent. No need to lobby Congress for a few thousand extra H-1B visas or navigate a lottery or complicated paperwork. Bill should just call Melinda and convince her to stop trying to transform academically-challenged Chicago students into software engineers. Instead, Bill would explain, their foundation would establish a national Bronx High Schools for Science network (BHSN 1.0) where admission would be exclusively by math/science test scores. Then, after a decade or so, there would be no need for endless demeaning pleas to Congress for expand H-1B programs. This, sadly, might not be a happy time in the Gates household. A defensive Melinda would probably fire back, "What about *you* Mr. Smarty Pants, the one who gave $120 million for college scholarships to barely literate Washington DC students? *Who*, Mr. Birdbrain, similarly squandered $1.8 *billion* on 1000 smallish high schools, with 500 more planned, with only a infinitesimal number catering to science and math though more than a few have phony 'high-tech' names ?" As tempers boil over, both might enter therapy for dysfunctional families.

Those outside of major universities or technology-dependent firms may barely grasp America's reliance on overseas developed cognitive talent. Consider some simple facts about earned doctorates. In 2006, 35 percent of all PhDs went to foreign born researchers, but, *non-citizens earned 43 percent of the doctorates in science and engineering and 70 percent of the PhDs in electrical, civil and industrial/mechanical engineering. In other engineering fields plus math, computer science and physics the figure was "only" 50 percent* (Lederman, 2007). In 2007 the number of science and engineering doctorates continued to increase, but those awarded to non-U.S. citizens grew at a far faster rate (Lederman, November 24, 2008). And these depressing statistics are only the beginning. Between 1990 and 2000, for example, the proportion of doctorate-level foreign-born employees in the US rose from 24 percent to 38 percent while nearly half of the National Institute of Health's doctorate level staff were foreign nationals. Fifty-eight percent of the post-docs, future scientists were foreign nationals. Among university science and engineering faculty, 19 percent are born overseas; in engineering this figure was a little more than a third (*http://www7.nationalaademies. og/internationalstgudents/*).

The contribution by imported talent is nearly invisible, and perhaps explains our indifference to the failed domestic crop. The label "Made in America" has almost become irrelevant, especially for innovations. Reports commissioned by the Kaufman Foundation and conducted by distinguished academics have detailed this staggering reliance (*http://www.kaufman.org/items.cfm?itemID=906*). Between 1995 and 2005, one in four of all the technology companies founded in America were established by an immigrant. The firms had 450,000 workers and generated $52 billion in revenue in 2006. Foreign nationals residing in the U.S. were named as inventors or co-inventors in 25.6 percent of all international patent applications in 2006, an increase of 7.6 percent over 1998. Well over half of all the patent applications filed by huge multi-national corporations such as General Electric and Merck were filed by foreigners. In 2006, 16.8 percent of all patents from the U.S. originated by a person with a Chinese heritage name. No doubt, the huge contribution would be even larger if those patiently waiting to get into the U.S. had been already admitted.

This influx of foreign-born scientific talent is relatively recent though a good case can be made that Nazi Germany refugees were vital to the World War II effort. In 1966 when the U.S. labored to send a man to the moon only 14.3 percent of the earned PhDs went to non-US citizens with a temporary residence; by 2003 the figure was a third. Comparable increases exist in nearly all areas requiring superior cognitive skill, and there seems to be no end in sight for this addiction. Post 9/11 visa restrictions temporally slowed the craving but most recent statistics show that foreign graduate students in engineering and science are again flooding American graduate schools. For example, in 2006-7, the number of U.S. citizens entering graduate programs in engineering increased by 1 percent; the increase figure for foreign born students was 7 percent. The ratio in the physical sciences was nearly identical, 1 percent versus 6 percent (Jaschuk, September 16, 2008). To repeat for the umpteenth time: it is just far easier to hire off-the-shelf superbly-trained Indians dying to come to America than prod domestic high schoolers to master calculus.

Still, these statistics undoubtedly underestimate America's dependence on foreign brain power. People familiar with elite research universities daily see that the best, most ambitious students in demanding technical fields are children of immigrants or themselves arrived in the U.S. as youngsters. Just walk around MIT, Cal Tech, or Stanford and listen to the languages spoken. At the super-selective University of California, Berkeley, a study found that nearly 12 percent of the enrolled were foreign born while 14.5 percent had at least one parent born overseas (Lederman, November 28, 2008). Particularly revealing is that while African-Americans are severely underrepresented at Berkeley, a third of this small group are either themselves born overseas or have a foreign-born parent. At New York City's elite public universities the influx of Asian and Russian students has similarly transformed an institution that nearly collapsed into, again, a stellar institution of higher learning (this resembled an earlier era when knowledge-hungry immigrant children created the "poor man's Harvard"). Recall the outstanding performances by children of the Vietnamese "boat people" in revitalizing "failing schools." The combination of innate cognitive ability and driving ambition can work educational miracles.

Unfortunately, cheaply importing brains may be ending as China and other cognitive talent exporters increasingly ship pajamas or vodka instead of super-smart graduate students. This type of talent, unlike trees, is not a self-regenerating resource. The National Academies Report cited above noted that from the mid-1990s to the middle of the first decade of the twenty-first-century, science and engineering (S&E) doctorates in Asia have *doubled* and the number of students in technical fields in China, South Korea, and Japan far outnumber those in the U.S. (these figure undoubtedly understate Asian preeminence since many "U.S. students" are actually from Asian nations).

Even Europe, which for decades lagged behind the U.S. in technology, is now out-producing the U.S. in science and engineering (S&E) doctorates. Several European nations have launched aggressive programs to attract technologically-talented immigrants so Indians or Koreans may now find Germany more hospitable. In Great Britain the number of foreign-born graduate students during 2005 increased by 36 percent; in France it was 30 percent. New Zealand now has a fast-track program quickly linking talented foreigners to awaiting jobs (Dalmia, 2008). One of America's advantages in this intellectual talent marketplace, English (since smart Asians are rushing to learn it) may be less important as English becomes the *lingua franca* in European technology and science.

Conclusions: Can the Infatuation with the Less Able Be Reversed?

The foolishness of the "war" against America's most talented is almost beyond belief, a relentless pursuit of an egalitarian fantasy at the expense of genuine educational accomplishment. It guarantees disaster though, like carbon monoxide poisoning, death may be slow and almost unnoticed. Can this imprudence be reversed? The simplest, and certainly most effective (and cheapest), would be to extend nationally New York state's 1971 law mandating objective tests as the exclusive requirement for admission to the City's elite math and science high schools. Laws will not transform dolts into geniuses or even wake up a daydreaming future Kepler, but at least they will ensure that budding scientists and engineers do not languish in the name of "equality." Unfortunately, the type of law guarantees a bitter political struggle since those benefiting from such protection will be far out-numbered by egalitarian educational professionals plus hordes of identity politics activists. Championing "elite" education is just incredibly unpopular in today's upside-down environment. Still, New York was a liberal state filled with anti-merit educators and activists when that law was enacted. The opponents have undoubtedly mounted every legal challenge to it, and its survival after nearly four decades offers yet more hope.

Perhaps another Sputnik-like wake-up call might do the trick. But, and we should be thankful, with the Cold War over, nothing so energizing looms on the horizon. What if Silicon Valley drastically constricted as locally-available talent evaporated? Would American consumers even notice? Probably not. What if sick Americans had to visit China since there were too few expertly-trained domestic MDs? But, unlike the threat of nuclear annihilation, this is a mere nuisance. In a pinch skilled Chinese doctors could cheaply treat visiting Americans on cruise ships just as Hong Kong tailors overnight supply custom-made suits.

If one had to predict the future consequences of the almost out-of-control voracious spending appetites and the penchant for effortless solutions, the best bet might be expensive cosmetic solutions. Gifted-lite, so to speak. This is especially true as urban school systems fill up with black and Hispanic children, the vast majority of whom cannot qualify for traditional IQ-based programs. A dystopian future of "gifted wars" is easy to visualize. Howard Gardner will be canonized, so we might see the Michael Jordan Academy for the Bodily-Kinesthetic Gifted or the Oprah Winfrey School for the Interpersonally Talented among countless others. Paradoxically, this transformation may be embraced by traditional gifted advocates since these "alternative" classes will remove the legal and political pressure to destroy conventional programs. Everybody now happily gets a piece of the gifted action. It will, to be frank, foster racially-segregated education under the guise of being sensitive to the unique talents of all children in a multi-cultural society. And, provided the resource allocation formulas are equal, and everybody gets an awards banquet, the political fallout of these empty calorie gifted programs will be minimal. Parents whose intellectually-mediocre mouthy offspring once struggled to master the basics can proudly boast that junior is now enrolled in a gifted program for those with unique verbal talents. Everybody will be contented, at least until after graduation.

6

The Museum of Failed Educational Reforms

A story is told of the great Yiddish stage actor Boris Thomashefsky who died in the middle of a performance. The theatre was in pandemonium, people were yelling and screaming and in the midst of all this, a voice came from the back of the theatre, "Give him some chicken soup, give him some chicken soup…" on and on without stop. The harried manager appeared on stage and called to the man, "Can't you see he's dead, what good will chicken soup do?" The man replied, "It can't hurt."

When a new drug comes out, you should use it while it works.
—Dr. Nolan D. C. Lewis

W. C. Fields once quipped that giving up drink is easy—"I've done it a thousand times," he confessed. Improving schooling—it would appear—is likewise a snap—proposed reforms are endless, though alas, they have about the same benefit as Field's struggle with sobriety. Admittedly, as Diane Ravitch shows (2000, Chapter 1) experts have endlessly fussed over our allegedly-broken school system, often harkening back to previous eras as a mythical "Golden Age." Nevertheless, current anxiety is not, we believe, yet one more crying wolf. Particularly as test scores go nowhere and private industry (and the military) must spend millions to teach what should have been learned in school. Proposing dubious if not guaranteed-to-fail transformations has erupted into a national obsession. Nothing seems to work and we often resemble a desperate alcoholic rummaging though the pantry looking for a buzz. Even if students are no worse than before, we spend unnecessary billions for mediocre outcomes, money certainly better applied elsewhere

A Quick Tour of the Museum of Educational Failures

Failed "guaranteed" educational reforms would fill a colossal museum and exhibits forever expand. Ironically, virtually every contemporary educational calamity was once heralded as the Messiah only to be discarded as a new and improved Messiah arrived. Among others, today's oft-criticized mega factory-like high school with its jumbled potpourri of electives was, at least according to Harvard's President, James B. Conant, the answer to the resource-deficient undersized scattered rural school. Now private foundations subsidize small, often theme-based "personal" high schools as supposed pathways to academic proficiency. Appetites for administrative centralization and decentralization have swung pendulum-like for over a century, and today's infatuation with accountability—strict, transparent measures of precisely-specified performance outcomes—was yesterday's hated dead-hand, innovation-killing bureaucratic micro-management. Ditto for centralized political control of schools versus non-partisan expert administration—each repeatedly comes and goes as *the* solution. A similar dialectic applies to treating school as vocational training versus "impractical" traditional liberal arts. The neighborhood school has periodically evolved from idealization—safe, nearby, parent-friendly while promoting community cohesiveness—to a bastion of racial homogeneity incapable of imparting survival skills in a multicultural world, among other evils.

The widely-condemned, mystifying, and innumeracy-producing "New Math" was the 1950s brainchild of distinguished mathematicians persuaded that it would propel the U.S. ahead of more numerate Soviet students. Indeed, fiddling with the math curricula appears to be an un-controllable habit. A recent report of the National Mathematics Advisory Panel, a distinguished group of professors and teachers, recommended that K-8 math teachers put more emphasis on whole numbers, fractions, and certain aspects of geometry and measurement, a pedagogy that goes back centuries. The recommendations claimed to be based on some 16,000 research publications and took 90 drafts to produce the final version. President Bush's Secretary of Education hoped that Congress would pass the President's budget request for the $100 million for the "Math Now" program reflected in the Report (Lewin, 2008). It goes without saying that what "Math Now" is supposed to replace what were once, too, sure-fire cures for national innumeracy.

Today's experts may complain about students' disliking homework but some early-twentieth-century educators condemned all homework for ruining the mental health of youngsters. A half century back the now largely forgotten "team teaching" was the rage *du jour* so students would benefit from narrow expertise just like hospital patients might see dozens of specialists. During the 1960s the Ford Foundation (which also bank-rolled the failed "team teaching" effort) convinced that they had the solution to deteriorating test scores, funded community control of New York City's public schools in African-American neighborhoods. This "reasonable sounding" scheme drew widespread business elite support, academic endorsements, and even the ACLU joined in (see Ravitch, 1974, Chapters 23-34). The outcome was violence, corruption, racial strife and a massive teacher strike with, critically, zero academic improvement. Bilingual education was once hailed as uplifting Hispanics falling behind because of faulty English skills; a half century later many criticize it as part of the problem, not the solution.

Radicals currently excoriating IQ or SAT tests as hindering the disadvantaged should remember that science-infatuated Progressives embraced objective tests to discover diamonds-in-the-rough among the poor. Today's widely-damned "social promotion policy" once elicited expert endorsement since it unquestionably benefited all students. Similarly, academic tracking, the *bête noire* of contemporary egalitarians was formerly a liberal innovation guaranteed to increase learning for everyone. Parental choice, the elixir for scores of contemporary conservatives, was once declared an illegal segregationist ruse. New York City's "open admission" to city-run colleges begun in 1970 would "surely" help the disadvantaged move up the economic ladder. Today it is remembered as an academic catastrophe harming all students, including the poor.

One set of such sound-bite proposals currently making the rounds is to increase time spent in school, an idea whose popularity rests on lengthier school years in Japan, Germany and Singapore where students outshine their American counterparts. That these school systems profoundly differ from American schools besides longer hours, or that more days in school requires arduous renegotiation of union contracts, goes unsaid in this almost panic-driven search for solutions. A similar glib tinkering concerns starting the school day later since teenagers, it is said, are seldom early risers. That a lack of "early to rise, early to bed, makes you healthy, wealthy and wise" mentality is something to be reversed, not accommodated, likewise goes unnoticed. Meanwhile Idaho has announced that all second and third-graders will soon receive instruction in chess though the State's Superintendent of Education admitted that no studies exist demonstrating that learning chess benefits children.

No doubt, absent a learning curve, much of what seduces today will be condemned tomorrow. To put today's sundry enterprises into context, a few additional snippets of wrong turns must suffice though, we admit, stalwart defenders of the ideas will reject the verdict as too harsh and premature. Others might claim that they "really did work" though not in ways traditionally understood and will require yet more time. Still, this catalogue of disappointments is huge and, sadly, grows. Our tour does *not* argue that reforms are generally hopeless so we might just restore one-room schoolhouses and save billions. We are clearly better off today than a century back though future progress is hardly guaranteed. Rather, exhuming past mistakes reveals that all that glitters is not gold and educators, including many of today's well-intentioned philanthropists, prefer self-induced amnesia or were asleep during the history of education lecture. Our brief excursion counsels caution and skepticism.

Progressive Nostrums

Let's begin on the ideological left. Critics of "Progressive Education" have had a justifiable feeding fest in cataloguing widely-adopted "made-in-the-academy," professionally-certified Progressive schemes that have, apparently, debilitated millions from achieving once-common basic academic competence. E. D. Hirsch (1996) summarizes multiple dubious pedagogies with the catchphrases favored by educators themselves and exposes the ineffectualness despite glittering hype. Prominent failure-engendering tactics include teaching students "at their own pace" (children learn only when they want to learn); "child-centered schooling" (tailoring subject matter to each child's peculiarities); "constructivism" (children autonomously discover knowledge and this acquisition outshines what teachers bestow); "open classroom" (students are ungraded and meander at their own pace); teaching "critical thinking" independently of imparting "mere facts;" "culturally-sensitive" curricula based on racial and ethnic traits, not vital common knowledge; "hands-on learning" (the superiority of physical activity versus mental exertion); and, the grand champion of toxic progressive educational objectives—building self-esteem by avoiding the inescapable pain that comes with genuine learning. Particularly evil for Hirsch is our Education School-concocted aversion to factual knowledge in favor of content-free "learning how to learn" plus the dogmatic belief that youngsters can be trusted to learn autonomously. Both philosophies, Hirsch insists, probably correctly, inevitably foster ignorance.

Incongruously, while rightfully damning Progressive ideas, Hirsch himself conjures up an alluring proposal to promote academic excellence—a compulsory, top-down formulated, nationwide common, content-based curriculum—that is equally quixotic. Like Progressive educators in the first half of the twentieth-century demanding a near Stalinist centralization of state authority over schooling, Hirsch loathes

America's fragmented educational system with its myriad provincial school boards and idiosyncratic standards. He also correctly notes that residential mobility, especially in the inner city, breeds a mish-mash learning as children frequently change schools.

Hirsch would replace harmful content-free idiosyncratic instruction with a European style, nationally-directed, detailed, fact-based lessons. Now federal (or state) bureaucrats would dictate what every American public school student in each grade learned daily. All fifth graders, for example, might learn when the Civil War began, prominent generals, major battles, and key legal quarrels, among other supposedly immutable facts. And, for good measure, conveying essential knowledge would restore our common heritage in an era of cultural fragmentation.

Unfortunately, Hirsch's prescriptions is just as pie-in-the-sky as when Progressives insisted that unscrewing desks from the floor would ignite passions for learning. Hirsch may be right in championing fact-based pedagogy, and his commitment to national greatness is unquestionable, but he lacks any political acumen. If miraculously imposed (very unlikely), it invites sabotage. It is pure fantasy to demand localities surrender authority to distant bureaucrats or ignore preferences for, say, more football and less calculus. Equally preposterous is the belief that elected leaders (or their minions) could determine precisely what should be taught in each grade across an entire nation without waging countless time-consuming political battles. Nor would many of today's free-wheeling (and poorly-trained) teachers suddenly submit to top-down imposed lockstep curriculums once the classroom door is closed. Interestingly, though a professor of education, Hirsch is also an entrepreneur currently marketing his own performance-boosting schemes which, he assures potential buyers, will clean up the mess left by Progressive miseducation.

The Addiction to Ineffectual Reform

Wandering through the over-stuffed educational reform museum has been depressing, and to be frank, the future looks bleak. Success rates certainly cannot exceed 10 percent, and if education were a corporation, shareholder suits would try to salvage assets prior to bankruptcy. American public schools perform reasonably, sometimes exceptionally well, *in spite of* reformers' "best efforts." There are also moral tribulations here. Today's students, especially African-Americans, are often treated as cheap, expendable laboratory research animals subject to endless and hastily-conceived experiments as if trying some fashionable gimmick in lieu of proven traditional approaches was risk free. This wasteful penchant for uncertain options speaks volumes about our indifference to academic excellence for African-Americans and others mired in failure, strident protestations to the contrary aside.

Perhaps like a comet, dubious panaceas travel on mysterious periodic cycles so that what disappoints today will be rediscovered a few decades later, fail again, be forgotten, and then inexplicably reappear. Meanwhile, to continue to the astronomical imagery, schools are occasionally hit with "meteorites"—paying students to read books, boosting self-esteem to jump-start a thirst for knowledge or varied technological gizmos—that enter the policy atmosphere in a blaze of glory and quickly burn up leaving behind only tiny iron/nickel rocks suitable for pedagogy museum gift shops. Let us pray that a giant dumb rock meteor extinguishing intelligent life altogether will not hit American schools. Over and above why each of these "sure-fire" cures fails lies a more fundamental question: what keeps the parade of failures going? Or, why are so many seemingly-smart people easily and repeatedly misled?

The Flight from an Awkward Reality

Americans are optimists, and infatuations with glittering promising novelties can, unfortunately, help avoid painful realities. It is just socially unacceptable, if not injurious to our national self-esteem, to confess that mediocrity is tolerable since that is really what most parents and students want. Optimism about some soon-to-be discovered, expert-provided gimmick enables denial and escape from drudgery. Compounding misplaced optimism is that erstwhile do-gooders seldom—if ever—suffer *any* personal consequences for pursuing damaging chimera. Actually, purveying educational fantasy has become a career choice with a bright future vis-à-vis the private profit-based sector since: (a) there is no stigma for advocating dubious fixes since "just trying" is business-as-usual; (b) ample "free" government money (versus scarce private capitalist investment) together with desperate schools almost guarantees that somebody, somewhere takes the enticing bait; and (c) some philanthropic benefactor will fund almost any sexy scheme "offering hope." A newspaper headline, "Test Scores Collapse, Education Industry Plans to Lay off Thousand of Reformers" is absolutely inconceivable. The opposite is more likely: "Test Scores Collapse, Desperate Industry Plans to Hire Hundreds of Reformers."

Elected public officials from the president on down are *never* vulnerable if they propose educational nonsense. In today's desperate environment it is better to offer something, no matter how ill-conceived or doomed to fail, since "doing nothing to help the children" may risk defeat. Schemes to improve education are primarily schemes to get elected, and voters probably grasp this and thus relax standards of accountability. Savvy candidates also know that the very nature of political squabbling, endemic thanks to pluralism and fragmented political power, create perfect alibis while facilitating an "A" for effort—one is held responsible only for trying. The scenario is as follows: candidate Smith pledges "to fix education" by handing out laptop computers, she is elected and quickly announces her plan, then political resistance delays everything, multiple qualms require adjustments, negotiations commence, a few laptops are distributed, most remain unused in storage, teachers struggle to master the software, and the union demands extra money for additional training. A year passes before there can be any noticeable impact, another six months go by while preliminary, partial data are analyzed, critics quarrel over the outcomes and methodology (what about students who had computers only for half the term?), changes correct initial glitches of design and administration, another eighteen months go by, more ambivalent ("he said, she said") results are in, and then its time for reelection.

If Ms. Smith is up for reelection, she can always brag about a few successes, justifiably claim that more time is needed, command the city's public relations department to hail "important first steps in bringing students into the twenty-first Century" and otherwise spin triumphs. Whatever the strategy's downside, these are undoubtedly smaller than refusing to embrace some mesmerizing (but futile) quick fix. And since Ms. Smith is a skilled politician, she has made sure that varied constituencies, including newly-hired bureaucrats and consultants, let alone computer suppliers, have materially benefited from her plan regardless of educational advances. Better yet, more attention-getting successes elsewhere, e.g., reducing crime or a booming economy, overshadow ambiguous educational outcomes. The bottom line, then, it is better for an office-seeker to suggest something, *anything* that sounds promising versus counseling surrender to sloth, and as one office-holder follows another, each with their alluring innovative panaceas, like rabbits in Australia, failed reforms multiply.

Academy Concocted Remedies

Perhaps nowhere is irresponsibility more encompassing than among academics in education-related fields. Almost *every* university career incentive distances researchers from actual outcomes, a sure recipe for ineffectual prescriptions. Academic survival, at least at prestigious schools that shape "serious intellectual discussions," means publication (and related professional activity like conference presentations and grant-getting), *not* enhanced K-12 learning. Of the utmost importance, getting ideas into print typically requires overcoming hurdles having *nothing to do with K-12 academic attainment.* A tenured professor (and professors typically spend most of their careers tenured) need not worry about offering disastrous recommendations and, ironically, incentives exist for nutty novelty since "creativity" often brings notoriety and such "fame" typically boosts career options.

Among the numerous academic gods to be honored are embracing prevailing ideologies (whether liberal or conservative), reaffirming professionally-certified wisdom, no matter how uncertain, to placate journal and grant reviewers, coddling influential professional factions (especially thin-skinned minority groups), and heeding prevailing norms regarding evidence, jargon, and statistical technique. One can spend an entire career advocating multiculturalism as "the cure" for dismal black academic attainment, receive countless honors, build a hefty vita, and otherwise enjoy the good academic life, including a handsome salary, without *ever* having to defend this failed nostrum before outraged disappointed parents.

The unfettered search for truth is thus subordinated to personal economic survival. If race/class/gender-based analyses are "in," rampant illiteracy has to be examined through that lens; perhaps a rational choice approach will dominate next year, and so the herd will move accordingly. All and all, better to be published in the right journals and get it wrong versus getting it right and remaining unpublished. Moreover, academic departments infrequently reward "real world" accomplishment, so even if one discovered the long-awaited magic bullet, pursuing this goal invites huge career risks; wiser to play it safe, honor the local ideological gods and just be "professional." If driven to speak the disconcerting truth, do it privately.

Out of Sight Means Out of Mind

Nor must wrong-headed advocates personally see painful calamities, a situation comparable to misguided foreign aid where "assistance" often exacerbates misery. In a pinch, a visiting "education mayor" with reporters in tow can observe carefully stage-managed "progress" as coached third graders recite Shakespeare to adoring teachers in squeaky-clean classrooms. The flight from consequences is particularly important for the long-term consequences of ill-advised nostrums. The "education mayor" need not worry that today's showcased bright-eyed students might decades later suffer as a result of this made-for-media "help." And, to be honest, who knows for sure what today's reforms will bring? Building a record for the upcoming election is far more important.

Nor will underlings bring bad news; the Emperor's New Clothes parable applies to educators with a vengeance. What brave careerist will tell New York City's Mayor Bloomberg that his merit pay plan (see Chapter 8) is probably pointless? It is unlikely that any ambitious subordinate ever tried to convince President Bush and his congressional supporters that NCLB invited wholesale data fabrication. Where evidence of failure may be decades away and readily muddied by statistical dexterity, whistle-blower honesty invites professional suicide. Brutal frankness might even be castigated as "disloyalty." The watchdog media is likewise advised to shun disconcerting news to sustain continued access to government. Cassandras are not invited to the ball; optimism in the face of almost-guaranteed failure is a prerequisite for those with an opportunistic bent.

Moreover, wealthy foundation executives funding iffy schemes can help their own children by moving to localities providing first-rate education, use private schools, hire tutors or otherwise exploit private sector services providing superb outcomes to the affluent. During the divisive push for racially integrating New York City public schools during the 1960s, not a single black civil rights leader had offspring in a public school (Ravitch, 1974, 290). *All* members of Congress or the president, including President Obama, enroll their children to elite Washington, DC private schools and, significantly, nobody is embarrassed by this revealing fact. Imagine if law-makers had access to miracle anticancer drugs or super-safe automobiles unavailable to ordinary folk—the outcry would insure wholesale political slaughter. Meanwhile other pontificators either have no school-aged children or are childless. Let's be clear: nearly all reformers are *profoundly* irresponsible. None need worry that Junior suffers if a far distant ghetto school dumbs down its curriculum to build self-esteem and thus "graduates" semi-literates. Perhaps the only guaranteed sure-fire way to overcome irresponsibility would be to legally require all educational pundits to subject their offspring (or children of close relatives) to pet panaceas, and make refusal a criminal offense. This "Hostage Reform" hearkens back to the era when Kings sent family members to foreign kingdoms to guarantee immunity from attack.

The Pernicious Role of Greater Government Funding

The far distant federal government's growing educational responsibilities makes a bad situation even worse. As any economist will confirm, "free money" promotes frivolity, and this certainly applies for putative education reform. Specifically, where local outcomes and made-in-Washington budgets are disconnected, local programs are readily judged less by demonstrable utility than by the "Washington will pay for it, so let's do it" criteria. If "free" Washington money suddenly dries up, political agitation might yet again restore millions in addiction-sustaining grants. It certainly makes better economic (though uncertain educational) sense to lobby for state or federal handouts, even when strings are attached, versus increasing one's own local property taxes.

Perhaps even more troublesome for academic progress, local educational options are increasingly being influenced by Washington-based lobbying. This is perfectly legal and commonplace across countless other policy areas. A *Washington Post* story told how the Voyager Expanded Learning literacy program gained adoptions thanks to the company's close political ties to the Bush administration (Grimaldi, 2007). Thousands in national campaign contributions now bring multimillion local dollar Voyager adoptions despite educators doubting the program's overall effectiveness. Some school districts did not even request this federally-funded "gift." No doubt, the role of political clout in local curricula choices will expand as Washington-centered generosity increases. Educational spending may eventually resemble military contracting—firms hiring well-paid lobbyists who ply legislators with favors while demonstrating that some outlandishly expensive "learning system" will shower jobs to thankful constituents. Since grants will include lobbying costs, "helping the children" now means helping the children of lobbyists. In a word, improving education becomes pork.

The plan-of-the-day industry would be profoundly transformed—though actual learning may be unaffected—if parents personally paid for alleged improvements over and above a plain vanilla status quo. Now Dad and Mom would annually receive, say, a $1,000 debit card to select educational extras from a "reform catalogue," and unspent funds could be pocketed or used to reduce taxes. Perhaps purchases could be restricted to school-related products, a tactic comparable to the Women Infants Children (WIC) subsidy program permitting parents with young children to buy certain foods at local stores. Passions for glittering untested innovation would surely vanish though skeptics would guess that "education" money might flow toward spiffier athletic equipment or lavish proms.

The downside of federal government lavishness hardly stops here. As cures grow costlier, securing funding requires ever more legislative arm-twisting, and made-in-Washington panaceas undoubtedly require the most arm-twisting. With billions at stake, one must fend off rivals elbowing their way to the public trough. Debating pedagogical merits is thus replaced by devising bills amenable to legislative logrolling, and this can be independent of pedagogical merit. A well-crafted "liberal" measure would, for example, draw support from the NEA, civil rights groups, and education school professors, even brokerage firms selling government debt. A "conservative" proposal, by contrast, must line up fans of local control, fundamentalist religious organizations, and similarly-minded coalition partners. Politics may also push legislative provisions to include purely-ideological addendums to sweeten the deal—teaching "social justice" for the left, permitting Bible instruction for the right. Like military contractors, big-time textbook companies and other purveyors of costly pedagogy may locate facilities in key legislative districts. Whether a particular educational reform passes may depend on bargaining unrelated to schools—extra preschool funding might be "paid for" by trading votes for relaxing automobile pollution standards.

The government's "free money" also affords an all-too-easy flight from confronting awkward tribulations; the fiscal tail now happily wags the educational dog. This is the classic chronic procrastinator tactic: avoid the unpleasant task by substituting something more enjoyable. For example, disciplining unruly students is hardly fun but what if a legislative provision subsidizes a conference to address the problem? Now the original (and serious) task is transformed into a more manageable logistical "problem": "Where to hold the meeting?"; "Which hotel?"; "What to eat?"; "Who will speak?"; "How many after-work parties?"; among countless other "fun" details, all divorced from the unsavory task of disciplining students. And, if educators are lucky, the conference's "success," as reflected by media coverage, published papers, and speaker prestige, might bring yearly meetings, all the while out-of-sight students run wild.

This solution-by-regression abetted by "free" government money was recently illustrated by one Washington, DC's effort to boost learning among its struggling students. The School Chancellor decided that "better principals" were necessary, so an $180,000 national advertising campaign was launched to attract talent (Labbé, 2008). This is "free" money since a $2 million federal grant paid for it. As of early 2008, some 500 applications were on file and this bountifulness will undoubtedly generate thousands of hours of scrutiny, meetings, memos, interviews, and discussions over applicable hiring criteria (and possibly a few lawsuits, to boot). All participants can now honestly claim to be "working hard to improve schools." This is an avoidance strategy: according to the education director of the Wallace Foundation, which has spent some $215 million researching leadership's impact on school performance, recruiting heroic principals is pointless. Not only does it fail; it merely reshuffles talent, so Washington, DC's "gain" is some other school district's loss. The musical chairs also raise salaries by promoting bidding wars with no corresponding educational benefit.

This new responsibility hardly ends the escapist busywork. The federal government's Accountability Office is pressing the DC district to develop a comprehensive plan, as if such a make-work document (apart from any implementation) would cure endemic problems that have resisted past multimillion-dollar solutions. And if hiring heroic principals and devising a plan fail to offer relief from confronting a troublesome reality, the DC's State Board of Education is pressuring administrators to revise its definition of a "highly-qualified" teacher. A cynic might guess that some bureaucrat deep in the bowels of Washington DC's education colossus burns the midnight oil inventing such running-around-in-circles tasks to escape distasteful realities.

Politicized funding makes some reforms political orphans regardless of demonstrated effectiveness—why struggle with unfunded projects, no matter how important, when extra money can be gained elsewhere? (And a knack for securing funds may be career enhancing, especially in idea-factory Education Schools.) This is comparable to students refusing to prepare for tests if no longer paid. Consider, for example, providing teachers greater disciplinary authority, a step that teachers universally welcome to improve academic proficiency. Implementation is cheap since nobody new is hired nor is anything built; a few new administrative rules and stricter enforcement suffice. Alas, no ready-made political constituency, let alone financial beneficiaries, exists for cracking the whip, while countless politically-influential opponents will resist. For big spending fans, imposing law and order might be a dangerous first step subverting the dominant "we need more money" mentality. ACLU-type groups and civil rights leaders who see "more discipline" as a code phrase for racial discrimination would likewise object. To be sure, "orphan" measures undoubtedly have advocates, but many of these "homeless" nostrums (e.g., a more disciplined classroom, or rigorous textbooks) can be better pursued outside public schools making it unnecessary to confront politically-entrenched forces. In the case of tougher discipline, just impose it at home or transfer Junior to a military school.

Imagine if strict discipline were transformed from an orphan to one with a constituency. Now, recognizing the importance of classroom decorum for learning, even the need for mild corporal punishment, Congress authorized a "modest" $100 million for the "The School Discipline Reform Act of 2014." It allocates $5 million for "best practices" research, a few more million on workshops and conferences, $10 million to train newly-hired "school discipline professionals," a million or two for lawyers to fret over school liability for injuries, plus pilot projects (selected via a national competition) to fine-tune programs. Despite initial mixed results, predictable glimmers of hope merge, and lobbying by the newly-fashioned "School Discipline Association" (SDA) helps raises funding to $120 million in 2016 (still less than one Air Force F-22 the SDA rightly claimed).

Now, sensing an opportunity to get in on the ground floor, educators once enamored of self-esteem discover the value of "tough love" and rush to join the SDA. A new refereed journal appears and scholarly papers linking paddling to test scores mushroom. Early movement enlistees become sought-after academic stars in this burgeoning trendy field. Furthermore, thanks to a sizable conservative Congressional bloc, no omnibus education bill could survive the legislative gauntlet without funding the new disciplinarians. After a decade or so, expanded funding becomes automatic and paddling and similar "tough love" measures are barely noticed.

The Vagueness of "Reform"

While everyone demands "improved education," no consensus exists on what, exactly, "improvement" means, so absent specifics, public discussion veers towards wooly cliché mongering. A Rorschach test quality masked by a superficially-common vocabulary infuses this enterprise, the equivalent of prescientific physics calibrating objects with terms like "big" or "hot." Nor does it take too much to package almost anything as a "reform," so both the latest fads and ultra-traditional measures are "reforms" to those disinclined to peer beyond slogans. It may be just a matter of time before the bare-bones one-room schoolhouse reappears as a cutting-edge corrective ("the chronologically-unstructured academically-integrated setting minimizing modern distractions").

More fundamental, disagreements exist regarding the central purpose of American education, and differing viewpoints profoundly shape attitudes towards reform. Powerful egalitarian and meritocratic ideologies (among others) flourish side by side. Measures that improve narrow academic skills may be "failures" to experts making psychological adjustment central and vice versa. Imparting unblinking patriotism, a great triumph for traditional educators, may be a disaster to preferring that American youngsters "think critically." Even among higher test score proponents, success or failure can reflect the widening or narrowing of race-related gaps, not overall upward movement. The heterogeneity of American education obscures these multiple divergent aims—we have both military academies and progressive schools—but this is of little help in public debates over "improving education." Conflicting visions mean that both successes and failures are inevitable so reform, then, approaches a zero-sum enterprise with one's expert's success being another's failure.

The exceptionally-low entry costs into the "reform industry" readily permits explosive conceptual clutter. This is not physics where someone ignorant of Joule's Law is too embarrassed to pontificate. Everybody, it would appear, is an expert with dozens of flippant opinions, always happy to offer them—"When I went to school...." This is the world of home-made kitchen cures, not the multi-billion dollar pharmaceutical industry. With blogs and small-sized family foundations, pushing dubious putative solutions is easy. Of the utmost importance, there is negligible professional gatekeeping if there is money to be had. Outside self-appointed experts may have little appreciation of the obstacles daily facing teachers and administrators, let alone the politically-protected bureaucratic inertia in every school district. Particularly in states facilitating charter schools (see our discussion of Arizona in Chapter 8) anybody can be "an educator" and almost nothing impedes dubious eccentricities.

To illustrate reform glibness, consider one such seductive cure-all that inevitably arises when debating "educational reform:" reducing class size. Judged by its popularity it seems a feel-good no-brainer: with fewer students per teacher, each teacher can devote more attention per student and thus increase learning. Unfortunately, reducing class size, like so many pat panaceas is deceptively complicated and often impractical. The easy cure *du jour* inevitably skips over these considerations: (1) countless new classrooms must be constructed to accommodate fewer students per teacher, a huge cost in urban areas; (2) the existing teacher supply is inadequate for a significant class-size reduction, and thus new teachers must be recruited, many of whom will be inexperienced or unqualified, and even then filling the ranks takes years; (3) classrooms now devoted to electives like music and art may have to be sacrificed and thereby end non-core instruction; (4) new job opportunities may draw teachers away from inner-cities to wealthier suburbs possibly exacerbating race-related differences; (5) no scientifically-demonstrated consensus exists between class size and learning; (6) other nations with stellar academics have much larger classes than the U.S.; and, finally, (7) class size in America has been declining for decades all the while test scores similarly drop.

Uncertainties also bedevil implementation. For instance, are reading and math specialists without fixed classroom assignments included in these ratios? Do we measure class size by official attendance lists of enrolled students versus pupils actually showing up on a given day? Nor can we specify optimal class size, and this figure might vary by subject and age, e.g., tiny for language instruction but much larger for history lectures. It is also plausible that class size is a proxy for classroom discipline—fewer students facilitate discipline, and so the underlying impediment is disorder, not class size per se. Nor can class size readily be disentangled from innumerable other conditions affecting academic performance. Finally, even if it did perform as advertised, this does not automatically mean that it is the superior allocation of scarce resources—perhaps the billions could be better spent elsewhere.

These inescapable complexities unfortunately get swept away in the frantic quest for "something that might work." Vacuous Babel becomes the default option. A televised debate of school reform might devote five minutes to class size, an amount wholly inadequate for the topic, and this is only one of a dozen reform options. And, if the patient TV station covered each topic adequately, the weary audience would dwindle. Nor does intelligent discussion prevail in more "serious" forums. No reform-minded public official would be foolish enough to bore the audience with, say, the uncertainties of preschool programs or the drawbacks of expensive technological fixes. Ditto for holding a community meeting to explain why "hiring the best teachers" is not as straightforward as it seems—who can oppose "good teachers"? Even staid university and think-tank conferences typically offer little more than fifteen-minute speeches (often to justify some pet nostrum) and brief Q and A on horrendously-complicated topics. *All* reform discussion must be dumbed down if anything is to be understood by educational consumers. The public side of the reform marketplace of ideas might be compared to beer marketing—airy slogans such as "less filling," "thirst-quenching," "full-bodied," and "smooth" that describe nothing in particular.

Rorschach-like labels afloat in a sea of verbiage virtually guarantees "reform-minded" educators toil at cross purposes, often without realizing it. While one set of do-gooders strive to boost math scores with repetitive drill (the "return to basics reform"), others insist on Progressive-inspired fun computer games that, they claim, will arouse future mathematical appetites. One school's progress-minded school principal recruits teachers who satisfy tough academic standards; across town a similarly reform-driven principal hires teachers who racially resemble her students, regardless of academic qualification, to push test results upward. Both administrators embrace the "reformer" label and, conceivably, they might exchange schools and upend previous reform-driven measures, all in the name of "reform." To repeat, *nothing* exists in education that cannot be twisted into "reform" and as we tirelessly repeat, last year's reform is often this year's vexation, and since no mechanisms exist to certify "reform" versus imposters, incoherence and failure are to be expected.

Terminal Research Inconclusiveness

If linguistic confusion were not sufficiently debilitating, the tribulations of assessing any reform's impact is often sufficient to confuse matters beyond all hope. Educational research is light years away from the physical sciences. Its jumbled nature ensures that multiple researchers can examine the same data yet reach different conclusions regarding outcomes and, to paraphrase Newton, for every finding there is an equal and opposite finding (Henig, 1994, Chapter 6 illustrates these quandaries). Chester Finn, a long-time educational reform insider noted sadly, "education policy-making proceeds in an environment of astonishingly little knowledge about what works…. We're in a primitive and politically dominated world" (quoted in Rotherham, 2005, 209-10). Indeed, as the subsequent two chapters will illustrate, if a prize were awarded for the world's most confusing, contradictory if not acrimonious research literature, the "what works in education" would win hands down. That this research is often sponsored by groups with an economic stake in outcomes, and authored by employees of ideologically-motivated organizations only compounds difficulties.

To appreciate the roots of this vexation, one must acknowledge the classic experimental design as the gold standard for calibrating any reform impact. It is simple in principle but a nightmare in practical implementation. Unfortunately, the gold standard experimental ideal is seldom realized, and most—if not all—investigations are only rough approximations. Cheating or laziness are not the problems; the practical impediments (including government-mandated privacy) are just extraordinarily daunting, so researchers must make assumptions, rely on proxies and inferences, leave critical factors unmeasured, and hope for the best. For example, testing a school's second-grade class and then retesting them a year later assumes that the two groups remain identical. This is seldom the case; some original second graders have changed schools while some of the third graders are newcomers, so apples are being compared to oranges. Nor is there any estimation of student potential, so even a tiny gain may be all that was possible. Similarly, creating precise control groups may be unworkable since students cannot be treated as guinea pigs for the investigator's benefit. Faced with multiple incomparability obstacles, researchers typically rely on far cruder evaluations, for example, comparing overtime aggregate progress at one school with national or state test scores though very little is known about this improvised "control group." In other instances "progress" estimates using different test instruments must suffice, the equivalent of, say, comparing "speed" on a 100-meter dash versus a 400-meter high hurdles dash. No doubt, the two "speed" indicators are probably correlated, but the inexactitude remains.

The upshot is, if put under a microscope, almost no study can survive close inspection. Inconclusive long-winded boring technical arguments inevitably bring frustrations and frustrated souls hankering "to save the children" readily relapse to simple-minded slogans—"abolish unions," "end teacher tenure," "give parents more choice," and the like. Eventually, not even the committed reformer might want to confront the mind-numbing Tower of Educational Reform Babel, and as serious discussion bores listeners, "reform" slides into battles between competing clichés and slogans.

Research confusion makes it almost impossible to "kill" failed reforms regardless of the damage. Educational reform is not akin to the automobile industry where Hudsons and DeSotos have long ago risen to the great junkyard in the sky. Being an "educational reformer" means never having to say "I was wrong." Since those who have built political or professional careers on some remedy can *always* discern research-based glimmers of hope, the passion lingers on. The dreaded "F" word (failure) never need be uttered; euphemisms abound. When New York City's Chancellor Joel Klein confronts static test scores after spending billions and haranguing educators, he simply says, "We have more work to do." Others prefer "The goal is too important to give up on." Educators possess an ample catalogue of handy excuses when plans go awry, and professional courtesy mitigates harsh criticism. Unlike the commercial marketplace, then, failures are not banished.

This almost built-in inconclusiveness was perfectly illustrated in 2009 when the federal government's Institute of Education Sciences issued a comprehensive analysis of eight of today's favorite panaceas (Viadero, 2009). The Institute applied the gold standard, i.e., randomized controlled trials, to assess programs such as school mentoring, various math curricula, the use of commercial computer software, intensive literary instruction, the impact of various teacher training methods among other interventions. Positive outcomes did occur, but only sporadically and it is unclear if these benefits outweigh monetary and opportunity costs. But, predictably, program defenders quickly challenged the findings, noting (apparently correctly) that the studies were flawed, even inappropriate given the intervention's aims (but nobody seemed to suggest that positive outcomes may also have been a result of poor research). In other words, despite millions spent on careful scientific evaluation, the "he said, she said" education reform industry marches forward, probably as if the Institute of Education Sciences never existed.

Foundations and Educational Reform

Foundation munificence strongly shapes today's educational reforms and this "help" explains why our museum overflows with disappointing panaceas. Like the chicken soup "cure" for Boris Thomashefsky's death, the billions in foundation grants are better understood as noble intentions than solutions for our educational tribulations. "Foundations" refers to what the IRS calls 501©3's (after the tax code section), more specifically private, family foundations (not "charitable foundations" like the American Cancer Society). Some—so-called "operating foundations"—actually run programs but the major benefactors—"grant giving foundations" fund others who direct programs. Both types are non-profits though not all non-profits are foundations. IRS tax regulations are complicated, but key elements include: a stipulated "public" purpose (i.e., education, religion, or charity) and this must exclude substantial political activity and the general requirement that 5 percent of assets be spent annually (else taxes are higher). Foundations also enjoy various tax exemptions for organizational income and donations. Annual reports must be filed and made publicly accessible. Still, and this is crucial, foundations benefit from ample spending discretion to accomplish stated missions and this is especially true compared to governments mired in gridlock facing multiple electoral pressures.

Thanks to recent prosperity plus America's donation-encouraging tax code, private foundations have multiplied. For the rich, endowing a foundation helps offset huge tax bills all the while providing opportunities to advance worthy public aims. Between 1975 and 2005, grant-making foundations increased from 21,877 to 71,095 while in inflation-adjusted dollars, grants increased from $1.9 billion in 1975 to $10.0 billion in 2005 (The Foundation Center, 2007). In 2005 the top philanthropic donor was the Bill and Melinda Gates Foundation that distributed some $1.4 billion (upped to $2.8 billion in 2006) while ranked 50th on the list of largest foundation was the GE Foundation that "only" awarded $70.6 million. The Rockefeller Foundation, long epitomized as "the" foundation in the public's mind was only 33rd on this list with grants totaling $111 million.

Foundations granted some $1.84 billion for primary and secondary schools in 2005. Though noticeably far less than government outlays in 2005 ($470.2 billion), this figure belies influence. Unlike widely-dispersed public funding, foundation grants are narrowly targeted and thus may comprise a large portion of a particular school's budget while permitting innovations lacking public money. "Free" grant money can also elicit favorable publicity which, in turn, can attract additional private funding. Adroit foundations create policy "atmospheres" by subsidizing like-minded think tanks or university centers which, in turn, issue research reports, hold conferences, and generate mass media exposure for the foundation's ideas (see Rotherham, 2005, pp. 213-23 describes this process). Foundations often speak of leveraging their gifts by getting others, including public agencies on board to multiply impact.

It is no exaggeration to say that without foundation support, the "choice" movement in K-12 education would barely exist. A 2007 National Committee for Responsive Philanthropy report noted that some 1,200 foundations had given $380 million to 104 organizations advocating school choice between 2002 and 2005 (Brodbeck, 2008). The Walton Foundation (the Wal-Mart fortune) led the way with $25 million and other major donors to the choice movement included the Gates Foundation, the Scaife Foundation, and the John Templeton Foundation. These mega entities also actively encouraged less prominent foundations and wealthy individuals to enlist in the choice movement, and judged by rising fervency, this tactic seems effective. (Nevertheless, long before free-market options grew popular well-established foundations were at the forefront of funding "liberal" education-related solutions such as day-care, multicultural education, community control of schools, and varied pre- and after-school enrichment programs.)

Does Foundation Money Help?

Unfortunately, upbeat claims by foundations themselves do not supply a straightforward answer to this fundamental question. Handsome annual reports hailing a success or two do not make for a transformation. Nor are these alleged successes always scrutinized by outsiders. One could certainly ask if all these billions performed as claimed, why are achievement trends so disappointing? Many grant recipients, whether well-paid program administrants or students visiting a spiffy grant-built library are certainly happier but happiness is not necessarily learning. Inconclusiveness acknowledged, several general factors counsel caution against foundation-supplied solutions.

IRS regulations are critical to understanding pessimism. Recall that foundations activity must conform to a stated mission while satisfying other purely-financial obligations. Still, despite countless strictures, *absolutely nothing in IRS rules pertains to program effectiveness.* IRS officials are concerned with possible tax scams, money laundering, and (recently) promoting terrorism, among other illegal activities; pedagogical soundness *is irrelevant* unless a mission statement is clearly a tax dodge. A foundation and a profit-driven capitalist firm differ profoundly. Foundations do not have "products" to sell finicky consumers nor can they be judged by the traditional capitalist metric, profits. No foundation risks trouble if its gifts have zero or even negative impacts, and even horrific publicity is financially inconsequential for foundation survival. Perhaps the worst that can happen is that the erring foundation might be threatened with losing its tax-exempt status but the odds of this actually happening are miniscule. As previously noted, the Ford Foundation sailed along unhampered despite bankrolling New York City's disastrous, racial strife-producing 1960s community control of schools, among other notable fiascos.

"Improving America's education" is also such a daunting and murky task that expectations of success are so low that failure is not stigmatized. Just "trying" generally suffices where disenchantment is customary and no unambiguous benchmarks signal victory. During the 1960s and 1970s the Ford Foundation poured millions into public schools to no avail. In 1993 the Annenberg Foundation gave some $500 million to help K-12 education (eventually leveraged into $1 billion), the results, as was true for the Ford effort, were meager (at best). Tellingly, the debacles have vanished from public memory, and both foundations soldier on. A cynic might claim that "improving educational achievement" is the perfect foundation mission since the challenge is eternal and the IRS tolerates futility provided paperwork is properly completed. Perhaps only "creating world peace" outranks reversing our educational calamities as lifetime employment.

IRS income distribution requirements (usually 5 percent) also dictate a financial grantsmanship strategy to improve schools. Reform, at least from the foundation perspective, is thus subtlety transformed from "What helps children learn?" to "How can we give away specified sums while keeping the IRS happy and, maybe, help children learn?" This shift can readily impede progress. For one, it is just administratively easier to distribute substantial grants to minimize administrative overhead, independent of achievement potential. A moderately-sized foundation might, for example, "solve" its annual $4 million financial obligations by funding two charter schools versus, say, a more labor-intensive hiring 50 researchers to probe successful school practices overseas and then publicizing these findings. And with general administrative expenses reduced, salaries for top officials can be increased since the total distribution is fixed according to IRS rules. Continuing the few but large grants strategy year after year further minimizes administrative costs. Small, family foundations with tiny staffs may find an automatic approach particularly inviting regardless of failures.

Though IRS rules permit ample mission leeway, deciding what, exactly, best "helps the children" is daunting. Dubious schemes abound, charlatans are everywhere so clutter-cutting shortcuts are inevitable, especially as hundreds of unsolicited requests for money arrive. It may be more efficient to join the big foundation bandwagon than start from scratch. Thus, if the Wal-Mart Foundation decides that enriching preschool helps, just follow on a smaller scale. Even with a more independent approach, the yearly pressure to distribute considerable sums may push funding into uncertain, hurried investments with minimal impact evaluation beyond ensuring that money was spent on proposed projects. Foundation executives cannot be faulted for believing that even uncertain charity outranks mailing a check to Uncle Sam.

The contrast between the aims of foundations and capitalism cannot be over-stressed. Business fortunes are largely nourished by sound ideas; in philanthropy, by contrast, the money made decades back generates today's ideas, and nothing suggests that billionaire entrepreneurs are especially insightful about educational achievement or can hire experts possessing answers. Being an "educational philanthropist" requires millions, but the intellectual hurdles to pontificate are minimal, and even off-the-cuff remedies might be intoxicating. Solving the reading woes of fourth graders seem almost effortless compared to conquering the dog-eat-dog world of computers, so a half-baked idea can easily pass muster. Conceivably, the billionaire's schemes may reflect romanticized memories of a 1950s rural school or a haphazard suggestion passed on at a health care charity gala. Nothing counsels reasonableness, let alone effectiveness. The multibillion-dollar Broad Foundation, for example, is committed to closing racial gaps in educational achievement, a goal that has defied hundreds of billions and, as we saw above, dozens of ingenious schemes (Hassett and Katzir, 2005, 228). Imagine a private firm pouring millions into risky ventures where dozens of predecessors have failed completely?

Consider the radically-different incentive structures in making money versus giving it away. The risks associated with making a fortune are huge, and every firm has experienced disasters and many have vanished as a result of stupidity. By contrast, *nothing* exists to impede foundation wasteful foolishness; foundation administrators and grant recipients have *zero* incentive to say, "This scheme may bring ruin, so perhaps we should study it more or drop it." A workaholic acquiring billions by carefully scrutinizing every option can blithely give away this fortune on whim, without any fear that rivals will pounce on ineptitude. No wonder creating foundations are so popular—this is great fun after the rigors of making money.

If anything, we suspect, well-paid foundation administrators may serve as clever flatterers to reassure donors of idea worthiness. Based on numerous first-hand interviews and long experience in this world, Joel Fleishman (a fan of foundation generosity) acknowledges that grant-makers can be whimsical if they so choose (Fleishman, 2007, Chapter 9). There is absolutely no downside to telling the benefactor that his or her ideas are "brilliant." Moreover, promoting educational amelioration is unlike, say, running an investment fund where trained, experienced financial experts carefully scrutinize, say, Stanley Kaplan, Sylvan Learning, or Edison Schools and other for-profit ventures, and if nothing looks promising today, park the money in U.S. Treasury bills until inviting opportunities appear. Investment-seeking firms routinely supply detailed business plans, audited financial statements, and similar data facilitating professional decision-making. If stock purchases turn sour, punishment is real: investors flee and the investment firm goes bankrupt. In other words, a rotten educational investment differs profoundly from investing in now bankrupt Enron. Foundations do, of course, disappear, but not from ill-advised helping efforts. A Merrill-Lynch analyst who regularly advised investing in disaster would soon be unemployed; not so for foundation officers. At least for-profit businesses learn from failures.

The "might not help but can't hurt" intellectually painless approach was exemplified by how the multibillion-dollar Atlantic Philanthropies in 2008 gave $18 million to five Chicago schools. This gift, moreover, was expected to generate an additional $15.8 million in matching public and private grants. Since routine expenses such as teachers' salaries are already funded, this "extra" $33.8 million, or $6.76 million per school, resembles winning the lottery. The commendable objective was to help disadvantaged middle-school children succeed academically while aiding the nearby community. The initiative, called the Integrated Services in School (ISS), provides comprehensive in-school health care, multiple non-classroom learning opportunities, mentoring by caring adults, plus ensuring that students and parents benefit from existing public programs such as health care and tax credits. Everything is off-the-shelf, so to speak. Numerous other local foundations, universities, community groups, and public agencies will also participate, and they probably developed many of ISS's administrative details (Atlantic refuses to consider uninvited proposals, so participation in the project was solicited).

Will ISS succeed? All the evidence, as Chapter 4 demonstrates, suggests that the academic portion will disappoint though students and parents might appreciate the added health care and other tangible non-academic benefits. If after-school programs and mentoring had any real academic value America's problems would have been solved decades ago. Meanwhile, federal and state governments offer abundant non-academic programs almost identical to what ISS supplies. Atlantic is lending a hand only at the margin in light of existing government-supplied help, and if these were successful, Atlantic's efforts might be redundant. Perchance Atlantic's grant givers understood these formidable obstacles, but with millions needing to be spent, even repeating past failures was worth a shot. And who knows, this time around it might succeed. In any case, the venture made perfect philanthropic sense regardless of outcomes. And why would any sane person reject "free" money, more local jobs, and the prestige that comes with winning multimillion-dollar grants? In other words, apart from actual progress, ISS will be a grand success.

A skeptic who viewed these and countless other iffy grants might opine that their real (and artfully-disguised) purpose is securing future political support from certain ethnic/racial constituencies, less to help struggling students. At least in some instances, this is the *only* plausible explanation. Consider, for example, the musings of Stanley Litow, a former New York City deputy school chancellor, now vice president of IBM's program for citizenship and corporate affairs (Litow, 2008). His concern is the paltry number of Hispanics in science and engineering. His recommendations would never pass muster as a business plan or a legitimate helping effort. He glibly announces that U.S. economic competitiveness requires children from all ethnic backgrounds to pursue science and technology careers, a totally unsupported if not half-baked claim. To accomplish this, he suggests a litany of doomed-to-fail nostrums: recruiting better (and more highly-paid) math teachers for schools with large Hispanic populations, more role models and mentors, help for parents so they can press schools for more attention for their offspring, more financial support for Hispanic college students, and promoting awareness among Hispanic students of lucrative technology careers. Other major corporations, notably Exxon Mobil, Lockheed among others, are joining the campaign. This is a venture to create education-related jobs for Hispanics, not push struggling Hispanics to master calculus as only a first step in a long road.

Nor are private foundations obligated to follow solid research findings or lose their vital tax-exempt status. The IRS does not oblige foundations to be open forums where experts deliberate solutions and only certified winners are funded. If Bill Gates fantasizes Washington, DC's struggling high schoolers will be energized by awaiting $122 million college scholarships, so be it—it is his money (on average only 9% of all those DC students attending college actually graduate). It gets worse. The Gates Foundation has poured $1 billion into 1,500 "small learning communities" and the executive director of the foundation publicly confessed that this was a waste—learning was no better than at traditional schools (Klein, 2006). A version of the Golden Rule prevails: he (or she) who has the gold makes the rules. The billionaire founder might solicit expertise, even heed it, but effective policy-making is optional. If staff members disagree, just hire more compliant ones. A foundation can quickly become a platform for doomed-to-fail schemes, and if people take the money, there is no corrective.

Sexy Fantasies Often Disappoint

New York City's application of philanthropic funds under Mayor Bloomberg illustrates the potential dilemmas of "free" money absent traditional political scrutiny. Here, thanks to several multimillion-dollar grants administered through the private Fund for Public Schools, the Mayor and School Chancellor Joel Klein now can pursue expensive risky schemes. One such venture, the $70 million Leadership Academy (begun with Wallace Foundation seed money), is supposed to train "super" principals. The Academy's admission standards were tough for the rigorous fifteen-month program and the Chancellor hailed the Academy's central role in saving the city's struggling schools. Alas, both the numbers eventually employed and the cost per graduate ($160,000 to $180,000) has proven a disappointment. A 2007 *New York Post* story four years after the Academy's creation recounts dismal academic performances by the Academy's graduates, varied problems dealing with parents and students plus sundry other troubles (Klein and Montefinise, 2007). Perhaps most relevant, despite Chancellor Klein's continued glowing endorsements, the city's test scores, including those schools run by "super" principals, generally remain static (Gootman, December 20, 2005).

Other high-risk education-related programs to emerge from the Fund have included rewarding students for passing tests and paying parents to take out library cards, attend a parent-teacher conference, or otherwise be engaged in their children's learning. Again, the impact of these novel ventures remains uncertain, and zero in the research literature suggests optimism. Though private money conceivably permits the autonomy necessary to correct deeply-rooted educational tribulations, it is equally plausible that trouble-free access to millions encourages unexamined flights of fancy unlikely to pass public scrutiny. Recall how Bill Gates wasted $1 *billion* on small schools that proved no better than larger ones. It is also arguable that *public* schools should not be the playthings of unaccountable *private* foundations. Nevertheless, squandering foundation money has few drawbacks provided improvidence is legal or avoids embarrassment; a taxpayer-funded boondoggle is a bit riskier, however, and may explain why elected officials love foundation grants.

The New York experience illustrates what might be called the "sexy money" problem. That is, generous donors frequently prefer "solutions" that attract media attention, are deemed "innovative" and otherwise might bestow personal fame. Given a choice between, say, updating a school's antiquated heating system or providing free state-of-the-art laptops, the latter might be more tempting despite shaky evidence of it helping. Laptops may even prove a costly distraction or invite rampant thievery. By contrast, imagine the photo ops with the school's custodian flipping the switch to ensure uniform temperatures and fuel oil saving versus seeing thrilled youngsters and their new toy. What modern philanthropist, especially one who made a fortune via inventiveness, wants a plaque on a basement boiler? "Sexiness" also applies to pursuing trendy ventures with little chance of success; futility itself may only add to the quest's "heroic' allure. For philanthropic deeds the "profit" is psychological, not material, so a "good reform" may just maximize self-esteem, not some stranger's future gain.

A prominent example of what can happen with billionaire-turned-school reformer is Eli Broad whose fortune comes from home construction and insurance. He and his wife Edythe through the Broad Foundation have, as of May 2007, given some $250 million to K-12 education and hope to spend most of their Foundation's $2.5 billion on that cause (Matthews, 2007). Besides his passion for schooling, Broad is an avid art collector who has lent his collection to over 400 museums, has helped reinvigorate downtown Los Angeles, been active in promoting cutting-edge biological science and research in inflammatory bowel disease plus generously funding varied higher education projects (*http://broadfoundation.org/eli/index.shtml*). Broad is also an extraordinary Democratic Party donor and counts the Clintons and other top elected leaders among his friends.

The Broad Foundation targets urban schools where it attempts to circumvent "meddlesome school boards" by instituting sound business practices, particularly by training future educational leaders with the tools for effective management, providing tangible rewards and showcasing successes (*http://broadfoundation.org/mission/index.shtml*). Broad sees himself as a mischief maker, a man of action who prefers quick, executive-led decisive action, not never-ending political haggling. Judged by his projects, he's convinced that American's educational woes result from inept leadership, and if the right, well-trained executives were turned loose on ineptly-managed public schools, learning would explode among invigorated students.

Among his concrete accomplishments has been an "urban school executive program" to prepare future school administrators (many graduates are former high-ranking military officers), an urban residency program, and institute for schools boards, a school superintendent's academy, and a million dollar annual prize for excellence in urban education. He has also funded various innovative charter schools. Along with Bill Gates, Broad created the Strong America Schools to elevate education to a national priority, and the two billionaires have committed $60 million for advertising and enlisting volunteers in both political parties to push their agenda (no candidates will be endorsed as per IRS rules). The campaign has drawn the endorsement of well-known Democrats and Republican office holders (Herszenhorn, April 25 2007).

The rise of the Broad Foundation, Wal-Mart, Gates and similar multibillion-dollar entities has made education grants a big business, a far cry from a few engineers with a shoe-string budget inventing the micro-processor. In 2004 the median Broad grant was $846,100 and this has probably risen as the Foundation's assets grow. With the odds of success low (12 percent of applications to Broad received funding in 2004), the entire grant process—from crafting proposals to evaluating them—grows more complicated and, undoubtedly, more bureaucratic since "amateur" efforts will surely be rejected (data are from Hassett and Katzir, 2005, 231). With the stakes high, grant getting becomes a professionalized, well-paid job, and an ability to sniff out opportunities, write proposals with the alluring jargon, and otherwise satisfy arcane technical requirements almost guaranteeing employment. Again, funding can shape ideas not vice versa: "what might work" becomes "what might work *and* be funded." And with the promise of continued funding on the line, powerful incentives exist to "make it work" regardless of the actual benefits, a strategy well-suited to an environment where achievement may be a decade away.

These countless millions, and the promise of more to come, have certainly had an impact, and graduates of various Broad Foundation academies are filtering into educational leadership. The Foundation has also attracted widespread educator attention, hardly surprising given the enticing millions. But, as always, it remains to be seen if this generosity brings academic achievement apart from just shaking things up and hiring fresh personnel. The most skilled, energetic administrator may not be able to motivate miscreants. The Washington, DC city school district where Broad has lately focused his attention is not KB Home or SunAmerica where Eli made his fortune as a hard-charging entrepreneur. Though he surely has access to leading educational pundits, all of the likely advice has been around for decades, and none has proven particularly effective. Nor is it evident how the $60 million effort to make educational insufficiency a national priority will invigorate a nation accustomed to a parade of "education presidents" and "education mayors." Thus far, Eli Broad certainly deserves an "A+" for effort but observers witnessing decades of comparable business-flavored advice might predict disappointment.

Such ego-boosting gestures can be far more wasteful than just disruptive meddling—they can needlessly risk lives. In 2007 the Woodrow Wilson National Fellowship Foundation, with major foundations backing, launched a $17 million-dollar program to entice graduates from top universities to teach in high poverty struggling schools. For $30,000 in educational assistance, graduates would be required to spend three years in troubled schools teaching math and science (Glod, December 20, 2007). These are risky, even life-threatening jobs (especially for young women), and zero evidence predicts that inexperienced teachers from elite schools will outshine replaced veterans. One can only wonder how much money it would take for well-paid foundation administrators to visit these hellish schools, let alone confront often violent students. These rookies are closer to cannon fodder to indulge some benefactor's whim than solutions to a probably intractable problem.

Non-Obvious Agendas

A particularly troubling feature of today's private foundation is a penchant for self-indulgence apart from "helping the children." At worst, efforts to improve education are just an excuse for less commendable aims, often little more than "photo ops." Observers of charities have long recognized that donor egotism, social climbing, publicity seeking, even personal greed can motivate ostensible altruism. Scores of corporations now rely on charitable tie-ins to sell merchandize. The GAP, for example, recently used the "RED" logo to indicate that some sale proceeds would help fight AIDS and HIV in Africa. The tactic now has its own name—cause marketing. In some cities charity may become handy vehicles to gain political access while elsewhere the goal is social prestige by favoring the "right" charitable cause so an *arriviste* gets his or her photo in the newspaper's "Society" section. Bountifulness also opens the door to lavish dinners and balls that provide superb business networking opportunities. And, as per John D. Rockefeller Sr., philanthropy can "rehabilitate" unsavory reputations.

The link between philanthropic programs and social standing is critical but difficult to untangle. Still, it is obvious that enhancing one's reputation steers assistance away from some paths and towards others. Few benefactors want their names associated with "controversial" initiatives and this can facilitate a gap between "what might work" versus "what might work *and* bring me mass media kudos." Not even "conservative" foundations might, for example, fund projects to restore corporal punishment, create schools heightening racial segregation, or similar "taboo" ventures. Even employment at a "controversial" foundation might forever tarnish a non-profit sector career, and no benefactor would risk angry protests at the annual black tie awards dinners. Ironically, though a foundation may boast of its "innovation" and "risk-taking," they gravitate to politically-safe nostrums, and these are not necessarily effective (if they were helpful, our woes would have vanished decades back).

This partially self-serving impetus certainly applies to "helping" struggling students. One conspicuous "mixed motives" example is the New York-based Robin Hood Foundation. Since its inception in 1988 to mid-2007 it has raised some $500 million and this money has been given to numerous New York City educational and child-welfare organizations. Beneficiaries include various charter schools, after-school enrichment programs, libraries, schools for potential drop outs, teacher training programs, literacy programs among (as of 2008) the 59 Robin Hood-assisted programs (*http://www.robinhood.org/programs/grant/. cfm?/portfolio=6*).

This is not scruffy folk in tights hiding in Sherwood Forest. It is a premier, high-profile foundation where elite members have enormous fun while doing good deeds to help the poor (thus the "Robin Hood" name). Super-rich Wall Street operatives or media celebrities like Tom Brokaw and movie star Gwyneth Paltrow are regulars. There was also money to be made, or at least until mid-2007 when unwelcome publicity from Congress altered matters. Until then much of its endowment was managed by Robin Hood's major donors, and while investments in the donor's own funds is prohibited, $14 million was paid for investment fees in 2005 (Donmoyer and Fitzgerald, 2007). This was legal, and Robin Hood fund managers secured above-market returns, but this helping the less fortunate also illustrated the old proverb that charity begins at home.

Robin Hood fund-raising events are million-dollar spectaculars, with thousands of guests, featuring such groups as the Rolling Stones, Aerosmith, and the Who. The June 2006 event raised $31.9 million and its over-the-top lavishness drew media attention galore. For $650,000 attendees "bought" 10 "power lunches" with high-profile corporate executives, lessons with champion surfer Kelly Slater, even a sea plane trip with the singer Jimmy Buffet. Beyonce, Jay-Z, and Jon Stewart provided entertainment. Naming rights for 30 school classrooms were auctioned off for $250,000 while larger facilities went for a million each (Beatty, 2006). At the 2007 benefit two attendees paid $400,000 each to sing along with

Aerosmith and with New England Patriot star quarterback Tom Brady egging on the audience, frantic bidding occurred for the opportunity to train with Mr. Brady, a flight in an L-39 jet trainer accompanied by an F-14 fighter pilot, a golf outing with Tiger Woods, and similar extravagant opportunities. More sedate bidders had the opportunity to have tea with the actress Gwyneth Paltrow and her husband, Chris Martin of Coldplay, who will also give a piano lesson. All told, $71 million was raised.

Whether this lavishness is or is not commendable is irrelevant; the millions certainly help somebody, including students, and, to repeat, "It can't hurt." But, consider the "logic" of this generosity. First, most Robin Hooders annually earn millions and without ample charitable deductions, the money just goes to taxes, so better get "something" for the money. Thus, the $400,000 Aerosmith sing-along probably only cost net $200,000 and donating that money to the Red Cross is probably less fun or memorable. Second, while all the money does, indeed, go to teachers, health-care workers, and others helping the poor, no assurances exist that allocations perform as claimed. Top business people attending the 2006 event—the head of J.P. Morgan Chase, the Chief Executive of Time Warner, and buy-out king Henry Kravis would *never* invest their own money on a scheme without due diligence, and, from all appearances, none is offered to Robin Hood benefactors other than all the money will be spent as claimed. Quarterback Tom Brady does not personally guarantee that the millions for classroom naming will go to the bottom line in improved test scores or any other academic return on investment. A guest familiar with the relevant educational research literature would probably conclude that this was all conspicuous consumption swathed with the all-too-familiar "it just might help."

Radically different is New York state-based Campaign for Fiscal Equity (CFE). Founded in 1993 by assorted educational advocates, it has received grants from major foundations including the Rockefeller and Schott Foundation. Whereas Robin Hood's merry men (and women) are moguls and celebrities, the CFE draws heavily from education professors, community activists, teachers' unions, and state politicians (*http:/www. cfequity.org/ns-board.html*). The CFE promotes the constitutional right of New York State's public school students to a sound basic education. In practice this means suing New York State to increase school funding dramatically and provide the underlying research justifying the huge increase. The constant litigation has brought in victories, then defeats, and then victories, and finally, in March 2006, matters were seemingly settled when the State's Appellate Division court ordered the state's operating education budget increases by between $4.7 and $5.63 billion plus adding $9.2 billion in capital outlays. On April 1, 2006 the legislature accepted the capital fund decision but not the operating budget funds. Litigation continues—a subsequent court order asked that the state consider $2 billion more for New York City and, in 2007, the Governor's budget included these huge increases but it is uncertain if they will ever be implemented.

This CFE-led battle is complicated. It is unclear whether a judge can force a legislature to spend money, and at least some legal experts insist that the doctrine of sovereign immunity permits the legislature to refuse the court order. Nor is it self-evident what a "right to education" means in terms of costs. More relevant here, however, is the exceptionally-dubious contention that massive spending increases will help. Convincing a judge does not make something true. Innumerable studies demonstrate a feeble link between outlays and outcomes, and New York is already exceedingly generous to its students. It is also undecided how this money will be used to improve education though CFE advocates insist that it will be spent "carefully." All and all, CFE seems to be wasting money.

A more hard-headed assessment is that CFE advocates are pursuing financial and ideological agendas. Robin Hood's Merry Gang just wants to have fun socializing or flying jets versus enriching Uncle Sam. CFE supporters are not multimillionaires so the tax advantages are less relevant. Instead, and this is speculative, they seek aggrandized power from dramatically expanding the educational workforce, from thousands of lowly unionized classroom assistants to dozens of university-based curriculum designers. Or, for contractors, architects, construction workers, and real estate experts, billions more in public capital expenditures (public buildings are notoriously expensive, and would probably be even more so with court-mandated funding). A cynic might also add that the extra billions are easily converted into legislative pork to impress voters and juice campaign contributions from potential beneficiaries. As Chapter 9 will show, much of today's educational reform is best understood as social welfare, and the CFE is the perfect "help the children" vehicle.

In the final analysis, burgeoning foundation assistance, much of it divorced from actually boosting educational attainment, encourages reforms galore, and while many certainly "help" (if only by spreading around wealth) in one form or another, the chaotic, uncoordinated often *ad hoc* approach foretells failure. Foundations, like all other educators, really do not have the magic bullet and the all-powerful IRS does not care. Countless foundation program officers continue to endorse Progressive education though the evidence of its deficiencies keeps mounting. Nor do donors seem angry if one nostrum after the next falls short—it is always possible to find some honoree for the annual banquet. And it goes without saying that few children of top foundation executives suffer the consequences of dreadful public education. Nor do foundations, unlike elected public officials, need worry that ill-conceived prescriptions will undermine a city's tax base or, as with the Ford Foundation's funding community control of New York's school, exacerbate racial strife. Futility can harmlessly be combined with risk and innovation. To be a tad vulgar, foundations can follow what has been labeled the pigeon approach to management: fly in, crap all over everything, and then fly out.

Conclusions

This has been a pessimistic tour, but, we believe, justifiably so. What underlies these failures is that, when all is said and done, educational excellence is not all that important. For countless reformers, radical, conservative, and middle-of-the-roader, the "it might help" is usually sufficient. Medical research is the exact opposite. Here failures—scores of dead bodies—are painfully real, and the "let's try it since it might help" occurs outside of science and, to be fair, it occasionally succeeds, just as "educational reform" occasionally succeeds.

But, as dreary as these conclusions may be, our search and destroy mission is hardly finished. The next two chapters closely examine two approaches that draw great enthusiasm from conservatives—namely accountability and school choice—and we shall see that these too are built on hope, not science.

7

Business-like Solutions to Academic Insufficiency

*Practical men, who believe themselves to be quite exempt from any intellectual influence,
are usually the slaves of some defunct economist.*
—John Maynard Keynes, *General Theory of Employment,* (1947 edition), Ch. 24.

Romantic progressives are not the only chronic, futility-inclined tinkerers. Self-proclaimed realists looking to business for guidance similarly substitute clichés and slogans for serious science. Only superficially do their "magic bullet" suggestions appear "realistic" compared to overblown romantic Progressive rhetoric. Tyack's (1995) overview of reforms describes America's long-standing but disappointing infatuation with technology as *the* solution for our woes. In 1841, for example, one pedagogical innovation was hailed as among the greatest benefactors of mankind—the blackboard (in some schools students wrote on sand using sticks). Many of today's taken-for-granted learning tools, available in every underachieving school—quick drying ink, crayons, cheap paper, and the like were all part of the heralded march toward educational excellence. In the 1920s Thomas E. Edison declared that motion pictures would replace textbooks and thus revolutionize education.

Naturally, as technology progressed, and automobiles replaced horse-drawn buggies, so did claims for imminent shortcut miracles to similarly upgrade learning. Just look at what works in commerce, write the check and test scores would skyrocket thanks to radio, riveting educational films, closed-circuit television, slide projectors, tape recorders, pre-recorded language lessons, hand calculators, video recorders, and, today, computers and the Internet. Unfortunately, technologically-minded reformers who look to business for inspiration rarely notice that academic performance has gone nowhere or declined as the marketplace grows ever more wondrous.

What Works in Innovative Businesses will Rescue Education?

The urge to apply "hard-headed" business practices to schools seems irrepressible. This mania was especially popular during the 1960s and 70s when "what was good for Texas Instrument would now invigorate K-12." Prestigious business schools gladly pitched in, and with client-seeking consulting firms and defense companies facing cutbacks as the Vietnam War wound down, the stage was, allegedly, set for educational breakthroughs. Three techniques then sweeping industry and business schools were particularly popular: Management by Objective (MBO); the planning, programming and budgeting system (PPBS); and zero-based budgeting (ZBB).

In MBO learning objectives were carefully quantified, and appropriate resources then assigned. In many ways MBO presages President Bush's ill-fated No Child Left Behind (NCLB) whereby in the name of account-ability state agencies stipulate test targets and schools strive to meet goals. Hopefully, as underperforming educational policies were junked thanks to not attaining MBO benchmarks, learning would soar. PPBS stressed incurred costs (including indirect ones) of existing programs and positing alternatives for reaching multiple short- and long-term goals. PPBS grew famous thanks to Robert McNamara's Department of Defense bean counters and other federal agencies soon followed. A PPBS-inclined educator might, for example, mull over multiple ways to teach mathematics, price each one (including, say, hand calculator thievery, stocking batteries, lost instructional manuals, annual upgrade costs, and required paperwork for each task) and then choose cost-effective routes. ZBB required every unit to annually justify its budget versus unchallenged incremental expansion. Now, advocates of once sacrosanct extracurricular programs would plead cases before skeptical school boards, and do so with hard figures regarding precise educational benefits, not with the usual "football is just our honored tradition."

All these rescues fell short, and even once-impassioned government agency advocates jumped ship. Corporations likewise grew uneasy with faddish bean-counting strategies to surmount substandard products or inept marketing. Schools, as one might predict, found profit-based tech-nocratic schemes inappropriate or were overwhelmed by mind-numbing paperwork. One California school district formulated fifty-eight separate mathematics-related objectives for its primary schools. Teachers wrestling with PPBS once described the paperwork as "Mickey Mouse in triplicate," and the exodus from this Promised Land was swift (Tyack, 1995, 197).

The disappointments were easily foreseeable. Applying trendy cures often imposed distracting opportunity costs—ZBB and the like cannot be mastered overnight and teachers are not CPAs with sufficient time for complicated paperwork. Nor were "scientific" solutions always legal. State requirements forbid shuttering bungling math departments or financially-starving terrible schools. Of the utmost importance, technocrats fixated on accounting rules sidestepped contentious school-related politics. Education policy cannot be dictated as one might manage a corporation. Parents voting on school boards have more on their minds than share price, and schools must satisfy multiple, often conflicting aims, not just pay dividends. Educational goals often defy quantification and are more psychological than tangible. Self-esteem champions are seldom swayed by cost-benefit analysis, and though one might document that the beloved but senile Mr. Rogers deserves termination to maximize budgetary aims, firing can be a bureaucratic and emotional nightmare. In sum, the business and education parallel is inappropriate.

Private Contracting

Nevertheless, hope springs eternal and the next "business-like" teacher-proof nostrum from the 1960s and 1970s was for-profit performance contracting. Here private firms announced learning targets, and were paid only for success. As with many of today's "business-like" reforms, the exact pathway to success was unspecified—"just do it." This approach was first tried in Texarkana, Arkansas where Dorsett Educational System agreed to bring slow learners up to speed on fundamentals (Tyack, 1995). In Dorsett's well-furnished Learning Center supervised by "instructional managers" (not "old-fashioned" teachers), each pupil had their own filmstrip and record, put on a headset, logged in to Dorsett's computer-like teaching machines, and if they mastered the day's lesson, the reward was ten Green Stamps. Feedback was immediate via the technology, and learning proceeded as if schools were automated assembly lines. Those advancing a grade level in math or reading received a transistor radio. The year's most accomplished student won a portable TV. In keeping with the then trendy vocabulary, the entire endeavor was a "learning system."

Other firms quickly joined the crusade, and industrial mass production was expanded to music, art, and physical education. The Nixon administration's Office of Economic Opportunity had thirty-one firms compete for contracts in eighteen selected school districts. Six won and agreed to forego compensation unless test scores improved by an entire year. Under Title 1 (a program assisting low-income students) twenty additional performance contracts were awarded, all with the by now familiar material incentives, programmable teaching machines, individual diagnoses, and small armies of technocratic supervisors. The industrial revolution had, seemingly, arrived at America's schools.

Grand promises aside, troubles quickly appeared though, to be fair, the government- mandated incentive structure hindered profits, and one participating firm soon went bankrupt (see Gramlich and Koshel, 1975 for these tribulations). Teachers and administrators repeatedly objected to the mechanical style of learning with its craven bribery, and occasional litigation over the abdication of public responsibility to a private firm killed off demonstration projects. Critics further insisted that progress was illusionary—teaching the test—and the results were Hawthorne effects resulting from all the razzle-dazzle. Measuring progress in complicated environments of diffused responsibility was also tricky, as was reaching a consensus on exact learning objectives. Foreshadowing NCLB, the produce-or-don't-get-paid approach promoted cheating—actual test items would appear in practice sessions.

The *coup de grâce* was that the contract system failed to boost learning vis-à-vis traditional classrooms. Government payments over and above normal education budgets brought careful auditing by both Washington and private organizations like Rand and the Battelle Memorial Institute, and the news was bad. Comparative studies found that performance contracting classes did less well than comparable classes relying on traditional pedagogy. By 1975 this "sure-fire" approach to uplift disadvantaged children via technology and cutting-edge business expertise ceased entirely.

A particularly revealing (though now long-forgotten) business-like reform from the 1980s into the 90s was Outcomes Based Education (OBE). The pattern here, yet one more time, foretells today's NCLB accountability-driven tribulations, including how educators can subvert "business-like" schemes. As usual, the impetus was widespread demands that officials "do something" about sorrowful academic performance. Though this initial "something" was enhanced traditional academic achievement, including hard-nosed tests to assess progress towards specific learning targets, the reform was soon transformed into something quite the opposite. Proficiency in mathematics, science, and literature soon gave way to assessments of "soft" accomplishments stressing feelings and social views. Thus, Johnny might be illiterate, but he could shine as a responsible family member or demonstrate positive strategies for his mental and social well-being. The politics of OBE could also be exasperating—when Pennsylvania adopted OBE in 1992 the state board of education listed some fifty-five desired learning outcomes but one month after this listing, the state legislature abolished it, and a year later a reduced set of requirements were adopted. These goals, especially since many are barely academic, were magnets for political turmoil.

OBE's popularity was brief, and opposition occurred nearly across the ideological spectrum. Hard-headed reformers objected to substituting vacuous aims for required traditional courses or eliminating guidance on how these aims were to be accomplished. OBE also seemed to be yet one more invitation to dumb-down education by politicizing standards. Still, OBE did not die instantly, and schools in some states embraced it despite dreadful outcomes elsewhere (Coulson, 1999, 117-19).

Perhaps there is just something seductive about magic bullet reforms depicted by acronyms and, sure enough, in 2007/8 the impulse resurfaced in Pittsburgh: Total Quality Management (TQM), Toyota's famous manufacturing method to build defect-free cars (Sostek, 2008). Central is continuous improvement towards specific goals via meticulous attention to correcting defects as they occur. In one first-grade classroom children keep personal binders showing learning progress so results can be compared week-to-week and pupils feel distraught if their "quality" lags behind the classroom norm. The local school district, aping *au courant* manufacturers, had mission statements and balanced scorecards. The American Society for Quality actually endorsed this approach and schools are eligible for its Malcolm Baldrige National Quality Award. Though test scores are up in Cedar Rapids, Iowa where TQM was implemented in 2004, Larry Cuban, the Stanford Professor of Education and long-time observer of educational reform, has his doubts and compares it to a Botox-like cosmetic gimmick.

Merit Pay Will Do It

Applying "sound" business principles to public education hardly ends with 1960-ish systems analysis and similar shortcuts. Tyack (1995, 204-9) describes now-forgotten failed experiments with merit pay for teachers, a panacea that yet again attracts widespread attention. In fact, this seductive idea has endured on the reform circuit, often adopted then dropped or just reduced to tiny salary differences (also see Hanushek, 1994, 95-9). Tellingly, a 2008 *Time* story quoted the Director of Vanderbilt's National

Center on Performance Incentives saying that there is little research on what makes for a successful merit pay system but, nevertheless, several factors *seem* critical (italics added, Wallis, 2008).

Nonetheless, since few object to handing out more money, the merit pay idea seems an irresistible force of nature. According to one website (*www.edwebproject.org*) some 46 states permitted some form of merit pay in 1986, so it is difficult to argue that adopting this policy reversed America's educational woes. In 2006 the Bush administration instituted a $99 million a year program to assist school districts that tied pay to performance. In 2007 Texas allocated $100 million to its Texas Educator Excellence Grant program targeting 1,148 schools. Houston, Texas thanks to a $3.2 million dollar grant from the Broad Foundation also had its own bonus plan supplementing the state-wide plan, and in January 30th, 2008, some 10,600 of the district's 14,000 school-based employed got some cash. Payments averaged $2,000 with the highest being $7,865 (Keller, 2008).

Though defenders portray this fix as "obvious," matters can be quite complicated and details may have little to do with financial incentives. Dumbed-down tests, the demographic mix of students, union rules, and administrative transparency can all shape merit pay impact. The causal links in this relationship may not be as commonly portrayed: motivated, talented teachers seek out smart students, many of whom live in affluent communities paying above average salaries, so the good-pay-leads-to-good-results relationships are spurious—good students brings higher pay. Perhaps the only indisputable case for merit pay concerns collegiate sports where winning records can be parlayed into multimillion-dollar compensation packages.

Equally relevant, few who enter teaching seek riches, so a few thousand dollars more is the wrong carrot. Surveys of teachers find that teachers primarily justify their professional choices with psychic—not financial—benefits, for example, job satisfaction or wanting to help children (summarized in Coulson, 1999, 139). Ample vacations and relatively short workdays are also attractive lures, and many competent teachers might change jobs or flee the profession altogether if excessively pressured to spend more time helping students. Nonetheless, the oft-made "scientific" justifications—people respond to incentives and education is no different—virtually guarantees endless rediscovery of this alluring wonder drug. Nervous office holders conceivably possess a hidden file folder labeled "Quixotic Good-Sounding Reforms Proposals for Emergency Use."

The script is totally predicable: school critics demand a salary-based teaching meritocracy ("it works perfectly in business"), and the teachers (and unions) justifiably resist by insisting that professional certification and tenure review adequately (though not entirely) culls out incompetence, unequal pay breeds morale-destroying strife, administrative judgments will be capricious, selective rewards makes progress a zero-sum game, evaluations involve excessive paperwork, and, most persuasively, a few extra dollars per week will scarcely alter behavior, especially when most teachers are already doing their best under trying circumstances. There are also opportunity costs since creating an incentive system satisfactory to all parties requires extensive negotiations and periodic adjustments, time perhaps better spent on lesson preparation or tutoring students.

The merit pay enterprise complexity was illustrated when Denver, CO adopted, after *seven* years of negotiations between the union, teachers, and public officials, the Professional Compensation or ProComp plan (Wallis, 2008). Experts on incentive plans even said if this failed in Denver, incentives would never work elsewhere. The arrangement offered nine ways a teacher could increase income that in ways that mimic factory piecework, and for rather modest amounts in today's economy. However, by the beginning of the 2008/9 school year the Denver plan was in shambles and a strike loomed. Some teachers even staged sick-outs and distributed flyers to parents denouncing the system (Simon, 2008). The Houston, Texas, plan mentioned earlier was likewise ensnarled in endless negotiations, disputes, and school resources had to be redirected to keeping everybody informed. Nevertheless, despite the exertion, many Houston teachers insisted that it made no difference, and while the extra cash was welcome, the system's complexity left many teachers in the dark regarding just how rewards were calculated (Keller, 2008).

The Milken Family Foundation has since 1999 also funded merit pay schemes. Their Teacher Advancement Program (TAP) as of early 2008 were used in 180 schools in 14 states (the US Department of Education has also contributed another $80 million to TAP). So far, the TAP results seem disappointing, though, as is customary, glimmers of hope can be found. In particular, a recent study using various statistical controls to hold constant student traits such as poverty found that TAP helps in elementary schools but middle and high school students in TAP lag behind—sometimes substantially—their peers with non-TAP teachers (Keller, 2008). One Missouri study involving some 500 schools over a nine-year period reported that its incentive-based program brought small grains in math but no progress in reading. Merit pay can also bring unintended consequences—in one North Carolina experiment teachers disproportionately left low-performing black schools since it was more difficult to receive bonuses there (Honawar, March 12, 2008). More generally, the Vanderbilt University conference at which these disappointing TAP results were presented included other similar studies of incentives, and the overall verdict was the by now familiar, "occasionally works, but rarely, and we really don't understand much about the entire enterprise" (Honawar, 2008).

Unfortunately, it almost goes without saying that where merit is defined solely by test scores, cheating will go up or teachers will take only assignments guaranteed to make the salary-enhancing numbers. And, as we repeatedly stress, education is one of the few endeavors where those receiving rewards are the same people certifying progress (especially where the entire school shared the bonuses). That an outsider might never know how slight tinkering with the curve can alter outcomes cautions further skepticism. To repeat, no hard evidence exists that incorrigible sloth can be reversed by bribing teachers, at least within permissible monetary ranges. Given what teachers themselves say about personal motivation, the most effective incentive might be to fill classrooms with students dying to learn!

Edison Schools

Beliefs that "business-style" pay-only-for-good-outcomes policies can work wonders are, apparently, irrepressible. The failed contracting out experiments of the 1970s and 1980s soon reappeared in the 1990s with Edison Schools. Surely, yet one more time it was reasoned, making a buck will conquer once-intractable obstacles. Beginning in 1992 the for-profit Edison schools volunteered to run often hopeless appearing schools, guaranteeing upbeat outcomes for less money, and for countless exasperated administrators, Edison seemed the savior. As an added incentive, disappointments could now be blamed on Edison, not bumbling public officials. Edison offered a persuasive pitch: longer school days and school year, extensive staff development, high levels of parent and community participation, national-based financial and pedagogical support plus its unique rigorous, research-based, technologically-enhanced curriculum. Classes were offered in character and ethics while instruction reflected multiple pedagogical approaches. Its Web site (*www.edisonschools.com*) boasted of combining the classic liberal arts tradition with skills needed for the twenty-first century, up-to-date vocational training, and relentless evaluation for students and school.

By 2006-07 Edison's schools had enrolled some 285,000 students in nineteen states and Washington, DC, and had even expanded to the U.K. (about half of these schools were charters while the rest were partnerships with only partial control). Judged by its own data, Edison appeared to produce an authentic miracle. For example, Edison students had averaged 7.7 percent gains on standard tests in one year while averaging 12.3 percent over two years. In Charleston, SC, Edison students performed well in mathematics tests, even better than non-Edison students in the district and the state. Meanwhile, those in its Newton program made truly spectacular gains in both reading and math during the 2004/05 school years.

Alas, if one prospers by promised outcomes, one dies by market failures, and Edison has faced storms of criticisms. Its financial practices have drawn SEC rebuke, its stock has declined sharply and it has lost millions. Still, perhaps reflecting America's growing desperation for quick cures, Edison schools often expanded, but many participating school districts have also ended agreements. Terminations often reflected substantial cost overruns. Elsewhere tribulations resulted from cash shortages, for example, in Philadelphia during 2002 a few days before classes were to begin, Edison sold off its modern equipment and textbooks to avoid bankruptcy (students were requested to work an hour a day without pay in school offices). In other school districts Edison schools performed so dreadfully on state-mandated exams that even desperate public officials accustomed to failure reasoned that even they could do better (Texas Freedom Network 2004-6).

Edison's record in Philadelphia has been especially dismal. In 2008 the city "de- privatized" six schools that had been given over to private firms and issued warnings to twenty other schools also under private control. Of the six schools shifted back to public control, four were Edison schools (Richburg, 2008). Twelve of the other schools put on one-year probation are also Edison schools, so only four of the initial twenty will continue on. These warnings followed a Rand Report that found that Edison schools generally did no better than public schools and, significantly, the threat of Edison acquiring public schools did not push public schools to improve.

More telling, ample non-Edison sponsored research has raised serious doubts about this putative marvel. Note well: assessments often rest on complicated methodological choices and occasional incomplete data but *none* confirm Edison's self-reported triumphs. An American Federation of Teachers (an Edison opponent) report found that Edison schools generally lagged behind comparable public schools with achievements notably worse for predominantly African-American schools (Nelson and Van Meter, 2003). Perhaps the most systematic, meticulous, and probably unbiased study of Edison's claims was offered by Miron and Brooks (2000) in their examination of ten schools over four years. These are complex findings that vary between types of standards and institutions, but the overall conclusion is that Edison schools fail to deliver the promised elixir. Edison students often advance along with others at their grade, but typically at a slower pace. Miron and Brooks categorize Edison's accomplishments as "mixed," and this judgment is typical of many other careful empirical studies.

One last item on this "private enterprise will do it" approach concerns a possible harbinger of future policy. Beginning in 2007 enrollments in twenty-seven largely-black, underperforming schools Washington, DC had so drastically fallen that eliminating them seemed compelling. A major budget shortfall also encouraged closings. Unfortunately for Chancellor Rhee, a furious "save our schools" campaign was launched with considerable local political backing. To escape the predicament, Rhee suggested that the appalling schools be turned over to private operators, even a university, who had taken on similar salvage tasks elsewhere. Though experts dismissed this stratagem as having a poor track record, the Chancellor nevertheless insisted that outsider management would "bring in their best practices, structures, curricula and themes" (Haynes, February 26, 2008). What makes this episode out of the ordinary is how it reverses the customary nationalization pattern. Now, rather than government taking over failing private business to rescue jobs, the government sells off government-run disasters to private firms to placate consumers, a tactic that can only delay the Grim Reaper. Perhaps a firm called "National School Liquidators" will arise to handle the unpleasant tasks, and one can only guess the financial incentives necessary to entice private firms to shoulder these politically-unpopular responsibilities.

New York City's Embrace of "Business-like" Solutions

Setting clear goals and then holding educators responsible with a mixture of carrots and sticks, is one of the most pervasive themes in the "business" approach to educational reform. Nowhere has this been pushed harder than in New York City under Mayor Michael Bloomberg and his School Chancellor, Joel Klein, and while New York City tribulations may be unique, they offer lessons to even the smallest rural school district. In a nutshell, though the City's advocates often insist otherwise, New York City's experiences show, yet one more time, that learning cannot be imparted top-down no matter how strong the threats or material incentives. This tale also illustrates the problems that arise when reformers ignore history.

In 2007 New York City Mayor Michael Bloomberg, having promised to turn around the City's troubled schools, rediscovered business-like approaches to education (that Bloomberg was wildly successful in business may explain this infatuation). Merit pay was one of the earliest nostrums. In Bloomberg's plan teachers in some 200 of the cities "high need" schools (read struggling poor black and Hispanic students) will be eligible for some $20 million in bonuses, or up to $3,000 per teacher, if they satisfy certain test score performance criteria (eligible schools would increase to 400 in the program's second year). Some 86 percent of the qualified schools quickly agreed to participate. The $20 million funding came from private sources, and the plan's originator said that if $3,000 maximum per teacher were insufficient, more could be raised. Unlike previous merit-based plans rewarding individuals, schools themselves receive the money, and it is then disbursed by a special four-person committee to individual union members, either equally or just to high performers (Gootman, October 17, 2007).

According to the Mayor and his school chancellor, this merit pay scheme was an "historic and unique" solution (Gootman, October 18, 2007). A glowing *New York Times* editorial welcomed the proposal as "…a good first step toward the goal of attracting teachers to the most challenging schools—and keeping them there" (*New York Times,* October 20, 2007). The *Times* then called for additional steps, namely reducing class size and augmented support services to sustain progress. Tellingly, the *Times* forgot to mention that past research demonstrates: (1) few teachers can be financially lured to dangerous underachieving schools; (2) money-minded teachers are better advised to take safe, well-paying suburban jobs; (3) reducing class size is unrelated to learning; and (4) the city's schools already overflow with social services, and if these did boost learning, learning would have skyrocketed as social workers and counselors multiplied.

A skeptic might predict that this incentive plan would disproportion-ately attract teachers approaching retirement given that bonuses would raise future pensions and pensions are calculated according to the final four years of employment (see Wolf, 2007 on this gaming). Though unions traditionally oppose merit-based pay, they embraced the Mayor's plan since substantial financial rewards were available only to union members. And the cost of securing union support was substantial, namely it lowered retirement age by ten years and boosted city pension contributions, while protecting job security. That this formula would encourage an exodus of experienced teachers to be replaced by rookies was left unstated. Likewise unsaid was since only union members could receive bonuses so incentive was created for union membership, and that unions typically hindered the administrative flexibility sought by reformers like Bloomberg and Klein.

The New York City "business-like" financial incentive plan was also extended to students so that fourth graders earned bonuses by passing math and reading tests. This could be as much as $50 per student, a pittance compared to the $3,000 the classroom teacher might "win" by improving test results. As of early 2008, some half a million dollars in prize money (all from private donations) has been awarded to 5,237 students in 58 schools. Though the lure has seemingly pushed students to master the exams, the long-term impact is unclear (Medina, March 5, 2008). One overview of this tactic found little reason for optimism though, as is typical with heralded panaceas, glimmers of hope abound (Singer-Vine, 2008). Even here, however, limits on research design and sorting out multiple causal factors counsel caution. Uplifting the most troubled students via cash bribery may be especially daunting. A study of a New York City program targeting poor black and Hispanic students found that when cash was on the table, the proportion of students passing AP courses actually declined compared to pre-bribery conditions (Gonen, August 20, 2008). Again, limits on cognitive ability and insufficient motivation cannot be overcome, even with generous bribes.

Critics argue, probably correctly, that linking learning to instant payoffs can only undermine long-term appreciation for education ("why learn if I'm no longer paid?"). This tactic also permits an easy escape from confronting harsh reality since it can always be argued that the bribery was too small or should consist of other incentives. Recall the problems of merit pay for teachers—thousands of hours haggling over details versus actually teaching children. A recently-proposed Washington, DC cash incentive plan relies on piecework—students can get paid for regular attendance, handing in work on time, displaying manners, and getting good grades (Haynes and Birnbaum, August 22, 2008). Alas, nobody seems to worry about adding paperwork to a school system that is barely able to perform its minimal responsibilities.

Nor is NYC's Mayor worried about schools—not parents—putting unrestricted cash into the hands of immature youngsters. These sums, around \$35 to \$40, may also grow if more is required to motivate lag-gards. Given that beneficiaries live in neighborhoods overflowing with dangerous temptations, let alone what can be purchased illegally, the prizes may eventually promote risky behavior or distractions like yet more video games. Depositing funds in a bank account with restric-tions may be safer, but pointless if only immediate gratification works. Ironically, some schools avoid the cash problem by awarding meals at McDonald's or pizza parties, just what increasingly-tubby American youngsters need.

Adding Accountability to the Reform Menu

Accountability is a powerfully-seductive but quite elementary idea: set tough standards, measure performance against targets, publicly post results, and then reward those meeting the standard. Unlike PPBS or MBO, however, accountability never rises above being a catchphrase and this fuzziness may help explain the allure. Capitalist greed is central—if you want the sales division to sell more cars, push them by rewarding the stars and if employees fall short, demote or fire them. At least super-ficially, accountability appears to be a no-brainer.

Surprisingly, its current widespread application to education is rela-tively recent. The first inkling appeared in the 1960s, but it was not until the 1990s that the idea gained prominence as states mandated testing and posted outcomes (see Foundation for Education Reform & Accountability, 2007 for a snapshot history). Perhaps the rise of extensive computerized K-12 testing facilitated this hold-their-feet-to-the-fire approach. The key watershed event was President Bush's NCLB that embodied account-ability as *the* solution for our national tribulations, and this multibillion dollar example was soon widely emulated. Now, at long last, the door to educational paradise was in sight, or so it seemed, and one political leader after the next joined the accountability stampede.

New York City's School Chancellor Joel Kline is one such reformer seemingly obsessed with accountability. Ironically, Klein is *not* a busi-nessman. He is an aggressive lawyer notable as the Justice Department Attorney who sought antitrust action against Microsoft, the firm that enriched thousands of its employees via accountability. All the same, his attempt to break up Microsoft aside, he insists that today's school system is anti-accountability thanks to lifetime tenure, lock-step pay, and seniority (Klein, 2007). He also asserts, sans *any* empirical evidence, that many of New York City's teachers don't try hard, and thus need a strong push. And like past incentive advocates, he thinks that teachers can be pressured to push harder for a few dollars per week after state and local taxes (a $3,000 annual bonus, the scheme's jackpot, is, after taxes, slightly more than a dollar per hour). Klein explicitly likens his plan to corporate stock options—the bigger the corporate gain, the higher the stock price, the greater the personal wealth (just like at Microsoft).

Accountable for "Just Doing It"

While accountability is abstractly alluring, the principle itself says nothing about *how* newly inspired teachers are to push pupils to greater accomplishment. It is thus a mandate lacking *any* implementing directions. Absent instructions, all the incentives and penalties, no matter how munificent or draconian, may just be empty rhetoric. Teachers and administrators are on their own, making it up as they go along, and hoping for the best, and it is uncertain whether a successful teacher can pass on what succeeds other than informally advise coworkers. Furthermore, nobody, especially those giving the marching orders, wants to confront this essential missing information, hardly a surprise since *nobody* really knows what produces the desired outcomes. It is just far more enticing to quarrel endlessly about administrative minutia over rewards and punishments as if "everybody" knows that malingering teachers possess magic bullets to boost performance.

The lack of specifics—what the newly cash-hungry teacher must do, exactly—is typically conveniently obscured by mountains of high-sounding verbiage. It is endless trial-and-error pedagogy of the most discouraging type, and would be as if a cookbook extolled pot roast, depicted its history and how it delights the palette without providing a single clue on cooking it. Consider, for example, the New York City Department of Education (DOE) website's accountability decree supplied years after NCLB hailed this panacea. The DOE boasts of giving schools increased autonomy, flexibility, and resources to improve the academic outcomes of all students. Furthermore, DOE will now provide schools with "an unprecedented" amount of information about student achievement plus "…intensively training educators and parents to use this information to accelerate student learning." Schools will be rewarded for their accomplishment, every student's progress will be tracked, high standards will be enforced, and every school will receive a Quality Review. To insure that no teacher is left behind, DOE will provide schools with new accountability tools to accelerate student learning. Again: *nothing* is said how teachers, many of whom are assumed to be sleep-walkers, are to accomplish the newly-demanded, and exceedingly-tough, mission.

Tellingly, the recent data-laden 216-page assessment of account-ability-driven NCLB mentions that much is being done to help under-performing schools, but it is impossible to even guess what this might entail concretely (Le Flock et al, 2007, xxvii). We are told, for example, that troubled schools were (somehow) improving curriculum, involving state and district officials in planning, better aligning curriculum with tests (i.e., teaching the test), implementing more regular testing (practice test-taking), increasing time spent on mathematics and reading (again teaching the test), even adding extra hours to the school day. Signifi-cantly, 80 percent of the surveyed K-12 teachers found that the NCLB tests provided useful pedagogical feedback. To be frank, though excep-tions certainly must exist, the technique that NCLB offers to teachers is to teach the test, and while this approach does impart knowledge, it is a far cry from supplying an effective teaching repertoire. To continue our food preparation analogy, this is the equivalent of telling the cook "use good ingredients" without any indication of what to buy.

The silence regarding useful teaching tools is profound given that scarcely anything on today's pedagogical agenda even approximates a sure-fire improvement recipe. The opposite is true: the existing stockpile of tips, including what the schools of education expertly advise, have pretty much done as much as they can though, like diet books, alleged "cures" endlessly proliferate. Ironically, as we saw in examining the professionally-certified literature on upping motivation, many histori-cally-proven remedies for sloth, e.g., shame and humiliation, are now expressly forbidden. A fantasy element informs this "just do it" thinking, something akin to conspiratorial claims that auto manufactures possess a secret cheap pill that with a little water replaces gasoline. What account-ability fans are really saying is, "try harder and *you*—not *me*—figure out what works." And while a small number of sleep-walking teachers may wander the hallways, no evidence exists that suddenly waking them up will transform students into outstanding young scholars. Few teachers are heroic figures, and even a miracle worker may only get a "D" student to do "C" work. The reverse is more plausible—intractable students make for zombie teachers, not the other way around.

Today's obsession with accountability also neglects non-material in-centives, and these can be vital even in economically cutthroat settings. Moreover, this noneconomic menu is probably far more relevant in edu-cation than any other field given multiple options in today's economy. This is not just rewarding star teachers with plaques or banquets (though these may help). Inner satisfaction—feeling good about oneself for a job well-done—can far outshine a dollar per hour extra. The experience of having a former student express profound gratitude, a "you changed my life" note, can keep the fires burning for years. Experienced teachers relish this feedback, but school chancellors and frantic mayors are, unfortunately, clueless about this motivation while today's job qualification tests are not geared to attract such inner-motivated teachers. Bloomberg and Klein may not even understand this non-monetary passion given their personal lucrative vocational choices. Ironically, transforming teaching into an economic piecework enterprise may do more harm than good by attracting only those motivated by money while discouraging those inspired by imparting knowledge.

The Inappropriate Education Accountability and Business Parallel

Though "accountability" is explicitly linked to America's business triumphs, a little thought shows that business and educational accountability share only common superficial vocabulary. Applying tools from the former to the latter is done reflexively, with scant research on transferability and also misperceives business. It is a cartoon-like vision, perhaps predictable since its adherents typically lack business acumen or, for those who know better like Mayor Bloomberg (founder of the highly lucrative Bloomberg Media), the manic urge to "do something and do it now" clouds judgment.

First, experienced bosses know you cannot endlessly squeeze employees, and to push beyond practical boundaries risks disaster. GM would be insane to insist that its dealers regain the 25 percent lost market share, or else! Too much pressure, even to rescue schools from impending catastrophes, might instigate mass departures, not new-found vigor. Much of the rhetoric is flippant grandstanding, and few experienced multibillion-dollar firms would launch a similar high-pressure incentive plan without additional research, notably, assessing staff potential, determining the most alluring incentives, or evaluating the full ramifications of chosen inducements. When Domino's Pizza tried free pizzas unless delivered in 30 minutes or less, it forgot about rewarding speed-demon drivers prone to expensive, litigation-generating accidents to save $6 on a pizza. Business lore abounds of similar tales of incentive programs gone awry.

Moreover, local labor conditions dictate recruit quality, at what salary, and companies routinely settle for subpar workers since stars capable of thriving under accountability would be too expensive, too demanding, and the extra productivity is thus cost *in*effective. During the Great Depression of the 1930s New York City and elsewhere could lure talented people unable to find private sector employment; today, schools must compete for skilled employees, and to be frank, no amount of bonus pay might be able to transform the perfectly adequate into stars. Denver's teacher incentive plan previously mentioned would pay an extra $1,067 (about $800 after taxes) per year to work in a "tough school." How many teachers would shoulder this potentially dangerous task for an extra $22 per week?

To appreciate the problem of applying incentives in education, compare teachers struggling with lethargic students (bonus plan targets) to commission salespeople who also must produce or starve. What happens when American Widget (AW) turns the screws on its sales force and despite more and more enticements to jump-start progress, sales move up only slightly? At some point, this strategy might be prudently abandoned since compensation costs mount but profit is not commensurate. Funds might now be reallocated to producing better widgets so as to enhance sales or widgets could be discounted to increase revenue via larger volume among other tactics. But, if executives thought like accountability-obsessed educators, and the screws were tightened even further on the sales force, and no other option perused, the likely outcome would be cheating, for example, widgets would be "sold" to customers unable to pay for them (apparent only after the commission were paid) or pressured sales people would just misrepresent the widget's virtues and let the lawyers handle the litigation.

If American Widget still experienced zero success, its Chief Financial Officer (CFO) might recommend abandoning the widget division and take the tax write offs. Or, as sometimes occurs with unproductive enterprises, the widget division could be spun off to its employees, sold to outside investors, or just dismantled for scrap. If the firm was still fixated on widgets, production could be out-sourced to China and sold only by Internet sans any sales force.

The Failed Application of Accountability to New York City Schools

Imagine a mayor actually behaving as a hard-headed CEO armed with traditional business-like powers. Faced with the city's chronically underperforming but increasingly-costly school system, the mayor calls a press conference to announce a quintessential business solution—sell underperforming assets and invest the saved money more productively. Horrible schools will be closed and the buildings auctioned off to real estate developers, displaced students and teachers will be offered transfers to the cost-effective Mexican Division (the "Learn in Cancun Program") while terminated teachers will receive a substantial one-time severance package. Below current market price office space, old furniture and surplus equipment will be sold to Stanley Kaplan, the Catholic Church, Edison Schools, the local teachers' union, among others. Nonessential staff—diversity specialists, program developers, AIDS educators, coaches, mentors, various bureaucratic coordinators—will be cut to the bone or eliminated altogether. This, the mayor, boasts, will save the city millions without hurting education since these de-invested assets were never profitable or essential to learning.

Needless to say, almost *nothing* in this business scenario can be applied to education. School administrators cannot fire underperforming students, entice them to Cancun, or even threaten classes taught by TV since miscreants don't care anyway. Educational assets are incredibly illiquid. Administrators can rarely shift funds from wasteful endeavors to those with demonstrably superior payoffs, e.g., quality health care for lousy but chronically-sick students, since educational functions are state mandated. If business and education were run according to the same laws, Congress might, Soviet-style, force domestic widget firms to produce them regardless of market demand or cost. All and all, while an executive who is judged by performance enjoys multiple proven options, and must choose the best, educators possess an exceptionally-limited array of alternatives, and it is no wonder that teacher cash incentives becomes *the* panaceas.

But, draconian "shut it down" business-like solutions aside, let us assume that the AW CEO is increasingly under the gun from angry stockholders since profits are falling and executive pay is rising. The stockholders' meeting draws closer and dissidents are growing bolder, so the panicked CEO might decide (among several possibilities) to book next year's expected revenue in the current year but not the associated manufacturing costs from future sales, and hope nobody notices. Here, alas, the business and education parallels are closer—just manipulate the books to show fictitious gains or hide losses. In fact, deviousness is far easier in education given the absence of General Accepted Accounting Principles (GAAP), SEC regulation, and multiple other financial strictures, some of which impose criminal penalties for malfeasance on business people. Nor are there education "stockholders" (i.e., parents) glued to their stock tickers wondering about collapsing stock prices or what happened to the quarterly dividend. We have already touched on various "make the numbers" tricks of the education trade but accountability brings its own special duplicity.

Cooking Books

New York City's embrace of accountability unfortunately illustrates how unrealistic pressure encourages dishonesty. Given the public's hunger for good news and unwillingness to scrutinize upbeat outcomes closely, such deceit is remarkably easy. Here's the recipe. First, devise a seemingly easy to understand rating system for schools, the well-known A to F scale. Second, just as any teacher might do, calculate grades according to multiple performance criteria. In school assignments this is so much for effort, so much or originality and so on. NYC's Department of Education formula initially gave 55 percent to improvement, 30 percent to actual test performance and 15 percent to school "environmental" factors such as attendance plus various surveys of teachers and parents (there is also an entirely discretionary fudge factor, "additional credit"). Also categorize schools according to student body ethnic composition and poverty level—called "peer horizon"—to permit additional creative comparisons. Third, wrap the final grade in statistical mumbo jumbo to befuddle or intimidate outsiders from inquiring how the educational sausages were made. Fourth, define the measure of success by bottom-up progress, not the gains made by the top, or for that matter, any absolute standard of proficiency. Finally, in what guarantees media attention, close "underperforming" schools to demonstrate that education is taken "seriously" and losers, just like in business, will get the ax.

Opportunities for deception abounded. To begin with, the "closed" schools are not shut since New York City desperately needs the classroom space and truly boarding up a building invites quick physical deterioration (many maintenance costs are unavoidable and abandoned schools invite vandalism). The old school is merely "reorganized" and quickly reappears under a new (often more alluring) name. Second, and most critical, *no* teacher becomes unemployed. According to the local UFT contract, half of the teachers in the old school must be rehired for the new one, and those not rehired must search for positions elsewhere in the system all the while at full pay (UFT teachers' assistants also enjoy considerable job protection). No money is saved, no inept teacher is sent walking; at most, local parents are needlessly panicked and the Chancellor garners some publicity for being "tough." Interestingly, these duplicitous elements are hardly hidden but this has not stopped this odd quest for "progress."

Note that there is absolutely nothing, *nothing* in this NYC scheme about how particular students perform. Nor is there anything whatsoever about a teacher transforming a student's life, outcomes that certainly deserve praise. Scores are *for schools, not students*, and concerned progress from 2006 to 2007. Targeting cohorts, not individuals, is almost an invitation to subterfuge since cohort composition can be malleable, that is, recruit a few bright students, subtract a few less able, reclassify a few malingerers as "disabled" so as to excuse them from testing, and suddenly, as if a teaching miracle transpired, scores are up. In fact, judiciously sprinkling a few academic stars around a district is akin to add a bit of sherry to an otherwise dull soup to provide some zest. Cohort-based accountability also assumes that the student population remains stable, a dubious presumption in today's mobile society, especially in many inner-city schools where families regularly relocate. Even without students changing schools, the normal fluidity of city life makes comparisons tricky—even a shift of a few city blocks in school boundaries to reflect recent immigration or construction can alter test outcomes apart from any individual change.

There is also a chance element here independent of what teachers actually accomplish. For example, talented teachers who pushed fourth graders beyond grade levels get collectively punished if their fifth-grade colleagues cannot maintain this difficult-to-sustain pace. The reverse is also possible—teachers "inheriting" ineptly-taught students can achieve artificial successes as students merely return to normal progress, so the teacher, regardless of special skills, receive a bonus. If not for the renaming and keeping of existing schools, a potential Zeno-like paradox lurks here: closing one school filled with underachievers sends these troubled students elsewhere, and recipient schools will now decline, too, and then also be shuttered. Now, underperforming students are shipped to a third school, which is then closed for "declining" scores, so the road show moves to a fourth school, and on and on, so like dominos, *every school in the city will eventually be closed as "underperforming"!* This might be called the pandemic scenario of educational excellence (or "plague model") by ending public education altogether.

Now for the secret of achieving cosmetic "success:" weight outcomes to reflect "improvement" at the bottom while totally ignoring accomplishment at the top. In classroom practices, this is identical to awarding gold stars to hard workers who have gone from "D" to "C" while ignoring steady "A" students. And since only helping laggards can produce bonuses, savvy teachers will reasonably target these students, even neglecting the "A" students, so fans of accountability can now proudly boast of their triumphs! This is an ingenious scheme and absolutely *guaranteed* almost regardless of classroom performance, incentives, or any other pressure. In betting parlance, it is a sure thing or, to be a bit harsh, "the fix is in."

Let us peek behind the curtains. Statisticians speak of a "ceiling effect." At some point, no room for upward movement exists, so, for example, a student with perfect test scores cannot perform better if only he or she studied harder or teachers were promised a Rolls Royce. Progress would be possible only by extending the scale to, say, 150 percent correct, a numerical absurdity or piling on extra credit for extraneous factors like "good attitude." In other words, an "A" is as good as it can possibly get. By contrast, a student with a 70 percent average might be advised to study harder, and, unlike the "A" student, can actually move upward. And the lower the score, the more potential for progress, so clever bonus-seeking teachers should avoid classes of super-bright students and Mother Teresa-like minister only to those furthest behind. Furthermore, normal statistical volatility (reliability, technicality) ensures that some scores go up and some will go down, regardless of effort or ability. Another statistical principle—the regression to the mean—also guarantees that the lowest will likely advance upward toward the mean if tested a second time (while the very best will fall back). Now, for multiple purely statistical reasons, having nothing to do with skill or effort, a teacher with the lowest of the low has the best chance of saying, "see, some did better thanks to my brilliant intervention."

Manufacturing Bogus Outcomes

In late fall 2007 this is exactly what the New York City Department of Education did to bedazzle skeptics. With great fanfare, school report cards were announced followed by a "hit list" of some sixty schools to be closed since they had "failed their students." According to Klein, these report cards are "...glue that holds together the entire effort to overhaul the entire school system ..." (Medina and Gootman, Nov. 4, 2007). A few days later he boasted that this was, "the best system for evaluating schools in the country" (Gootman and Medina, Nov. 6, 2007). Outwardly, accountability seemed to succeed—those teachers and administrators who had successfully pushed the bottom upward now anticipated their prizes while schools unable to respond to enticements were put on probation or awaited the Grim Reaper. Next year, no doubt, teachers and principles, like those harried commissioned salespeople desperately hawking widgets, might finally get serious about educating students.

Alas, demonstrating that "accountability works" via gaming the system was too transparent, too cockeyed and dissatisfaction was immediate. At one New York City Council meeting the DOE's Chief Accountability Officer (James Lieberman) was repeatedly booed and hissed at by irate parents while various disgruntled City Council members joined the anti-DOE fray. Parents afterwards tried to present him with a 7,000-signature petition to protest the report cards but Lieberman had fled (Medina, Dec. 11, 2007). Perhaps the city DOE should have followed the old cheating adage—don't overreach or it will be obvious and you'll get caught. Only a few samples exist of this bizarre twisting of academic sloth into achievement, or, on the other hand, punishing stellar schools must suffice.

Specifically, more than half the schools that the state or federal government (which employs an absolute performance standard) labeled academically weak received an A or B while 99 schools in good standing according to these state and national standards received a D or F (Ravitch, 2007). Similarly, 20 percent of the City's "A" schools were failing according to New York State criteria. Intermediate School (IS) 289, an exceptional, Washington-designated "blue ribbon" school (the only one in NYC) was hit with a "D." In fact educators from around the country regularly visit IS 289 to shadow its teachers for tips on how to succeed (Medina and Gootman, 2007). Surely a "D" is inappropriate for IS 289 since "only" 84.2 percent of its seventh graders met the state's reading standard while the comparable citywide figure was 50 percent. Similarly, a Staten Island school where 85 percent regularly pass the state tests was awarded an "F" while the Peninsula Preparatory Academy (a charter school), received an "F" though about 70% of its students passed the state's math standard, a commendable accomplishment in the city's schools (Medina, December 20, 2007). By contrast, the East Village Community School received an "A" rating since the proportion of children passing the reading test went from 46.3 percent to 60 percent. Stuyvesant High School, the elite of the elite math and science academy—it had four of the forty national finalists for the Intel Science Talent Search in 2008—was originally scheduled to receive a high "B" but the school's principal intervened for "extra credit" for its college courses, etc., and the grade was raised to an "A."

It gets worse. Franklin D. Roosevelt High School scored an "A" though it graduated a mere 50.4 percent of its students (Gootman and Medina, November 6, 2007). The South Bronx Academy for Applied Media is a museum-quality nightmare—half the faculty quits every year; crime and violence, including attacks on teachers, are commonplace; and New York State has classified the school as "persistently dangerous," one of fifty-two in the entire state (Freedman, 2007). Classrooms often lacked books and a school focusing on the media had no Web site. Just 17 percent of its students were at grade level in reading. Nevertheless it, too, got an "A." Meanwhile, Bard College's Early College High School received a "C" and was "under review" for possible closing. This occurred in spite of a truly outstanding academic record—students pass the tough state Regents examination by their sophomore year (a feat beyond most city seniors) and after four years those with diplomas have earned two years of college credit (Gootman, Nov. 9, 2007).

Expensive Deviousness

What is most revealing about New York City's experiment in accountability is its calculated deviousness in transforming shoddy academic performance into progress, and at a cost of $88 million, to boot. It would be as if American Widget claimed to cure cancer since most of its customers were cancer-free. One duplicity indicator is that the DOE commissioned a poll to demonstrate public endorsement of report cards, and it did find a 75 percent support level, but it is extremely unlikely that any of the respondents fully and accurately grasp how these complicated ratings were calculated. Tellingly, of the 1,007 voters polled, only 143 were public school parents (Medina, Dec. 11, 2007). As for giving an "A" to unsafe schools, a true oddity given parents' justifiable concern with school safety, the DOE's Chief Accountability Officer downplayed safety altogether. According to his twisted logic, administrators in smaller, better schools, unlike their compatriots in crime-ridden schools, were more sensitive to safety issues and thus reported more infractions, so including safety in the ratings would distort reality (Gootman and Medina, September 27, 2007). That school safety might be determined by outsiders, say the NYPD, not on the school's staff was conveniently off the agenda.

Another event hinting that school closings are basically publicity stunts comes from the "closing" of the Bronx's PS 79, an "F"-rated school. The school, which was in the lowest 2 percent of all city elementary schools, enrolls some 1,000 students K-5, and local parents were distraught when informed of its closing. But, alarmed parents were soon officially assured that nothing of the sort was planned, DOE proclamations aside. Instead, two "new" schools would soon be established in the same building serving K-2, and then these "new" schools would add grades three to five, so students would again attend PS 79 though "PS 79" would vanish as a label (Bleyer, 2007). Since these "new" schools will hire many of the same teachers from "old" PS 79 (required by union contract), this is, as the saying goes, largely old wine in new bottles. As with some primitive religious ritual, an effigy of PS 79 had been taken to the altar, and with great public ceremony sacrificed to appease the Accountability God.

Regrettably, such chicanery easily passes unpunished since educators, unlike merchants, are not liable for consumer fraud or regulated by multiple government agencies. Imagine the AW CEO explaining that the rash of defective widgets sold to trusting customers "merely" reflected the firm's new and improved quality control procedures, not shoddy widgets. Nor can defrauded parents seek damages as they can sue drug companies. Lawyers do not advertise in subways, "Has your child been miseducated? We have won millions for past malfeasance." In fact, when confronted with these bizarre outcomes and the rising chorus of bewilderment, Klein backtracked from previous euphoria and promised a "more sophisticated" version next time around and further added, "You have to start somewhere" (Medina and Gootman, Nov. 4, 2007).

These misadventures in accountability did not, however, stop Bloomberg and Klein from trying other "business-like" tactics to pressure teachers without providing any clues regarding what might prove effective. One can only be reminded of a Spanish Inquisition interrogator who, failing to extract confessions with boiling oil, threatens the rack, and if that should fail, promises the Iron Maiden. Specifically, in 2007 the New York City DOE instituted a program in which 2,500 teachers, *unbeknownst to them*, were graded according to their students' academic performance, progress in meeting proficiency standards and gains compared to what students did in other classrooms. The test outcomes, it was hinted, would not only determine rewards (including the granting of tenure) but might be made publicly available for everyone to see. According to the Deputy School Chancellor, publicizing teacher test scores would be a "…powerful step forward" to insure that teachers did their jobs (Medina, Jan 21, 2008). Needless to say, this teacher-based accountability system suffers from the same flaws as the school-based version, namely it penalizes teachers inheriting good students (the ceiling effect), disproportionally rewards those starting with the worst of the worst while opening the door to statistical manipulation via weighting. It also may encourage cheating since a few spectacular "successes" in a small class can send averages skyrocketing (expelling a few disasters can produce the identical outcome, too). Savvy teachers might also demand the dumbest students at the beginning of the school year to maximize "progress."

Not surprisingly in early 2008 Klein substantially revised this once-heralded scoring system to assuage parent, administrator, and union sensibilities (Green, 2008). Now it would be easier for schools to receive higher grades since more credit would be given to progress from special education students while a slight downturn among top scorers would not be penalized. Four separate grades would also be handed out so like distraught students with a generally bad report card, a school might find some nugget of achievement. To repeat a by now familiar point, testing in American education has evolved into a tactic to placate varied interests, not measure some well-defined learning according to a strict standard.

In September 2008 the Education Mayor and his school Chancellor predictably resorted to the time-honored solution to placate those angered over low grades: just award high grades to nearly everyone. Now nine of the schools receiving "Fs" in 2006-7 miraculously received "As" in 2007-8; only one dropped from "A" to "F." Almost 80 percent of the city's schools "earned" an "A" or "B" though 30 percent of these "A" schools were deemed failures under NCLB. One "F" to "A" marvel occurred in PS 5, a school famous for dreadful academics (meanwhile, one newly-certified "F" school, PS 8, continued to have outstanding test scores but these had fallen slightly as per ceiling effect). Tellingly, the scoring system's architect explained the variability by admitting that scores were adjusted according to "demographic peer performance," a polite way of saying that if dullards now showed some sign of life, they can be certified as smart (Medina and Gebeloff, September 17, 2008). The march toward excellence even picked up. In late 2008 Bloomberg and Klein announced that thanks to the "new and improved" grading system 83 percent of all schools received an "A" or "B" while 57 percent of all schools either moved up a grade or maintained their "A" status. No doubt, the city's schools will soon resemble Harvard where yesterday's "F" is often today's "C" (Medina and Gebeloff, November 13, 2008). One can only conclude that Bloomberg and Klein just don't care about academic excellence and believe the public is so stupid that the ruse will satisfy parents who conflate a convoluted "A" with genuine learning.

This accountability gone wild case study is, admittedly, a harsh indictment but make no mistake, the strategy's devious character was self-evident at the very beginning. And while our account has centered on New York City, the same outcomes are likely elsewhere if pushed with a comparable take-no-prisoners mentality. Its purpose was less to enhance learning but to show cleverly how a trendy scheme could produce "results," and judged by the initially upbeat publicity it appeared that Bloomberg and Klein had, indeed, struck gold. An almost desperate quality infuses this "accountability works" enterprise. Anybody familiar with statistics knows about ceiling affects, measurement unreliability, the difference between comparing cohorts versus individuals, and regression toward the mean. Interpreting simplistic poll responses to extract evidence showing public endorsement for alluring but dimly-grasped statistical models is an equally-obvious manipulative device.

A never-voiced irony is that a superb, effective and easy-to-implement accountability system *already* exists in New York City and every other school in America. It is, moreover, cheap, statistically reliable and produces absolutely transparent results for individual students. It is called grades and it makes students, not schools, accountable. Here's how it works. First, teachers assign tasks, students perform them, and teachers decide who gets what grade. Those who excel gain personal satisfaction and perhaps classmate respect. A few build stellar academic records and eventually enter college. Laggards, by contrast, receive extra help or are stigmatized for laziness. This "innovative" system can be customized to the unique abilities of every student. Teachers know who can do what, and thus might shower praise on a less-talented student who does "B" work while pushing the class brain who lazily earns a "B." This "reward good students, punish the bad ones" system also costs less than $88 million per school district and teachers have already mastered it. And unlike what is offered by Joel "The Terminator" Klein, cheating, other than plain-to-see grade-inflation, is usually caught and punished, and teachers being teachers—not lucre-motivated commissioned salespeople—can gain immense personal satisfaction, not perhaps a dollar per hour more, by witnessing youngsters learn.

Does It Work?

What does this New York City experience suggest about applying the accountability panacea more generally, particularly in NCLB-like measures? The news is pretty grim. The National Assessment of Educational Progress (NAEP) report released in September of 2007 was, at best, decidedly mixed regarding overall progress though, predictably, NCLB defenders crowed about minuscule gains (Holland, 2007). For example, between 2005 and 2007 fourth-grade and eight-grade math scores rose two points on a 500 point scale. Reading test outcomes between 2005 and 2007 showed similar tiny 2 point gains. To be sure, math results have moved upward since 1990, but most of this came twelve years before the accountability obsessed NCLB. By contrast, long-term reading results were flat despite billions in extra funding. Perhaps the best news was a small narrowing of the racial gap in fourth-grade math.

A massive, detailed, and exacting study on NCLB released in late 2007, relying on both surveys of educators and testing data, confirmed growing skepticism (LeFloch et al, 2007). The good news for accountability fans is that NCLB mechanics—establishing content-based tests for reading and mathematics for fourth and eight graders—are now in place nationally and as required, many schools were notifying parents of school failures. There are also some advances in establishing school reporting mechanisms and in targeting resources to lagging schools. Progress is also occurring in extending tests to other grades plus devising English proficiency standards. But, a national standard still remains beyond reach as individual states vary considerably in test toughness, and this can seriously distort assessments of progress. In fact, without a uniform clear standard, the incentives to dumb down the test remain as powerful as before.

When we turn to actual academic outcomes, the news is less upbeat though, as we tirelessly repeated, compelling incentives exist for educators to shoot bad news messengers. In a nutshell, while administrative procedures expand, students are more resistant to change. First, while the overall rate of Annual Yearly Progress (AYP) was high, this was shockingly low in some states or school districts—less than 10 percent of school districts in Alabama, West Virginia, and Florida. Second, and particularly relevant for egalitarians, schools in high-poverty urban areas still dramatically lagged behind despite all the targeting of resources though, on the plus side, about a quarter of the deeply troubled high-poverty schools did improve. Nor did these disappointing results reflect failures in just one sub-group or two; most of the failures to make progress reflected shortcomings in the entire student body.

Some seven years after NCLB, only 32 percent of fourth graders, according to the National Assessment of Educational Progress (NAEP), are reading at or above proficiency while 38 percent are at this level in math. Racial gaps, the *bête noire* of the NCLB, remain largely unchanged, for example, 52 percent of white fourth graders read at proficiency or above compared to 16 percent of African-Americans. According to one 2007 report regarding trend lines, overall gains in reading achievement (fundamental to other learning) have been marginal, sometimes up, sometimes down depending on the state, with performance declining among eight graders. On the plus side, math scores are up a bit (Dillon, 2007). Lastly, though exact comparisons across languages are difficult, international test data show that compared to 2001 and NCLB, American fourth graders have gone nowhere on reading, even falling further behind age-mates overseas (*Associated Press*, 2007).

Writing in early 2008, Helen Ladd, a professor of public policy at Duke University, offered a general assessment of the entire accountability movement as embodied in NCLB. It certainly energized educators and did help boost some math (but not reading) scores a bit, and may have helped African-Americans a bit, but the general verdict is disappointing. As she put it, "Test-based accountability has not generated the significant gains in student achievement that proponents—however they perceived the problems to be solved—intended." Ladd did not reject testing *per se,* but suggested that it be combined with numerous other interventions, for example, having schools evaluated by outsider experts and more early intervention. Whether these proposals will perform is, of course, just speculation.

Repent: The End is Near

The NCLB legislation faces major obstacles in securing reauthorization and opposition cuts across party and ideological lines, so the education reform cemetery may soon have a new resident. President Obama has yet to endorse or reject it but his Secretary of Education, Arne Duncan, suggests that the program's reputation is sufficiently awful to warrant a new name (contempt has even brought facetious suggestions like "Act to Help Children Read Gooder" and "All American Children are Above Average"). Still, the lure of "accountability" remains as enticing as ever. Perhaps the term's draw just hinders clear thinking. Interestingly, the reauthorization debate has drawn suggestions to gut the bill's original tough academic mission, for example, including portfolio assessment, the use of non-English in testing, a national standard for "environmental education" among other "soft" measures (Lips, 2007).

All and all, business-style accountability will probably fade into the background once today's enthusiastic political leaders depart. It has not rescued America from academic insufficiency though its defenders currently insist otherwise, often, alas, by imposing low-bar standards or selective interpretation. Critically, over and above the wasted billions the opportunity costs have been huge, and the emphasis on "failing schools" not "failing students" may have corrupted public discussion on education for decades to come. Eventual shortcomings were certainly predictable given past performances and the clear inappropriateness of the education-business parallel. The fervent insistence on following this slapdash gimmick only reveals our refusal to look in the mirror. It is one thing for worried parents to be hoodwinked into some miracle-like device hawked on late night TV, quite another for putative experts to fall pray to such a simplistic "business-like" schemes.

8

The Alluring Choice Solution
or Why Educating Students Is Not
Manufacturing Cheap Flat Screen TVs

The believer is happy; the doubter is wise.
—Old Hungarian Proverb

You got to be careful if you don't know where you are going because you might not get there.
—Yogi Berra

As contemporary reformers lurch from one ineffective reform effort to the next, at least for some, "school choice" becomes the Messiah *du jour*. Judged by advocacy vitality, its legislative successes despite often intense opposition, school choice, even more so than accountability, has become *the* conservative nostrum to cure America's educational woes. The February 2008 edition of *School Reform News*, a leading school choice campaigner, lists some eighty-five state and national organizations promoting this agenda. It is also a foundation favorite while polls periodically confirm majorities, particularly among African-Americans, yearning for more schooling options. The justifying logic seems indisputable: break the government's near schooling monopoly, give educational funds directly to parents, and let schools battle for students as businesses compete for customers, and *voilá*, educational excellence! Just look at commerce—we have progressed from expensive tiny black and white TVs to affordable flat screen room-filling monsters. Unfortunately, as is true for past business-analogy reforms, seductive parallels are misleading. The real problem is not lack of supply; it is insufficient demand for academic achievement.

Immense School Choice Already Exists

Choice advocates believe that too few educational options exist. This is factually incorrect. Educational choice *currently* abounds; Americans are not prisoners of the state, and while satisfying educational preferences is hardly effortless, it is regularly accomplished. Moreover, recall from our discussion of how parents (85 percent of them) prefer local schools even if "bad," so choice champions are pushing a product with weak demand. That status quo preference understood, piling on yet more choices with vouchers and charters will unlikely boost academic success. Slackers avoiding today's ample, often free opportunities to learn will not suddenly acquire academic appetites if enjoying an even wider option menu. Nor will many parents of struggling students make even the small effort to help Junior utilize the new-found opportunities. To be impolite, hankering after "more choice" is just a socially-acceptable way of avoiding the real culprit, intellectually-mediocre students who disdain learning. Demanding more "choice" is akin to insisting that Americans would eat more healthy meals only if more restaurants offered these options.

The smoking gun evidence that widespread, reasonably affordable choice thrives without the formal mechanisms championed by choice advocates is the paltry numbers of white students in nearly all large city public schools. If no choice existed, why are white enrollments in many urban public schools half or less of the total local white school population? Are white kids simply playing hooky? Hardly. A "government monopoly" would suggest rough proportionality, and this rarely occurs. In fact, government policies like court-mandated bussing or magnet schools to achieve racial integration exist to *prevent* parents from exercising free choice and these measures have, obviously, largely failed.

Innumerable private schools exist, including many inner-city Catholic schools offering generous financial aid to impoverished students, many of whom are not Catholic. The ease by which parents can pick and choose is apparent when scanning America's varied religious schools. The Department of Education catalogues these schools, and in 2003/4 they reported some 30 schools run by the Islamic School League of America with 3,179 students; 35 schools run by the Council of Islamic Schools with 4,567 students; 179 schools under the auspices of the National Society of Hebrew Day Schools with 18,552 students plus innumerable other religious schools, many of which provide excellent educations on bare-bones budgets. Admittedly, private sectarian school enrollments are tiny compared to public school populations, but their variety and geographical dispersion disproves the government monopoly argument. Nor do these schools require major investments, so demand, not endowments, is critical. Religious schools often operate rent-free in church basements, are staffed by teachers accepting below market wages and heavily rely on parent volunteers. Choice requires wanting something badly enough to forego competing enticements so it is just a matter of priorities.

It is almost impossible to depict the variety of America's schools. The Amish, for example, have for over a 100 years run schools that have scarcely left the early nineteenth century. Hasidic Jews similarly prefer their offspring to study the ancient Torah and Talmud, not modern knowledge. One under-the-radar manifestation of this freedom are the 200 Afrocentric schools (both public and private) that have opened between 1996 and 2004. At the Milwaukee's private all-black Blyden Delany School, for example, students observe a code of silence when walking halls bedecked with African masks, second-graders begin each day counting to 10 in Swahili, and memorize poems by African-Americans while focusing on their African heritage to build self-esteem. The Afrocentric message also dominates Milwaukee's public Martin Luther King, Jr. School (Sykes, 2004).

Especially relevant for exasperated parents truly wanting superior educations for their offspring, relocating for better schools—whether for academics, athletics, art, or anything else—remains a viable, popular option. This is less troublesome than it might appear since most cities are surrounded by hundreds of suburbs so the educational bill of fare is reasonably full, and residential choice may pose little hardship in terms of travel, shopping, taxes, and similar considerations. Even if one lives amidst lousy schools, not all is lost. Countless localities permit non-resident children to enroll in public schools by paying local tuition if space is available. This is a popular option in the Washington, DC area so families can give their children a superior public education without using even more expensive private schools (de Vise, 2008).

Choice proponents similarly ignore American education's localism and how minimal state-mandated requirements regarding attendance and required subjects permit ample flexibility. Untold small towns place sports ahead of academic rigor and states almost always bend laws to accommodate voters. Other localities push high quality academics at the expense of non-academic frills like sports. Thus, to insist that Americans truly crave academic excellence but just don't seem able to find it is preposterous. *They just don't want it, at least if it requires unpleasant work or modest personal sacrifices.* Millions readily get what they want in schooling though they will tell pollsters that they crave academic excellence.

Non-School Options

Even among the poorest of the poor the public school is not the exclusive education option. Those thirsting for knowledge trapped with indifferent teachers can, for example, visit local libraries that typically offer conveniently scheduled courses ranging from basic reading to computer literacy while librarians might provide one-on-one tutoring. Libraries often supply free Internet connections and assisted Web surfing, so it is hard to insist that a "rotten school" denies access to knowledge. The Massachusetts Institute of Technology now offers K-12 science courses (including video) *free* to students nationally via the Web, so if Bart is confused by his fifth-grade biology teacher, he can visit MIT for the best of the best.

Moreover, an already huge for-profit non-school industry exists seemingly hidden from critics bewailing America's insufficient educational choices. The most notable are chains like Stanley Kaplan (and its Score affiliate teaching high-school subjects) and Sylvan Learning while most Yellow Pages supply a treasure trove of choices. Kaplan offers after-school coaching for state-mandated tests (especially reading and math) and, given that parents demand results for their out-of-pocket fees, Kaplan's pedagogy (and technology) is constantly updated. Sylvan Learning Centers have more than 1,100 locations in the U.S. and Canada, with after school, evening, and weekend hours, offering various courses, including study skills.

A quick Web search for New York City's "trapped parents" uncovers multiple options for frustrated parents, e.g., A+ Home Tutoring, Forde's Professional Tutoring, ClubZ! Home Tutoring Services among countless others. SMARTHINKING is a private online firm that since it's founding in 1999 has provided over a million lessons on multiple subjects. A similar web-based firm is Blackboard offering interactive instruction between students and teachers. Tutor.com advertises online supplementary instruction 24/7 and private firms advertise of a willingness to accommodate customers with special needs, e.g., meeting pupils at community centers. Parents unhappy with local math instruction can help junior by logging on to *http://artofproblemsolving.com* that offers advanced math for talented youngster grades 6-12 (as of February 2008 there were 37,000 registered users). The site offers math books, competitions, and a gateway to mathematics organizations.

Defenders of adding yet more "choice" would, of course, insist that this private tutoring is beyond struggling students in poor neighborhoods. This is absolutely false—under NCLB it was freely available until late 2008 to students in "failing" schools, and at no cost but, with few exceptions, students just rejected it. Even thousands of entrepreneurs who stood to gain financially could not entice these youngsters to enroll, let alone complete the courses. City after city reported a nearly identical experience: huge numbers of lagging students were offered a free tutoring option, often in the school they already attend, but only about 10 percent signed up, and even then, most dropped out after a few sessions (see, for example, Saulny, 2006). California in 2004 had some 397,000 eligible students and 20,000—5 percent—sought assistance, or at least signed up. Even these paltry numbers exaggerate the demand for "choice" since many enrolled thanks to cash incentives or were pushed in by school officials at the bequest of for-profit tutoring services. Yet one more time: it is demand, not supply that drives choice.

Home school's burgeoning popularity (over a million students) has generated thousands of instructional programs in every imaginable subject with every type of pedagogy, Web and non-Web, available even to isolated rural parents worried over Junior's mis-education in government "monopoly" schools. Numerous, widely-sold books can help parents navigate homeschooling. Gifted children, even average ones wanting a challenge, can easily find serious academics provided, of course, that this is wanted. Several firms—Prufrock Press, Free Spirit Publishing, and Great Potential Press—specialize in books for gifted children, and a magazine exists—*Gifted Child Today.* Parents of gifted children also have state and local organizations supplying resources and tips. The National Association of Gifted Children's 2008 national convention in Tampa, Florida had some 77 private firms, university centers, institutes, publishers, and foundations in their exhibit hall, some 3,000 experts in gifted education plus an opportunity for parents to socialize with others in similar situations. Even without spending a nickel, Mom and Dad can certainly help with homework or pool neighborhood talent to compensate for lousy government-paid instruction (many private schools begin as informal collective tutoring).

So-called "cram academies" are especially popular in neighborhoods with education-hungry Asian immigrants but many also attract ambitious non-Asians. A *New York Times* story tells of some 138 cram academies listed in a New York City Korean business directory (as of 2003) and the total number must far exceed that figure (Luo, 2003). Score, one such after-school "cram academy" has a branch in New York City's largely black Harlem neighborhood, and these services were once free if a student's school failed under NCLB standards. They regularly teach the full array of academic subjects, not just mathematics. Significantly, many New York City cram academy students (an estimated 15 percent to 25 percent) are of a different ethnicity than the school's majority, and enrollees include many African-Americans. The available *à la carte* approach (e.g., studying reading at Sylvan, calculus at the Korean-run Elite Academy) may, admittedly, challenge parental initiative and scheduling, but it *already* incorporates essential features that choice proponents crave and, critically, without all the political lobbying.

To illustrate this bountifulness, consider one such cram academy, Score, in New York City's Chinatown neighborhood. It offers three levels of instruction (prices are from 2008). The Online Plus Tutoring option provides unlimited access to online tutoring plus for multiple subjects two visits per month for personal instruction (with a student/teacher ratio of 3:1) and costs $119 per month. The Online Program Only alternative costs only $29. Finally, intensive personal tutoring costs $50 per hour. Score's costs for the first two options certainly comparable with, say, a middling cell-phone or Cable-TV packages and today's poor often avail themselves of these "luxuries." Moreover, recall that these services were free if schools are failing under NCLB guidelines. Put bluntly, many poor parents must choose between extra academic help for junior versus cable TV or a cell phone, so to insist that they "lack choice" only flatters their disdain for education.

The Friedman Solution

The contemporary (conservative) justifications for uprooting the state's educational monopoly are traceable to Milton Friedman's influential essay, "The Role of Government in Education" in his *Capitalism and Freedom* (1962, originally published in 1955). Here Friedman distinguishes between government-funded schooling (almost always worthwhile) from state-administered schools, a non-essential, generally inefficient arrangement. The term "voucher" is introduced as the mechanism permitting both government funding and parental choice to overcome monopoly conditions. Friedman offers no reorganization blueprints, let alone innovative pedagogy, and instead tries to anticipate and rebut objection to ending state control for both K-12 and higher education, for example, non-state schools will neglect a common curriculum and thus undermine democratic society or that choice exacerbates social stratification.

Though Friedman may be the choice movement's Founding Father, his seminal essay was *not* about promoting intellectual excellence, today's paramount choice justification. His over-riding concern was personal *freedom, not top test scores,* and the primacy of freedom was crystal clear. Schools, he argued, will surely improve with competition and become more efficient, but this means greater variety, more flexibility and educators securing market-determined wages (93). The neglect of academic excellence is not an oversight since Friedman's celebration of individuality forbids raising any one value to the highest priority. The single reference to academic excellence concerns a bright, ambitious student unable to get a superior education at the local state-funded school but the opposite is conceivable—a duller student transferring to a less demanding school.

Friedman, moreover, says absolutely *nothing* about choice uplifting chronic laggards, today's obsession among choice advocates. Friedman concedes that schools unhindered by government might offer frivolous basket weaving and social dancing, but, "I hasten to add that there can be no conceivable objection to parents spending their own money on such frills as they wish" (94). Let there be no mistake: *consumer choice and academic excellence are not identical and may even be antithetical.* Pushed to its logical limits, since freedom to choice means freedom to choose (almost) anything, virtually *any* school outcome would satisfy Friedman provided parents wanted it.

Neglecting intellectual distinction was hardly an oversight to be corrected. Writing some fifty years later Friedman reiterates his central point—"The Role of Government in Education" was about "…the philosophy of a free society," not a recipe for achieving academic excellence (Friedman, 2006). He also admits that when the essay was written in 1955, he and his coauthor wife were satisfied with the quality of public education, both what they had personally received and what then existed in the U.S.

Friedman hardly disdains academic excellence; rather, the two ideas now inseparably linked in the minds of countless free-market reformers—choice and stellar academics—were *never* connected by the champion of vouchers. Friedman *only* claims that school choice will enhance parental control over their children's education and thus enhance personal freedom. In retrospect, the choice=academic quality link probably grew seductive more as a desire to solve burgeoning academic tribulations, less as a result of empirical studies or careful theory building. There is nothing logical about this link and while choice advocates routinely invoke Friedman's towering prestige (he is a Nobel Prize winner) and readily suggest alluring economic analogies, the academic benefits of choice is but a hypothesis, and an iffy one at that.

Exaggerating the Power of Markets

It is all too easy to be intoxicated with choice as a magical elixir—just observe improvement in consumer electronics. This indisputable progress does not, however, demonstrate that rivalry can universally square circles. Since the 1970s, for example, automobile manufactures have relentlessly competed to boost fuel economy while not sacrificing other attributes, and billions await anybody who can design a 75 mpg vehicle without compromises elsewhere, but the intensely-sought aim remains unreachable. Competition, no matter how fervent, cannot surmount the laws of physics, the laws of economics or reverse human nature. Markets are wonderful for expanding choice *but not for performing the impossible.*

Even if we assume that market competition powerfully pushes excellence, progress says absolutely nothing about what "excellence" comprises. Academic distinction is only one of many—perhaps dozens—of traits that schools might maximize, and given what we know about public appetites for intellectual accomplishment, it is probably pretty far down the public's wish list. A more clear-eyed guess would be that in a *laissez-faire* educational marketplace the most intense competition would be in sports, country-club-like recreational facilities, lavish monthly proms, gourmet food, and "educational" travel. If schools were pressed to up academic achievement, many might be tempted to just inflate grades and put everyone on the honor roll lest disgruntled "customers" flee elsewhere.

What markets can accomplish with those disdaining learning is severely limited. If competitive pressure itself did the trick, every Harvard-obsessed parent would succeed in getting junior off to Cambridge. To return to the car parallel, if initial progress via the market guaranteed future success, the modest mpg gains of the 1980s would have resulted in today's cars achieving 75 mpg, tomorrow's cars 100 mpg and, eventually, almost energy-less cars. Actually, everything known about efficiency patterns suggests the Law of Diminishing Returns. That is, already huge educational outlays and the myriad (failed) reforms depicted in Chapter 6 suggest that with existing levels of intellectual talent a point of diminishing return may have been reached years ago. Keep in mind that the automobile manufactures who frantically competed to build gas-saving vehicles in 1980s when gasoline prices shot up eventually turned to gas-guzzling SUVs in their profit-driven competition for customers. Market competition says nothing about hankering after "good" goals.

This "competition will do it" mentality in education also ignores bearable cost. That rivalries might bring improvements does not mean that potential consumers will buy competition-produced upgrades. No doubt, even today's impressive technological marvels are too expensive for some despite sharply falling costs—some people are content to wait for powerful laptops under $100 and refuse to budge until they arrive. To reiterate yet one more time, millions of students and parents surely crave a first-rate schooling but simply refuse to pay necessary, often painful costs, i.e., arduous study versus socializing, even if the formula were handed to them. To insist that more competition will eventually reduce learning costs so everyone, regardless of intellectual apathy, will "buy" a first-rate (and effortless) education is dangerous fantasy. Abundant choice can *never* make learning painless. Even bribery may not convert those disdaining academic achievement since the hard work entailed by learning is inescapable.

A wide open, weakly regulated marketplace hardly foretells a mass rush to superior schools and this has troubling implications seldom admitted by choice advocates. In particular, racial segregation will appear with a vengeance as gifted white and Asian students gravitate to these top-notch schools. Meanwhile, barring a major redirection of academic inclinations, struggling blacks and Hispanics will enroll in more culturally attuned schools that are, to be frank, generally academically less demanding.

This sorting will be voluntary, just as people diverge on nearly all consumer choices but the logic of unhampered economic competition can be grim for racial egalitarians. Imagine a charter school advertising itself as the *ne plus ultra* of academic rigor and happily sacrifices sports, cheerleading, soft courses like yearbook, while students are relentlessly pushed to the breaking point. Competition is fierce, and parents wisely pay only for a reasonable shot at admission to Ivy League schools. Under these "produce or go broke" conditions, *administrators can ill-afford catering to those years behind who nevertheless might benefit from pressurized opportunities.* Reputation is everything, so why risk it by enticing the academically troubled? Business is not charity. If such troubled students were admitted (and with scholarships, too), full-pay parents of high achievers might rightfully complain of new-found discipline problems, excessive time wasted on review, the hiring of expensive non-academic support staff, all of which detracts from the school's advertised narrow aim. Even government subsidies to enroll strugglers will probably be rejected since this will dilute product quality, and top quality is the school's *raison d'être.*

Competition will push academically-oriented schools to use brutal tests and to publicize the outcomes (even sponsor brainy Olympics akin to TV's College Bowl to attract students). Cheating would risk everything. This is economic self-interest at its best since the more arduous the test, the greater the score dispersion, so those craving first-rate academic reputations will insist on tough exams to certify themselves as, indeed, the *very* best of the best. Though politically-sensitive legislators may reject grueling tests since they dread awkward outcomes, nothing can stop private firms like ETS from providing brain-busting exams provided a market exists.

Meanwhile on the other side of the divide, non-academically oriented schools will likewise push for high standards to burnish marketable reputation but these will *not* be academic standards. Such schools might distribute handsome brochures boasting of graduates receiving college athletic scholarships or commission surveys to demonstrate improved self-esteem. Free-market fans have it wrong when they dream of markets uplifting everyone academically—a tiny handful will now excel but the intended beneficiaries of this magic bullet *du jour*, namely struggling blacks and Hispanics, will probably be worse off academically and greater market choice will be the culprit.

What Does Freedom of Choice Mean for Academic Performance?

Has parental choice delivered improved academic performance over and above offering parents a modicum of personal freedom? There is no simple answer here since judging the success of choice reforms is deceptively complicated, perhaps even impossible (Henig, 1994, Chapter 6 covers some of these hurdles). If, as per Friedman, we use "freedom of choice" as the yardstick, success can be readily determined—do parents enjoy desired educational variety as they possess multiple consumer-type options, even if not availing themselves of the options? So, just tabulate the number of options until "enough" is reached, whatever that might be, according to each individual. A further, and inevitably neglected, serious complexity is calibrating "choice" in the context of non-educational lures. How does one classify a mother who could have junior expertly tutored for $200 a month but instead buys new clothing? Does Mom "lack choice" since anything less than free is totally unattractive? There is also the quandary of how much choice is sufficient to satisfy choice champions, no small matter since choice advocates can only explain away failure by insisting that "yet even more choice was necessary." After all, even the most wide-open marketplace lacks something, so a parent with esoteric needs "lacks choice."

All these tribulations far exceed the usual measurement obstacles when assessing choice options. Indeed, assessing how much choice exists can be a quagmire. To illustrate these problems, consider a student, Dick, who elects a school stressing music, just what he and his parents want while his brainier sister, Jane, attends a tough science-based academy. Both exercise choice but the choice payoff is fundamentally different for each. Dick's dismal science test scores are irrelevant—it is Dick's chance to play the Tuba that counts, and for good measure, it is only opportunity that matters, not his eventual Tuba skill. Dick's sinking science scores do *not* discredit the value of choice (and the same would be true for Jane's declining musical attainment). Going one step further in this measurement mess, Mom and Dad complain that their public schools lacks a Tuba program for Dick but unbeknownst to them, a local music teacher offers inexpensive lessons, so Mom and Dad really have a choice but don't realize it.

Going even further, some parents may *want* a school where cronies get contracts; teachers hired according to race and academic outcomes are judged disasters according to middle-class "good government" standards. Make no mistake, this *is* choice though not what choice champions envision. As our subsequent analysis of schools as social welfare will show, efforts in New York City and Washington, DC (and surely elsewhere) show that shuttering horrific schools inevitably draws public opposition. That such anti-academic preferences may be publicly denied adds yet one more tribulation to calculating choice outcomes. The predicament of evaluating multiple goals permitted by freedom is probably beyond resolution. Perhaps only a mind reading of every person's unique personal goals and aligning them to educational opportunities would suffice. *Any educational arrangement, no matter how good or awful, can satisfy Friedman's demand for more "choice."* When all is said and done, however, Friedman would insist that market entry and cost accessibility are the standards, not test scores. Keep this in mind as we review the research literature—it all may be irrelevant to "school choice" correctly understood.

The Empirical Evidence

Leaving aside the specter of any arrangement satisfying choice, does enhanced parental choice produce academic excellence? Herbert Walberg

(2007) is a fervent choice advocate and offers his take on this complicated, sprawling literature. Not surprisingly given his predispositions, he gives glowing marks to school choice in all of its varied forms as the academic savior. Charter schools, he argues, academically outperform traditional government-run schools despite spending far less and their newness (30). He cites a meticulous study by Caroline Hoxby of 99 percent of the nation's charter schools showing that their students, when matched with public school pupils, performed slightly better in both reading and math, and that these gains grow slightly larger the longer a school has existed. Gains were especially notable for black and Hispanic students, and, significantly, were better where charter schools enjoyed ample autonomy. Equally important, urban charter schools were more rigorous judged by course requirements, more discipline, and greater testing (31-2).

Walberg also approvingly cites a meta-study of twenty-six rigorous studies by Bryan Hassel who concluded in sixteen of the twenty-six cases, charter schools equaled or outperformed their public rivals (34). Meanwhile, a one-year over-time study in eleven states found that charter school students surpassed their public school compatriots by three percentile points in math and two points in reading (35). Similar upbeat news comes from an experimental design study of the Chicago International Charter School where students gained five to six points in both reading and mathematics, a shift that cut in half the gap between black and white students (37).

Walberg also assembles varied studies showing that vouchers likewise improve test scores. One such study matched students in Washington, DC, New York City, and Dayton, Ohio and found that, thanks to vouchers, African-Americans modestly outperformed public school compatriots though this did not occur for white students (52). Research in several other cities finds comparable improvements for African-American students, usually about an 8 percent or 9 percent boost. In 2001 Jay Greene summarized the results of eleven voucher studies and concluded that there were academic benefits in ten of them and no study reported any academic harm (54). Careful analyses across multiple studies reiterates this racial pattern, i.e., vouchers perform best for low-income blacks but not elsewhere, and while these gains diminish the black/white gap, most of the gap remains even after two years (55-6).

A more encompassing approach is offered by Foster (2007). Written under the auspices of the Milton and Rose Friedman Foundation, it utilizes data from the government's Educational Longitudinal Study (ELS) to track individual high school students in both private (including "choice" schools) and public schools. Basically, even after taking myriad factors into account (e.g., race, income, family composition, parental education), the private side outperforms government schools academically. Admittedly, per grade academic gains may be modest, but they cumulate so that by graduation private school students are well ahead of public school peers. Private schools also were superior in retention plus various "civic values" such as tolerance for the rights of others while having no ill affects on the quality of race relations. And, for good measure, they were cheaper than comparable state institutions.

Still, upbeat assessments are hardly universal, and this includes researchers with no ideological stake in the debate. Eric A. Hanushek et al (2005) offers a review of charter school studies and reports that they were less effective vis-à-vis government-run schools in North Carolina and about the same academically in Florida. Texas charter schools, he notes, have been repeatedly scrutinized and while the news compared to traditional schools is positive, this positive assessment depends on several statistical adjustments. He and his colleagues' own analyses find that within two years after being created Texas charter schools are just as effective as public schools. Perhaps the most negative assessment comes from the American Federation of Teachers (AFT) Report, hardly surprising given the AFT's opposition to school choice (Nelson, 2004). Using NAEP data for 2003 the Report finds that fourth- and eight-grade students in charter schools perform less well on both reading and math. Significantly, the charter-public school gap held for poorer students as well, and while a racial gap in performance also existed, it was not statistically significant. The poorer or equal charter school performance compared to public schools also seemed unrelated to charter school autonomy.

A recent summary report (eighty-seven studies were examined) issued under the auspices of both Arizona State University's Educational Policy Research Unit and the Education and Public Interest Center at the University of Colorado (Boulder) illustrates this maddening quandary regarding choice effectiveness (Viadero, 2008). Taking a broad perspective on various choices measures—magnet schools, charter schools, open enrollment, tuition tax credits and the like—one author concluded that "progress" all depends on how programs are specifically designed. Some programs, for example, might foster racial segregation; others promote integration. Innovation can occur but sometimes it is stifled. Test scores sometimes go up; sometimes they go down. Meanwhile, while home schooling often receives high marks in the mass media, studies examining actual impact are methodologically flawed, according to this overview. Elsewhere the role of advocacy groups in sponsoring studies raises suspicions regarding scientific neutrality. Overall, according to one lead author, the literature has yet to show "clear and unambiguous factual statements of achievement across any of the key types of school choice." But, and totally predictable, this very mixed assessment was rejected by school choice proponents who noted that it was funded by the NEA, which opposes choice. Another researcher not connected to the report confirmed the overall mixed verdict though adding that some bias was probably present.

A more recent professionally-executed study of several hundred charter schools across five large school districts plus Florida, Ohio, and Texas similarly reported disappointing results (Viadero, 2009). Here and there some upbeat news could be found, for example, charter graduates were more likely to attend college in some instances, but the overall conclusion is the all-too-familiar one: no appreciable improvement. The researchers admit that some signs of progress may be buried in the data, but an impartial expert analysis cannot find them.

Two recent studies from Washington, DC also cast doubt on school choice as the elixir to uplift troubled students (Glod and Turque, 2008). In one program 1,903 children from low-income families were given $7,500 for tuition and fees at participating schools. The results showed little if any overall academic gains. Another study conducted by the Institute of Educational Sciences (the Department of Education's research arm) found that students who had received scholarships did no better on various tests such as the Stanford Achievement Test than peers who had applied for scholarships but were not chosen in the lottery. On the whole, as one would expect given all the myriad possibilities, glimmers of hope could be found side by side with disappointments. Those who did well before receiving the scholarship improved the most (perhaps the Matthew Effect) while those furthest behind went nowhere.

Contradictory findings are predictable and, critically, a likely permanent feature of this debate. Endemic uncertainty flows from two factors. First, the absence of clear research standards makes it very difficult to uncover smoking gun proof. An improvisational quality infuses this research literature and with so many jumbled, difficult-to-measure factors to be assessed, uncovering rock-solid truth requires a near miracle. Second, investigations with an ideological stake in the outcome frequently conduct these studies and are unlikely to bite the hand that feeds them. School policy is big business and careers can depend on results, and with the underlying phenomena so complicated, it is all too easy to shade findings. In the final analysis political muscle, not objective science, will probably determine policy.

To illustrate this evaluation process, consider two reputable accounts of the identical situation. A 2007 *Wall Street Journal* Op-ed by two academic experts, using what they claimed were state-of-the-art statistical techniques, hailed the progress made in Philadelphia's for-profit schools (Peterson and Chingos, 2007). About eight months later a *Washington Post* story recounted how Philadelphia city officials reclaimed six privatized schools and put twenty on the shape-up-or-else list (Richburg, 2008). All had dreadful test scores. Only four of the schools were allowed to continue and even then with a threat of closure hanging over them. Are the academic experts correct despite the disasters recounted in the *Washington Post*? Are municipal officials cooking the data depending on who asks? Who can say, and such disputes are typical.

Still, let us assume the best and conclude that various limited, experimental choice programs—both vouchers and charters—can boost academic attainment, particularly for African-Americans. That acknowledged, has America finally arrived at the true pathway to higher achievement? Maybe but given the eventual failure of countless glittering "guaranteed" panaceas, prudence is advised. Even if we assume that the formidable school choice foes will not sabotage it, tribulations may await as this alternative is scaled up. Keep in mind that as of 2007 the number of charter schools was tiny—some 4,046 with 1.1 million students in 40 states and Washington, DC, only 2 percent of all students (Smarick, 2008). Matters can change drastically when we move from a few experiments with very limited alternatives to a wide-open system involving millions of students. Better to be cautious at the beginning than, as has so often happened, immense resources are committed for "well, it seemed a good idea at the time."

Caution begins by reiterating that Friedman championed freedom, not necessarily academic excellence. This point is downplayed by today's voucher advocates but it remains unavoidably central, and choice *qua* choice, not academic rigor, may be the impetus for many charters. It may therefore be inappropriate to assess academic performance then by solely according to test scores. In one of the disappointing Washington, DC studies mentioned above, parents of those receiving scholarships to escape public schools were more satisfied than those stuck in the old public system. Conceivably, charter schools work fantastically but satisfy endless idiosyncratic goals such as student safety or social prestige. This is not hair-splitting; it goes to the very heart of "choice." The multiplicity of *valid* aims cannot be dismissed by saying "academics should be paramount" or "America needs better educated citizens." For choice advocates to compel bookishness is, Friedman would insist, just as nefarious as insisting that children attend football factories. Walberg and his ilk *hope* that academics will be central, but experience—sad to say—suggests otherwise. Unleashed, choice can prove hostile to academic excellence, not its savior.

The choice/academic excellence disconnect is readily visible in the thousands of American colleges, all of whom, like charter schools, compete for enrollees bringing their own funds (i.e., vouchers). Here intellectual pursuits are seldom paramount though, to be sure, all colleges possess libraries, offer courses, hire professors, and grant academic degrees. But, it is widely recognized that the academically-elite schools are few in number. Innumerable colleges enjoy well-earned reputations as party schools, centers for libertine "alternative life-styles," sports factories, degree mills, comfortable surroundings to acquire future spouses, opportunities for networking, and even possibilities of college credit political activism. Hundreds of schools subordinate solid scholarship to religious devotion and consciously reject mainstream science in favor of theological orthodoxy. And, as any professor will tell you, anti-intellectualism is hardly hidden and is often readily admitted by students themselves.

Can the Educational Marketplace Perform?

If we momentarily assume that nearly all parents genuinely crave top academic quality the question still remains whether it can be bought in a wide-open marketplace. Choice fans often point to the consumer marketplace that strives to please varied customers as a parallel, but school shopping is *profoundly* different. And it is doubtful that these "shopping" impediments can be overcome for all but a handful of determined parents. It is a serious mistake to insist that since disgruntled parents willingly flee a public school in favor of a non-government school that achievement would soar if *dozens* of choices, all hawking distinct wares, were available.

Keep in mind that today's proffered choice menu remains minuscule, a far cry from the fantasized commercial marketplace parallel, so extrapolating from today's limited experiments is risky. There are also practical considerations especially for those unfamiliar with education. Imagine trying to assess genuine academic excellence at a "school fair" held in a convention center where hundreds of schools handed out four-color brochures, imprinted canvas bags, pens, key chains, and other promotional lures. And none of these claims can be verified by shoppers. Not even the most fervent choice advocate might require schools offer guarantees as is common with consumer goods, and if Dick and Jane have a rotten third-grade experience, they cannot take their refund and repeat the grade elsewhere (guarantees often inhibit iffy marketplace claims). Actually, the home school market does occasionally organize such fairs on a state-wide basis, but home school parents tend to be better educated and more focused than those mired in academic misery, the usual target of choice reformers. One might want to visualize such a fair in slum neighborhoods where the entreatments are likely to favor non-academic enticements such as spiffy facilities and entertaining after-school programs.

The educational choices and the economic marketplace differ profoundly insofar as there is no handy pricing-to-benefit mechanism in the former, and this absence seriously undermines market rationality. If Homer visits Sears for Lisa's new bicycle, he easily compares price and features, calculates marginal cost benefits, and certainly asks Lisa her preferences. Lisa may even take a test drive. Everything is immediate and concrete, not a future bike delivered twenty years hence when Lisa's tastes may have changed. "Investing in education" is, by comparison, a pig in a poke, a huge and inescapably uncertain long-term venture.

The world is filled with adults who decades later appreciated receiving a once-loathed education (or kick themselves for skipping Latin). Even a CPA may be challenged to put a future dollar figure on a $50,000 per year Phillips Exeter Academy education versus the humdrum free local high school. A prestigious Phillips Exeter education is undeniably better academically, but is it $200,000 better? The CPA might also be challenged to value the extra tuition cost versus acquiring a new computer, psychological therapy to cure Junior's aversion to homework or a multitude of other learning-enhancing options. And, perhaps the Exeter's education value is short-lived. Without clear price-to-benefit ratios, momentary nonrational criteria, e.g., prestige, sports prowess, easily dominates and this, as we often repeat, is exactly what at least some parents desire. Clearly, while a fool can maximize benefits per dollar when buying a TV, or at least be assured that the purchase is guaranteed, a genius might be befuddled when shopping the education market. The commerce analogy is misleading.

A more appropriate parallel than TV shopping is choosing a college—parents often feel overwhelmed by colorful embellished brochures, unverifiable claims, carefully stage-managed site visits, and similar hype. Parents in the K-12 marketplace may eventually become quite savvy at discerning academic excellence amidst accompanying bragging about athletic facilities, food service, stunning architecture, fawning deans, available social services, and all other potential but fundamentally non-academic lures, but this enlightenment typically arrives only after disappointments, and wasted school years cannot always be made up. Especially for the most desperate for educational excellence (the targets of choice advocates), shopping a medieval fair for herbal cures may be a more appropriate parallel—so, *caveat emptor* (buyer beware).

It is not that some information about a specific school is unavailable, especially to sophisticated savvy parents willing to spend hours getting it right. Today's accountability mania plus the Internet have decidedly improved information flow though, it cannot be overstated, the information is almost entirely school-supplied and thus often sugarcoated or incomplete. On the plus side, however, many cities now have web pages describing individual schools and two national websites—education.com and Schoolsmatter.com—can supplement official statistics. Especially in more affluent communities where school quality sharply affects housing prices, local realtors are probably quite knowledgeable. Still, observing conditions on the ground coupled with interviewing teachers, administrators, and parents may still be advisable though seldom practical.

Potential information acknowledged, however, "being a wise educational shopper" may still challenge parents with limited education and computer skills while those flustered by statistics and educational jargon are almost doomed. Choice may not even be particularly pertinent for this population since residency (which can dictate school choice) may be driven by housing costs, access to employment, affordable neighborhood stores, community amenities, and other non-school factors. Possible language barriers for both the parents and offspring can be especially decisive for immigrants. It is not that choice is foreclosed in such circumstances (recall that even the very poor enjoy non-school options). The point is merely that exercising choice entails costs, and providing an ever-expanding cornucopia of options does not reduce decision-making burdens; it may even raise them, and ironically, those who might benefit the most from proliferating alternatives may be the most challenged at sorting through these options.

As an experiment in what a school shopper might encounter with available net-based resources, I assumed that a mythical family—the Bundy Family—planned to move to Manhattan's Upper West Side. One attractive locale was in the 90s, and this raised the possibility of Kelly and Bud attending PS 75, the Emily Dickinson School (K-5). (Disclosure: I graduated from PS 75). An hour or two of research provided some valuable information, for example, PS 75 performs moderately well according to the NCLB Annual Yearly Progress standards on all tested fields, and has a fairly racially- and ethnically-diverse student body (14 percent were white, the rest largely black and Hispanic). The student teacher ratio was 16:1 and most of the 800+ students were sufficiently poor to be eligible for free or reduced price lunches. Crime was almost nonexistent according to the official statistics. Also on the upbeat side were several attractive after-school programs: chess and varied music activities, daycare, Spanish language classes plus an active PTA and links with twenty-five community-based organizations.

Nevertheless, Peg Bundy desired the best academically for Kelly and Bud, and she grew suspicious when probing deeper. There are no parent comments on the two websites describing the school so official statistics and pronouncements were the only story. SchoolMatters.com had one terse parent rating (basically average across the board) but other information was almost nonexistent. That the nearby neighborhood according to her boots-on-the-ground tour is overwhelmingly white yet the white enrollment is relatively small (14 percent), which suggests that local whites, who tend to be affluent (determined by rental prices), generally avoid Emily Dickinson. Similarly disquieting was NYC private school skyrocketing tuition that suggested an exodus by the affluent, more education-minded from public education. Going beyond speculation in explaining this flight was vital but beyond Peg's talents. A trendy cliché quality also infuses PS 75's mission statement—the principal speaks of creating an environment celebrating diversity, and while test results are satisfactory by hazy government criteria, many students, a third to a quarter, still fail despite small classes and ample resources.

Sports-minded Al Bundy was even more worried since government-supplied data ignored athletics, possibilities for Bud to find well-mannered friends (he needs some civilizing influences), and other largely-social benefits (Al had read Milton Friedman and was therefore immune to Peg's entreaties about academic excellence being the paramount criterion). Both Al and Peg decided to continue investigating but just limiting it to Manhattan's Upper West Side (District 3). Again, the results were frustrating. All told, using the NYC Department of Education's website, there were some nineteen other potential schools for Bud and

Kelly, and sad to say, information was usually dated or, more commonly, nonexistent, far less than what PS 75 supplied.

Exasperated, they Googled private schools in the neighborhood, and a web search found some twenty-two possibilities plus two Catholic grade schools, but this only deepened aggravation. Here, too, personally relevant information—critical for Al given his Friedmanesque leanings—was lacking; if provided, descriptions favored inane verbiage; and as with public schools, everything was school-supplied and thus to be ingested with a grain of salt. Accounts usually resembled flattering brochures, e.g., pictures of bright-eyed multiracial students happily studying, well-dressed teachers attentively tutoring yearning pupils and banal feel-good school mission statements. Unfortunately, since Al and Peg (as average parents) lacked the resources vital for anything more, they decided to remain in the Chicago suburbs amidst familiar if mediocre educational terrain. All and all, absent Herculean efforts that might include extended visits to each school, this is probably as good as it gets for savvy decision-making.

Al and Peg unfortunately neglected to ask if choices existed beyond school walls, and if they had looked around, they would undoubtedly found many more options (see above). It was just a matter of expending extra effort, spending a little money, and the "state monopoly" could have been easily defeated. Perhaps Al and Peg had labored too long reading gloomy think tank reports how New York City parents "lacked educational choice."

Disentangling claims and counterclaims is also daunting work and inescapable if academic excellence is to be made supreme. Consider, for example, a recent "math war" controversy, one of many such curriculum battles that choice-minded parents would have to face (Green, 2007). This battle was a relatively high-profile one unlike much of what occurs over curriculum choices. In the newspaper-reported saga, Texas dropped its "Everyday Mathematics" program, the book adopted in New York City schools in 2007 under Mayor Bloomberg. According to Texas critics, it failed to teach youngsters even basic multiplication. One Texas State Board of Education member called the book the "very worst book" ever submitted for review. A New York University professor of computer science who advises both New York City schools and the federal government on mathematics education praised the Texas decision (and some New York schools rejected the book). Yet, the book's pedagogy does enjoy expert backing. The US Department of Education called it more effective than some traditional programs and "potentially positive." The book's publisher, McGraw-Hill characterized their book as a "proven rigorous program." A New York City educator defended "Everyday Mathematics" for successfully raising fourth-grade test scores. In police language, this is classic "He said, she said" and cannot possibly assist anxious parents wanting the best for junior.

The Arizona Wild West

To appreciate the difference between today's constrained vanilla or chocolate choice menu and what might happen in a "Wild West" choice environment, consider Arizona where charter schools flourish almost unimpeded and can be created by almost anybody, profit or non-profit (Hassel and Terrell, 2004). On average, some three-quarters of charter school applications are approved and no limits govern the number of schools. Nor is local demand a prerequisite. This is the choice advocate's Heaven on Earth, or for public school champions, the nightmare of nightmares. What happens in this *laissez-faire* world?

First, any results from Arizona are to be treated cautiously since the students enrolled comprise less than 10 percent of all students though this type of school abounds. Moreover, the legislature periodically changes the rules, so over-time comparisons can be tricky. Charter and public school students can also be quite different demographically. Still, does this cornucopia of choice boost performance just like competition makes for better TVs? As is commonplace in the entire choice debate, much of these data has a "he said, she said" quality, and research sponsorship clearly seems to shape final verdicts. Assessments also reflect time period, specific proficiency measures, and multiple other key research choices that can easily tip the evidence in a positive or negative direction. The uncertainty here is deceptively consequential for assessing the pro-choice agenda. After all, how can parents choose wisely if expert researchers cannot even agree on basic measures (e.g., "proficiency") or their implications?

At least some of the academic performance data are encouraging though a bit murky (Hassel and Terrell, 2004). According to one overview, schools large enough to participate in the state accountability program (40.4 percent) generally outperform public competitors, and students initially learn at a faster rate, while parents seem generally satisfied (keep in mind however that most schools—still very few students—remain outside this official accountability). Test improvement, moreover, was not a result of charter schools enrolling better students compared to public school pupils (actually, entering charter school students generally have lower test scores). Charters in the accountability system also did well according to NCLB progress criteria although it should be noted that Arizona schools generally lag behind the nation as a whole, so progress is easier.

On the downside are several cautionary studies. A study cited in the *New York Times* (Winerip, 2003) found charters more than twice as likely to be "underperforming" compared to Arizona's public schools. A handful of charters are unmitigated disasters rivaling even the worst public schools—almost nobody can read or write despite all the instruction. An *Associated Press* account for 2005-6 reported that 40 percent of students in charter schools passed the state's AIM math test compared to 72 percent at state-run schools (*AP*, July 13, 2006). Some evidence suggests, however, that the low performance reflects less able students leaving state-run schools and enrolling in charters (and these schools often lack the resources of state schools). Other studies show that while Arizona charter grade schoolers are catching up with their public school peers, student scores plummet when they reach high school (*AP*, July 19, 2007).

Paralleling test score accounts are the "bush fires on the frontier" as Arizona educators call them. The wide-open arrangement has produced countless scandals, notably public officials on the sly selling school charters and collecting supervision fees for doing nothing, instances of egregious financial misconduct, illegal religious instruction (e.g., teaching Creationism), and discriminating against disabled students. The absence of employment contracts and unions to enforce them has sometimes brought high instruction staff turnover so students must adjust to a confusing parade of teachers. Iffy finances have occasionally resulted in sudden mid-year school closings leaving parents befuddled about where to turn next.

Nor are teachers required to be certified except those participating in federally-funded programs for the disabled. The same is true for administrators—anyone in Arizona can be an "educator." While standards exist regarding academic progress and annual report cards, the sheer number of charter schools coupled with limited state oversight means that many schools escape supervision. The extent of corruption and dishonesty is difficult to assess given the lack of accountability, and to compound matters, very few charter schools are closed by the state or voluntarily cease operation though standards have been tightened in response to multiple scandals.

A Future Educational Dystopia?

Foreseeing the future is problematic, and administrative details can be critical, but the Arizona experience bodes poorly for students and their families mired in academic tribulations. In a nutshell, some will undoubtedly gain, some will lose, but choice is not the long-awaited savior. To repeat a warning that cannot be reiterated enough, *everything* we know about those with limited education strongly predicts problems in navigating copious, unregulated choices, especially absent personal experience with demanding academics. Recall the disaster of African-American community control in New York City during the 1960s, a novelty popular with parents and endorsed by leading local civil rights activists: corruption and incompetence everywhere and, glittering assurances aside, learning plummeted. Given that this experiment financially benefited many locals at the expense of learning, a cynic might aver however that this "choice option" was *exactly* what many in the community desired.

The very idea of government-enforced consumer protection, everything from banning dangerous toys, dubious patent medicines and dishonest advertising to truth-in-lending regulations, is essentially aimed at the poorly educated, the target of today's choice advocates. Swindlers praying upon the unsophisticated are a mass media cliché for the TV journalist needing a quick outrage story. The current subprime mortgage loan mess in which those of modest means were tempted to take on huge mortgages with deceptive "teaser rates" once more illustrates the probable gullibility and vulnerability. Actually, those seduced by cheap interest rates were at least rational in the sense they knew what they wanted—a better house. It is less clear what a "good education means" and thus the possibilities of irrationality are greater. The risks of inept school choice are huge if Arizona-style choice becomes the national norm, and if this comes to pass we may hanker after the "good old days" when public control insured a minimum of educational responsibility. Actually, if the idea of personal freedom becomes the supreme value, just as the choice advocates wish, it is just as plausible that millions of students will drop out rather than shop the market for academic excellence.

Defenders of markets as the great elixir conveniently forget that vigorous markets are highly vulnerable to difficult-to-control fraud. Dishonesty *inescapably* comes with the territory. When public appetites are whetted for "new and improved," and progress—say the advertisements—seems effortless, charlatans easily prey on the gullible. Dishonest firms have long exploited the educational marketplace, particularly poor people seeking shortcuts—the door-to-door salesman who convinces mom and pop that Junior will excel academically if they buy a $3,000 encyclopedia. The FTC has long waged legal battles against proprietary schools promising far more than they could possibly deliver. During the 1960s the rage was speed reading—totally digest a 300-page book in an hour—until thousands of disgruntled customers forced deceptive firms out of business.

Not only might gullible parents be hoodwinked by bogus educational claims, but the financial fraud generated by a barely regulated system with tens of thousands of schools and millions of students may be huge. Consider just one possibility, collecting public funds for "ghost" students. Texas recently sued seven charter schools for $16 million for allegedly providing inflated attendance figures (Hargrove and Gavinoff, 2008). This malfeasance was hardly just sloppy record keeping. Houston's Gulf Shore Academy simply "re-enrolled" recent graduates to boost attendance. Even honest public schools collect money for students whose sole act of "attendance" is to sign in and then leave. Existing problems with tracking dropouts suggests the dishonest educators may have a gold mine here since a student can enroll in several schools simultaneously, hardly ever show up at any of them, but be counted for purposes of receiving public funds.

A remarkable feature of the choice debate is how champions "defend" the public's capacity to choose wisely. This is advocacy research and, sad to say, typical of the ideologically-driven battle over choice. Most notable in these "defenses" is that absolutely nothing is said about *individual* decision-making skill on anything vaguely related to education. This is a far cry from, say, asking supermarket shoppers to choose wisely among competing products or understand labels. It is always assumed that parents, even those befuddled by earning a living and staying out of legal trouble can choose wisely when it comes to education. Pro-choice researchers also glibly assume that first-rate education is truly desired. Needless to say, both assertions—sufficient decision-making skill and desire for academic excellence—are highly debatable.

When defenses regarding education-related consumer ability are supplied, they are limp and basically *non sequiturs*. Coulson (2006), for example, defends the skill of the less well-educated by insisting that: (1) public schools, too, sometimes act foolishly; (2) private schools are more attuned to parental desires and drop foolish ideas faster; (3) private schools are superior in educating students and; (4) state-run schools in Africa and India are less likely to teach English, a necessary skill in today's world, than private academies. Neal McCluskey of the pro-choice CATO Institute reviews several cases of private schools victimizing parents, together with comparable incidents from public schools (2005). His point is that while abuses occur in choice schools, they are even more likely in the public sector where layers of bureaucracy shield perpetrators (his examples suggest that fraud, both in public and charter schools, probably reflect local culture, not a school's legal standing). Again, proof is supplied by mere assertion.

Lieberman (1993, 293-4) spends two pages on this topic, half of which (oddly) covers student loan defaults and he concludes that nobody really knows if fraud would be more prevalent with freedom of choice. He also claims, without evidence, that deception would be more likely exposed in competitive settings (that hyper-competition encourages fraud is never considered). Another study by three academics seemingly addresses this "can they decide wisely?" question directly but rather than evaluate the quality of the choice (i.e., receiving the best education for a students ability, interest and circumstances), they instead ask if parents were personally satisfied with their choices and if they actively sought information (see Drummer, 2007 for details). This approach oddly assumes that (a) "satisfaction" equals a sound choice and (b) soundness can be properly assessed long before the educational outcomes are discernable. That even well-informed parents make ill-advised choices about their offspring's college selection seems unthinkable. Given the possible consequences of massive ill-advised choice, such glibness regarding choice sagacity is deplorable and reflects the religion-like character of the choice movement.

Widespread gullibility may well destroy public education as it currently exists, especially if Milton Friedman's standard is seriously applied. Keep in mind that when Friedman in the mid-1950s called for abandoning state-administered schools he expressed satisfaction with it so, as the old adage goes, you may not know what you have until it's gone.

Finally, the alluring "choice means lower prices/better quality means improvement" parallel drawn from economics is not as one-sided at it might initially appear. Markets are not cost-free miracle devices; every market-generated benefit has a cost (recall the Bundys' time-consuming but ultimately futile struggle above). It is indeed odd that this "economic" approach to education slights costs. Myron Lieberman (2007, Ch. 9) is typical in this one-sidedness when he compares the benefits of choice to easy-to-see progress in automobiles, telephones, copying, frozen foods, pharmaceuticals, travel, computers, and similar goods and services. The characterization of progress is absolutely correct but, alas, it is incomplete—facilitating consumerism brings liabilities. Cheaper food may reduce hunger, but after a point it can facilitate obesity and other eating disorders. Aggressive marketing can encourage heavy debt. Today's electronics are, indeed, inexpensive technological productivity-enhancing marvels but whether a house full of giant TVs and similar gizmos has actually improved human existence is hardly self-evident. And, for good measure, rapacious consumerism has often been "paid for" with high environmental costs, e.g., mountains of discarded electronics as improved models emerge every two years, and soaring energy demands, not to mention unwise indebtedness of many poor people. It is a bit incongruous that many of those believing that wide-open competition will insure academic excellence simultaneously bemoan America's deteriorating public culture, a decline clearly facilitated by mass access to high-quality, inexpensive, competition-produced electronics.

This gloomy assessment does *not* claim that academic excellence will be corrupted by markets as hyper-competition seemingly debases popular culture. Without doubt, many parents genuinely crave excellent academics, know how to find it and will pay the necessary prices, so choice will facilitate quality. The size of the elite market cannot be foreseen but it will surely be modest—perhaps no greater than 10 percent of all schools. But, whether progress can be sustained post-choice creation is uncertain. Our analyses of efforts to narrow racial achievement gaps suggest endless assaults on these schools to "help the less fortunate." The war on merit brings the same assault—why should smart (white and Asian) kids "have all the advantages." In other words, unless those wanting undiluted distinction can exclude fans of watered-down standards ("different talents"), market-based solutions to our educational malaise will, like so many other reforms, fail.

A Conclusion: Free Market Education versus Liberal Indoctrination

Expanding choice will not cure academic insufficiency and it may even open the door to extensive quackery. Nor is it absolutely vital to academic excellence since the smartest of the smart can now find what they want even if "imprisoned" in state monopoly schools. The capitalist spirit always finds a way, and with today's technology, this becomes easier by the day. The state may generally supply education but it does not have a monopoly. Nobody has ever averred that teaching third-grade arithmetic is covered by so many patents and trademarks that a freelance tutor might have to battle a Microsoft-like colossus defended by hundreds of lawyers. Nor must this entrepreneur join the union to practice his or her craft. In other words, we now live in the Golden Era of educational proliferation though we might not realize it. Build the rent-free church basement tutoring center with volunteers and they will come *provided they want to learn.* Home schoolers and educationally-driven poor Asians have triumphed *without* charters, vouchers, and all the rest. In economic terms, for the umpteenth time, it's the lack of demand, not inadequate supply that drives our dismal achievement.

The skeptical explication of free-market solutions may appear depressing, but there is a sunnier side. An obscured, perhaps consciously so, agenda may inform its advocacy: insulate instruction from the liberal (if not radical) ideological domination imposed by today's left-leaning education establishment. From this perspective, academic quality is merely the movement's public relations savvy face. Though speculative, it may nevertheless explain the ideological (versus pragmatic) rancor often infusing the battle. For radical educators, permitting parents to select among a dozen or more competitors undermines *their* monopoly on indoctrination. Choice may occasionally improve academic performance, and some choice advocates sincerely insist that academics are paramount, but—to reiterate—this aim may only be the public rationale. In this unstated scenario today's public school obsessions with multiculturalism, "social justice," race and gender oppression, secularism, anti-Americanism, and similar subversive radical views can *only* be defeated by breaking the government's educational monopoly.

Permitting charter schools, vouchers, and the like can thus defeat radical ideological indoctrination. If non-government school choice abounds, a handful of radical professors ensconced in leading teacher's colleges (and their union allies) will lack access to millions of "imprisoned" students save co-believing parents preferring left-of-center messages. Choice advocates assume—probably correctly—that most parents reject leftish ideology, but must tolerate it given the paucity of alternatives. Such ideological baggage is also a luxury to be discarded as schools vigorously compete over price and service. How many parents, for example, will pay for multiculturalism if their children cannot read? Perhaps some will insist on such non-academic ephemera, but probably fewer than what occurs today where parents have little choice. But, with charters and vouchers, those unwilling to pay for such ideological "extras" can readily flee it, and while Junior may not necessarily learn more, he or she eludes the unwelcome proselytizing.

Ironically, the identical logic applies to parents wanting to circumvent "conservative" indoctrination in public schools. That is, parents who abhor creationism, hyper-patriotism and similar "right-wing" views may now find it easier to escape thanks to vouchers or charter schools. Thus while the future is always uncertain, this escape from ideological proselytizing, whether from the right or the left, may benefit everyone. At a minimum it will free schools from wasteful political battles (e.g., so-called "curriculum wars") and educators can now concentrate on education. Hopefully, such "free time" will bring improved academic performance.

9

Reforming Education Is the New Great Society and Why Fixing Schools May Well Subvert the Social Peace

Deep Throat: Follow the money.
Bob Woodward: What do you mean? Where?
Deep Throat: Oh, I can't tell you that.
Bob Woodward: But you could tell me that.
Deep Throat: No, I have to do this my way. You tell me what you
know, and I'll confirm. I'll keep you in the right direction if I can,
but that's all. Just ... follow the money.
  —*All the President's Men,* Bob Woodward and Carl Bernstein

That today's educators keep spending ever more money without much academic gain is one of today's great anomalies. This oddity is hardly a mystery, however: much of what is labeled "education" is less about enhancing learning than enlarging the current social welfare system which, in turn, helps keep the peace. "Reforming education" has grown into an anti-poverty program in sheep-skin clothing. Measured against this yardstick, what appears to be failure is often actually a triumph—the clueless ones are idealistic reformers, not educators with rapacious appetites. This substitution is hardly a nefarious public robbery; all modern societies justifiably (and lavishly) spend on social welfare and conceivably, the U.S. now spends too little. Nor is it a catastrophe that should be undone. Government has long supplied make-work jobs and we are certainly not attempting to roll back kindness by exposing how it has slyly corrupted education. Rather, *many educational reforms will inevitably fail, no matter how technically adroit if they ignore education's intractable social welfare component.* If reforms are to succeed *educationally*, we should at least recognize the formidable obstacles faced by those anxious to fire thousands from decent jobs that they might not otherwise hold.

The Education Social Welfare Colossus

Consider some key features undergirding what uncharitably might be labeled The Failed Educational Industrial Complex (FEIC). Begin by recognizing that "education" is close to a sacrosanct budgetary item across the entire ideological spectrum. In early 2009 with the economy collapsing on all fronts, Congress remained as intent as ever to insulate education from financial carnage. The final $787 billion stimulus package passed enacted in February 2009 allocated some $115 billion for education-related projects, from higher education to daycare and special education, and much of it (specifically $39.5 billion) was to help local school districts avoid teacher layoffs. New construction and renovation were also generously funded while schools at the very bottom were to receive an additional $6.5 billion in both 2009 and 2010 though decades of such largesse had shown the futility of additional spending. New York City, Los Angeles, Washington, DC, and other cities whose school enrollments have been shrinking while budgets expanded naturally welcomed this rescue. Hard, business-like choices were yet again off the menu thanks to "helping the children." Schools were not GM or Chrysler where bankruptcy would allow them to shed thousands of jobs and close unneeded factories.

Classifying a public expenditure as "education" is a huge political accomplishment. Not even skin-flint conservatives dare challenge a few million for some fine-sounding " help the children" program, and it is thus almost 100 percent bullet-proof. (Ironically, the Pentagon's budget includes millions for education yet this is classified as "military spending" and condemned by erstwhile educators since they don't get a piece of this pie). Polls endlessly demonstrate the public's reflexive appetite for more bountifulness, and perhaps only healthcare—"saving lives"—shares this privileged status.

"Education" is also remarkably expandable to include activities that barely affect classroom learning and gullible taxpayers seldom appreciated the elasticity. A planned cutback in Medicaid funds under the Bush administration highlighted this education/social welfare link, a relationship perhaps inconceivable to many Americans perceiving Medicaid as helping sick adults. Though reductions excluded physical and speech therapy or transportation for medical treatment, the new Medicaid's reimbursement policy would cut $635 million from school budgets nationwide (and $3.6 billion over five years). Proposed cutbacks targeted schools that had cleverly pushed varied humdrum expenses on to Medicaid, e.g., construction costs, the school nurse's supply of antacids tablets, and lice combs (Glod, 2008). School officials were outraged over this cutback while "pro-education" law-makers depict this tightening of medical reimbursement rules as thwarting hungry-to-learn youngsters.

Following in the footsteps of past school-based AIDS programs, the blending of health and education may be a growth industry since multiple illnesses (e.g., diabetes, heart conditions, and lung cancer) are partially self-inflicted and consequently might be cured by "more education." In 2005 New York State launched its school-based Activ8Kids to fight obesity and promote healthy lifestyles and, as typical in contemporary education, a cornucopia of jobs flowed. The program's brochure stated that schools were to create teams of parents, administrators, teachers, and community members (among others) to fight fat. A wellness plan was to be developed, data collected from students, and measures implemented, all coordinated with myriad state and federal agencies. A toolkit supplied nutritional guidelines for vending machine snacks and how to encourage physical activity (*http://health.state.ny.us/prevention/obesity/activ8kids/index.htm*). That lethargy might be addressed at a pittance by requiring mandatory outdoor recesses with no cost calisthenics seemingly failed to be noticed by experts sitting around devising ways to energize youngsters.

Washington, DC's schools, many of which deal with students from dysfunctional families are often indistinguishable from social welfare agencies. A *Washington Post* account listed various in-school services, for example, one school has a LifeSARTS program to supply used clothing to neglected students, many of whom had drug-user parents. Several DC schools provide free groceries to take home, a place to sleep or a ride home if parents "forget" to pick them up. Monitoring parental abuse is now a major, legally-required school responsibility and school social workers (117 plus 31 supplied by the DC Department of Mental Health) justifiably feel overwhelmed. The District also contracts with outside therapeutic service firms for after-school, holiday break, and summer treatment for children abused at home. Three Charter Schools (District funded) now administer homeless shelters. Schools also keep food handy when parents "forget" to feed offspring plus showers for those needing them (Pierre, 2008). Another DC program launched in 2008 is D.C. Start. It would draw together some 17 local agencies to send specially-trained counselors into the homes of troubled students to address substance abuse, public aid problems, and the like. The hope is to cure student problem before they erupt in the classroom. Pilot programs will begin in five elementary schools at a cost ranging from $500,000 to $750,000 per school and will be extended if proven effective (Haynes, March 19, 2008).

This may only be the beginning. Washington, DC has now extended "educating youngsters" into "educating parents on how to educate youngsters." The newly-created "Education Excellence: All Students, All Parents, all Families" is a Saturday program involving 25 local government agencies to instruct parent in basic parenting skills, e.g., read to them, help with homework. So no parent would misinterpret these complicated points, translations were available in French, Vietnamese, Arabic, and Spanish. A fair with 50 exhibitors allowed parents to sign up for various government agencies such as free lunches and subsidized childcare (Marcias, 2008).

Washington, DC's approach may be the wave of the future. The school superintendent in post-Katrina New Orleans, Paul G. Vallas, has proposed transforming schools into substitute families with three meals a day, medical and dental care, even keeping school open during dinner, and eleven months a year (Noseiter, 2007). When the head of New York City teachers union assumed the presidency of the 1.4 million member American Federation of Teachers, she called for abandoning President Bush's focus on standardized tests and instead transforming schools into community centers dispensing medical, dental, psychological counseling, and other services to the poor (Dillon, July 15, 2008).

Nor are skeptics worried about taxes inclined to delve into complicated budgets to disentangle fat from muscle, assuming that the two are separable. Creative politicians can, for example, subsidize local museums by insisting visits "help children expand their horizons" while professional conferences can provide vacations at public expense. For good measure the rhetorical defense arsenal for budgetary largesse is often irresistible: fixing schools will cut crime and multiple other costly social pathologies ("schools not prisons"), enhance U.S. economic competitiveness, sooth lingering civil rights animosities, promote patriotic assimilation (and thus defeat terrorism), and promote just about any other imaginable virtue. If ethnic animosities turn violent, the solution is always more education. Even bankruptcy may be insufficient to turn off the faucet given judges' power to order tax increases or further borrowing regardless of legislative miserliness.

Education is also remarkably impervious to modern cost-cutting strategies so expansion only slows but almost never reverses, even as enrollments decline. Saving jobs can be ingenious. In Washington, DC, for example, termination requires an investigation, which, in turn, requires paperwork detailing past performances. According to the current School Chancellor Rhee, administrators would "forget" these regular reviews, or the files would vanish, so it was legally impossible to terminate even the most inept employee. When in 2008 Chancellor Rhee got "serious" about axing incompetents, one price she had to pay for future staff reduction was agreeing to hire yet more staff to counsel teachers who had already been identified as inadequate to provide one last, final, absolutely ultimate opportunity to upgrade skills. She also agreed to establish a new teacher evaluation system so as to cull ineffectual teachers more effectively, and this, guaranteed, will soak up additional funds (Turque, October 25, 2008).

The incredible hostility to terminating unessential, even incompetent teachers was recently exposed in New York City, perhaps a result of proposed budget cutbacks. The City Department of Education has fourteen "Temporary Reassignment Centers," (more commonly known as "Rubber Rooms") for teachers (plus assorted guidance counselors, psychologists, even secretaries) not teaching but still on the payroll (average salary is about $70,000 per year). A spate of newspaper exposés in 2008 estimated the number at about 700 with the cost ranging from $40 million to $65 million per year though the local union claims that "only" $18.7 million is spent (Einhorn, May 4, 2008; Green, May 5, 2008). These Rubber Room occupants, all drawing full pay and benefits, include those who cannot find employment within the system since no school wants employees disciplined for infractions ranging from chronic lateness to sexual impropriety. Several remain there for two or more years and pass the time playing cards, doing puzzles, and sleeping. Half do not even bother to apply for vacant teaching positions. The Rubber Room can be dangerous and demoralizing and recently some occupants sued the board claiming that assignments there violates teachers' rights.

But, what happens to these rubber room residents when educational funding must be drastically cut? Not much, it seems. In late 2008, with the city's Department of Education facing as much as $435 million in cuts, the school chancellor negotiated a union-approved settlement that would, supposedly, "save" the city millions (Medina, November 19, 2008). Nobody would be fired, and no rubber room resident evicted but to encourage schools to hire these idling residents versus cheaper rookie teachers, central administration would pay the difference between rubber room veterans and new-hire salaries for up to eight years. To sweeten the deal, the principal of the school doing the hiring would receive a discretionary bonus equal to one half the hire's annual salary. To be sure, the principals for one year retained the option of firing the rubber room hire (though his or her salary would, of course, continue). All and all, this is how, at least in New York City, one "saves" education money amidst a huge financial crisis: leave waste untouched but spend even more money but call this fresh funding "less than hiring even more teachers."

Perhaps nowhere in the U.S. is this tacit jobs, jobs, jobs, social welfare function more pronounced than in Washington, DC. When the city's mayor planned to close 23 of the city's under-enrolled facilities so as to upgrade instruction elsewhere ($50 million alone in utilities would be saved), a reasonable step given utilization, widespread outrage greeted the plan. Through the Coalition to Save Our Neighborhood Schools parents and community activists launched a citywide campaign, including radio commercials. School officials (nearly all of whom were black) were accused of racism and secretly planning to sell schools to real estate developers for gentrification. Many parents kept Junior home for the day to protest announced closings. The anti-closing campaign also drew support from DC's city council (Haynes and Stewart, 2008; Stewart and LabbA¿, 2008).

Quickly, however, even without the closings, the job-creation machine was back on track (Haynes, February 18, 2008). A grand new educational agenda was announced for the 2008-09 school year. The smorgasbord of labor intensive proposals (all uncertain, limited, or proven to be ineffective) included scripted lessons for some elementary school teachers, extra evening, weekend and summer instruction for select middle-school students, school-within-school career-themed academies (with separate administrators). This was in addition to hiring literacy and math coaches plus other specialists in all "failing" schools. Meanwhile, "overage students" notorious for bullying others would be enrolled in Twilight, a supposedly intensive math and reading program to prevent them from dropping out. Not all parents were satisfied with the menu, and they too had ideas, all of which, naturally, cost money. One suggested hiring an outside consultant with a record of helping at-risk students. A PTA president recommended expanding their child's high school course offerings to include culinary arts, business, media, and barbering/cosmetology.

Now, thanks to political indignation, what began as an effort to cut unnecessary expenses, or at least allocate resources more productively, was quickly transformed into an even greater (and pointless) expansion of employment. It was as if School Chancellor Rhee was throwing raw meat to placate wolves nipping at her heels. Why should "overage" bullies be kept in school? Are not math teachers "math coaches"? That the DC district faced a financial shortage apparently was irrelevant—failure was again reflexively attacked with bigger budgets. One might speculate that program advocates are incapable of calculating costs or just believe that "somebody else" (i.e., Uncle Sam) will pick up the check. At a minimum, adding extra hours of instruction requires additional pay for teachers and schools-within-schools means administrative duplication. And, to repeat, absolutely nothing about these "improvements" guarantees progress other than progress for expanding the educational workforce.

K-12 education is one, if not the most, labor intensive industry, and this trend seems to be increasing (see Lieberman, 1993, 257-8). At least in the 1990s, personnel costs in education amount to some 93 percent of output value compared to 54 percent for all private businesses. While private industry on average invests some $50,000 in capital per employee, the education's figure was $10,000, a pittance even in other labor intensive industries. This is a far cry from what transpires in the rest of the economy, even medicine where cost cutting is vigorously pursued though lives are involved. But, when it comes to education, today's reform agenda, namely smaller classes, one-on-one counseling, innovative pedagogy, multiple enrichment activities, and the like, are exactly the *opposite* of what is preached elsewhere. If schools operated like GM the latest Chevy would be horrendously expensive, almost all hand-crafted, burdened with useless gimmicks, unreliable and, if customers resisted, educators would demand larger government subsidies since, after all, "cars are critical to our nation—see the USA in your Chevrolet." Discussions commonplace in industry over slashing per unit labor costs or squeezing suppliers to cut prices, are unthinkable in education where soaring labor costs are equated to "commitment to progress."

Part of this attachment to extravagant practices, no matter how deficient educationally, is explainable by what economists call surrender costs, a powerful psychological force almost divorced from rational economic calculus. That is, handing back an existing benefit will require more compensation than original cost (i.e., a benefit costing $5 might require $20 for it to be returned, not the original $5). A recent budget cutback in New York City illustrates this principle and how reductions can be as painful as a drug addict reducing the dosage. Here the City's Department of Education announced a 1.75 percent budget cut resulting from the 2007 economic downturn, a pittance since the pro-education Mayor Bloomberg had boosted school spending some 72 percent since 2002. But, returning the bird in hand was extraordinarily unpopular, undoubtedly far more unpopular than if the mayor had increased spending by 70.25 percent. Thousands of parents, teachers, and students protested in front of City Hall shouting in English and Spanish "Keep the promises." One parental coordinator told the press, "You can't cut off people's legs and expect them to succeed." The City's principals union president said that his group had been suffering and waiting too long (Medina, March 20, 2008). Perhaps Bloomberg should follow Machiavelli's advice that benefits should be ladled out in small increments but bad news announced all at once.

Cost-cutting is not about imposing ruthless business practices on the schoolhouse. The aim should be changing the culture from one where budgetary expansion indicates progress to honoring those able to trim without hurting actual learning. It is hardly mean-spirited to follow the Japanese practice of cheap bare-bones black/white textbooks. Or downloading daily lessons from a CD and printing them with high-speed printers so teachers could print library books on demand to eliminate ordering, cataloguing, and replacing lost books. Instead, textbook companies, with full education establishment encouragement, compete by hiring experts to tweak pedagogy, add riveting graphics, or cater to noisy racial/ethnic constituencies. The possibility of replacing bloated, expensive textbooks with cheap DVDs is unthinkable. It would take little to enlist former Wal-Mart executives notable for cost-reduction ingenuity, but that policy is far less alluring than, say, hiring additional special counselors for troubled students.

Some Statistical Snapshots

A little statistical data exposes these rapacious appetites. Though comparing educational expenditure over decades can be tricky given changing requirements (especially teaching disabled students), how inflation is calculated, and shifting public expectations, the overall spending increases are indisputably huge. If private donations, gifts-in-kind, and volunteer labor are included, these numbers would be much larger. Further add the considerable remedial educational expenses shouldered by the military and private firms, including basic literacy that should have been accomplished by grade schools. But, just sticking to official statistics, the U.S. educational honey pot's growth is large enough. In 1919-20 the cost per pupil in constant (2005-06) dollars was $668; by the beginning of WWII it had risen to $1,404. Upward movement continued so in 1949-50 it was $2,188 and by 1959-60, $3,190 per pupil. By the end of the twentieth century it hit $10,000 and by 2003-05 it was $11,000 (Digest of Educational Statistics, 2006, Table 167). Keep in mind that this is per pupil, and inflation adjusted.

Eric Hanushek (1994, Chapter 3) calculates that between 1890 and 1990, educational spending grew at a rate three times that of GNP growth, so in 1890 education consumed 1 percent of the GNP compared to 3.6 percent in 1990. Education munificence, according to Hanushek, has even outstripped health care appetites. We are also spending more on buildings and facilities. In 1990, the inflation adjusted per pupil outlay for K-12 for construction was $481. It has risen steadily, and by 2002 it had more than doubled to $903. In Washington, DC, which leads the nation in public school ineptitude, the figure for 2002 was $2,552 (NCES, 2007, Table 7c). Moreover, the student-to-teacher ratios over the last half-century have fallen sharply, and with no academic improvement, despite the oft-repeated claim that smaller classes would do the trick.

These dollar figures obscure how "education" entails far more than teachers helping students learn. The classroom with its teacher is, to invoke a hoary cliché, just the tip of the iceberg. Hanushek (1994, 27) notes that in 1940 instructional costs (e.g., teachers) comprised about two thirds of school budgets but the figure had fallen to 45 percent by the mid-1990s. Keep in mind that expansion occurred when class size dropped sharply, and smaller classes required more teachers to teach the same overall number of students, so the shift away from direct instructional costs is greater than these statistics indicate.

Gone are the days when schools consisted of teachers, a few administrators, maybe a guidance counselor and a custodian or two. Today's facilities overflow with specialized staff catering to the complicated psycho-social needs of pupils who were, allegedly, ignored a generation back. This is very different from Japan where parents shoulder many tasks that would otherwise occupy teacher time such as ensuring that students are prepared for school. Japanese students even help with custodial work. In the U.S., by contrast, people are paid to contact parents and otherwise spark interest in their children's education. And to insist that American students pick up trash ("demeaning"), this cost-saving measure would probably instigate a union-led demonstration (and if implemented, rest assured, somebody would be hired as "student work coordinator").

Some settings, especially where "at-risk" students are involved, now even rival luxury resorts where attendants outnumber guests. In 1949-50 when Ozzie and Harriet sent David and Ricky off to school, the ratio of pupil to school staff member was 19.3 to 1; by 2004 it had fallen to 8 to 1. In the 1960s when the Fonz, Lavern, and Shirley of *Happy Days* all hung out, there were barely any "instructional aides" (1.3 percent of all staff); by 2004, nearly one of eight staff members was an "instructional aide" (11.7 percent). In per pupil terms, the figure had gone from nearly 800 per aide, to 69 (Digest of Educational Statistics, 2006, Table 77). In fact, primary school classroom teachers, the soul of "grade school," may eventually become a minority of K-12 personnel if trends continue: in 2003, for example, there were a shade under two million full-time elementary teachers but closing in were 857,000 support staff.

The enterprise's labor intensive nature can be discerned from job descriptions and pay scales. New York City is a leader in the expansive social welfare-as-education enterprise, and many positions are available to those with modest training or a high school equivalence certificate. Job descriptions include "Teaching Assistant," four distinct levels of "Educational Assistant," three levels of "Education Associate" and two types of "Auxiliary Trainer." There are also varied "Family Assistants" hired *per diem*. Salaries (as of 2008) for all these helping jobs range from just over $20,000 per year to $31,000, hardly middle-class in New York City but with benefits (a choice of three health plans, disability insurance, a pension plus multiple other benefits), a decent job for many. The police department also supplies school safety positions such as crossing guards (who are Teamsters Union members). To be sure, better positions require some college credit, but not the degrees, and credits can be earned gradually at minimal cost at numerous open-admissions community colleges throughout the city.

The formidable obstacles awaiting anybody who seeks cost/benefit efficiencies was strikingly illustrated in 2003 when the New York City Department of Education sought to outsource some public school maintenance (Herszenhorn, 2003). If salary were any indication of worth, more is involved than pushing a mop. Base pay in 2001 for custodians was between $58,000 and to $92,000 per year, considerably more than what the city's teachers earned (Kelley, 2001). Custodians can also supervise more than a single school, and thereby boost earnings well into six figures (Gootman, September 26, 2003).

More important, cost-cutting measures that would usually pass unchallenged in private industry brought outrage when applied to school employees. Local 891 of the International Union of Operating Engineers denounced the alleged money-saving plan and filed a lawsuit to prevent outsourcing. It also instigated a city council hearing on the subject and organized protest meetings outside of city hall, again tactics unthinkable in the private sector. Local 891 further enlisted support from the powerful UFT union representing the city's teachers plus the head of the principals union. Meanwhile parents representing several schools protested the outsourcing and newspapers told how private custodians endangered the health of students.

In early 2004 a State Supreme Court Justice ruled in the union's favor and declared that the outsourcing contract violated the New York state's competitive bidding rules. The city said it would appeal the verdict but this may drag on for years. The ruckus also highlighted certain custodial practices regarding just how janitorial work is performed in the city's schools. This is truly enlightening. Custodians are forbidden to do all but the most minor repair work, leaving the tasks to union carpenters, union electricians, and other specialists. Interestingly, unionized custodians are also school-financed "capitalist" entrepreneurs, if not empire builders, a throwback to the earlier patronage-based system. Each receives a lump sum annual budget to hire assistants and to pay for cleaning supplies. Unfortunately, fiscal discretion has brought payoff scandals and accusations of hiring subordinates with criminal records. In other words, a neighborhood school, thanks to the janitor, now becomes an employment center where locals, regardless of qualifications and backgrounds, can find work and contracts.

Leaving "lowly-paid" custodians and moving up the social class hierarchy are school-based positions whose existence New York's taxpayers probably barely suspect. Positions include alcohol and substance abuse counselors, school medical inspectors, sign language interpreters, education officers, and pediatric nurse associates, among others (UFT, 2008). Further add graphic artists and editors preparing all the handsome upbeat reports issued by the Department of Education, website experts, researchers, lobbyists, statisticians, and media liaisons.

Solid upper middle-class jobs also exist for this rush "to help languishing children." New York City's central educational administration has recently added several new positions whose responsibilities, at least according to a *New York Daily News* story, baffles parents and are undoubtedly redundant (Einhorn, December 26, 2007). Among them are a Chief Accountability Officer ($196,000); a Chief Knowledge Officer ($177,000); a Chief Talent Officer ($172,000); a Chief Portfolio Officer ($162,000); A Chief Family Engagement Officer ($150,000) and a Chief Equality officer who in 2007 worked for free but will earn $195,000 in

2008. All told, eighteen of the City's top education bureaucrats earned more than $190,000, a salary more than the city's police and fire commissioner (Einhorn, December 18, 2007). This is on top of the seven education consultants, each being paid $1 million plus expenses.

These salaries are only part of the freshly created and ever-expanding bloat; each Chief surely requires a retinue of assistants, secretaries, computers, cars and drivers, and, no doubt, expense accounts while occupying hyper-pricy New York City office space. A cynic might also predict yet more appointments to coordinate relationships among these newly-hired chiefs or settle turf battles. Imagine Mayor Bloomberg running his lucrative media empire by hiring people with murky job titles and big salaries whose responsibilities were already performed elsewhere? A "Chief Profit Maximizer"? Perhaps New York City's highly-politicized education dictates bringing potential troublemakers on board at decent salaries.

Schools have also become restaurants, not lunch rooms where grade schoolers ate home-made sandwiches while older students just visited the neighborhood diner. In 2007, New York City schools served some 640,000 lunches and 191,000 breakfasts during the school year, most of which were subsidized. The Big Apple is hardly exceptional in making "eating" a school-run activity. Since 1969 student participation in the national school lunch program has dramatically expanded (along with student waistlines, it should be added) and so has the proportion of subsidized meals. According to the Department of Agriculture that administers the program, the proportion of free or reduced-price lunches nationally has gone from 15.1 percent in 1969 to 58.8 percent in 2007. The breakfast program has meanwhile exploded by a factor of 43, and by 2007 nearly all (80.8 percent) are free or at reduced cost (*www.fns. usda.gov/pd/slsummar.htm*). No wonder today's youngsters do poorly at economics—they are incredulous when told there is no such thing as a free lunch.

The "children can't learn on an empty stomach" claim is hardly self-evident given that students once survived—even thrived—without school-supplied meals. Nor can it be argued that the U.S. has slipped into such dire economic straits that schools must do double duty as soup kitchens. Have parents forgotten how to prepare peanut butter and jelly sandwiches? A more plausible explanation is that putting food on the students' table also puts food on countless other tables. As a formidable military bureaucracy stands behind each combat soldier, supplying meals entails far more than telephoning Pizza Hut. The school's gastronomic commitment means hiring kitchen staff, clerks to order food and equipment, dieticians to plan meals and supervise special dietary needs, accountants to monitor expenses and payroll, extra custodians, lunchroom monitors to prevent food fights, inspectors to report rats and improper food preparation, plus central administrators to handle Department of Agriculture subsidies. Resistance has emerged to schools-as-restaurants, but objections concern the poor nutritional values of these meals and proposed solutions include fewer pre-packaged meals, using locally-grown fruits and vegetables, more organic foods, educating students about healthy diets among other measures, all of which will boost costs. No doubt, a small fortune could be saved by giving students free McDonald's or Burger King gift certificates.

The rise of employees performing work once largely done by classroom teachers is hardly accidental, especially where the newly hired must join the union. To repeat, this is job creation, not necessarily better education, and the greater the number of workers, the greater the number of union dues payers who vote. The current New York City UFT contract explicitly prohibits teachers from performing tasks that once came with the job. Article Seven excludes teachers from study hall service, handling, storing or inventorying books, scoring achievement tests, or preparing postcards to be sent to the homes of truants. Even duplicating classroom material—personally photocopying materials rather than having a specialist do it—is forbidden. Meanwhile, teachers of disabled students are barred from helping their students on or off the bus except in contract-specified circumstances and, thankfully, emergencies. Likewise, as per UFT contract, paraprofessionals who assist in regular teaching responsibilities are not permitted to perform office work, lunch room duty, and hall and potty patrol while enjoying considerable job security (*http://www.uft/member/publications/paraprofessionals/you_uft_para/print.html*). The venerable "It's not my job" is now a protected right.

New York City is hardly unique in transforming "education" into job machines. The US Department of Labor regularly estimates future job growth, and those seeking careers in today's uncertain economic times are advised to enlist in the "Help the Children" crusade. For example, while the demand for teachers in general will grow by 12 percent from 2006 to 2016, job increases will be even greater in "less desirable urban and rural school districts." Job prospects are also above average for future preschool and Kindergarten instructors thanks to federal largesse. In fact, teaching math and science to inner-city students, no matter how unwelcomed by lesson recipients, is the best bet, and virtually a sure thing if one is a minority or bilingual. Though many Americans complain about relying on immigrants for skilled workers, many of whom are here illegally, the demand for vocational teachers will *decline* by an estimated 5 percent. In other words, for those contemplating a career in education, it is better to teach science to bored sixth graders than to impart marketable skills.

Particularly helpful for uplifting poorer Americans is for schools to hire teacher's assistants, workers with limited schooling for whom a $24,000 job with decent benefits and job security helps to escape poverty. According to the Department of Labor, the growing attention to disabled and non-English-speaking students will require additional school personnel, and the teaching assistant, who can draw half a teacher's salary, is the answer to these expanding needs. More help is also needed for government-funded after-school programs, summer catch-up programs, tutoring students on standardized tests and here, too, the teaching assistant fills the bill. Job prospects are likewise excellent for more middle-class workers in the "helping professions," e.g., counselors, social workers, family workers, and psychologists (U.S. Department of Labor. Occupational Outlook Handbook, 2008-09 Edition).

The trend toward narrowing responsibilities and adding yet more workers to shoulder tasks rejected by others is exactly the opposite of current private industry practices. Private-sector down-sizing without diminishing output means that, for example, five employees do the work that once required seven or eight. Even in universities, hardly grim profit-driven factories, professors use computers and high-speed printers to replace secretaries. Airlines permit carry on luggage to cut labor costs and advise passengers to buy sandwiches before boarding. Recall that Japanese schools demand students clean up their classrooms. Schools today overflow with innovative job descriptions but "cost cutter" is not one of them. Educators by the thousands may attend conferences on the latest pedagogical innovation, but it is unlikely that school administrators would visit religious schools (let alone Wal-Mart) renowned for superb results on a shoestring. "Inappropriate" would be the rejoinder if this site visit were suggested.

The Financial Benefits of Educational Disasters

To appreciate further the money to be extracted from terrible schools, consider school security. Official government figures confirm what is widely suspected—many urban schools with impoverished students are increasingly prison-like, and educational incarceration does not come cheap. In these urban schools nationally, 16 percent have bars on windows, 45 percent employ security guards, 12.8 percent have metal detectors, 15.6% use security cameras, 36.6% fence off the entire school, and 21.7% monitor the parking lot (US Statistical Abstract 2007, Table 219).

In New York City 82 percent of black and Hispanic high schoolers pass permanent metal detectors, all staffed by security personnel and others who keep this safety enterprise afloat. In New York City's 2008 budget, some $221.7 million was spent on school safety when including the services provided by the City's Police Department. No doubt much of the maintenance staff works to repair vandalism or willful neglect of equipment in addition to other humdrum activities. Watching over Big Apple students is a growth industry—since 1998 when the New York City Police Department took charge of security, more than 1,600 new security personnel have been added (Tarleton, 2007). NYC's school security is now the *fifth* largest police force in America.

These security costs are deceptively far-ranging. Over and beyond the initial material costs for cameras and fences, for example, there is ongoing training (fourteen weeks in NYC for the school police), hiring specialists to adjudicate incidents, and yet more lawyers to both assess disputes and defend the school from litigation-prone groups such as the ACLU. Add counselors to mediate the inevitable clashes between security and students, and the bureaucratic overhead to hire employees, assign guards, and perform dozens of other new-found tasks. Janitors may now receive extra training for graffiti removal while many schools rely on the local police department's anti-gang units. Schoolyard ethnic tensions may also soak up resources by paying teachers extra for lunchroom or playground duties.

More pernicious than converting policing into "education" is how dependency and job creation merge. This is self-evident but never acknowledged: students are "trained" for dependency, and this helplessness generates ever more employment. This is a win-win policy from the perspective of an expanding welfare state—students are allowed to be irresponsible while the once unemployed gain jobs. As is so often the case, Washington, DC is the poster child (NBC4.com). In 2008 it was discovered that a quarter of the city's 2,000 seniors were in danger of not graduating due to insufficient course credits. This was previously handled by a modest summer school program, but with heightened pressure to make the graduation numbers, more was now required, and the job creation machine quickly geared up. Now all 12 of DC's high schools will offer summer programs to some 8,000 students (an increase of 1,000 over the previous year), decrepit schools will be repaired, new air-conditioning will be installed, and schools will serve breakfast and lunch. Private businesses will supply tutoring help. The cost of this extra effort will be $7 million and will focus on basic literacy and math skills.

The underlying reward structure here invites disaster; it is not "compassion." Given awaiting rescues, it is perfectly rational for school officials to be lackadaisical in ensuring that seniors graduate on schedule or, for that matter, students learn their lessons on time. With self-induced failures come summer teaching and administrative opportunities, contracts for businesses (who are probably well-connected politically), and other tangible rewards. Parents may appreciate free meals and knowing that their children are safely under adult supervision for a few hours per day. One could only imagine if the summer program beneficiaries were legally required to work during the summer without pay as a penalty for prior ineptitude (with the meals prepared by parents out-of-pocket who neglected Junior's progress).

Money into Toilets

It may be awkward to admit it, but the physical tribulations bedeviling many schools populated by black and Hispanic students are, sad to say, probably incurable and thus a near permanent source of income. Media accounts of visitors being shocked by dilapidated schools in New York City, Paterson and Newark, NJ, Chicago, Washington, DC, St. Louis, and elsewhere have a generic quality. Facilities are nearly always in deplorable shape: toilets overflow, graffiti everywhere, broken windows, too few textbooks and inoperable equipment, broken heating systems, random vandalism, and even gang-infested "no go" zones. Having depicted the hellish environment, the outraged visitor proclaims that learning is impossible under the appalling conditions, and when the story breaks, embarrassed officials promise to correct deficiencies "immediately" and contracts are soon awarded. Critically, absolutely nobody objects to repairing overflowing toilets or fixing dangerous stairways and all else.

Keen observers know that these scandalous conditions are virtually identical to what is found in nearby non-school venues. A word-processing program could substitute "public housing" for "public school" and scarcely any newspaper reader might notice. Playgrounds blocks from schools display similar disarray—broken equipment, litter, mindless vandalism, graffiti, and a sense of immanent violence. Happily for those on the payroll, interventions to improve non-school settings likewise almost always fail, and in a few cases the only "solution" (as in St. Louis and Chicago) was to demolish public housing which, to be frank, only relocated pathologies elsewhere. But while the local playground may go unfixed, the moral impetus to repair schools is indisputable—education is just "too important." Teachers would undoubtedly privately confess that patching broken equipment or shipping in fresh supplies is only temporary since, as we showed in discussing bad students versus bad schools, it is the students, not shoddy equipment that are the calamity's source. Toilets elsewhere work for years with only minor, if any, maintenance.

Pouring money into brand-new facilities that will quickly return to their decrepit state-of-nature can verge on self-imposed mental illness. Washington, DC officials plan to level H.D. Woodson High School and replace with a new and "better" facility (Haynes, June 11, 2008). Woodson is only 36 years old and was once offered a swimming pool, air conditioning, escalators, and similar amenities "guaranteed" to help the children. The original principal sought to impart strong academic values and racial pride—red, black, and green were the school colors—and discipline was firm. Alas, the familiar urban pathologies eventually appeared, including drug-related killings, and the facility crumbled. Heralded amenities such as the air conditioning and the pool are broken and Woodson has repeatedly failed NCLB standards. Does anybody *seriously* believe that its expensive replacement will escape these calamities? Will new escalators help move the same students toward academic proficiency?

Compare how the public views repairing shoddy schools and funding yet more social services for troubled students versus tackling out-of-control welfare spending. Beginning in the 1970s it became increasingly clear that existing welfare policy fostered a downward pathological spiral—generosity discouraged employment, and without regular employment, dependency bred countless bad habits and this soon became a way of life. Finally, in 1996, with bipartisan support, Congress ended this cycle by permitting states to restrict time on welfare while requiring job training and employment as a precondition for assistance. Support for welfare reform reflected both a moral imperative—punish sloth—and the practical realization that long-term generosity sustained human misery. Thanks to reform, welfare rolls dropped sharply and once "incurable" pathologies declined.

Education is different. The very idea of skimping, unless revenues precipitously decline or no more bonds can be issued, is almost unthinkable. In 2006 New York City hired a consultant to "cut fat" (Einhorn, December 18, 2007). The upshot was not reducing the budget, but shifting funds from the central administration to the schools themselves, perhaps the equivalent of an obese person "cutting back" by stealing somebody else's food. The pro-spending chorus, regardless of outcomes, is deafening. Vandalized toilets, to take but one odious example, will be fixed, and fixed again even if students themselves daily destroy bathroom facilities. If toilets remain broken, some bureaucrat will be threatened and action probably taken, but the student culprits will probably continue as before. Schools may even invest in finding a vandal-proof toilet which, rest assured, will be ten times as expensive as the normal one, but surely "the children are worth it." Nobody is willing to say, "Perhaps the best response to bathroom vandalism is to lock all inside restrooms and replace them with schoolyard port-a-potties." Ditto all other self-inflicted harm: let students suffer the consequences, including the incarceration for mischievous behavior, and they will soon learn that bad behavior is not rewarded but this is, naturally, just daydreaming.

Administrative ineptitude, like learning itself, can be its own reward. Without competent oversight, the money flowing through schools can easily disappear so "helping the children" becomes personal enrichment. Washington, DC is justly famous for Third World style looting but it undoubtedly exists elsewhere where hiring policies disdain merit. A *Washington Post* account (Fallis and Witt, 2007) tells of rampant stealing from student activity funds, money collected from private donations, and student-run activities for yearbooks, class trips, and similar activities. Activity funds can amount to several hundred thousand for high schools, and while strict control and audit rules exist, the district's central administration just ignores thievery or is totally inept when investigating criminality. In fact, several activity fund monitors were convicted felons and record-keeping was so sloppy that uncovering the stealing was impossible. In recent years, despite rampant larceny (and myriad highly-suspicious activities) only a single person has been prosecuted. Money is just deposited in a bank account, and culprits (sometimes several in a single school) use ATM cards for withdrawals to finance expensive personal indulgences.

To focus just on stolen bake-sale revenues ignores the larger point: the entire administration, from top to bottom, can be "organized" to extract personal gain under the guise of educating students mired in failure. Boosting learning thus serves as the socially commendable stick-up weapon. The *Washington Post* runs a cottage industry depicting incompetence so far-ranging, so tolerated, that it can only be deemed a morally acceptable culture. One typical story told how the school's transportation division paid millions in unauthorized, undocumented, unjustified overtime while not bothering to check if drivers possessed required commercial licenses (most did not). Not surprisingly given the predatory culture, more than half of the time-sheets for overtime had disappeared (Editorial, 2006). Elsewhere fiscal bountifulness included non-existing personnel in budgets, gross over-staffing, employees without clear job responsibilities, and countless other instances of mismanagement (Lipscomb and Emerling, 2007). What perhaps sustains this incompetence is that firing administrators is difficult, and if demoted for ineptitude, he or she keeps the higher salary, so the ranks continue to fill with inept workers while the payroll increases.

The popularity of the Failed Education Industrial Complex (FEIC) is totally predictable: all those feasting off failure, including their families, are potential voters (and requiring city employees to reside where they work compounds this pressure). Filling the government payroll to ensure reelection is hardly a novelty, and education may be one of the few remaining places where patronage can still thrive. Education as social welfare even outshines over-staffed municipal hospitals since the damage inflicted by schools is almost invisible compared with filthy operating room carnage. The closest business parallel is the employee-owned firm where efficiency may run counter to economic self-interest. But, even then, owner employees may accept that it may sometimes be necessary to amputate a limb to save one's life.

The Anti-Drop Out Employment Machine

When expanding jobs for "education" nothing outranks the strategy of pushing students to remain in school—it is the full employment perpetual motion machine and has been growing thanks to NCLB rewarding retention. In his first address to Congress, President Obama made retention a priority: "This [a high drop out rate] is a prescription for economic decline, because we know that countries that out-teach us today, will out-compete us tomorrow." And, he added, the U.S. will have the world's highest proportion of college graduates by 2020, as if a high school or college degree somehow magically certified competence. This "body-count" obsession may put food on the table but it is a horrendously wasteful academic quality benchmark, a measure akin to Soviet factories filling production quotas by manufacturing millions of ill-fitting left shoes. The jobs awaiting saviors may even explain the paradox of Hispanics (among others) overwhelmingly demanding "more education" while their offspring flee school—tangible benefits accrue to those trying to keep students in, not the students themselves.

Actually, accurate figures are unreachable, and numerous incentives exist to fudge the data, so we squander huge resources not knowing what we are accomplishing. An odd parallel exists between America's dropout statistics and Soviet-era industrial production figures. It is even unclear exactly what "dropping out" means since a student may disappear from one school, arrive at another and then a year later leave for a third—two "drop outs" for only a single student. A *New York Times* account told how states routinely and admittedly keep two or more sets of books with real attrition rate often dramatically higher than the official figure (Dillon, March 20, 2008). Despite NCLB mandates for statistical accuracy, and a 2005 agreement among governors to improve the data, unchecked dishonesty continues and myriad technical problems, e.g., tracking itinerate students, makes the quest Utopian (Neal, 2007).

Unfortunately, the economically-driven "we must force them to get the degree" argument has risen to an article of faith, a set of undocumented clichés. Henry M. Levin, a Stanford University Professor, is typical when he proclaims, "The rising number of at risk students and their continuing failure will have severe ramification for the United States" (Levin, 1996, 227). Superficially, this oft-stated view seems self-evident. It is hard to imagine a modern, productive economy staffed by illiterate, innumerate workers. But, matters are not so obvious. For one, the U.S. economy has grown substantially while millions flee school and, conceivably, the skills contributing to this growth have *nothing* to do with a diploma. Certainly many economically-relevant skills are acquired on the job or in apprenticeship programs. Second, many school-related deficiencies can be overcome via technology or outsourcing, so armies of drop outs need not be economically fatal. Finally, curing the drop out disorder may misallocate precious resources. Perhaps the millions spent here could be better invested in, say, rebuilding America's deteriorating infrastructure or some other venture promoting economic growth (and construction workers could be those unable to get the high school diploma). Remember, if economic efficiency is paramount, the question is always the *best* investment, and anti-drop out champions *never* assemble the relevant data.

The tip-off that anti-drop out measures entail more than "saving young minds" becomes clear when we recognize that keeping every teenager in school counters history and, undoubtedly, human nature. Compulsory schooling is *compulsory* because absent legal sanctions the flight from academics would be a jail break. No educational system, past or present, *ever* judged educational progress by the more-the-merrier criterion, and justifiably so. European schools routinely permit students who would be likely drop-outs by American standards to leave school by fifteen or so. Some—perhaps most—youngsters abhor school, and they cannot be convinced otherwise. That they want to run off as quickly as possible should be perceived as an enduring human condition, the historical default option. It is *not* a correctable defect that has suddenly and mysteriously plagued American society.

Futility is further deepened if the IQ is factored into this equation. Intelligence and dropping out are strongly related—among those at the bottom of the IQ distribution the drop out ranges from 35 percent to 55 percent versus nearly zero for those with IQs above 117 (Gottfredson, 2003). This is absolutely commonsensical: less bright students are exasperated by repeated failure and *rationally* see no point in listening to what sounds like gobbledygook. By contrast, bored but smarter student can slide through with minimal effort. Boosting retention among those with low intelligence thus requires either (a) upping IQ or (b) making complicated lessons clear to the bewildered. Unfortunately, neither option is viable and pessimism reflects hundreds of billions in failed government programs.

A clear-eyed (and *rational)* economic analysis of life options might also suggest the futility of keeping many students, especially those living in dangerous crime-ridden neighborhoods, in school. The oft-made argument—you can take home a few dollars more over a lifetime with the degree—will fall flat to those who might *immediately* earn far more by dropping out. A full-time gang-banger running drugs can probably earn more in a single year than the marginal lifetime increment earned by a compatriot who struggled to acquire a high school diploma. Even if criminality is eschewed, the available job market in fields like construction and agriculture are indifferent to diplomas, and if work experience is essential, the drop out may *rationally* elect to start his or her career a few years before the graduation date.

Positing the diploma and future earnings link also reflects economic naïveté. Gary Becker (1993, Chapter 7) shows that the incremental value of a high school diploma greatly shifts as economic conditions fluctuate, and no reason exists to suppose an upward trend or even steady positive yields on investment. The opposite is more likely if anti-drop out advocates triumph. That is, if the marketplace will now be flooded with recently manufactured "graduates" so the degree's value is necessarily diluted (simple supply and demand). Going a step further, the presence of these fresh diploma holders, many of whom received it by the skin of their teeth (or official duplicity), would doubtlessly encourage employers to substitute their own tests for the diploma and thus substantially reduce the value of the *ersatz* degrees. This is merely government-produced educational inflation to create jobs.

Claiming that "having a degree" in and of itself bestows knowledge and motivation is akin to primitive people believing that pen ownership signifies literacy. A New York expert on retention spoke of having the diploma—not knowledge or discipline—as the crucial first step in socioeconomic advancement (LoMonoco, 2008). She also depicted the problem as having nothing to do with the students themselves. Everything was a matter of resource insufficiency, e.g., a lack of collaboration between varied government and community agencies, as if the students on the edge had nothing to do with their plight. All of this analysis was, naturally, economically self-serving since her job depended on this characterization of the problem. The time-honored "let them drop out and see what happens, then welcome them back" solution was probably unthinkable—no jobs there.

Predictably, the education establishment happily manufactures studies galore to justify "keep them in at all costs" (Drop out studies are multiplying and a fuller picture can be found at the California Drop Out Research Project at *http://www.lmri.ucsb.edu/dropouts/pubs_reports. htm*). That these studies are conducted by educators themselves whose profession materially benefit from keeping bodies in school represents a clear, though never acknowledged conflict of interest. Picture these educators confronting global warning research sponsored by coal companies—cries of bias would be immediate. Nevertheless, leaving aside self-interest, the methodology employed to reach these upbeat conclusions is hardly persuasive. This is advocacy research sold to a happy-to-believe public.

One overview drawing widespread publicity summarized several studies relying on multiple interventions, e.g., preschool, smaller classes, more dedicated teachers, encouraging parental involvement, to prevent attrition (Belfield and Levin, 2008). Here's how the case was made. First, the total per student cost of each extra assistance effort is calculated over the program's lifetime. For example, in the Chicago Child-Parent Center Program the price tag of the supplied services was $4,728 per student. But, since most of those exposed to the program failed to stay in school, the cost per actual graduate was $67,714. Next, compare high school graduates vis-à-vis non-graduates on multiple indicators, from taxes paid on income to the cost of incarceration. Predictably, those leaving school early are over a lifetime especially burdensome to society. With the calculated cost to society of drop outs in hand together with the price of preventing the flight, the cost/benefit ratios of intervention can be calculated.

The investment payoffs are truly impressive, or so it would seem. For example, the Perry Preschool program showed that every intervention dollar produced $2.31 in benefits, i.e., those who would not have otherwise graduated paid more taxes, consumed less public welfare, committed fewer crimes, etc. The Chicago program produced slightly over $3 per intervention dollar. When actual per student dollar figures are multiplied by the number of "saved" students, the alleged savings are staggering. In California, for instance, the intercessions would save the state some $46.4 billion annually, an incredible bargain for a small investment. Savings are, moreover, particularly impressive for low-income students whose lack of a high school degree is especially expensive.

Another example of this research approach comes from a report entitled Fight Crime: Invest in Kids California, and is strongly endorsed by the Los Angeles County Sheriff. The report insists that the "drop out crisis" comprises a "substantial" threat to California's public safety (Bagchi, 2008). It further claimed that cutting the dropout rate by 10 percent would reduce murder and assault by 20 percent—500 fewer murders per year, to be exact. The suggested recipe for saving these 500 lives per year and other crime costs was the (predictable) high-quality preschool, and dramatically expanding the Check & Connect program in which monitors checked on school attendance while connecting potential fleeing students to needed social services. The report even claimed that for every dollar invested in preschool, California taxpayers would save $2 to $4.

These studies are prime candidates for the "too good to be true" museum. The method of calculating benefits is seriously deficient. The proper methodology would be to randomly select a representative sample of children, subject another random sub-sample to the anti-drop out measures (preferably in varied combination), follow all groups for about thirteen years (K-12), and then statistically disentangle the impact of each treatment. Then "saved" students would be matched against students lacking the assistance over, say, twenty years, to chart variations in income, criminality, welfare use, and all the rest. An accurate answer thus requires about thirty-three years, though much less if intervention begins in high school, and even then, sorting it all out is a statistical nightmare. And keep in mind that it is almost impossible to follow individuals for such lengthy periods and this, in turn, requires dozens of adjustments and guesses.

Needless to say, the save-the-drop-out "studies" fall well short of this standard; they are not even within hailing distance. Biases are everywhere and verge on deceit. As one might predict from the "spend more" economic motives of these education researchers, the reduced tax outlays that come with fewer high school enrollees is excluded from the "benefits to society" ledger. Letting millions easily flee versus holding them back will trim down the required number of teachers, free up classroom space, and permit schools to fire countless administrators specializing in retention. School safety costs would also be lowered and, critically, those remaining might learn more thanks to teachers freed of trying to teach those rejecting education. All and all, a tax-saving bonanza.

Faulty assumptions are just piled one on top of another. Can we assume that one-time interventions like a year of preschool or a better trained fifth-grade teacher outweigh hundreds of other uncontrollable, long-term influences? Why must we presuppose that the "saved" high school graduate is no different than his or her classmate who fled degree less? It is bizarre to assume that "saved" students are intellectually or psychologically comparable to those actually graduating sans intervention. That they differ cognitively and morally, among other differences is far more credible. Nor can it be taken for granted that tactics monotonically cumulate so, say, a class-size reduction adds so much, after-school tutoring so much, parental outreach so much, and the effort's total yield comes by mechanically adding up all three. Nor is there any evidence that bits and pieces of unaudited upbeat news, culled from a few localities, can be applied state-wide, let along nationally. Keep in mind that research on drop outs has been ongoing for years while the drop out rate has soared.

Nor is it axiomatic that these save-the-drop-out intercessions competently use taxpayer money. Especially when these newly manufactured "graduates" are enticed to attend colleges, the savings quickly evaporate. One study of remedial education in America's colleges put this bill at between $2.3 billion and $2.9 billion. A different study using federal data found that some 43 percent of community college students and nearly 30 percent of four-year college students require remediation (cited in Pope, 2008). While this shifted burden might be judged just robbing Peter to pay Paul, it is doubtless popular among thousands of academics who survive by instructing indifferent students in subjects they have encountered two or three times before.

Perhaps requiring potential drop outs to enroll in for-profit vocational schools (which are often cheaper than public schools) is a more efficient, cost-effective strategy. Hiring more police and tougher law enforcement may reduce criminality more cheaply than "fighting crime" by forcing students to stay in school. Welfare costs might be more efficiently reduced by tougher eligibility standards, not better preschool. Moreover, since many high school dropouts are Hispanic immigrants, and if saving public money is the sole criterion of a program's success, more forcefully stopping immigration would undoubtedly outshine trying to graduate immigrants post-arrival. In fact, deporting students here illegally may be cheapest solution to many of our social tribulations versus spending even more to keep them in school.

More telling, the oft-remarked link between keeping kids in school and economic progress is not nearly as valid as it appears. Actually, it is incorrect though it has become a cliché. That prosperous nations keep students in school does not mean that welding doors shut brings economic bountifulness. A detailed long-term analysis using fifty countries did find a small relationship between time spent in classrooms and economic growth—each additional year added .37 to GDP (Hanushek et al, 2008). Make no mistake, this tiny amount is important over the long haul but it says nothing about actual learning. As the authors note, a year of schooling in Papua New Guinea is not the same as a year in Japan. When cognitive skill—what is actually learned—enters the equation, actual learning has a far greater impact. With high achieving students the GDP increases a percentage point per year for each year in school. Of the utmost importance, once actual learning is taken into account, the time spent in school has no value for GDP. The authors are frank: "A country benefits from asking its students to remain a longer period of time *only if students are learning something as a consequence*" (italics added). The authors also found that immigrants who arrived in U.S. already well-educated added to the GDP but they contributed little if their education was acquired here. This last item is crucial since so much of the anti-drop out effort is directed at recently-arrived Hispanics. In other words, this effort, no matter how noble, makes no economic sense.

Moreover, American schools are geniuses at offering empty calorie classes that entice bodies from fleeing. Those "rescued" by endless interventions may owe their diploma to a steady diet of dumbed-down instruction, credits for fluff yearbook and cheerleading courses and easy grading. It resembles the old Soviet era factory adage: they pretend to pay us, and we pretend to work. Absent clear national tests, this strategy is also undetectable except when employers are exasperated when hiring ill-educated "graduates." Certainly nobody on the school payroll will blow the whistle.

Research on alleged benefits aside, however, the retention-at-all-costs strategy is a god-send to armies of job security-seeking bureaucrats. A particularly insidious example of this jobs *über alles* mentality is the growing reluctance to expel troublemakers. Not only does keeping miscreants in school generate state-supplied revenue but, often thanks to advocacy and "rights" groups, fresh staff can be hired to protect schools against litigation. A favorite to total expulsion is to create an entire labor-intensive "alternative school" to house delinquents, complete with psychological specialists and monitors. Ambitious alternative schools may even hire consultants to cure anti-social behavior with wilderness treks or self-esteem building exercises. Los Angeles recently allocated $200,000 on an anti-drop out marketing campaign that includes commercials on hip-hop radio, cell phone text messages, and YouTube videos. This is in addition to lots of new staff (e.g., a diploma project advisor) plus capital intensive building projects (Hoag, August 19, 2008). A few chronic mischief-makers if compelled to stay in school can probably support entire families for years.

This retention-at-all-cost feeding fest received fresh meat in April 2008 when AT&T announced a $100 million grant over four years to keep students in school otherwise inclined to drop out. These funds will go to America's Promise Alliance (APA), headed up by Colin L. Powell that also receives millions from the Gates Foundation for the anti-drop out crusade. Awash in cash the APA plans a national campaign with "summit" meetings in all 50 states and 50 key cities over the next two years. These will be celebrity-style events (Oprah Winfrey is included) drawing together civil rights groups, talk-show personalities, community organizations, varied philanthropic groups, students, parents, teachers, faith-based organizations, and similar concerned citizens (Maxwell, 2008). The director of the AT&T philanthropic fund also hoped that the company's employees would help mentor 100,000 students in grades 9-12 to prevent their dropping out.

The APA's solutions appear to be a rehash of previous failures, e.g., combating poverty, more support for struggling students, encouraging greater parental involvement, and overcoming student boredom. Other remedies on the "10 Point Plan" seem antithetical to retention, e.g., raising the compulsory school age and pushing a college-oriented curriculum, though they will surely generate additional educational jobs. In a telling comment, the AT&T foundation director said that by exposing students to a tech-oriented workplace, students might be convinced to remain in school. It is equally arguable that this experience may whet appetites for abandoning boring school work (Howard, 2008). The program also calls for more accurate statistics, a long-time quest that has repeatedly fallen short.

Though the millions will undoubtedly be spent (hundreds of conferences require ample hotel rooms, food and drink, speaker fees, planning costs, and transportation) it is difficult to see how the assorted personalities, all representing divergent constituencies can agree on anything, let alone discover what works when offered proposals have terrible track records. Cliché mongering will be the norm and media-monitored forums will draw publicity seekers galore. What, for example, would a civil rights activist add to the shopworn menu of more diversity, more affirmative action, or greater spending? Does Oprah have some unique insight? With tempting millions before them, groups will probably pursue thinly-disguised economic self-interest, e.g., church groups will push for religion-based solutions while unions will insist upon bigger bureaucracies.

The well-intentioned program also deepens dependency under the guise of helping. The D.C. College Access Program (part of the ATA) recently boasted of its success in turning once troubled students into college graduates (Bhanoo, 2008). The amount of effort exerted by those assisting the students was prodigious. It began with counseling in high school, college tours, pre-college parental workshops plus tracking academic progress. Once enrolled in college, there was financial aid, more monitoring, and similar pushes to securing the diploma. One lesson from their experience is crystal clear: I can succeed provided I have lots and lots of expert help to push me. One might guess that when these endlessly-assisted graduates enter the workforce, they will rationally expect similar help and, if it is not forthcoming, may be clueless on surviving on their own.

Graduating those prone to flight can also be an economic boon to fourth-rate colleges, especially enrollment-driven community colleges. With the "stay in school for as long as possible" message volume turned up, many "graduates" might be enticed to attend nearby two-year state colleges. Besides automatically upping per pupil state assistance, the woeful academic preparation of these fresh recruits justifies hiring additional staff, funding yet more remedial programs, and otherwise conflating academics with social work. A recent story from Washington,

DC perfectly illustrates how ill-prepared high school "graduates" can be a financial lifesaver for a university about to go under. Here Trinity University, a once elite women's Catholic sister school to Georgetown University, experienced severe enrollment declines during the 1970s and 80s. It went coeducational but that scarcely helped. Recently, however, it discovered the path out of bankruptcy—it has reinvented itself as a largely black/Hispanic school catering to local low-income students (Redden, 2008).

Though it remains to be seen whether Trinity teachers and administrators can reverse twelve years of bad habits, the prospect of economic security has brought an enthusiastic welcome. The dean of arts and sciences called this influx a "radical and exciting transformation" and she is excited about the wholesale revamping of the curriculum to build "foundation skills" (e.g., learning how to read and write). She further adds that the "urban learners" have, despite acknowledged deficiencies rendering them unprepared for college work, "amazing assets," notably their resilience and persistence. Their predictable shortcomings have even generated an academic conference paper. Though data on progress are incomplete, faculty and administrators are upbeat, especially since extra specialists have been hired to offer additional lab work. Meanwhile, the once-hidden away Academic Services Unit has been resurrected to handle student shortcomings. Perhaps the Holy Sisters of Trinity decades back prayed for a miracle to save Trinity, and sure enough, the sky opened and thousands of ill-prepared students arrived to keep the institution going for eternity.

Trinity College's salvation is hardly unique. All across California community colleges are benefiting from foundation support to teach basics to those who missed them the first, second, and third time around (Redden, 2008). In 2007 the Carnegie Foundation for the Advancement of Teaching together with the Hewlett Foundation has allocated some $300,000 to instruct elementary math and English skills. Other foundations joining this quest include the James Irving Foundation, the Walter S. Johnson Foundation, and the Packard Foundation. In Detroit an organization called Detroit College Promise is similarly trying to push high school graduates into community colleges with the lure of free tuition (Associated Press, August 19, 2008). The Gates Foundation sensing a grand opportunity to squander hundreds of millions has predictably joined the futile but job-generating campaign. In November 2008 it announced that it was committing hundreds of millions to help students in community colleges obtain the degree (Jaschik, November 8, 2008).

Melinda Gates opined that just getting poor and disadvantaged kids to college was insufficient; they must graduate if they are to get a job with a "family wage." That this diploma may merely be high school remediation or, worse, a worthless piece of paper issued by enrollment hungry schools was obviously off the agenda. The degree itself just bestowed vocationally-relevant knowledge.

A recent study of remedial efforts on nearly 100,000 Florida students confirms the futility of manufacturing college graduates (Calcagno and Long, 2008). The good news was that remediation in math and reading could help troubled students remain in school a bit longer, no small benefit for teachers hungry for extra enrollees. But, in the final analysis, remedial classes did not produce a college degree or even help pass additional college-level courses. The research confirms what every college instructor already knows—those unable to do college-level math or read complicated material cannot be upgraded by extra attention. Perhaps extra English instruction might help a recent immigrant, but an eighteen-year-old still unable to read is a lost cause. If these students had the ability, they would have mastered these skills years before showing up.

Educators toiling "to save the drop outs" are silent regarding the huge academic benefits of permitting easier flight from school. Clearly, opening the schoolhouse door would enhance average test scores while assisting those staying put by banishing miscreants soaking up teacher time and resources. This is one educational reform that really does have a legitimate money-back guarantee. It will not, however, be embraced for the simple reason that it is too risky. Though NCLB would reward test-score progress, it simultaneously punishes the higher drop out rate. This exchange of higher test scores for lower enrollments would not, however, be a wash. The tie-breaker is that fewer enrollees means fewer jobs, and since NCLB may vanish tomorrow while enrollment-based employment is forever, better to keep the mischief-makers locked up.

Job apprenticeships, a traditional cure for those hankering to escape school *never* emerges in laments about wasting essential national talent. The assistant vice-principal for student retention may incessantly complain about finding a skilled auto mechanic, and even hear about students skipping school to customize cars, but complaining is never translated into, "Perhaps we should let potential drop outs leave school and work with local car dealers so I can get my Honda fixed in a day, not a week." Inner-city school administrators bewailing broken toilets should consider apprenticing students to the local plumbers union so as to help reduce repair costs and thus have more funds for staff salaries.

The issue is not being frugal since costs may be a wash; nor is the question of whether apprentice programs work (they, too, can be sabotaged by slothful students). Rather, apprenticeship programs would defund schools, and this means job reductions, so broken cars and vandalized toilets will have to wait.

Defending the School's Social Welfare Function

Transforming schooling into social welfare is not necessarily evil or wrong-headed. It is certainly arguable that the early nineteenth-century Jacksonian spoils system helped democratize America and cement immigrant attachments. There is also a more contemporary sturdy non-educational defense: it sustains the social peace. This is an updated Great Society-style mollification of potential violent discontent, an insurance policy to avoid the urban, heavily racially-tinted upheavals of the 1960s. Actually, the idea is hardly original idea and certainly not a "right-wing" one. Over thirty years ago this rarely articulated purpose was advanced by two radical professors—Richard A. Cloward and Frances Fox Piven in their widely read *Regulating the Poor.* For them social welfare was less good-hearted humanitarian aid than a mechanism to mollify potential social unrest—when the poor grew restless, mail out more welfare checks, and when matters calmed, cut them back. From that perspective, all that has changed is the form of the bribery.

The evidence here is substantial though hardly admitted. We repeatedly saw how huge sums were invested in doomed-to-fail projects, and funds still continue to pour in despite futility. Washington, DC with its large poor black population exemplifies this "foolish" enterprise. Bloated, unproductive school payrolls exist as a form of socially-acceptable bribery for those otherwise incapable of achieving a decent middle-class life. Watered-down diplomas similarly provide the happy illusion of "education" to youngsters who might otherwise be driven to mayhem. "Educational reform" is a tactic, perhaps a cynical one, of social control, and tranquility, not a path toward higher test scores. Frustrated reformers are thus applying the wrong yardstick.

From this perspective educational "reform" has achieved its aims regardless of academic achievement. "Urban riot" now has an antique quality, and "long hot summers" are no longer greeted with trepidation by big city mayors. Radical violence-threatening Black Panthers and their ilk are history. It is an incredibly cost-effective solution—millions are squandered so that billions are saved on riot control and restoring torched neighborhoods. Though students might learn little, nobody dies or is injured by educational inefficiency. In an emergency, as we saw, smart people can be imported via increased immigration.

Paradoxically, expensive "reform as peacekeeping" may be wealth-producing, fiscal waste aside. Making money in peacetime is always easier than with a tumultuous home front. In New York City domestic tranquility that results from calming troubled waters via proliferative educational spending has helped instigate a real estate boom which, in turn, means higher municipal revenue via higher tax assessments plus innumerable capitalist gains. Educational reform is thus economically a positive sum game. Try imagining New York if Chancellor Klein slimmed down the school system as many financial firms trim staffs in lean times—the overall financial costs of controlling outrage and diminished taxes from lower property assessment may far exceed ended "waste." "Excess" school employees are also avid consumers and thus help drive the city's thriving retail sector. Salaries are merely recycled. The exploding economy built on social peace certainly permits middle-class parents almost painless escape from dreadful public schools. Savvy elected officials perhaps unconsciously sense that a "bang-for-the-buck" cost-cutting school reform will reignite 1960s urban turmoil, and to be frank, no superior way of allocating funds exists to uplift the intellectually averse bottom. Social peace via "waste" thus yields the most optimal outcome possible.

Some Disturbing Implications

Today's school reformers inevitably begin as optimists—surely, they insist, schools could do better while saving millions, so why can't we roll up our sleeves, commission rigorous scientific studies, figure things out, and impose necessary changes. That approach inevitably brings disappointment and erstwhile reformers lash out at what they consider obstacles to change: teachers' unions, entrenched bureaucracies, antiquated laws, public ignorance and all else sustaining the flawed status quo.

Reformers typically misconstrue the obstacles they confront. For them the core problem is to uncover effective policies and then convince policy-makers to heed expert advice. This is the universe of scientific reports and the Progressive belief that technical excellence must ultimately triumph; all executed by talented, well-paid people *whose livelihood does not directly depend on education budgets*. Those experts, moreover, assume that academic superiority is the highest priority for everyone, and it would be even better if progress could be achieved at the lowest possible cost. This *weltanschauung* is incredibly naïve; for every think tank wizard or Education School professor demanding quality and efficiency there are thousands of school janitors, bus drivers, classroom assistants, lunchroom workers, curriculum coordinators, guidance counselors, school psychologists, and on and on who may have few options outside of school-based employment. Unlike these reformers, inept teachers, clueless principals, and all the others living off of "wasted" expenditures are totally uninterested in the latest study showing the inverse relationship between spending and accomplishment. Those perpetrating ignorance just don't care—bread on the table counts more.

This plain-to-see social welfare fact has powerful and dreary implications for those embracing Milton Friedman's quest for economic efficiency. Privatization is especially anathema where school payrolls are vital to the local economy, and this doubtlessly includes dozens of cities with a majority of the nation's pupils. Voters will not vote themselves out of work nor will politicians endorse firing constituents. Wal-Mart is scary enough in New York and Chicago; schools run like cost-obsessed Wal-Mart are a hundred times more terrifying. Once given, publicly-supplied benefits such as jobs and contracts are almost eternal and quickly evolve into rights and entitlements. Keep in mind that that hyper-expensive over-staffed school systems with armies of barely competent teachers and administrators would require the most pruning, and employees about to be marched off to the gallows are not about to go quietly. Tribulations faced by downsizing corporations—union opposition, bad press, towns devastated by closings, hoards of unemployable middle-aged workers, closing expenses—are child's play compared to slimming down a distended, incompetent school system. GM can always correctly insist that looming bankruptcy gives it no choice, and even unions accept that half a loaf is better than none. This is far less true for schools—they always have the option of drawing more from the public treasury, even if this requires a court order, often conveniently secured by a "do-good" foundation.

Dreary news also awaits reformers favoring tougher job requirements. These reforms, no matter how obvious or rational, will meet ferocious and probably successful resistance for the very simple reason that the least able, those most dependent on public sector jobs, are the most likely to be terminated by staff upgrading. Marginally-qualified workers might also be the most likely to be disruptive, often thanks to demagogic local leaders. Education, unfortunately, is not professional sports where cutting marginal players, even beloved over-the-hill veterans, to win championships is heralded. If anything, as we argue, much of today's education is expressly designed to shield the barely competent from market forces. Similarly, boosting salaries will necessarily increase competition and, again, this is bad news for those just hanging on. In many cities a principal who received a generous bonus for sharply curtailing labor costs or raised standards so that only non-locals could fill positions would need armed guards.

The ramifications of having to keep the inept are deceptively serious. Reformers and most educators live in different universes, the former see education as primarily about academics while the latter see it as a source of jobs, and east is east, and west is west, the twain shall never meet. For the umpteenth time, quality education and an inclusive personnel policy are antithetical. This is sad news for boosting achievement but probably inescapable.

10

Hope?

Belling the Cat

*Long ago, the mice had a general council to consider what measures they could
take to outwit their common enemy, the Cat. Some said this, and some said that;
but at last a young mouse got up and said he had a proposal to make, which he
thought would meet the case. "You will all agree," said he, "that our chief danger
consists in the sly and treacherous manner in which the enemy approaches us. Now,
if we could receive some signal of her approach, we could easily escape from her. I
venture, therefore, to propose that a small bell be procured, and attached by a ribbon round the neck of the Cat. By this means we should always know when she was
about, and could easily retire while she was in the neighbourhood."*

*This proposal met with general applause, until an old mouse got up and said: "That
is all very well, but who is to bell the Cat?" The mice looked at one another and
nobody spoke. Then the old mouse said:*

"It is easy to propose impossible remedies."

—*Aesop's Fables,* by Aesop
translated by G.F. Townsend

Books on education policy usually conclude with a litany of vacuous
homilies peppered with good-sounding, endlessly repeated panaceas absolutely guaranteed to fail. We eschew this honored tradition and instead
offer some harsh commentary for those all-too-rare souls who genuinely
want better academic performance. We also confess that achieving this
aim may be too arduous even if possible and this grim assessment hardly
condemns Americans. Academic attainment is hardly so sacrosanct or
vital to human existence that it must dominate our national agenda.
So, with America being a democracy, the required diligence cannot be
government imposed. We get what we want, and top-notch schooling is
just not our national obsession. For millions of Americans a championship football or basketball team may be more appreciated than, say, a
dozen Merit scholarships, and rest assured, if given a chance, hoards

of youngsters will skip math classes to secure a spot on championship team rosters.

The Academic Achievement Equation

Recall that our Human Capital understanding of academic achievement:

$$Achievement = 8 \text{ Intelligence} \times 4 \text{ Motivation} \times \text{Resources} \times \text{Pedagogy} \times \text{Instruction}$$

Both liberals and conservatives fret over the equation's last three elements and, sad to say, all have been pretty much maxed out. This is the gist of our depressing tour of today's extensive reform menu. Pouring billions more into spiffier schools, higher teachers pay, accountability incentives, more choice, and new instructional gimmicks (among hundreds of alleged panaceas) will scarcely help without touching intellectual ability and motivation. Glimmers of hope occur largely from lying or lowering the bar to produce illusionary progress. Elsewhere progress is often cherry picking a few items in a sea of unreported failures. This is hardly good news, but like hapless dieters misreading the scale, Americans happily accept modest accomplishments.

Our analysis has, we confess, only made an indirect case for this vision. We have argued that today's claim that the last three components of right side fail to perform as advertised. They cannot make so-so students inherently smarter or dull the pain of serious learning. It is not that they are irrelevant since some of these remedies, under certain conditions and with certain students, can help (and others can make matter worse). But, to insist that tinkering with these components can yield dramatic improvements is usually vacuous political rhetoric.

Matters are not hopeless; everything depends on altering the mix of smart and not so smart students, and then somehow pushing the intellectually-talented to even greater achievement. This is feasible *provided* the political will exists and, sad to say, this may be asking for too much. It is unlikely that an "education mayor" will run on a "time to kick butt" platform or advertise for a "high school quality control expert" whose job will require throwing out underperforming students, firing now surplus teachers and all the others who existed to help these slackers. Genuine reform would be cheap and less able students might be encouraged to enroll in vocational schools where their training would far outshine a bogus academic diploma. If talented students refuse to make the effort, return to traditional motivational practices like scorn and ridicule, tender egos and delicate self-esteem be damned. Perhaps the lessons of what occurred in America immediately following Sputnik should be read aloud once a year to all educators and, if that is insufficient, explain how our technological advantage may vanish if we can no longer import brains as we now import oil.

If there is an elephant in the room it is America's rapidly-changing demographic. The government's own data paint a picture that may shock today's adults who attended school thirty or more years ago. Specifically, in 1975 84 percent of all seventeen year olds were white, 11 percent black and just 3 percent Hispanic. By 2008, the proportion of whites had fallen to 59 percent, blacks were up slightly to 15 percent, and the Hispanic proportion had soared to 18 percent (*http://nces.ed.gov/whatsnews/sat-chat/users/index.asp?auto=true*). As of 2006, some 21 percent of all elementary students in public elementary schools were of Hispanic origins (these and similar data are available at *http://www.census.gov/population/www/socdemo/school.html*). In a nutshell, to speak the virtually unspeakable, if average IQ test scores for blacks and Mexican and Central American immigrants are to be taken as valid indicators of cognitive ability—about 15 points lower than whites—the average IQ of the school-aged population has dropped, and this, not resources, pedagogy and all the rest, probably explains most of our tribulations.

This decline in cognitive ability is only the beginning, however, though keep in mind that IQ is hardly destiny. Recall how New York City now must educate 15,000 students who barely speak English and are unacquainted with what classroom behavior entails. And New York City's vexations are common elsewhere. Especially where Hispanics have congregated, notably large cities like New York and Chicago, plus southern California and Texas, where they are close to a majority. Many struggle with English, frequently change schools as a result of parent job opportunities and, as their high dropout rates attest, seemingly devalue the vital trait of tenacity. And as these difficult-to-teach youngsters grow in number, more academically-attuned students flee, and the obstacles to imparting knowledge multiply. Reversing this downward trend is exceedingly difficult. When you combine struggling Hispanics with native-born (but not immigrant) African-Americans, more than one in three elementary public school students comes from a racial/ethnic background that has long struggled with schooling.

National discussion of "educational reform" would differ radically if America were suddenly flooded with students from Finland, Korea, Japan,

Australia, and Switzerland, all nations where students excel in math and science (see McKinsey & Company, 2009 for these comparative data). Further imagine that current students from Mexico, Guatemala, Honduras, and other Third World nations suddenly all voluntarily returned home. Professional educators would be congratulating themselves on the dramatic turnaround and nearly all of today's reform agenda would quickly vanish. Yet, this possibility can only be uttered in the most hushed conversations since it hints that human beings are not interchangeable in terms of cognitive ability. To be blunt, better to pour billions into futile reforms than broach taboo topics.

This demographic shift is reinforced by parallel cultural deterioration. With scant exception, little pressure exists in today's culture to "be smart" aside from ambitious immigrant children. Recall Lawrence Steinberg's extensive analysis of American high school students—being a "brain" is unimportant if not widely condemned. Athletics far outranks scholarship and this occurs in so-called "good schools," not inner-city "bad schools." Today's public culture heroes are drawn from entertainment, sports, and elsewhere where being super smart is almost irrelevant. Celebrities are often famous for being famous and their silly public utterances often contribute to their fame. And, whatever natural intellectual ability and ambition young Americans possess has been undermined, especially among the intellectually less able. Subversive forces would include loosened family bonds, single-mother families, the rise of violent gangs, cheap, readily available dumbed-down pop culture with its multiplying distractions from schoolwork, debilitating drugs, and countless other modern attention-deficit disorder inducing pathologies. These forces powerfully shape motivation, and as Chapter 1 argued, Calvinism often substitutes for modest smarts and at least in some settings such as the renowned KIPP academies, it can be instilled.

Nor is there much pressure to reverse these dumbing-down trends. No Sputnik-like wake-up appears on the horizon, and to be blunt, even if it did, many Americans just don't care. The War Against Gifted Students chapter showed that we happily import brains and this dependence on foreign-born talent (or the children of immigrants) embarrasses nobody. Matters hardly differ at the personal level—few youngsters are discomfited by their inability to calculate a 10 percent discount on an iPod. Scary rhetoric about the "need for a good education for a good life" aside, the modern and (so far) prosperous welfare state insulates dolts from catastrophe. Though millions of semiliterate youngsters are officially unemployed, even unemployable, America has not returned to a Dickens-like England where armies of paupers begged for handouts; drop outs are more likely to suffer obesity than starvation. Crime now provides a viable alternative to holding a job requiring a decent education. Decades of economic prosperity have cooled the passion for reading and writing, and millions of Americans hardly care.

Correctly Measuring Our Alleged Failures:
It May Be Better than It Seems

The prevailing wisdom is that America is bumbling along educationally. This is, alas, true but that admitted, it does not follow that we could do any better. Rather, improvement efforts must be judged by what is feasible under trying circumstances, including what schools can reasonably impart when functioning in often hostile settings. From this perspective even decline may, in fact, be a "success" since without all the seemingly wasted billions, matters may be worse. To be frank, existing data tell us almost nothing about realizing academic potential, not its absolute level, but at least in principle an answer is not especially difficult, either collectively or individually. Indeed, it is remarkably easy so perhaps we just don't want to hear unwelcome news. Hugh McInnish, an engineer, did precisely this with a few back-of-the-envelope calculations for twenty-five elementary schools in Huntsville, AL (McInnish, 2008). He simply took each school's Standard Achievement Test (SAT) and the Otis-Lennon School Ability Test (OLSAT) off the state's Department of Education Website (OLSAT basically reflects IQ). He then developed a measure called "Teaching Effectiveness" which is simply achievement divided by ability multiplied by 100. What he discovered was that five of the six schools with the highest test scores were actually operating *below* their average cognitive potential while four of the six schools at the bottom were *above* their IQ-predicted performance levels. This pattern is hardly surprising given America's obsessive passion for uplifting the bottom at the expense of the smart.

A different analysis comparing U.S. youngsters in grades 8-10 of varying races to compatriots in Canada, France, Japan, Italy, and Germany reports that white students, but not blacks or Hispanics, more than hold their own (save against the Japanese) in reading, mathematics, and science (Boe and Shin, 2005). To be politically incorrect, America's education woes vis-à-vis foreign economic rivals largely reflect the U.S. having large black and Hispanic populations, both of which perform below average on tests. America's schools are conceivably doing a fantastic job given our demographically-related obstacles. If our lazy, least capable students were subtracted (many of whom should not have been in school in the first place), the outcome might be spectacular. We might justifiably spend a year holding banquets honoring once castigated educators as newly recognized "Heroes of Knowledge." Throw into the equation a cultural disdain for academics, and America's accomplishments, modest as they are, may be off the charts for doing so much with so little.

Of course this "positive" assessment would devastate the educational reform industry since their livelihoods depend on the "we can, we must do better" assumption. Remember: *Bad news extracts the dollars.* So, without this sky-is-falling research, public officials might just conclude that our educational woes can be cheaply fixed via immigration and incentives for smart people to have more children. After all, why spend millions concocting expensive interventions if they have minimal impact other than sustaining today's costly education-flavored Great Society? An act of Congress could swell the number of ambitious, higher IQ students, and while the assimilation costs are not zero, they are trivial compared to present-day efforts to extract proficiency from those often challenged by the basics. As is true in other nations, just make immigration policy skill-driven. This cheap solution also wonderfully avoids all the totalitarian dangers lurking below today's panaceas—state intervention in child-rearing, cultural engineering to inculcate the "right" academic values, and other Marxist-lite "solutions." The strategy is routine in industry—at some point you cannot wring more from obsolescent equipment, so just replace everything. In sum, restock schools with what always worked in the past—ambitious smart immigrants.

Are We Using the Wrong Yardsticks?

Our alleged deficiencies can, however, be viewed from a sunnier perspectives. There is what might be called the fluid yardstick dilemma. While standards regarding certain abilities, for example, reading, are invariant, others properly shift, and it is unclear whether yesterday's seemingly sacrosanct benchmarks remain appropriate. This is not an attack on fixed standards *per se*; the issue is *what* fixed standards? Consider mathematics, a seemingly permanent subject: 2+2=4 is forever. Yet, it is plausible that conventional, especially advanced mathematics is essentially a nineteenth-century endeavor and which is less relevant than computer programming skills only loosely related to 2+2. Similar cases can be made for other modern skills, for instance, Internet building or computerized graphics. Unfortunately, no methods currently exist for testing or even defining these economically valuable quantitative skills, so to conclude that Americans trail Japanese students in solving quadratic equations, while ignoring writing programming code, may undervalue America's educational accomplishments. Applying obsolete standards may explain the oft-noted paradox: our schooling's decline on traditional measures while we simultaneously lead the world in technological innovation. Perhaps NCLB should add a "Geek Test."

The predicament of viewing "educational attainment" in a rear-view mirror may be intractable. Emerging accomplishments may still be murky as they surface, and proper measurement may have to wait decades, so perhaps fifty years hence worried educational researchers will marvel over how American schools once imparted the hyper-entrepreneurial spirit making the U.S. technologically preeminent or how teachers helped ordinary students master complicated electronic gadgets "so vital to human existence." A distinguished panel of mid-twenty-first-century experts might issue a thick report: "A Nation in Crisis: Why Americans Cannot Invent New Video Games, Let Alone Excel at Historic Ones." A possible evolving standard does not justify contemporary imperfection; it merely cautions against judgments based on past, conceivably antiquated, criteria.

It is also arguable that present proficiency levels, no matter how low, suffice for our national needs. It is unclear just how many "brains" America needs and it is undeniable that top schools with world-class hard-working students abound in America, and these include hundreds of schools not dominated by knowledge hungry immigrant children. Plausibly, the "we must do better to be globally competitive" argument is more akin to education job-generating PR than a clarion call. Since the 1960s the American economy has overall soared all the while academic attainment has held steady or declined. To be sure, beginning in 2008 there was widespread economic dislocation, but nobody has suggested that shoddy schooling is the culprit. "Necessary levels of education to produce outcome X" is fundamentally an *empirical* question, and cannot be settled by Amen platitudes about modern techno-society needing ever more well-trained people to survive. Cliché mongering is not educational analysis. If anything, modern society does *not* require armies of highly-skilled workers. As the venerable Yogi Berra said, you can see a lot by just looking around. Massive stupidity can be circumvented via automation, outsourcing, or just abandoning the task. Entire industries, e.g., construction, agriculture, food service, transportation, among others, can survive with workers challenged by high school exit exams.

Economies, especially modern ones, adapt, even when facing illiteracy and innumeracy. It is no accident that books with "For dummies" and "Idiots" in their titles are best sellers. Money is to be made from surmounting stupidity, and so experts will figure it out. Commerce once required armies of skilled typists, and every year thousands dutifully learned to type 60 words a minute without errors to keep businesses going. Today, "typists" as a job classification has virtually vanished as literate executives type on computers where mistakes are easily (or automatically) corrected. McDonald's uses simplified, pictograph cash registers in lieu of trying to impart numeracy to its sorrowful teenage help. In the final analysis, a handful of very smart people may be able to compensate for thousands of dummies, and educating these smart people may be a far better strategy than imploring the latter to shape up.

Truly Serious Obstacles to Reform

Still, leaving aside an upbeat scenario of an ill-educated nation collectively thriving despite individual academic insufficiency, can *anything* be done to improve matters? Past chapters on narrowing the racial gap in achievement and motivating students abound with helpful advice while chapters on past reforms provide ample warnings of what to avoid. Rather than repeat these prescriptions, let me offer some broader observations regarding our tribulations. These have nothing to do with school administration, private vs. public schools, money, teacher training, or all the usual suspects rounded up for speech-making occasions. We will also set aside the contentious issue of immigration, so we assume that America's demography will continue to shift. The focus here is on self-inflicted wounds.

First, current education-related discussions are racked with dishonesty, spinning, and other tactics to escape reality. To draw an economic parallel, we are trying to build a capitalist economy awash with counterfeit currency, dishonest business practices, false financial statements, idiosyncratic weights and measures and all else plaguing mired-in-poverty inefficient Third World nations. This is so debilitating that even keeping two sets of books, an honest and a dishonest one, would bring improvement since it might be possible to know the truth. Further add a system that rewards dishonesty so the most craven advance upward. It is pointless to even talk about improvement if we insist on surreptitiously lowering standards on tests to achieve "fairness." Same is true for twisting definitions of "gifted" so as to appease racial and ethnic sensibilities or saying that black children will excel only if teachers take more sensitivity training to value their raucous church-related classroom behavior. Meanwhile, our overview of accountability showed how pressure to produce near miracles made data fudging a career requirement. That even good, honest educators can be corrupted is perhaps the system's worst feature.

These deceitful habits exist across the political spectrum and infuse the entire educational establishment, top to bottom. A pressured teacher has lots of "role models" if he or she elected to cheat. How is a New York City school teacher to react when hearing George W. Bush's Secretary of Education blithely announce that black students years behind in reading and math require additional AP courses to catch up to whites academically? How should he or she respond when Jeb Bush, the former "education governor" of Florida, is honored in a gilded hall in an exclusive Park Avenue club and tells an appreciative audience that Florida's education will improve if all high school graduates attend college? That many of these already enrolled cannot do college work except via dumbed-down Mickey Mouse courses or by taking extensive remedial work is irrelevant. We suspect that everybody in the audience recognized the lying, but nobody risked belling the cat. Indeed, those who cheered on the governor most enthusiastically were probably on his or her way to a stellar career in education. In a nutshell, to lie is to get "with the program."

In the economy such deceit is relatively easy to combat. A combination of government regulations (including criminal sanctions) and sullied reputations for deceit usually suffice. Education is different: *we want to wallow in dishonesty and condemn those who bring bad news.* A thriving market for mendacity exists among professional educators whose jobs depend on uncovering calamities and then demonstrating how their pet nostrums work wonders. The trick is to change jobs before the ruse is uncovered. Further add egotistic philanthropists looking "to do good" who just want to hear upbeat news and will happily hire experts to supply it. Meanwhile, parents will relish cheerful news about their children even it is fiction. Educators have long discovered how to quiet restless consumers—inflated grades, meaningless diplomas, generous honor roll standards, inclusive definitions of "gifted," and all the rest that puts psychological satisfaction above the rewards of hard work to gain just morsels of knowledge. Few object when classrooms deteriorate into mindless fun and games so as to "motivate" youngsters. Who will organize rallies on behalf of teachers who flunk half the class? By contrast, harsh graduation standards are to be overcome with litigation, not greater diligence. Among many racial/ethnic activists, a cheery educational result is a right, something automatically bestowed by government, not a sign of hard-earned accomplishment.

Appetites for counterfeit accomplishment are bad enough but, as they say on TV "infomercials" for miracle products, "wait, there is more." No honest assessment of our academic woes can omit what transpires in our "better" schools of education. Over a decade ago Rita Kramer's *Ed School Follies* exposed this gross stupidity in detail, but her warnings went unheeded. The nonsense continues to spew forth, almost none of it helpful. In psychobabble speak, Education Schools are "enablers." Perhaps it is time again to sound the alarm about these dangers. Generously pensioning off all faculty *immediately* would be far cheaper in the long run, the equivalent of retiring the horse cavalry when tanks arrived. If these professors refuse to go quietly into the night, make them financially liable for their recommendations and force these institutions to buy malpractice insurance. Unfamiliar outsiders who think that this medicine is too strong are advised to reread our chapters on motivation and school reform; better yet, visit a library and just randomly peruse the latest education school devised advice manuals. With slight exception, this "literature" is gibberish, often incomprehensible, unscientific banalities overflowing with ideologically-flavored platitudes and so contrary to common sense and history, that it defies comprehension.

Sadly, the rubbish is most fervent when directed toward those most in need of solid, useful advice. Recall how professional champions of black gifted children slighted the importance of hard work in favor of celebrating traits having zero to do with academics (e.g., interpersonal skills or dancing). The only plausible explanation is that churning out this rubbish is necessary for one's academic career, and that institutions of higher learning tolerate nonsense of this magnitude says mountains about how Americans disdain real education. It is absolutely, positively unthinkable that a university's medical school would permit similar quackery, approaches such as "faith healing." The piles of dead bodies and expensive law suits would soon end it. Most university sports programs are less forgiving of gross incompetence than their School of Education. Losing football and basketball coaches are fired; Education School professors spewing fashionable nonsense that makes matters worse have grand careers.

Reversing the public's craving for sham news about everybody being above average and shuttering horrific advice-giving toxic schools of education is unlikely to occur. As with those struggling with obesity, serious dieting begins tomorrow, perhaps with a visit to the bookstore to buy the latest no-effort, quick weight-loss book. America is stuck with these two giant millstones around our necks and, truth be told, we've grown accustomed to these burdens.

A Modest Reform Proposal: Professionalism

The urge to suggest at least something to improve matters is irresistible, so we conclude with a single modest idea: apply the consumer safety model to educational tinkering to at least exclude dubious crazes from the marketplace. Consider airplane safety beginning from the make-it-up-as-you-go-along Wright Brothers days to largely self-regulating engineering geniuses like Howard Hughes to the contemporary FAA. An FAA-like government agency—the National Bureau of Education Reform (NBER), we'll call it—could, with minimal ideological bias, scrutinize all proposals, assemble relevant past experiences, scientifically define key terms, calculate accurate cost to benefits ratios vis-à-vis alternatives, and then arrange field tests for promising candidates. NBER might even help the IRS certify educational foundations as "crackpot" (disallowed tax deductions could even help pay for NBER).

Actually, the National Center for Educational Evaluation already exists, but seems limited to analyzing government programs, not certifying FAA-like a wider range of proposals. Like many professionally-staffed regulatory bodies, civil service rules could promote a modicum of political insulation. Going further, assessing reform proposals, like auditors calculating profits and losses, would be professionalized so would-be experts would have to pass rigorous examination in statistical analysis, research design, and other relevant technical skills including detailed knowledge of past fiascos. To prevent evaluators from being swept up in fads, the bane of educational reform, designated Devil's Advocates might challenge all proposals, even those arriving with "absolute guarantees."

Promising pilot projects could be cautiously scaled up with particular attention to local conditions. Failures, like airplane crashes, would garner intense security, technical reports on malfunctions together with suggested corrective measures. Participating educators would keep detailed, periodically outside audited records—the equivalent of airplane "black boxes" and maintenance logs for jet engines—for accurate diagnoses. Regular outside reviews, including civil or criminal penalties for fraud, could ensure honesty. Since no obligation exists to participate in reform experiments, paperwork burdens would be self-imposed and participants might receive compensation, a small price to pay given the gargantuan costs of past failure.

The NBER would welcome all proposals though a serious review would require greater justification than the ubiquitous blithe "it might help, so let's try." Given the dismal past record of philanthropists and ambitious mayors, let alone presidents and Education School professors, we'd guess that only a handful would be field-tested, and faced with awaiting rejection, ineptly devised *ad hoc* plans might happily decline. For good measure foundations and private individuals operating outside schools themselves could have to undergo scrutiny too. If Bill Gates again wanted to give Washington, DC children millions for college scholarships, though many can barely read, his foundation would have to justify this potentially-disruptive meddling. Religious institutions and schools receiving no public funds might be freed from NBER oversight. To really be draconian, the NBER law might permit parents to sue school administrators for damages if they used non-NBER reforms. Now, at least, if some ambitious professor wanted to experiment on African-American youngsters with some off-the-wall pedagogical fad, he or she would have to run a fairly demanding scientific gauntlet (and be personally liable if he or she did not secure NBER certification).

These hurdles will, hopefully, sharply reduce today's reform clutter. It is not that bad advice should be officially excluded from the market-place. After all, little can stop a crackpot blogger and freedom of speech is freedom of speech. Rather, proliferation of unscientific, impromptu foolishness seriously hinders uncovering what might actually work. A comparable stamp-of-approval screening already flourishes in higher education via multiple accreditation agencies for colleges, for-profit vocational schools, and professional programs. Standards are enforced by regular inspections and they provide minimal assurances: that few parents enroll offspring in unaccredited colleges speaks to the value of this tactic. Law, medicine, accounting, engineering, and countless other professions impose strict licensing tests to discourage quackery. That this hard-nosed approach has not reached the school reform industry is remarkable, perhaps a testament to the low priority given achieving academic excellence or the political clout of the snake oil industry.

An Honest Political Platform

To bring this all together, here's a suggested political platform regarding education that a truly serious political candidate can advance:

> Ladies and gentleman, for the last half century American has been addicted to endless educational reforms, gimmick after gimmick, with negligible success. Despite glittering promises, matters get worse while we spend ourselves into bankruptcy.

There are no easy answers. To be frank, many—perhaps most—of our problems are self-inflicted. Millions of students abhor learning while making education impossible for others. We must certainly try to help all students, but at some point we must admit that we've tried hard enough, and all the extra spending is futile and best allocated elsewhere. As they say, you can take a horse to water.... Better yet give these currently indifferent students no expiration date vouchers for private vocational education.

Improving begins by determining what has succeeded or failed and if elected I will create a non-partisan, non-ideological federal agency modeled on the FAA that will insure that our children are not, yet one more time, treated as guinea pigs in a risky, hare-brained educational experiment. No more stupid experiments! Our children are not laboratory rats!

I cannot say what will boost achievement, but whatever we try, it should be thoroughly tested and results made plain-to-see. This approach has succeeded with aviation, pharmaceuticals, and consumer products, among many other areas, and it is time to apply it to education.

Our present generous system, sad to say, keeps on rewarding the failing, including students, and as any economist will tell you, if you reward it, you get more. If students refuse to attend school, forcing them is wasteful and hurts those wanting to learn. Schools must build academic excellence, not just create community jobs though rest assured, many people need decent jobs, and government can help, but this payroll padding undermines quality education. Education is not an anti-poverty program! Running a school is not the Job Corps! Nor should education be the plaything of wealthy philanthropists.

Nor must we be obsessed by closing gaps between blacks and whites, rich and poor or boys and girls. Leveling may be seductive, but attempts to achieve it are doomed to fail. This is the lesson we draw from the misguided Soviet experience. Everybody deserves the best possible education for them personally, but people will always differ in talent and inclination, and to pursue leveling, long after this is found to be impossible, brings everybody down. This may make some uncomfortable, but it is reality.

Our present system has, unfortunately, been endlessly compromised by politically-manipulated rubber yardstick measures of accomplishment and shoddy diplomas. If the food industry followed these standards, people would die. Education is certainly just as important. Under my administration the Department of Education will partner with states and localities for an incorruptible gold standard for academic achievement—we reject feel-good self-delusion.

None of this may be successful, but expensive banging our heads against the wall hoping for an Education Savior does nobody any good. In the meantime students, since the magic "smart pill" has yet to be invented, should just hit the books, and for parents, stop taking to the streets to demonstrate for "better education" and just help Junior.

Works Cited

"A Plan for Success: Communities of Color Define Policy Priorities for High School Reform," Campaign for High School Equity, nd.

Alderman, M. Kay. 2004. *Motivation for Achievement: Possibilities for Teaching and Learning.* 2nd edition. Mahwah, NJ: Lawrence Erlbaum Associates.

Ali, Aisha. 2008. "Guns, Knives and Education: Violence Erupts in D.C. Public Schools," *The New York Examiner.* December 3. Online at *examiner.com.*

Allen, Charlotte. 2007. "Read It and Weep: Why Does Congress Hate the One Part of No Child Left Behind That Works?" *The Weekly Standard,* July 16, 22-32.

Anna, Cara 2007. "Among Black Students, Many Immigrants," *Washingtonpost. com.* April 30. Online version.

Arenson, Karen W. 2003. "Colleges Struggle to Help Black Men Stay Enrolled," *New York Times,* December 30. Online version.

Arenson, Karen W. 2004. "In a First, 2 of Nation's New Rhodes Scholars Come from CUNY," *New York Times,* November 22. Online version.

Armor, David J. 1995. *Forced Justice: School Desegregation and the Law.* New York: Oxford University Press.

Ascribe. 2006. "Report Calls for Changes in No Child Left Behind to Help Children Move From Bad Schools to Good Ones." June 15. The report is available at *http://www.equaleducation.org.*

Asimov, Nanette. 2007. "Summit Called to Address Racial Disparities in Academic Performance," *SFGate.com.* (San Francisco Chronicle). November 17. Online version.

Associated Press. 2006. "Charter School 10th Grade AIMS Scores Still Lagging," July 13. Online version.

Associated Press. 2007. "Fourth-Graders Fall Behind in Literary Test," *Wall Street Journal,* November 29.

Associated Press. State and Local Wire. 2007. "AIMS Shows Elementary Students Improving," July 19. Online version.

Associated Press. 2008. "Group Plans Detroit College Promise Scholarships," August 19.

Baez, Benjamin 2006. "Merit and Difference" *Teachers College Record,* 108. Number 6, 996-1016.

Bagchi, Sanjit. 2008. "Improving Graduation Rates Can Cut Crime," *School Reform News,* Vol. 12, March, 16.

Baker, Joanie. 2008. "WKU Gets $2 Million Grant to Help Low-Income, Minority Students in Math, Science." *Daily News* (Bowling Green, KY), November 11. Online at *bgdailynews.com*.

Bautz, Greer. 2005. "University to Address 'Achievement Gap Issue': Initiative will Synthesize Research" *Harvard Gazette Archives,* April 28. *http://hno. harvard.edu/gazette/2005/04.28/13-gap.html*

Becker, Gary S. 1993. *Human Capital: A Theoretical and Empirical Analysis with Special Reference to Education*, Third Edition. Chicago: University of Chicago Press.

Bedford, Ryan. 2008. "New York City Beefs Up Efforts to Get Poor Teachers Out of Class," *School Reform News*, Vol. 12, No. 2 February, 10, 11.

Belfield, Clive R. and Henry M. Levin. 2007. "The Return on Investment for Improving California's High School Graduation Rate," *California Dropout Research Project,* UC Santa Barbara, Gevirtz Graduate School of Education, Policy Brief 2. August.

Belluck, Pam 1999. "Reason is Sought for Lag by Blacks in School Effort," *New York Times,* July 4. Online version.

Bhanoo, Sindya N. 2008. "Graduates Honored for Drive, Degrees," *Washington Post.* June 17. B07. Online at *washingtonpost.com*.

Blankstein, Alan M. 2007. "Terms of Engagement: Where Failure Is Not an Option" in *Engaging Every Learner*. Edited by Alan M. Blankstein, Robert W. Cole, and Paul D. Houston. Thousand Oaks, CA: Corwin Press.

Bleyer, Jennifer 2007, "A School Gets an F, and Parents Worry about What Comes Next," *New York Times,* December 9. Online version.

Blum, Edward and Marc Levin. 1999. "Washington's War on Standardized Tests," *Wall Street Journal*, May 26.

Boe, Erling and Sujie Shin. 2005. "Is the United States Really Losing the International Horse Race in Academic Achievement?" *Phi Delta Kappa*, 86, 688-95.

Brodbeck, Meredith. 2008. "Philanthropy Watch Dog Says Choice Donors Do More Than Give Money," *School Reform News*, January, 13.

Caplan, Nathan, John K. Whitmore, and Marcella H. Choy. 1992. *The Boat People and Achievement in America: A Study of Family Life, Hard Work and Cultural Values.* Ann Arbor: University of Michigan Press.

Ceci, Stephen and Paul B. Papierno. 2005. "The Rhetoric and Reality of Gap Closing: When the 'Have-Nots' Gain but the 'Haves' Gain Even More" *American Psychologist*, 60(2). 149-60.

Chandler, Michael Alison. 2007. "In This Class, Math Comes with Music" *The Washington Post.* October 23, B01. Online version.

Chandler, Michael Alison. 2007. "Lingering Academic Gaps Riles NAACP" *The Washington Post,* November 6, B01. Online version. *Washingtonpost. com*.

Cho, Jenna 2008. "Are Gifted Kids Shortchanged Academically?" *The Day* (Connecticut), July 13. Online version.

Chub, John E. and Terry Moe. 1990. *Politics Markets and American Schools.* Washington, DC: The Brookings Institution.

Ciotti, Paul. 1998. "Money and School Performance: Lessons from the Kansas City Desegregation Experiment" *Policy Analysis 298.* March 16. Washington, DC: CATO Institute.

Cloud, John. 2007. "Failing Our Geniuses" *Time.* August 27, 41-46.

Clowes, Barbara Barksdale. 1981. *Brainpower for the Cold War: The Sputnik Crisis and National Defense Education Act of 1958.* Westport, CT: Greenwood Press.

Corno, Lyn and Mary M. Rohrkemper. 1985. "The Intrinsic Motivation to Learn in Classrooms," in *Research on Motivation in Education*, Vol. 2, *The Classroom Milieu.* Edited by Carole Ames and Russell Ames. Orlando: Academic Press.

Coulson, Andrew 1999. *Market Education: The Unknown History.* New Brunswick, NJ: Transactions Publishers.

Coulson, Andrew 2006. "A Critique of Pure Friedman: An Empirical Reassessment of 'The Role of Government in Education' in *Liberty & Learning: Milton Friedman's Voucher Idea at Fifty.* Edited by Robert C. Enlow and Lenore T. Ealy. Washington, DC: CATO Institute.

Covington, Martin V and Karen Manheim Teel. 1996. *Overcoming Student Failure: Changing Motives and Incentives for Learning.* Washington, DC: American Psychological Association.

Covington, Martin V. 1998. *The Will to Learn: A Guide for Motivating Young People.* Cambridge, UK: Cambridge University Press.

Crompton, Karin. 2007. "Closing Education 'Achievement Gap' is Group's Objective" *The Day.* January 25. Online version.

Curry School of Education. 2008. "U.Va. Professors Moon and Brighton Get $2.2 M to Develop STEM-Focused Curriculum for Elementary School Students," October 23. Online version.

Dalmia, Shikha 2008. "Scarp the Visa Cap," *The Wall Street Journal,* April 5.

De Vise, Daniel. 2007. "Area Schools' Success Obscures Lingering Racial SAT Gap," *Washington Post*, September 10. A01. Online version at *Washingtonpost.com*.

De Vise, Daniel. 2007. "To Be AP, Course Must Pass Muster" *Washington Post,* March 25, A1, A17.

De Vise, Daniel. 2008. "D.C. Parents Look Outside the Box for Public Education," *Washington Post,* March 30, A01. Online at *washingtonpost.com*.

De Vise, Daniel. 2008. "Montgomery Erasing Gifted Label," *Washington Post,* December 16, B01. Online at *washingtonpost.com*.

deCharms, Richard and others. 1976. *Enhancing Motivation: Changes in the Classroom.* New York: Irvington Publishers.

Deci, Edward L. and Richard M. Ryan. 2002. "The Paradox of Achievement: The Harder You Push, The Worse It Gets" in *Improving Academic Achievement: Impact of Psychological Factors in Education.* Edited by Joshua Aronson. Amsterdam: Academic Press.

Dillon, Sam. 2003. "States are Relaxing Standards on Tests to Avoid Sanctions," *New York Times,* May 22.

Dillon, Sam. 2007. "Report Finds Better Scores in New Crop of Teachers," *New York Times,* December 12. Online version.

Dillon, Sam 2008. "New Vision for Schools Proposes Broad Role," *New York Times,* July 15. Online version.

Dillon, Sam 2008. "States' Data Obscures How Few Finish High School," *New York Times,* March 20. Online version.

Dillon, Sam 2009. "'No Child Left Behind' Is Not Closing Racial Gap," *New York Times,* April 29. Online version.

Dillon, Sam. 2007. "Math Scores Rise, but Reading Is Mixed," *New York Times,* September 26. Online version.

Drummer, Lori, 2007. "Low-Income Parents Make Informed Education Decisions for Their Kids," *School Reform News,* April, 13.

Editorial. 2006. "What a Waste," *The Washington Times,* June 25. B02. Online version.

Editorial. 2007. "Rewarding Good Teaching," *New York Times,* October 20. Online version.

Einhorn, Erin. 2007. "18 Ed Dept bigs making at least 190G," *Daily News* (New York) December. Online version.

Einhorn, Erin. 2007. "Education Jobs Stump Parents," *Daily News* (New York), December 26. Online version.

Einhorn, Erin. 2008. "Teachers in Trouble Spending Years in 'Rubber Room 'Limbo that Costs $65 M," *Daily News* (New York), May 4. Online version.

Epstein, Marc. 2007. "Dumbing Down the Regents" *City* Journa,l July 18. Online version.

Epstein, Marc. 2008. "Ignorance Is Bliss on the State Regents History Exam," *Daily News* (New York), July 22. At *dailynews.com* (Opinion).

Fallis, David A. and April Witt. 2007. "Student Money Vanishes, but Few Are Punished; Activity Funds Are Often Plundered by Adults," *The Washington Post*, November 9. Online version.

Ferguson, Ronald F. 1998. "Can Schools Narrow the Black-White Test Score Gap" in *The Black White Test Score Gap.* Edited by Christopher Jencks and Meredith Philips. Washington, DC: Brookings Institution Press.

Ferguson, Ronald F. 2001. *A Diagnostic Analysis of Black-White GPA Disparities in Shaker Heights, Ohio.* Washington, DC: Brookings Institution Press.

Fessenden, Ford 2003. "How to Measure Student Proficiency?" *New York Times,* December 31. Online version.

Finkelstein, Barbara. 1989. *Governing the Young: Teacher Behavior in Popular Primary Schools in Nineteenth-Century United States.* New York: The Falmer Press.

Fleishman, Joel L. 2007. *The Foundations: A Great American Secret.* New York: Public Affairs Press.

Fletcher, Michael A. 1998. "A Good-School, Bad-School Mystery," *The Washington Post*, October 23. Online version.

Ford, Donna Y. 1996. *Reversing Underachievement among Gifted Black Students: Promising Practices and Programs.* New York: Teachers College Press.

Ford, Donna Y., Tarek C. Grantham, and H. Richard Milner. 2004. "Underachievement among Gifted African American Students: Cultural, Social and Psychological Considerations," *In the Eyes of the Beholder: Critical*

Issues for Diversity in Gifted Education. Edited by Boothe, Diane and Julian C. Stanley. Waco, TX: Prufrock Press.

Foster, Greg. 2007. "Monopoly Versus Markets: The Empirical Evidence on Private Schools & School Choice," Indianapolis, IN: Milton and Rose D. Friedman Foundation.

Foundation for Education Reform & Accountability. 2007. "Grading Education: Making New York's Schools More Accountable," March.

Frasier, Mary M. 1997. "Gifted Minority Students: Reframing Approaches to Their Identification and Education," in *Handbook of Gifted Education,* second edition. Edited by Colangelo, Nicholas. and Gary A. David. Boston: Allyn and Bacon.

Freedman, Samuel G. 2005. "The Achievement Gap in Elite Schools," *New York Times,* September 28. Online version.

Freedman, Samuel G. 2007. "How a Middle School Can Be 'Dangerous' and Still Get an A," *New York Times,* December 19. Online version.

Fried Robert L. 2001. *The Passionate Learner: How Teachers and Parents Can Help Children Reclaim the Joy of Discovery.* Boston: Beacon Press.

Friedman, Milton 2006. "Prologue: A Personal Perspective," in *Liberty & Learning: Milton Friedman's Voucher Idea at Fifty.* Edited by Robert C. Enlow and Lenore T. Ealy. Washington, DC: CATO Institute.

Friedman, Milton with the assistance of Rose D. Friedman. 1962. *Capitalism and Freedom.* Chicago: University of Chicago Press. ("The Role of Government in Education" was originally published in 1955 in another volume.)

Fryer, Alex 2007. "Racism Tough to Tackle—or Even Talk about—for Seattle School Board," *The Seattle Times,* March 29. Online version.

Gallagher, James J. 1997. "Issues in the Education of Gifted Students" in *Handbook of Gifted Education,* second edition. Edited by Colangelo, Nicholas and Gary A. David. Boston: Allyn and Bacon.

Gallagher, Mary Campbell. 2000. "Lessons from the Sputnik-Era Curriculum Reform Movement" in *What's At Stake in the K-12 Standard Wars: A Primer for Educational Policy Makers,* edited by Sandra Stotsky. New York: Peter Lang.

Glod, Maria. 2007. "To Draw Top Teachers to Troubled Schools, Foundations Will Offer $30,000 Stipends," *The Washington Post*, December 20. A07. Online version at *washingtonpost.com.*

Glod, Maria. 2008. "Area Schools Set To Lose Millions Under Medicaid Policy Changes" *The Washington Post,* February 2. A01. Online version at *washingtonpost.com.*

Godwin, R. Kenneth and Frank R. Kemerer. 2002. *School Choice Trade-off: Liberty, Equity, and Diversity.* Austin, TX: University of Texas Press.

Goldstein, Joseph. 2007. "Supreme Court May Take Up New York City Teacher Exam," *New York Sun,* December 4, 5.

Gonen, Yoav. 2008. "Schools' Cash-to-Kids Plan Doesn't Pay Off," *New York Post,* August 20. Online version.

Gootman, Elissa. 2003. "School Custodians Object as City Hired Private Firms," *New York Times*, September 26. Online version.

Gootman, Elissa. 2005. "City Officials Put Academy for Principals under Review," *New York Times*, December 20. Online version.

Gootman, Elissa. 2006. "In Elite N.Y. Schools, a Dip in Blacks and Hispanics," *New York Times,* August 18. Online version.

Gootman, Elissa. 2007. "Bard President to Meet with City over C Grade" *New York Times*, November 9. Online version.

Gootman, Elissa. 2007. "Bloomberg Unveils Plan for Performance Pay for Teachers," *New York Times,* October 17. Online version.

Gootman, Elissa. 2007. "For Teachers, Middle School is a Test of Wills," *New York Times,* March 17, A1, B5.

Gootman, Elissa. 2007. "Teachers Agree to Bonus Pay Tied to Scores" *New York Times,* October 18. Online version.

Gootman, Elissa and Jennifer Medina. 2007. "New York Grades Set Off Debate on Judging Schools," *New York Times*, September 27. Online version.

Gootman, Elissa and Jennifer Medina. 2007. "50 New York Schools Fail Under Rating System." *New York Times,* November 6. Online version.

Gootman, Elissa and Jennifer Medina. 2007. "Schools Brace To Be Scored on a Scale of A to F." *New York Times,* November 4, 37, 42.

Gootman, Elissa and Jennifer Medina. 2008. "6 City Schools Designated by State as Failing," *New York Times,* February 7. Online version.

Gootman, Elissa and Robert Gebeloss. 2008. "Gifted Program in City Are Less Diverse," *New York Times,* June 19. Online version.

Gootman, Elissa and Sharona Coutts. 2008. "Lacking Credits, Some Students Learn a Shortcut," *New York Times*, April 11. Online version.

Gottfredson, Linda. 1994. "Mainstream Science on Intelligence: An Editorial with 52 Signatories, History and Bibliography" *The Wall Street Journal,* December 13.

Gottfredson, Linda S. 2003. "The Science and Politics of Intelligence in Gifted Education," in Colangelo, Nicholas and G. A. David, eds., *Handbook of gifted Education.* Boston: Allyn and Bacon.

Grabar, Mary. 2008. "Assaults on Teachers: Not Just for Crackers Anymore," May 10. *Townhall.com.*

Gramlich, Edward M. and Patricia P. Koshel. 1975. *Educational Performance Contacting.* Washington, DC: The Brookings Institution.

Green, Elizabeth. 2007. "Rule Change is Mulled for School Tests," *New York Sun.* December 12, 1, 4.

Green, Elizabeth. 2007. "Texas Challenges City on Math," *New York Sun,* November 20, 1, 4.

Green, Elizabeth. 2008. "Fewer Blacks, More Whites Are Hired as City Teachers," *The New York Sun,* September 28. Online version.

Green, Elizabeth. 2008. "High Test Scores, and Criticism, Follow a South Bronx Principal," *New York Sun,* June 30. Online version.

Green, Elizabeth. 2008. "Mayor Sees a Test Score Triumph" *New York Sun,* June 23. Online version.

Green, Elizabeth. 2008. "Report Cards on the Schools Will Be Revised by City," *New York Sun*, February 29, 1, 3.

Green, Elizabeth. 2008. "Teachers Union Fights Effort to Stop Paying Reserve Pool," *New York Sun*, May 5, 2.

Green, Jay P. with the assistance of Greg Forster and Marcus A. Winters. 2005. *Education Myths: What Special Interest Groups Want You to Believe About Our Schools—And Why It Isn't So.* Lanham, MD: Rowman & Littlefield.

Grimaldi, James V. 2007. "A Reading Program's Powerful Patron," *Washington Post*, December 20. A01. Online version at *washingtonpost.com*.

Gross, Jane 2002. "Paying for a Disability Diagnosis to Gain Time on College Board," *New York Times*, September 26.

Hampel, Robert L. 1993. "Historical Perspectives on Academic Work: The Origins of Learning" in *Motivating Students to Learn: Overcoming Barriers to High Achievement* Edited by Tommy M. Tomlinson. Berkeley, CA: McCutchan Publishing.

Handbook on Research on Improving Student Achievement. Third Edition. 2004. Edited by Gordon Cawelti. Arlington, VA: Educational Research Service.

Hanushek, Eric et al. 1994. *Making Schools Work: Improving Performances and Controlling Cost.* Washington, DC: The Brookings Institution.

Hanushek, Eric A. 2007. "Selling Adequacy, Making Millions," *Education Next*, Summer. Online version.

Hanushek, Eric A., John F. Kain, and Steven G. Rivkin. 2004. "Why Public Schools Lose Teachers," *The Journal of Human Resources*, 39 (Spring), 326-54.

Hanushek, Eric, Dean T. Jamison, Elliot A. Jamison, and Ludger Woessmann. 2008. "Education and Economic Growth," *Education Next*. Vol 8:2. Spring. Online version.

Hanushek, Eric, John F. Kain, Steven G. Rivkin, and Gregory F. Branch. 2005. "Charter School Quality and Parental Decision Making with School Choice," National Bureau of Economic Research, March.

Hargrove, Thomas. 2008. "Inflated School Attendance Spark Refund Push in Texas," Scripts Howard New Service, Oct 31 at *scriptsnews.com*.

Harmin, Merrill. 1994. *Inspiring Active Learning: A Handbook for Teachers*. Alexandria, VA: Association for Supervision and Curriculum Development.

Hart, Kim. 2008. "Gates Calls on Congress for Science Education, Visas," *Washington Post,* March 13. D03. Online version.

Hassel, Bryan C. and Michelle Godard Terrell. 2004. "The Rugged Frontier: A Decade of Charter Schooling in Arizona," Progressive Policy Institute, June 3.

Hassett, Wendy and Dan Katzir. 2005. "Lessons Learned from the Inside," in *With the Best of Intentions: How Philanthropy is Reshaping K-12 Education.* Edited by Frederick M. Hess. Cambridge, MA: Harvard Education Press.

Haynes V. Dion 2008 and Michael Birnbaum. 2008. "D.C. tries Cash as a Motivator in School," *Washington Post*, August 22, A01. Online at *washingtonpost.com*.

Haynes V. Dion. 2008. "A Landmark's Looming Demise," *Washington Post*, June 11, B01. Online version at *washingtonpost.com*.

Haynes V. Dion 2008. "New Program to Take Early Action to Help Those Failing," *Washington Post*, March 19. B02. Online version at *washingtonpost. com*.

Haynes V. Dion. 2008. "Outside Help for Schools Possible," *Washington Post*, February 26, A01. Online version at *washingtonpost.com*.

Haynes V. Dion. 2008. "Rhee Weighs Ideas to Fix 27 Schools," *Washington Post*, February 18, B01. Online version at *washingtonpost.com*.

Haynes, V. Dion and Aruna Jain. 2007. "Whatever Happened to the Class of 2005?" *Washington Post*, October 7. A01. Online version at *washington-post.com*.

Haynes. V. Dion and Nikita Stewart. 2008. "Boycott Set for Hearings on School Closing," *Washington Post*, January 8. B01. Online at *washingtonpost. com*.

Henig, Jeffrey R. 1994. *Rethinking School Choice: Limits of the Market Metaphor*. Princeton, NJ: Princeton University Press.

Hernandez, Javier C. 2008. "New Effort Aims to Test Theories of Education," *New York Times*, September 25. Online version.

Hernandez, Javier C. 2009. "Study Cites Dire Economic Impact of Poor Schools," *New York Times*, April 23. Online version.

Herszenhorn, David M. 2003. "School Janitors Sue over Hiring of Outsiders," *New York Times,* November 21. Online version.

Herszenhorn, David M. 2004. "Union and Lawmakers Attack Use of Private Custodial Services in Schools," *New York Times*, February 12. Online version.

Herszenhorn, David M. 2007. "Patrons' Sway Leads to Friction in Charter School," *New York Times,* June 28. Online version.

Hess, Frederick H. and Thomas Gift. 2008. "School Reform That Can Work," *The Insider.* Winter, 16-17.

Hirsch, E. D. Jr. 1996. *The Schools We Need, and Why We Don't Have Them.* New York: Doubleday.

Hoag, Christina. 2008. "An Inner-city LA High, nearly 6 in 10 Drop Out," *Associated Press.* August 19.

Holland, Robert. 2007. "2007 NAEP Scores Show Spending Increases Haven't Produced Results," *School Reform News*, December, 1, 4.

Holland, Robert. 2007. "Teachers Union Pushes Rollback of NCLB Standards," *School Reform News,* October, p. 12.

Honawar, Vaishali. 2008, "Performance-Pay Studies Show Few Achievement Gains," *Education Week,* March 12. Online version.

Honawar, Vaishali. 2008. "Performance-Pay Results Show Need for More Work on Concept," *Education Week,* March 3. Online version.

Hood, John. 1992. "The Head Start Scam" Policy Analysis number 187. Washington, DC: CATO.

Howard, Anne. 2008. "Corporate Fund to Spend $100 Million to Prevent School Dropouts," *The Chronicle of Philanthropy, News Updates.* April 16.

Hu, Winnie. 2007. "Statistics Pinpoint Problems in Patterson Schools, and No Excuses are Allowed," *New York Times*, Sunday December 2, 39, 40.

Hu, Winnie. 2007. "To Close Gaps, Schools Focus on Black Boys," *The New York Times,* April 9. Online version.

Husock, Howard A. 2007. "Stock Market for Nonprofits," *Society,* March/April, 16-23.

Hwang, Suein. 2005. "The New White Flight," *Wall Street Journal*, November 19. A1. Online version.

Hwang, Suein. 2007. "Anxiety High: Moving for Schools" *Wall Street Journal*, February 2. A1, A15.

Jacobs, Joanne. 2004. "Importing Smart Kids" *Fox News.com*, July 26. Online version.

James, George. 2002 "Communities; In Milburn, the Accent is Russian," *New York Times,* October 6. Online version.

Jan, Tracy 2007 "Minority Scores Lag on Teaching Test; Panel to Study Failure Rate, Bias Complain," *The Boston Globe*, April 19. Online version at *boston.com.*

Jaschik, Scott. 2007. "Should AP Add African-American History?" *Inside Higher Education.* August 7. Online at *http://insidehighered.com/news2007/08/07/ap.*

Jaschik, Scott. 2008. "Gates Foundation to Spend Big on Community Colleges," *Inside Higher Education,* November 12. Online at *insidehighered.com.*

Jaschik, Scott. 2008. "Graduate Enrollments Are Up, but Uneven," *Inside Higher Education,* September 16. Online at *http://insidehighered.com/layout/set/print/news/2008//09/16/grad.*

Jaschik, Scott. 2009. "Black (Immigrant) Admissions Edge," *Inside Higher Ed.* March 17. Online version.

Jensen, Arthur A. 1980. *Bias in Mental Testing.* New York: Free Press.

Jensen, Arthur R. 1998. *The g Factor: The Science of Mental Ability*. Westport, CT: Praeger.

Johnson, Gayle. 2009. "Seattle Public Schools Plan to Close African American Academy Misguided," *The Seattle Times,* January 27. Online at *http://seattletimes.newsource.com/cgi-bin/Print/Story.pl?dicument_id=2.*

Keller, Bess. 2008. "Less Improvement Seen in Secondary Schools Using TAP," *Education Week,* March 3. Online version.

Keller, Bess. 2008. "Houston, Denver Move into Next Stage of Pay Plans," *Education Week.* February 8. Online version.

Kelly, David. 2006. "U.S. Asians Drawn to Life in Irvine," *Los Angeles Times, Home Edition,* October 29. Online version.

Kelly, Tina. 2003. "Arrests Near in Kickbacks At City Schools," *New York Times*, December 11. Online version.

Klein, Joel. 2007. "Pay for Performance" *New York Sun.* October 23, 9.

Klein, Malcome. 2006. "Education Epiphany of Bill Gates," At *http://campus-reportonline.net/main/.*

Klein, Melissa and Angela Montefinise. 2007. "Principal Training 'Leads' Nowhere," *New York Post*, November 11. Online version.

Knight, Heather. 2006. "San Francisco; School Plans Hits Black Neighborhoods; Closure Include Western Addition, Bayview," *San Francisco Chronicle*, January 6. Online version.

Koretz, Daniel, 2008. *Measuring Up: What Educational Testing Really Tells Us*. Cambridge, MA: Harvard University Press.

Kosters, Marvin and Brent D. Mast. 2003. "Closing the Education Achievement Gap: Is Title I Working?" *American Enterprise Institute for Public Policy Research*, May.

Kramer, Rita. 1991. *Ed School Follies: The Miseducation of American Teachers*. New York: The Free Press.

Kriz, Vicki. 2008. "A Crime of Fashion," *Teachers Magazine*, Web Watch, August 5.

Kruger, Justin and David Dunning. 1999. "Unskilled and Unaware of It: How Difficulties in Recognizing One's Own Incompetence Lead to Inflated Self-Assessments," *Journal of Personality and Social Psychology*, Vol. 77, No. 6, 1121-1134.

Labbé, Theola 2008. "Principal Recruitment another Move in Reform," *Washington Post*, March 16, C05. Online at *washingtonpost.com*.

Ladd, Helen F. 2008. "Rethinking the Way We Hold Schools Accountable," *Education Week,* January 22. Online version.

Ladner, Matthew. 2004. "States Lower Accountability Bar to Boost Pass Rates" *School Reform News*. September, 5.

Le Flock, Kerstein Carlson et al. 2007. "State and Local Implementation of the *No Child Left Behind Act.* Volume III—Accountability under NCLB: Interim Report. Washington, DC: US Department of Education, Office of Planning, Evaluation and Policy Development, Policy and Program Studies Service.

Lederman, Doug. 2007. "More Doctors of Philosophy (and Science)," *Inside Higher Ed at insidehighered.com.* November 21. Online version.

Lederman, Doug. 2008. "Berkeley as the 'Immigrant University,'" *Inside Higher Ed* at *insidehighered.com.* November 29. Online version.

Lederman, Doug. 2008. "Doctorate Production Continues to Grow," *Inside Higher Ed* at *insidehighered.com*, November 24. Online version.

Levin, Henry M. 1996. "Economics of School Reform for At-Risk Students," in Eric A. Hanushek and Dale W. Jorgenson eds. *Improving America's Schools: The Role of Incentives.* Washington, DC: National Academy Press.

Levin, Tamar and David M. Herszenhorn. 2007. "Money Not Race, is Fueling New Push to Bolster Schools," *New York Times*, June 30, A10.

Lewin, Tamar. 2008, "Report Urges Changes in Teaching Math," *New York Times,* March 14. Online version.

Lieberman, Myron. 1993. *Public Education: An Autopsy.* Cambridge: Harvard University Press.

Lieberman, Myron. 2007. *The Educational Morass: Overcoming the Stalemates in American Education.* Lanham, MD: Rowan and Littlefield.

Lips, Dan. 2007. "NCLB Reauthorization Stalls on Capitol Hill," *School Reform News*, December, 3.

Lipscomb, David C. and Gary Emerling. 2007. "Surplus Revenue Eyed for Schools; Spending Earlier 'Understated,'" *Washington Times*, October 4, B01. Online version.

Litow, Stanley. 2008. "A Silent Crisis: The Underrepresentation of Latinos in STEM Careers," *Education Week*. July 21. Online version.

Lohrfink, Kimberly J. 2006. "Next Generation Venture Fund: Empowering Under-Represented Scholars to reach their Academic Potential," Paper presentation at the 2006 Annual Conference Eastern Educational Research Association.

LoMonoco, Paulette. 2008. "Tackling the Dropout Crisis Comprehensively," *Education Week*. June 6. Online version.

Luo, Michael. 2003. "Taking Lessons from Another Culture: For Students of Many Backgrounds, a Study Tool From the Far East," *New York Times*, October 20. Online version.

MacDonald, Christine. 2004. "More Mich. High Schools Fail," *The Detroit News,* November 5. Online version.

MacDonald, Heather. 1999. "How Gotham's Elite High Schools Escaped the Leveller's Ax" *City Journal*, Spring. Online version.

Macias, Verónica. 2008. "School Workshop Aims to Help Parents Help Their Kids," *Washington Post*, September 18. DZ03. Online at *washingtonpost. com.*

Marcus, Amy Dockser. 1999. "Standardized Test Guide Could Lead to Lawsuits," *Wall Street Journal*, May 26.

Matthews, Jay. 2007. "Putting His Wealth to Work To Improve Urban Schools," *Washington Post*, May 30. Online version at *washingtonpost.com.*

Maxwell, Lesli A. 2008. "Dropout Campaign Envisioned for States, 50 Key City Districts," *Education Week*, April 9. Online version.

McCluskey, Neal. 2005. "Corruption in the Public Schools: The Market Is the Answer," *Policy Analysis.* Number 542. Washington, DC: CATO Institute. April 20.

McCombs, Barbara L. and Jo Sue Whisler. 1997. *The Learner-Centered Classroom and School: Strategies for Increasing Student Motivation and Achievement.* San Francisco: Jossey-Bass Publishers.

McInnis, Hugh. 2008. "Sailor is Right: Measure School Achievement Relative to IQ" at *http://vdare.com/mcinnish/080702 iq.htm.*

McKinsey & Company. 2009. *The Economic Impact of the Achievement Gaps in American Schools,* April.

Medina, Jennifer 2008. "Reading and Math Scores Rise Sharply Across N.Y." *New York Times*, June 24. Online version.

Medina, Jennifer. 2007. "At Canarsie High, Now Marked for Closing, Loyalty Prevails." *New York Times*, December 24. Online version.

Medina, Jennifer. 2007. "Charter Schools Outshine Others as They Receive Their First Report Cards," *New York Times*, December 20. Online version.

Medina, Jennifer. 2007. "Defending School Report Cards, Over a Chorus of Boos" *New York Times*, December 11. Online version.

Medina, Jennifer. 2008. "New York Measuring Teachers by Test Scores," *New York Times*, January 21. Online version.

Medina, Jennifer. 2008. "Next Question: Can Students Be Paid to Excel?" *New York Times*, March 5. Online version.

Medina, Jennifer. 2008. "Thousands Protest Budget Cuts Aimed at City Schools," *New York Times*, March 20. Online version.

Medina, Jennifer. 2009. "In School for the First Time, Teenage Immigrants Struggle," *New York Times*, January 25, 1, 30.

Medina, Jennifer and Robert Gebeloff. 2008. "Finding Jobs for Teachers Already on City's Payroll," *New York Times*, November 19. Online version.

Medina, Jennifer and Robert Gebeloff. 2008. "More New York Schools Get A's" *New York Times*, September 17. Online version.

Medina, Jennifer and Robert Gebeloff. 2008. "Most City High Schools Improved This Year," *New York Times*, November 13. Online version.

Meenan, Michael. 2008. "Will City's Expanded Gifted Be Enough to Boost Minority Participation?" *NY1 News*, April 16. Online version.

Mehta, Seema 2007. "ACLU Targets Tustin Unified's Gifted Program," *Los Angeles Times*. February 20. Online version.

Meyer, Jeremy P. 2008. "Minorities, Poor Get 'Highly Gifted' Lifted," *The Denver Post*, March 4, in *denverpost.com*.

Mielczarek, Natalia. 2008. "Gifted-education Chief Wants New Path for Program," *Tennessean.com*. June 28. Online version.

Miron, Gary and Brooks Applegate. 2000. "An Evaluation of Student Achievement in Edison Schools Opened in 1995 and 1996," The Evaluation Center, Western Michigan University, December.

Murray, Charles. 2008. "On Requiring Every Child to Be Above Average," *The New Criterion*, May.

Nakamura, David. 2008. "Bush Proposes Giving D.C. $32 Million More to Boost School," *Washington Post*, February 2, B02. Online version at *washingtonpost.com*.

Nbc4.com. 2008. "D.C. Summer School Program Shaken Up: About 500 Seniors Failing, Survey Says," April 18. *http://www.nbc4.com/print/15926870/detail.html*.

Neal, Richard G. 2007. "Congress May Act to Define Graduation Rate" *School Reform News*, October, 8.

Nelson, F. Howard and Nancy Van Meter. 2000. "Update on Student Achievement for Edison Schools, Inc." American Federation of Teachers.

New York City Department of Education. 2007. *Fair Student Funding: Fair Funding for All*. January.

NYC Public School Parent. 2009. "Closing the Achievement Gap—DoE Discussion Series," January 8. Online at *http://nycpublicschoolparent.blogspot.com/2009/01-closing-achieve...*

Office of Student Research. 2003. "Statistics on Immigrant Students at UCB," May 5.

Ogbu, John U. 2003. *Black American Students in an Affluent Suburb: A Study in Academic Disengagement*. Mahwah, NJ: Lawrence Erlbaum.

Page, Clarence. 2007. "Black Immigrants Collect Most Degrees" *The Chicago Tribune,* March 18. Online version.

Page, Ellis. 1986. "The Disturbing Case of the Milwaukee Project," in Herman H. Spitz *The Raising of Intelligence: A Selected History of Attempts to Raise Retarded Intelligence.* Hillsdale, NJ: Lawrence Erlbaum Associates.

Palevsky, Stacy. 2006. "Gifted Student Programs Let Students Pursue Excellence" *Tri-City Herald* (Kennewick, WA), April 28. Online version.

Parker, Paige. 2006. "Portland Schools Try to Tag More Gifted Students," *The Oregonian*, October 31. Online version.

Peak, Lois. 1993. "Academic Effort in International Perspective," in *Motivating Students to Learn: Overcoming Barriers to High Achievement.* Edited by Tommy M. Tomlinson. Berkeley, CA: McCutchan Publishing.

Pear, Robert. 2007. "High-Tech Titans Strike Out on Immigration Bill," *New York Times*, June 25. Online version.

Peterson, Paul E. and Matthew M. Chingos. 2007. "Educational Rewards," *Wall Street Journal,* November 7. Online edition.

Plomin, Robert 1997. "Genetics and Intelligence," in *Handbook of Gifted Education,* second edition. Edited by Colangelo, Nicholas and Gary A. David. Boston: Allyn and Bacon.

Pope, Justin 2008. "Colleges spend billions to prep freshmen," *Associated Press*, September 15.

Powell, Arthur G. 1996. "Motivating Students to Learn: An American Dilemma" in *Rewards and Reforms.* Edited by Susan H. Fuhrman and Jennifer A. O'Day. San Francisco: Jossey-Bass Publishers.

Puko, Tim 2008. "Duquesne Science Camp Struggles for Applicants," *Pittsburgh Tribune-Review*, June 22. Online version.

Raffini, James P. 1996. *150 Ways to Increase Intrinsic Motivation in the Classroom.* Boston: Allyn and Bacon.

Ravitch, Diane. 2003. *The Language Police: How Pressure Groups Restrict What Students Learn.* New York: Alfred A. Knopf.

Ravitch, Dianne. 1985. *The Schools We Deserve: Reflections on the Educational Crisis of Our Time.* New York: Basic Books.

Redden, Elisabeth. 2008. "Rethinking Remedial Education," *Inside Higher Education,* January 29. Online at *http://www.insidehighereducation.com/layout/set/print/news/2008/01/29/cali...*

Redden, Elisabeth. 2008. "The Foundations of General Education," *Inside Higher Education*, April 4. Online at *http://insidehighereducation.com/news/2008/04/04/trinity.*

Redelman, Derek. 2003. "Using Statistics to Subvert NCLB," *School Reform News.* Vol. 7, no. 10, November, 1, 6.

Reid, Keith. 2006. "GATE Expansion May Narrow Choices for Some," *The Record* (Stockton, CA), December 17. Online version.

Richburg, Keith B. 2008. "Setback for Philadelphia School Plan," *Washington Post.* June 29, A03. Online at *washingtonpost.com.*

Richer, Matthew. 1998. "Busing's Boston Massacre," *Policy Review*, November/December. Online version.

Richert, E. Susanne. 2003. "Excellence with Justice in Identification and Programming. In *Handbook of Gifted Education.* Edited by Colangelo, Nicholas and Gary A. David. Boston: Allyn and Bacon.

Rief, Sandra and Julie Heimburge. 1996. *How to Reach and Teach in the Inclusive Classroom.* Nyack, NY: The Center for Applied Research Education.

Rimer, Sara. 2008. "Harlem to Antarctica for Science, and Pupils," *New York Times*, March 28. Online version.

Rotherham, Andrew J. 2005. "Teaching Fishing or Giving Away Fish? Grantmaking for Research, Policy and Advocacy," in *With the Best of Intentions: How Philanthropy is Reshaping K-12 Education.* Edited by Frederick M. Hess. Cambridge, MA: Harvard Education Press.

Rothstein, Richard, Rebecca Jacobson, and Tamara Wilder. 2006 "Proficiency for All—An Oxymoron" Paper presented for Symposium, "Examining America's Commitment to Closing Achievement Gaps," sponsored by the Campaign for Educational Equity, Teachers College, Columbia University, November 13-14.

Ryan, Richard, James P. Connell, and Edward L. Deci. 1985. "A Motivational Analysis of Self-Determination and Self-Regulation" in Education in *Research on Motivation in Education, Vol. 2, The Classroom Milieu.* Edited by Carole Ames and Russell Ames. Orlando: Academic Press.

Sadowski, Connie. 2007. "Vouchers for At-Risk Students Proposed in Texas," *School Reform News*, May, 5.

Sanbonmatsu, Lisa, Jeffry R. Kling, Greg J. Duncan, and Jeanne Brooks-Gun. 2007. "New Kids on the Block," *Education Next*, Fall. Online version.

Sarich, Vincent and Frank Miele. 2004. *Race: The Reality of Human Differences.* Boulder (CO): Westview Press.

Saulny, Susan 2006. "A Lucrative Brand of Tutoring Grows Unchecked," *New York Times,* April 4. Online version.

Schemo, Diana Jean. 2004. "Schools, Facing Tight Budgets, Leave Gifted Programs Behind," *New York Times*, March 2. Online version.

Schouten, Fredreka 2003. "Reform Punishes Diversity, Study Say." *The Detroit News* (*Detnews.com*), December 23. Online version.

"Seeking Excellent; Bad Schools vs. Good Schools Not a Solution" *San Diego Union-Tribune,* January 21, 2007. Online version.

Shapiro, Julie 2008. "In Its 2nd Century, School Thrives in the Area Now Called Chinatown," *Downtown Express*, May 2-8, 1, 8, 10.

Silverman, Julia. 2008. "Ore. Students Set to Get Choice of Graduation Test," *Associated Press.* June 21.

Singer-Vine, Jeremy. 2008. "When Schools Offer Money As a Motivator," *Wall Street Journal,* August 21, D1, D2.

Smarick, Andy. 2008. "Wave of the Future" *Education Next,* Winter, Vol. 8. Online version.

Snell, Lisa. 2005. "How Schools Cheat: From Underreporting Violence to Inflating Graduation Rates to Fudging Testscores, Educators Are Lying to the American Public," *Reason,* June.

Sommers, Christina Hoff. 2000. *The War Against Boys: How Misguided Feminism Is Harming Our Young Men.* New York: Simon & Schuster.

Sostek, Anya. 2008. "Management Philosophy Applied to Schools," *http://www.examiner.com/a-1237665~Management_philosophy_applied_to_schools.html.*

Sowell, Thomas. 1993. *Inside American Education: The Decline, the Deception, The Dogmas*. New York: The Free Press.

Spitz, Herman H. 1986. *The Raising of Intelligence: A Selected History of Attempts to Raise Retarded Intelligence*. Hillsdale, NJ: Lawrence Erlbaum and Associates.

Stein, Letitia. 2006. "School Newspaper Censored," *St. Petersburg Times*, October 24. At *tampabay.com*.

Steinberg, Lawrence with B. Bradford Brown and Sanford M. Dornbusch. 1996. *Beyond the Classroom: Why School Reform has Failed and What Parents Need to Do*. New York: Simon & Schuster.

Stephens, Scott. 2007. "Forum Aims to Uplift Black Males" *The Plain Dealer (Cleveland)*, May 30. Online version.

Stern, Sol. 2007. "The Bush Education Reform Really Works," *City Journal* Winter, 100-7.

Stevenson, Harold W. and James W. Stigler. 1992. *The Learning Gap: Why Our Schools Are Failing and What We Can Learn from Japanese and Chinese Education*. New York: Simon & Schuster.

Steward, Nikita and Theola LabbA. 2008. "Hearing on School Closing Is Long and Emotional," *Washington Post*, January 15. B01. Online version at *washingtonpost.com*.

Sykes, Leonard Jr. 2004. "In Seeking Best Education, Some Choose Segregation," *Milwaukee Journal Sentinel*, March 13. Online at JSOnline.

Tarleton, John 2007. "NYC Security by the Numbers," *The Independent,* November 15-December 5, 4.

Tarm, Michael. 2008. "Call for Chicago Students to Skip First Day of School," *Associated Press*. Available online at *http://apnews.myway.com/article/20080729/D9275U8GO.html*.

Teacher Magazine. 2008. "A Different Approach to History," December 8. Online at *www.Teachermagazine.org/tm/articles/2008//12/08/pittshist_ap....*

Texas Freedom Network. 2004-6. "Briefing Paper: Edison Schools, Inc. Privatization Earns a Failing Grade," *http://ftn.org/publiceducation/privitization/edison*.

Thernstrom, Abigail and Stephen Thernstrom. 2003. *No Excuses: Closing the Racial Gap in Learning*. New York: Simon and Schuster.

Thernstrom, Stephen and Abigail Thernstrom. 1997. *America in Black and White: One Nation, Indivisible*. New York: Simon and Schuster.

Thompson, Ginger. 2009. "Where Education and Assimilation Collide," *New York Times,* March 15, 1, 21-2.

Tobin, Thomas C. 2007. "Special School Programs for Blacks: Racist or Essential?" *St. Petersburg Times*. March 25. Online version.

Tomlinson, Tommy. 1993. "Education Reform: The Ups and Downs of Good Intentions" in *Motivating Students to Learn: Overcoming Barriers to High Achievement*. Edited by Tommy M. Tomlinson. Berkeley, CA: McCutchan Publishing.

Tomsho, Robert and Daniel Golden. 2007. "Educating Eric: A Troubled Student Was Put into Regular Classes. Then He Killed the Principal," *Wall Street Journal*, May 12-13, A1, A6.

Toppo, Greg. 2009. "A Few Word for Obama on Closing the 'Achievement Gap,'" *USA Today,* January 14. Online at *http://usatoday.com/news/education/2009-01-14-obama-achievement_N.htm.*

Toppo, Greg. 2007. "School Test Scandal Claims Decorated Principal," *USA Today*, December 21. Online version.

Turque, Bill. 2008. "Long Battle Expected on Plan to Fire Teachers," *Washington Post*, October 25, B01. Online at *washingtonpost.com.*

Tyack, David. 1995. "Reinventing Schools" in Diane Ravitch and Maris A. Vinovskis, *Learning from the Past: What History Teaches Us about School Reform*. Baltimore: Johns Hopkins University Press.

University of California, Office of the President. 2007. "Statistical Summary and Data on UC Students, Faculty and Staff. At *www.ucop.edu/ucophome/uwnews/stat.*

US Department of Labor, Bureau of Labor Statistics, *Occupational Outlook Handbook,* 2008-9 Edition. At *http://www.bls.gov/oco/ocos069.htm.*

US Statistical Abstract. 2007. The National Data Book. Online version.

Vanderkam, Laura. 2003. "The Challenge of Being Gifted" *Washington Times*, July 8. Online version.

Viadero, Debra. 2009. "Study of Charters in 8 States Finds Mixed Effects," *Education Week*, March 18. Online version.

Viadero, Debra. 2008. "'Scientifically Based' Giving Way to 'Development,'" *Education Week*. January 27, Online version at *http://edweek.org/ew/articles/2009/01/28/19rd_ep.h28html.*

Viadero, Debra. 2008. "Program Design Called Crucial across Array of School Choices," *Education Week,* March 25. Online version.

Viadero, Debra. 2008. "Scrutiny Heightens for 'Value Added' Research Methods," *Education Week*. May 5. Online version at *http://wws.edweek.org/ew/articles/2008/05/0736value.h27html.*

Viadero, Debra. 2008. "U.S. Position on Research Seen in Flux," *Education Week*. March 4. Online version at *http://wws.edweek.org/ew/articles/2008/03/05/26research_ep.h27ht...*

Viadero, Debra. 2009. "'No Effects' Studies Raising Eyebrow," *Education Week*, April 1. Online version.

Walberg, Herbert. 2007. *School Choice: The Findings*. Washington, DC: The CATO Institute.

Wallis, Claudia. 2008. "Bill and Melinda Gates go Back to School," in *CNNmoney.com*. November 26. Online version.

Wallis, Claudia. 2008. "How to Make Great Teachers," *Time* (in partnership with CNN), February 13. Online version.

Warner, Matt 2007. "Court-Ordered Funding Increases Are No Remedy for Ailing Schools," *Reform School News*, March, p. 17.

Webb, Florence R., Martin V. Covington, and James W. Guthrie. 1993. "Carrots and Sticks: Can School Policy Influence Student Motivation" in *Motivating Students to Learn: Overcoming Barriers to High Achievement*. Edited by Tommy M. Tomlinson. Berkeley, CA: McCutchan Publishing.

Weiss, Bari. 2008. "Ivy Graduates Earn Big Fees As N.Y. Tutors," *New York Sun,* September 22, 1, 3.

White, K, R. 1982. "The Relation between Socioeconomic Status and Academic Achievement," *Psychological Bulletin*, 91, 461-81.

Whitman, David 2008. *Sweating the Small Stuff: Inner-City Schools and the New Paternalism,* Washington, DC: The Fordham Institute.

Wickstrom, Clifton D. 2004. "Give Us the Best and the Brightest, But…A Historical Review of U.S. National Policy on Education for the Highly Capable," *In the Eyes of the Beholder: Critical Issues for Diversity in Gifted Education.* Edited by Boothe, Diane and Julian C. Stanley. Waco, TX: Prufrock Press.

Williams, Walter E. 2008. "Black Education" July 23. Column released by Creators Syndicate. At *http://gmu.edu/departments/economics/wew/articles/08black....*

Winerip, Michael. 2003. "On Education: When It Goes Wrong at a Charter School." *New York Times*, March 5. Online edition.

Wingert, Pat. 2008. "My Trip Inside," *Newsweek*, August 25. Online version.

Witt, April. 2007. "Worn Down by Waves of Change," *The Washington Post*, June 11, A01. Online version at *washingtonpost.com*

Wolf, Andrew. 2006. "Equity for the Gifted," *New York Sun*, May 12. Online version.

Wolf, Andrew. 2007. "Gifted, but No Cigar," *New York Sun,* November 16-18, 11.

Wolf, Andrew. 2007. "Socialism for Schools?" *New York Sun*, October 19-21.

Wolf, Andrew. 2007. "The Numbers Game," *New York Sun*, March 23-25, 7.

Zimmer, Amy. 2007. "Unsafe at School?" *Metro*, October 10, 3.

Index